Modern Magazine Design

Cover of the Saturday Evening Post, illustrated by Norman Rockwell, September 1961. In this self-conscious celebration of the magazine's new look, design consultant Herb Lubalin is shown reworking the logotype – part of a modern format with which he took the magazine into a new decade.

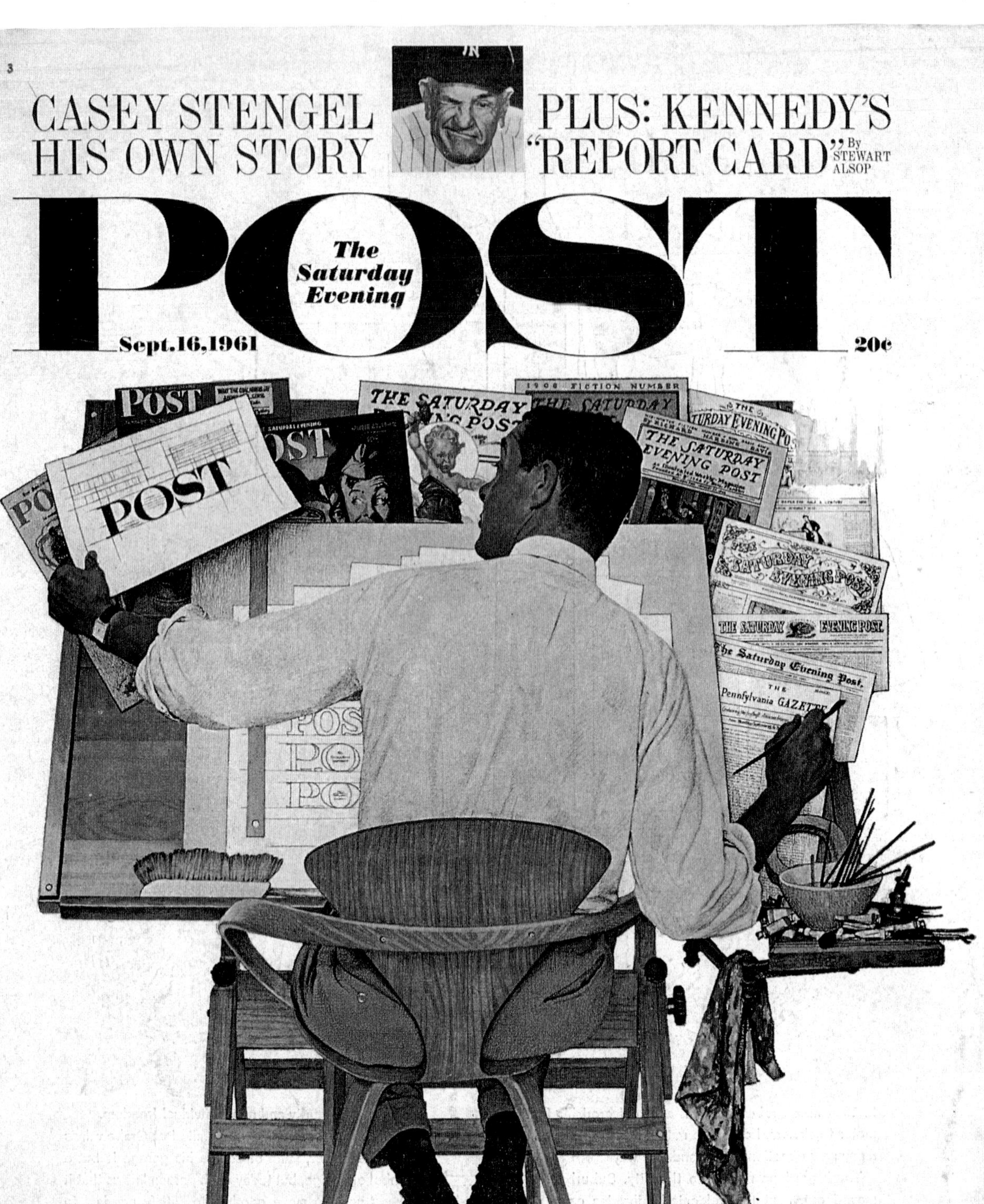

William Owen

Modern Magazine Design

RIZZOLI
NEW YORK

First published in the United States of America in 1991 by RIZZOLI INTERNATIONAL PUBLICATIONS, INC.
300 Park Avenue South, New York, NY 10010

Library of Congress Cataloging-in-Publication Data

Owen, William, 1957-
Modern magazine design/William Owen.
p. cm.
Includes bibliographical references.
ISBN 0-8478-1385-1
1. Magazine design.
I. Title.
Z253.5.084 1991
741.6'52--dc20
91-2257
CIP

This book was produced by Laurence King Ltd, London

Picture research by Lucy Bullivant
Designed by Esterson Lackersteen
Printed and bound in Singapore by Toppan Printing Co. Ltd

Front jacket
Background picture: photograph Phil Sayer
Top inset: cover of the Russian constructivist magazine *Novy Lef* designed by Alexander Rodchenko, 1928 *(courtesy David King Collection, London)*
Second inset: photomontaged cover for *Harper's Bazaar* by Herbert Bayer, art directed by Alexey Brodovitch, 1940 *(courtesy The Hearst Corporation © 1940)*
Third inset: cover of *i-D* designed by Carol Thompson and Eamonn McCabe, art directed by Terry Jones, 1985 *(courtesy i-D Magazine, London)*
Bottom inset: cover of *Metropolis*, art directed by Helene Silverman, 1987 *(courtesy Bellerophon Publications Inc., New York)*

Back jacket
photograph Phil Sayer

Acknowledgements
Special thanks are due to Rick Poyner, with whom I started this project, and to Simon Esterson, with whom I finished it. Both offered encouragement, good advice, source material, and made suggestions and corrections at the proof stage. Simon's assistance with picture selection was invaluable. The other major contributors were Lucy Bullivant, for diligent picture research and constant support; Jane Havell, my editor at Laurence King; photographer John Barlow, and Luke Hayman at Esterson Lackersteen. Ken Garland, David King and Lorraine Wild made further corrections to and comments on sections of the text. Any inaccuracies or omissions are of course mine, and not theirs.

I would also like to thank the many designers who generously gave of their time and knowledge in interviews: Walter Allner, Walter Bernard, Derek Birdsall, Roger Black, Neville Brody, Rod Clarke, Clive Crook, David Driver, Ken Garland, Malcolm Garrett, Milton Glaser, F. H. K. Henrion, David Hillman, Will Hopkins, Alex Isley, Terry Jones, Willem Kars, David King, Mike Lackersteen, Kathy McCoy, Pearce Marchbank, Regis Pagniez, Roland Schenk, Helene Silverman, David Sterling, Derek Ungless, Rudy VanderLans, Max Whitby, Henry Wolf, Tom Wolsey, Frank Zachary and Lloyd Ziff.

For their assistance in supplying or obtaining picture material I would like to thank David King/David King Collection; Ken Garland; Pearce Marchbank; Lorraine Wild; David Bishop at Richard Booth Books, Hay-on-Wye, and Derek Ungless (for political support). In addition, grateful thanks for picture material are due to Stephen Male; Otto Storch; Bill Cadge; Paul Rand; Paul Davis; Alan Pipes; Killian Jordan at WBMG; Jacques Koeweiden and Paul Postma; Wallace Grevatt; Hans-Georg Pospischil; Wolfgang Behnken; Lies Ross and Rob Schroder; the Multimedia Corporation; Roger Black; Henry Wolf; Frank Zachery; Dugald Stermer; R. Roger Remington of the Department of Graphic Design, Rochester Institute of Technology, New York; Ko Sliggers; Terry Jones; Melissa Tardiff and Colin Osman. Helpful advice was provided by Daniel Forte at The Art Directors' Club, New York, and Bride Whelan, Society of Publication Designers, New York.
William Owen
London, 1991

Contents

Preface

This book is a history, together with an analysis of contemporary magazine design: two parts which have as a single theme the development of magazine design from the latter part of the industrial revolution to the present day.

That the design of this ubiquitous print medium has been given no systematic history or critique is something of an anomaly, to say the least. The poster has one concise design history, the newspaper at least two, and the book too many to count. Therefore this work can at least atone for a sin of omission. The magazine constitutes a lively and fascinating part of our intellectual existence, and has played a crucial role in moulding the social and cultural forms of the twentieth century. Yet despite the important part that magazines have played as laboratories of experiment, especially in the development of modern design principles and visual expression, the technical, journalistic and artistic evolution of magazine design has received only the marginal treatment that general graphic design histories can provide. The aim of this book is to re-address the balance if it can, for the purposes that are outlined below.

Where historical and contemporary material is included within the same publication it is inevitable that comparisons will be made: some care is required in doing this. Editorial context, commercial circumstance and methods of production have changed considerably. Thirty and forty years ago art directors suffered severe technical restrictions, struggling with inferior inks, paper and print methods, and, if we are to believe what we are told, they also enjoyed a relatively greater editorial freedom. Advertising knew its place, which was at either side of the editorial well; editors not publishers controlled the content; and readers had quite different expectations. Magazines also fulfilled some of the roles that have since been assumed by television. What was useful then is not necessarily useful now, and almost certainly not in the same form. It would, therefore, be foolhardy to view both the immediate post-war period and contemporary magazine design from an identical critical viewpoint, just as it is useless and reactionary to bemoan the loss of an heroic age which quite probably never existed in the way we perceive it today.

The "great age" of magazine design – a commonly accepted proposition – ran from around 1945 to 1968, and it hangs like a necklace of retribution around the heads of subsequent generations. This was the period in which magazine design matured after a short adolescence lasting little more than fifty years – the time since the introduction of photography to pictorial magazines. It should not, however, be viewed as the summit of achievement. Nevertheless, and regardless of circumstance, much of contemporary magazine design has been disparaged for its lack of a comparable simplicity and intensity, for its absence of wit, for its fussiness; for being alternatively unadventurous, undramatic or overwrought; and divorced from the great design tradition established in the mid-century. At a symposium on magazine design organized by the

American Institute of Graphic Arts in 1985, a roll-call of the great names of the past vented their feelings: "Magazines today are timid. They have no self-confidence" (Cipe Pineles); "Something happened to the magazine in the Sixties; it was the loss of potency" (Milton Glaser); "Today the advertising departments run magazines, but once there was a kind of congressional immunity for editors" (Henry Wolf); "I feel like an old fuddy-duddy talking this way, but nevertheless, there were once basic aesthetic standards for magazine design that do not exist today" (Will Hopkins).[1]

Given the poverty of commercial magazine publishing in the 1970s, and – probably – a lack of awareness of developments in the independent press in Europe, these viewpoints are at least understandable, but that does not make them right. The old guard's criticisms are sometimes deserved, sometimes not. There is today a greater depth of technical competence, if not always of talent. Equally, there is undoubtedly a strong argument that an important heritage has been discarded, often involuntarily. Magazine design, however changed, must be informed by its past.

There have been two jarring dislocations to the forward march of graphic design this century which have combined to interrupt continuity and shatter the confident optimism of the modern movement: first fascist repression; more recently the upsurge of revivalism and eclecticism in the 1960s and 1970s. Both these amnesiac events were followed by periods of ignorance and a subsequent upsurge of naive if unfettered creativity. Many of the discoveries of visual science had been lost and the wastage of invention in magazine design, because its documentation is so sporadic, was particularly flagrant. As a result, too often young designers are forced to rediscover that "the world is round, like an orange". Continuity and tradition are essential even if they exist only to be demolished. An essential component of the creative process is deracination. Creativity consists of observing, learning and changing existing methods to adapt to new circumstances – a spiral pattern of subtly changed repetitions. It is a struggle between subconscious ideas and intellectual analysis, and between the conventional and the unconventional. It is, however, impossible to struggle in a historical vacuum. Push against nothing and you fall.

This is also an apposite time for reappraisal. Today, in all the arts, we have reached a moment of dissolution and uncertainty. There is no dominant philosophy of design and, if we take magazine design as our paradigm, a characteristically fragmented selection of pragmatic, revivalist, expressionistic, neo-modernist, unstructured and deconstructed approaches emerges. The narrow technocratic pursuit of efficiency has been largely superseded, too often by mere ostentation, sometimes by beneficent inquiry. There is a discernable shift from rational to sensual cognition, an apparent will to test the bounds of perception with a more complex array of words, images, signs and symbols which attack the instinctive rather than the logical mind.

In the hiatus between the breakdown of old belief systems and old technologies and the foundation of the new, in a time when the influx of influences and ideas is too great to be assimilated and acted upon with any consistency, such diversity is inevitable and not to be decried, as long as this aesthetic energy has graphic intelligence and is applied to political and social purpose.

A successful search for new forms which apply to different production methods and unfamiliar contexts requires experiment and a degree of indulgence, and has to be viewed from a short critical distance. This is why, in the second section of this book dealing with contemporary design, the perspective is altered. There is a much looser interpretation of the cardinal points of functionalist design – that is, of what is appropriate, simple, ordered – except where a problem-solving approach is evidently essential to lucid communication and as long as there is some purpose to invention.

And so the second part of this book is called "New magazine design". What is so new about it? The answer is: at the moment, there is no more than a hint of the new. Because only revolutionary situations create revolutionary ideas it is not surprising that in thirty or forty years we have seen only a gradual evolution in magazine design or graphic design *per se*. However, there has at least been a technical revolution. We are now well down a path that will lead to radical change in the commercial and technical environment in which magazine publishing operates. Start-up costs, even in large publishing houses, have been reduced massively by desktop publishing and this will have a profound effect on the scope and spread of magazine editorial. New markets will open up for new kinds of magazine, which will require new design structures. The same technology has given designers an unprecedented control over the production process, which has already led to a corresponding richness and variety of visual expression. And there are more fundamental changes approaching, which will have an effect in some ways comparable to the design revolution – the New Typography – which began in the first decade of this century and which was itself ignited by the advent of the new technologies of photography, lithography and industrial-scale printing. That is, the addition of digital distribution to digital composition – the substitution for paper of electronic media.

The paper magazine will not be replaced – it is far too convenient. But it will be supplemented by the electronic magazine, the first experimental examples of which have already been produced. Electronic distribution brings with it the opportunity to create entirely new typographic systems, new information structures, and new syntheses of text and image. For the first time, it introduces qualities of animation and interaction to typography. It also raises problematic questions about the mutability of data and information. These are issues which affect all graphic media but are of particular interest to magazines which have structures so amenable to the new "hypermedia". This is a digression born of enthusiasm. The subject is addressed more fully in the last chapter.

There are four riders to add to this introduction. Firstly, the text has an unfortunate but inevitable bias towards the Western design tradition. American design is observed closely, for the obvious reason that the great power and resources of American magazine publishing have created a corresponding strength in design. The remaining emphasis is largely on Western Europe and in particular Britain, where the author lives and works and therefore has a wealth of information on which to draw. The important Russian contribution is examined only up until 1941 and post-war developments in Eastern Europe are also omitted; this is due to lack of information rather than inclination; and the same problem, exacerbated by distance and language difficulties, applies to South America, Africa and Asia. Examples of Japanese design are included in the contemporary design section.

Secondly, there is the question of how the term "magazine" is defined. Rather than become entangled in an etymological debate which is in any case dealt with in "Journalism and art" (pages 126 – 157), it is only necessary at this point to say that, as a general rule, weekly reviews printed on newsprint, or adopting a "news" format (i.e. a hierarchy of separated stories on a single page) are excluded, as are illustrated comics on the one hand and "learned" journals on the other.

Thirdly, there is a limit to what can be achieved by photographic reproduction. The images in the book can provide only a two-dimensional representation of covers and spreads, whereas magazines have other important properties of touch and texture, size and weight. The paper is an essential component of the design, as is the quality of the print and the contrasts and consistency of the ink. The priorities of layout are subject to the physical size of the page, but this factor cannot be truly represented by a scaled-down reproduction. More importantly, magazines have a sequential structure to which a single page or spread can do no justice. So, if they can, readers are strongly advised to find the originals.

And finally, throughout this book its subject is treated seriously, which might imply that magazines are an essential – not ephemeral – element of human existence and vital to the sustainment of life. Well, they are – if not in such a profound way as books – and they certainly are to the people who depend on them for their jobs and careers. But while magazines inform they are primarily an entertainment, and when they inform they should also intrigue. Magazine design might be an excrutiatingly painful process and the source of much wailing and gnashing of teeth in editorial offices, but the way a page was designed never broke a reputation or changed the world. This is what gives the magazine designer such considerable leeway to experiment, to learn and develop, and to indulge a sense of humour. The ephemeral nature of magazines is their strength – there is no better place to make mistakes.

London, Summer 1990

Part one

A history of magazine design

Prologue: a new synthesis

The magazine has no true antecedent in pre-industrial printing. It is an invention of the industrial revolution, and as such it has matured in a relationship of mutual dependence with the modern movement in graphic design. The history of magazine design is one of a struggle to relinquish traditional book and newspaper typography and create a new synthesis of text and pictures.

The social conditions and technical processes required for the production of modern mass-circulation magazines existed only from the last decade of the nineteenth century. As the bastard offspring of the book and newspaper, upstart brother to the literary journal and poor cousin to the poster, the magazine lacked a unique visual format; as a consequence it became an ideal medium for graphic exploration. This was a new type of information source applicable to the requirements of a highly structured but rapidly changing society. In the machine age, the age of mass education and mass politics, of specialization,

In the early 20th century magazines assumed new importance as a pictorial and written medium of communication, extending to all classes of society. Two peasants (right), in 1929, study the Soviet anti-religious magazine Bez Bohznik.

it was necessary that the picture acquire equality with the word.

The modern magazine grew directly out of the invention of photographic reproduction and the automation of printing. The new technologies were assimilated through experiment in original forms of typography and spatial composition, and so contemporary magazine design evolved largely according to the new aesthetic developed in Germany, Russia and the Netherlands immediately after the First World War. In the mid-1930s the creative centre moved to New York. The modern format of integrated elements – in which visual and textual components were amplified through combination – was refined and applied commercially to popular magazines in the giant publishing conglomerates of the United States.

While magazine design remained a craft activity it was inevitable that composition would take on traditional, bookish forms. Few of the graphic characteristics individual to magazines were established before 1900. The magazine was distinguished from the book only by its flimsy cover; the headline resembled a chapter heading; the arrangement of type was symmetrical; text was wrapped from top to bottom in single or double columns in the bookish manner; and illustrations were placed over a full page opposite the text, or united with it only insofar as type was carried in a dog-leg around the picture. Most of these traits persevered well into the new century and today, in technical and literary journal publishing, they remain stubbornly, if sometimes appropriately, intact.

The impact of the new printing methods, of photography and photomechanical reproduction, was at first restricted to the production, print and distribution cycles. Publishers utilized the new technology to increase circulation, respond faster to events and incorporate illustration, but presentation and layout were largely unaffected. The traditional decorative and symmetrical style persisted as long as page make-up remained the prerogative of journalists and craft printers. Design, except in the matter of covers, was not recognized as a separate activity.

The division of labour was narrowed over a considerable period of time, beginning with the Arts and Crafts Movement. Aubrey Beardsley was described as "art editor" of *The Yellow Book* (a periodical) in 1894.[1] One of the earliest uses of the title in America was in *The Burr McIntosh Monthly* of 1908,[2] and the illustrator John Sloan was *de facto* art editor (unpaid) of the radical New York monthly *The Masses* from its launch in 1911. The great American typographer Will Bradley, better known for his work for the American Type Founders' Chap-Book, was from 1907 art editor of *Collier's* and, from 1910 to 1915, of five magazines in the Hearst organization – *Good Housekeeping, Metropolitan, Success, Pearson's* and *National Post.*[3] His systematic styling of *Cosmopolitan* magazine in 1916 anticipated the innovations of Dr M. F. Agha at Condé Nast by fifteen years – Bradley broke the conventions of the illustrated magazine by treating the double-page spread as a single unit.

Bradley, who from 1920 to 1930 was typographic supervisor of all Hearst publications, was the exception that proves the rule. The use of the term "art editor" and the existence of such a position was a rarity until the late 1920s when the first commercial art directors overturned craft conservatism and brought a modern sensibility to magazine design.

Illustrated magazines and the photographic revolution

The earliest "magazines" were literary or political journals published exclusively for the rich, and priced too high for broader circulation. The industrial revolution widened the social horizon. In Europe, the creation of an educated middle class and a small layer of skilled workers encouraged the invention of a new type of magazine distributed by the railway networks. Cheap weekly periodicals "devoted to wholesome popular instruction, blended with original amusing matter",[4] surfaced from 1832 in England with circulations of up to 100,000. They broadcast a patronizing morality and specialized in utilitarian miscellanies of fact, and quite naturally soon fell from favour with their readers.

The first sustained wave of popular magazine publishing was provided by the illustrated news weeklies. Their success coincided with the rise of the European popular democratic movements, and with technical advances in print and pre-press which made their production possible: paper manufacture was mechanized; all-iron lever presses improved efficiency and speed; and type composition was partially automated. Together, these developments allowed more resources to be devoted to illustration, which remained a time-consuming hand-worked process.

The prototype was the *Illustrated London News*, founded (or perhaps more accurately, invented) in 1842 by Herbert Ingram in association with topographical draftsman Ebenezer Landells, the man behind *Punch*. The illustrated magazines provided a novel, rapid and above all vivid weekly news service in a period of political upheaval. They were started in many European cities: *L'Illustration* in Paris and *Die Illustrierte Zeitung* in Leipzig both in 1843; *Fliegende*

McCLURE'S *for* AUGUST

The Business of Being a Lady

by Anna Steese Richardson

THE real thing in McClure's for June is Mrs. Anna Steese Richardson's article, or story, or whatever else you may call it, entitled "A Man in Her Life." It is a straightforward and deeply moving revelation of a woman's mind in respect to certain matters, and if we had our way would be read from every pulpit in the land which reaches out to, and does what little it can, to blister the gossip, the scandalmonger, the busybody, and all other newspeakers generally."

Arthur Spencer Morley, in The Boston Post.

McCLURE'S *for* AUGUST

McClure's

August 1916

designer unknown

The McClure's format represents a transitional stage, with evidence of the development of a distinct magazine typography. The type hierarchy incorporated headline, byline and introduction, usually centred at the top of the page but in this example sandwiched asymmetrically between picture and gutter. The picture arrangement, however, is eccentric and ill-defined.

Leslie's Weekly

21 May 1903

designer unknown

The utilitarian simplicity of this cover, with a single bleed photograph over which logotype, fudge and caption are superimposed, marks a profound change in cover design, away from the norm of engraved illustration surmounted by ornate titlepiece.

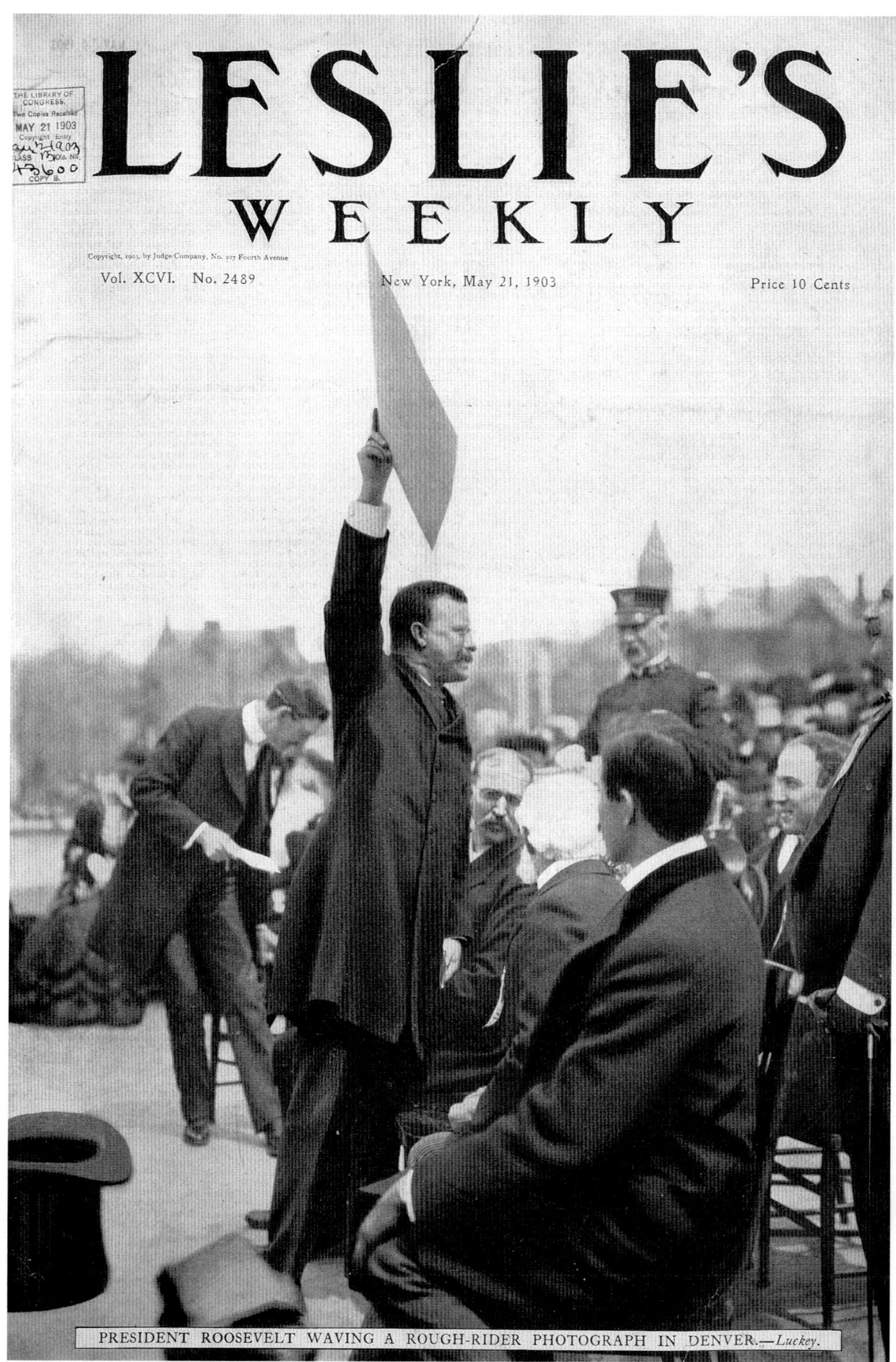

LESLIE'S
WEEKLY
Vol. XCVI. No. 2489
New York, May 21, 1903
Price 10 Cents
PRESIDENT ROOSEVELT WAVING A ROUGH-RIDER PHOTOGRAPH IN DENVER.—Luckey.

Blatter in 1844 and *Kladderadatsch* in 1848, also in Germany; the Spanish *La Ilustracion* was first published in 1849, and in the 1850s Frank Leslie's *Illustrated Newspaper* and *Harper's Weekly* appeared in the USA. These were the forerunners of *Life*, *Paris Match* and *Picture Post*, with the essential difference that the printed word retained its primacy in a typographical format borrowed from the newspapers of the day.

The 16-page *Illustrated London News* was produced only by the expedient of concentrating groups of four or more engravers on separate portions of each wooden block.[5] The process was extremely expensive and time-consuming and in 1848, the year of revolutions, the magazine was priced at sixpence, or about half the day-wage of a labourer; fifty years later the use of multiple illustrations was commonplace. Whereas at the beginning of the nineteenth century a wooden block took between a day and a month to cut, depending on its size; one hundred years later a photographic halftone could be prepared in hours and by 1890 magazines such as *Berliner Illustrierte Zeitung*, *Harper's* and *Leslie's* were making extensive use of photography. Moreover, magazines were universally affordable; the average cover price had dropped to threepence in Britain and to ten cents in the USA.

The photographic revolution was enforced against the will and without the understanding of many magazine editors of the time. From the invention of the daguerreotype onwards, a battle ensued between photography and illustration in which, intriguingly, each took on the characteristics of the other. Craftsmen wrought such miracles of cross-hatched toning that illustrations achieved a quality of realism rarely superceded by early photography, and the photographic facsimiles printed in magazines were so heavily touched up as to resemble drawings. Much of the photography published in the weeklies was treated as illustration. Inexplicably, to the modern eye, the dynamism of photography was emasculated by encasing pictures in a decorative frame.

Photography was first used in magazines to reproduce illustration, to transfer drawings to the sensitized surface of a woodblock in a mechanized engraving process. In 1872 zincography was invented, which created wholly new design opportunities by combining photography and line engraving so that pictures could be sized up or down to fit by the printer.[6] A variety of screenless techniques were used throughout the 1850s and 1860s, but any magazine attempting to reproduce photographic images faced the difficulty that screenless photoglyph prints required special paper and a separate press for printing the image; it was therefore impossible to produce both images and text on a single press using ordinary paper.

412 A Lady of Comedy

comedy rôles with Mr. Drew, I had a brief experience with 'The Rangers,' a play by Augustus Thomas, and a good-sized experience as leading lady with Francis Wilson in 'When Knights were Bold.'

"With Mr. Drew I have played in 'Jack Straw,' 'Smith,' 'Inconstant George,' 'A Single Man,' and 'The Perplexed Husband'—quite a sufficient variety to keep *ennui* at a distance for the time being, I can assure you.

"They say my little madcap Micheline in 'Inconstant George,' was just the opposite of my real self," continues Miss Boland, in her demurely sincere manner, "but that there was a whole lot of me in Miss Hazeltine, she of the simple faith and true love deferred, in 'A Single Man.' Maybe that is the way others see me. For my own part, this Kalleia means more to me than both the other rôles put together. Not that I imagine I am expressing myself in playing her—no ambitious actress wants to do that sort of thing. What I mean is that Kalleia is to me an actual, live woman, fascinating just because she is different. And at the same time I incline to be personally in sympathy and accord with her views—or, rather, the author's views, on the woman question, which he expresses in this character study, and in the whole play."

"In other words, then, you are an anti-suffragist?"

"I suppose I am. Of course I realize that the woman movement is running on its own motive power whether we 'believe in it' or not. I approve of work and a free field for women, but not brutalization. Just suppose the militants should win out, and women get the vote and the upper hand generally. Why, there would have to be a new man to fit in with the new woman. And I don't think men are changing. Do you?"

Kalleia, the ardent typewriter girl, with an artistic temperament under imperfect control

Vivacious Vivian

A "TOT" actress, a little player-child of the golden-haired and blue-eyed type such as the "Home Magazine" page of the family newspaper loves to portray by the three-color process, Miss Vivian Martin was never allowed to grow up, professionally, until Charles Frohman decreed that she should be a Maude Adams in miniature, playing Peter Pan in some important provincial circuits which Miss Adams has not yet gotten around to.

This is not the paradox that it seems on the face of it. For, while Peter Pan is the symbol of the eternal "kid," it requires a mature *artiste*, and even then some more, to put Peter over the footlights.

Miss Martin, although hardly yet out of her teens as the actual count of years goes, is in other respects the mature *artiste* with a full decade of professional experience behind her.

She started with Mansfield in "Cyrano de Bergerac," and during the past season has been seen in the rollicking hue and cry of an up-to-date Broadway farce called "Stop Thief!" The interval between these two engagements affords a diversified chapter of contemporaneous stage history, which the young *comédienne* sketches for us autobiographically, in her vivacious way:

"I was born in sunny Michigan. As far back as I can remember, my mother was never opposed to my going on the stage—rather the contrary, bless her heart!

"I may as well tell you, I was NOT educated in a convent. In fact, I was in danger of not being educated at all, except for home teaching, if my mother had not retired me from the theater for a couple of years and sent me to school.

"And I was a little school-girl with a past I can

Vivian Martin, a comédienne who yearns to play strong, temperamental parts

413

Cosmopolitan
August 1913
designer unknown

By 1913 Cosmopolitan had already developed an understanding of graphic unity, illustrated by this montage of right-facing silhouettes arranged, over a diamond-shaped vignette, across the spread. The differential scale provides depth and the cut-out pictures are integrated with text by extraordinarily elaborate, staggered typesetting. Three years later Will Bradley's styling took the process further by taking single pictures across the binding.

L'ASSIETTE AU BEURRE

LES STATISTICIENS.

— Rappelez-vous : lorsque Kock découvrit sa tuberculine, le nombre des tuberculeux diminua brusquement.
— Je vous crois : ce fameux traitement les tuait presque tous aussitôt !

L'ASSIETTE AU BEURRE 453

LES PROFESSIONNELLES.

— C'est tout de même rigolo... ils en parlent tous !... Interrogez-les individuellement, pas un seul ne vous déclarera *qu'il l'a*.

L'Assiette au Beurre

October 1910

designer unknown

L'Assiette au Beurre ("the butter dish", or colloquially, "graft") was a splendid leftist satirical magazine published in Paris from 1901 to 1912. Its full-page colour litho illustrations combined the naturalistic freedom of L'Art Moderne with the exaggerated forms of Art Nouveau. The illustrator was B. Galanis.

Practical photoengraving of black and white photographs with text was made feasible by the halftone screen process which remains in use today. The grid-patterned screen, first tried commercially in the USA in 1880, was in general use in magazines by 1895.[7] It was cheap and it was quick. In 1900 the American magazine *The Century* is said to have paid $300 for a full-page wood engraving and only $20 for a photographic halftone.[8]

During the three decades from 1870 to 1900, whilst printers struggled with crude halftone screens, magazine illustration had its golden age. Colour lithography, born out of experiments by Jules Cheret in Paris and London in the 1860s, brought colour to magazines for the first time and provided an artistic freedom on which many of the innovations of the modern movement in graphic design were founded. Lithography, always associated with Parisian art magazines of the late nineteenth century, was in fact used for a wide variety of short-run magazines printed on sheet-fed two-colour presses which gave

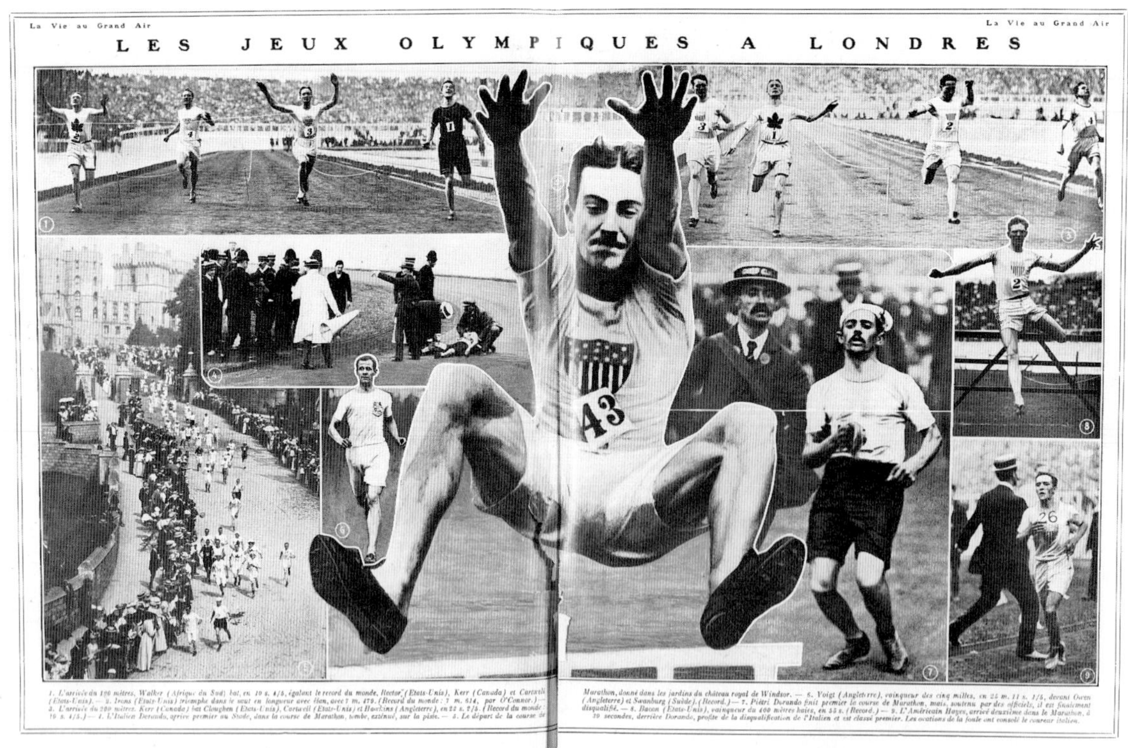

La Vie au Grand Air

July 1908

designer unknown

The French sports magazine anticipated the new dynamic of montage and the expression of movement. This spread exhibits many of the qualities of modern magazine design: the two pages are treated as a single unit; there is minimal decoration; photographs are locked together both as a grid and by the cut-out heads of the athletes; and the whole construction is unified by a tremendous action picture of a long-jumper bursting out of the page.

5,000 to 8,000 impressions per hour.[9] Colour was no longer a luxury.

Colour lithography was adopted by the early moderns as a means of propagating the natural style, and the magazine was a fitting vehicle for the new mode of painted reportage. Major impressionists – Manet, Degas, Monet, Sisley, Pissarro and Renoir – contributed frequently to *La Vie Moderne* (from 1879) and Toulouse Lautrec to several magazines beginning with *Le Mirliton.*[10] *Le Rire, Figaro Illustré, La Revue Blanche, Paris Illustré* and the British *Graphic* provided an essential platform to European artists; the role of the Parisian magazines in disseminating the modern art movement is well documented, but of more significance to magazines and magazine design was the establishment of a new rank of secondary artists – Renouard, Rochegosse, Forain, Boyd-Houghton – who grasped magazine illustration as a livelihood and founded a new mode of stark and realistic illustrative reporting in *Graphic* and *Harper's*, and in satirical political weeklies such as *L'Assiette au Beurre* and *Simplicissimus*.

L'Art Moderne broadened the role of the magazine as a documenter not only of news but of popular culture and common experience. The art magazines ignored convention, reworking the cover – once, typically, a standard ornate engraving used week after week (as in *Punch* or *The Strand Magazine*) – into a topical, vibrant, illustrated poster. The art monthlies maintained high standards of design and production, and contributed to the division of labour which ultimately enabled art editors to squeeze out some editorial power. Illustrators took on the role of art editors: Charles Parson on *Harper's Weekly*; John Heartfield on *Die Neue Jugend*, de Vinne on *Scribner's* and *The Century*, Ozenfant on *l'Elan*, as well as Sloane at *The Masses*.[11]

The general improvement in quality of production was given further impetus by the Arts and Crafts Movement. Aubrey Beardsley's *The Studio* (c. 1888), the German *Jugend* (1896), the exquisite *Ver Sacrum*, the magazine of the Vienna Secessionists (1897) and Bradley's *Inland Printer* (from c. 1890) paraded a commitment to fine typography, design, paper and printing during a period of rapid and traumatic industrialization. But the legacy of the Arts and Crafts Movement to modern design should not be confused with its direct contribution to magazine design, which was negligible. These publications may have encouraged the expressionist use of type which later proved of such value in creating magazine identity, but their designers were concerned rather more with reinventing the incunabulum than with the composition of the modern periodical.

Illustrated London News
April 1939
designer unknown

The "art treatment" of pictures: this is a classic example of turn-of-the-century photographic arrangements with oval vignettes, decorative borders, perfect symmetry, no evidence of cropping and no variation of scale. The date proves the immunity of some magazines to modernist notions of asymmetry and contrast, or to the advances made by German and Russian picture magazines in the previous decade.

MADRID FALLS TO GENERAL FRANCO AFTER 33 MONTHS OF WAR: SCENES OF ENTHUSIASM IN THE CITY AS NATIONALIST TROOPS MARCH IN.

THE CHIEF STRONGHOLD OF REPUBLICAN SPAIN SURRENDERS: NATIONALIST TROOPS GREETED BY THE INHABITANTS OF A "FRONT-LINE" CITY.

The development of magazine layout proceeded separately from that of the illustrated art magazines. Technology had created the potential for high quality, lavishly illustrated mass magazines: hot metal composition was introduced in 1896; the new high-speed rotary presses were capable of spitting out millions of copies a day; and in 1890 Karel Klic had demonstrated the industrial application of rotary photogravure.[12] Rotogravure was first used commercially in 1910 by Eduard Mertens on a section of *Freiburger Zeitung*,[13] and was adopted by *L'Illustration* and *J'Ai Vu* one year later.[14] The technique offered high-quality reproduction of type and photography printed from a single plate. Gravure, often used in combination with letterpress, became the primary method of producing colour magazines and its dominance was not broken by four-colour offset lithograpy until the 1960s.

In the news weeklies, editors were forced by the corresponding increase in the use of photography to re-consider page formats, although their response was usually to revert to traditional arrangements of pictures. Photographs were given what has come to be known as the "art" treatment, in which every image was decked out with an extravagant ornate border and portraits were displayed in oval vignettes in the manner of miniature paintings. The purpose was evidently to dignify the photograph with the label of art (illustrations were rarely disfigured in this way). Photographs were hung on the page as if on a gallery wall, with no consideration of visual priority or picture size, and no conception of the crop. One rare exception to this rule was *Leslie's Weekly*, which published front covers of shocking and utilitarian simplicity.

There is evidence in the first decade of the twentieth century that new forms of page composition were being developed in commercial publishing quite independently of the academic *avant-garde*. A still more remarkable pioneer of modern design was the French sports magazine *La Vie au Grand Air*, founded in 1890. By 1908 it had adopted an entirely original style of layout which was a direct precursor of the early photojournalistic magazines. *La Vie au Grand Air* used photomontage, sequences of squared-off photographs, tight crops and inset pictures to amplify the motion and action of sports photography. Nothing quite like it appeared again for twenty years. Not until the pre-industrial definition of "art" was swept aside, and a modern art was properly articulated, would the uninhibited and aggressive use of photography accompany the printed word.

A dynamic iconography: magazines and the modern movement

Veshch
1922
designer El Lissitzky
An early exercise in dynamic graphic composition for the titlepage of Veshch [Object], the international review of modern art.

Magazine design was transformed by the modern movement. The cubo-futurist doctrine of plastic dynamism[1] and the new, objective typography were primary forces in the liberation of magazine design from its traditional constraints. Asymmetric layouts created the potential for a fluent and dynamic visual vocabulary, and offered infinitely more compositional possibilities than the static, monolithic classical style. Similarly, the exploration of typographic relationships undertaken by Theo van Doesburg, El Lissitzky, László Moholy-Nagy and others[2] presaged the creation of a new hierarchy of type which was suited to the particular requirements of the magazine.

In his *Messaggio* of 1914, the Italian Antonio Sant'Elia articulated an ideological framework for the new design movement. The manifesto, by an architect associated primarily with futurism, introduced pioneering ideas which anticipated constructivism and elementalism. He wrote: "I affirm…

"That the new architecture is the architecture of cold calculation, temerarious boldness and simplicity, the architecture of…[materials] that make for the attainment in maximum elasticity and lightness.

"That real architecture is not, for all that, an arid combination of practicality and utility, but remains art, that is, synthesis and expression.

"That decoration as something superimposed on or attached to architecture is an absurdity, and that only from the use and disposition of raw, naked and violently coloured materials can derive the decorative value of a truly Modern architecture.

"And finally I affirm that just as the ancients drew their inspiration in art from the elements of the natural world, so we – materially and spiritually artificial – must find our inspiration in the new mechanical world we have created, of which architecture must be the fairest expression, the fullest synthesis, the most effective artistic integration."[3]

Each of these precepts can be transferred without loss from architecture to graphic design. The quintessence of modernism is the liberating facility of the machine. The "attainment in maximum elasticity and lightness", a basic component of the new aesthetic, is achievable in print through the use of photography, lithography, Linotyping, ultimately photo-typesetting (which was already anticipated) and by digital page composition (which was certainly not). The goal of the modern aesthetic is the creation of a different kind of balance, which expresses not a harmony of sheer mass, or monumental stasis, but change, movement, the constant revolutions of the machine age: to use the fundamental elements of the page to express tension as well as strength, and achieving a synthesis from those separate elements.

The "new typography" was both an expression and a vehicle of change, suited to new production methods, new kinds of printed matter, and to altered political and social perceptions. In its superficial mannerisms it celebrated the machine; in its appearance it exploited the capabilities of the machine; and its underlying impetus was the rationalist end of improving the organization and communication of information. Where the latter goal was absent it became mere stylistic fetish.

The revolution was ignited by futurists, Dada and cubists, by the suprematist Malevich, and the De Stijl group, fractious and contradictory movements which found their nexus in constructivism and, ultimately, elementarism, the doctrine of the unity of design elements propounded by El Lissitzky and László Moholy-

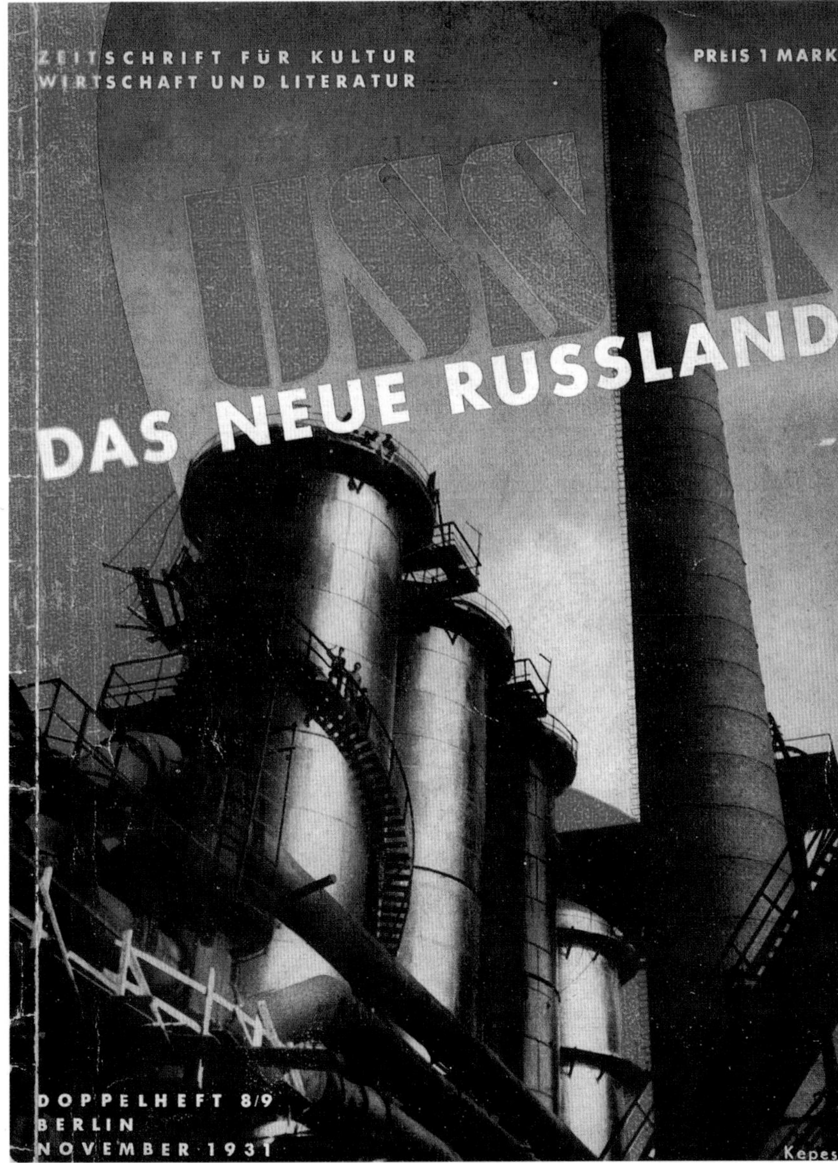

Das Neue Russland

November 1931

designer Gyorgy Kepes

Application of the principles of plastic dynamism to print: wide-angle distortion of the photograph is echoed in the placement of the type on a diagonal axis.

Nagy.[4] If modern graphic design can be summarized briefly it should be as, primarily, a democratic, egalitarian force which eliminated frivolous embellishment – expressions of class or privilege – in order to stress the true function of printed matter, in which the object, not its ornamentation, was the principle art form; as a search for a rational, objective means of communicating ideas through the appropriate application of printing technologies; and as the destruction of the old aesthetic, shrugging off outmoded prejudice and forme-bound ways of working which, in printing, could be described as the tombstone mentality – the crushing of type in the straightjacket of symmetry.

The impact of modernist design practice on magazines was all the greater because of their peculiar structure. The page was traditionally given an upright, columnar structure with no integral visual relationship with its opposite number across the spine – except reflection. The system works in a conventional book, where each page is merely one element of a series; and in a newspaper, in which many stories compete with each other on a single page according to established typographic rules. By contrast the magazine article is – in its ideal form – a self-contained body of text and pictures occupying a double-page spread. The article may often be related by subject and by format to the rest of the magazine, but it remains semi-autonomous. It therefore requires a distinct *mise en page* which floods across the rectangular spread, defying the symmetrical approach; and it requires a hierarchy of type which accommodates all the elements of a story in one view: heading, introduction, body text, sub-heads, captions.

These conditions inform all magazine design and determine the pace and continuity of the magazine.

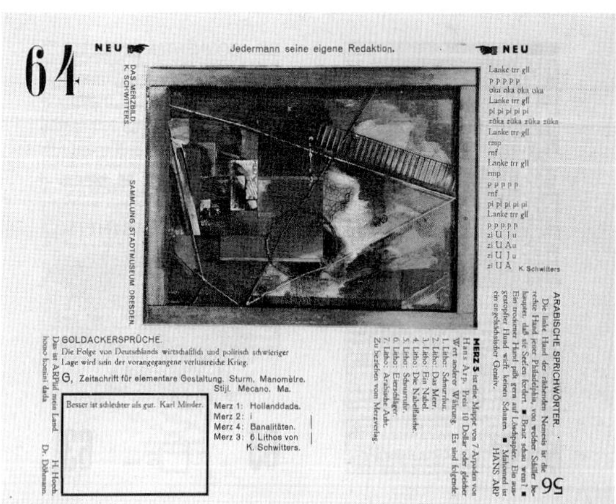

Merz

no. 6 October 1923

designer Kurt Schwitters

Merz (the title is an ironic contraction of "Commerz") was a Dada offshoot founded in Hanover by Kurt Schwitters. This centre spread includes one of Schwitters' "Merz" collages, and is characterized by the iconoclastic order of Dada typography.

Merz

no. 11 1924

designer Kurt Schwitters

Dada is superseded by constructivist influence in this later cover, for an issue devoted to the new typography in advertising.

The magazine is a continuum of cover, contents page, minor features, major features and miscellany, with a specific architectural integrity which, in this respect, differs from other forms of printed matter. This is why the grid takes on a double function in the magazine. The underlying geometric framework suggested by the work of the synthetic cubists and rather more directly by the compositional studies of Mondrian and van Doesburg, could be utilized as an anchor of constancy, or point of reference, within unrestrained asymmetric layouts.

The notion of linear continuity within print was addressed by El Lissitzky in the pages of his magazine *Veshch/Gegenstand/Objet* (1922) and in his pictorial book *The isms of art* (1924), which employed a consistent grid system of three vertical columns with an identifying horizontal bar at the top of each outer column. The design is balanced asymmetrically across each double-page spread. The same constructional tools were employed in the quarterly Bauhaus magazine which first appeared in 1927. The use of horizontal and vertical grid systems had already been exploited by the magazine's designer, László Moholy-Nagy, in the Bauhaus book *Malerei, Photographie, Film*, a graphic storyboard which used a grid to associate disparate elements in both space and time. This cinematic device became a model for the complex organizational requirements of the formatted magazine.

This rational approach had as its opposite, and as its precursor, the wilful caprice of futurists and Dadaists: perpetrators of crimes of such typographic disobedience that the limits imposed by the printers' forme were entirely disregarded. The chaotic, destructive, iconoclastic tendencies were dedicated to the extermination of the old order, and in many

7 dnei MKT

no. 15 1924

designers
V. and G. Stenberg,
K. Medunetskii

In 7 dnei MKT [Seven Days at the Moscow Kamernyi Theatre], heavy rules and blocked type build a solid constructivist architecture, practically applied to differentiate text, and creating powerful contrasts of black and white.

1928
2. jahrgang nr. 4
einzelheft preis rmk. 1.20

inhalt

bescheidene malerei von ernst kállai	seite	**1**
gestaltung? von n. gabo	seite	**2**
probleme um die lichtreklame von hugo häring	seite	**7**
internationaler kongreß für neues bauen	seite	**8**
reihenhausprojekt für tel aviv von ph. tolziner, bauhaus	seite	**10**
entwurf zu einer siedlungsschule von ernst göhl, bauhaus	seite	**11**
bauen von hannes meyer	seite	**12**
möbel aus holz oder metall oder?? von gustav hassenpflug, bauhaus	seite	**14**
ein beliebter vorwurf gegen das bauhaus von ernst kállai	seite	**15**
interview mit bauhäuslern	seite	**18**
glossen	seite	**23**
bauhausnachrichten	seite	**24**
buchbesprechungen von ludwig hilberseimer	seite	**26**
über herwarth walden	seite	**28**
kunst und sport	seite	**29**
33 abbildungen		

die bauhausbücher

verlag albert langen, münchen, hubertusstr. 27
schriftleitung: w. gropius und l. moholy-nagy

band 1 **walter gropius, internationale architektur** (zweite auflage) geh. 5 in leinen geb. 7 rmk.
band 2 **paul klee, pädagogisches skizzenbuch** vergriffen
band 3 **ein versuchshaus des bauhauses** vergriffen
band 4 **die bühne des bauhauses** geh. 5, in leinen geb. 7 rmk.
band 5 **piet mondrian, neue gestaltung** vergriffen
band 6 **theo van doesburg, grundbegriffe der neuen gestaltenden kunst** vergriffen
band 7 **neue arbeiten der bauhauswerkstätten** geh. 6, in leinen geb. 8 rmk.
band 8 **l. moholy-nagy, malerei, photographie, film** (zweite auflage) geh. 7, in leinen geb. 9 rmk.
band 9 **w. kandinsky, punkt und linie zur fläche** (zweite auflage) geh. 15, in leinen geb. 18 rmk.
band 10 **j. j. p. oud, holländische architektur** geh. 6, in leinen geb. 8 rmk.

neu erschienen ist:

band 11 **k. malewitsch, die gegenstandslose welt,** begründung und erklärung des russischen suprematismus geh. 6, in leinen geb. 8 rmk.

in kürze erscheinen:

band 12 **w. gropius, bauhausneubauten in dessau**
band 13 **a. gleizes, kubismus**
band 14 **l. moholy-nagy, von kunst zu leben**

die sammlung wird fortgesetzt

die bauhaus-zeitschrift erscheint vierteljährlich
bezugspreis jährlich rmk. 4.—
einzelnummer rmk. 1.20
preis dieser nummer rmk. 1.20

abonnements bei dem verlag oder durch den buchhandel

verlag und anzeigenverwaltung: dessau, zerbster str. 16
postscheckkonto: magdeburg 16662
telefon sammel-nr. 3106
für den anzeigenteil verantwortlich: hermann steffen, dessau.

bezugs- und zahlungsbedingungen:
abonnements haben geltung bis ende des laufenden kalenderjahres. abonnements, die 30 tage vor ablauf des laufenden kalenderjahres beim verlage schriftlich nicht gekündigt sind, gelten als um das nächste kalenderjahr verlängert. erteilte rechnungen sind so zeitig zu begleichen, daß der verlag spätestens 8 tage nach rechnungsdatum über die rechnungsbeträge verfügen kann. überfällige forderungen erhöhen sich um mahn- und inkassospesen. ausfall der zeitschriftenlieferung ohne verschulden des verlages (streik, höhere gewalt usw.) berechtigt nicht zum verlangen nach minderung des bezugspreises oder schadenersatzleistung. erfüllungsort und gerichtsstand für beide teile ist dessau.

sendungen an die redaktion: bauhaus dessau
für die redaktion verantwortlich: ernst kállai, dessau.
für unverlangte beiträge und rezensionsexemplare keinerlei gewähr.

alle rechte vorbehalten

nr. 2/3 1928 der bauhauszeitschrift ist vollständig vergriffen!

Bauhaus

issue 2 1928

designer Joost Schmidt

The contents page of Bauhaus bears the hallmarks of the new typography: lower-case lettering, asymmetric composition, a very advanced sans serif form and heavy horizontal rules. Note the architecture of the page, in which the second column is held up by a pillar of vertical type.

Bauhaus

issue 3 1929

designer Joost Schmidt

A simple and versatile cover format, with the logo reversed out of a left ranging black bar, which served as a model for later magazines. The primitive collage form used to illustrate this issue was enthusiastically adopted by American designers, including Paul Rand and George Giusti.

Novy Lef

1928

designer
Alexander Rodchenko

Cover of the Russian constructivist arts magazine Novy Lef [New Left Front of the Arts]. The eye is the most potent of visual symbols.

respects were premature – if only because the expressionistic application of type in disjointed curves and diagonals across a sea of white space, its formlessness, its subliminal mode of communication, was better suited to a time (like our own) with the appropriate technology and individualistic response. Dada-esque exuberance could not be practically sustained when letterpress remained the primary means of printing. Dada, which was founded in Zurich in 1917, had all but liquidated itself by 1922, along with the magazine of the same name (1917-21). It had fulfilled its political and artistic purpose but left important enduring influences. The group "helped to free typography from its rectilinear restrictions",[5] primarily via the influence of the closet Dadaist van Doesburg;[6] and it "reinforced the cubist idea of letterforms as a visual experience"[7] – Dada word pictures became a staple of the magazine designers of the expressionist New York School in the 1950s and 1960s. Yet the movement's great contribution to magazine design was the application of collage and photomontage to print and the use of photographic sequences as the prototype of magazine photojournalism. Experimentation with composites of type and photography using photograms, montage and juxtaposition was continued by constructivists, at the Bauhaus, and popularized by the Dadaist John Heartfield in magazines.[8]

The Dadaist magazine *Merz* personified the flight of one wing of the movement into the arms of the New Typography. Between 1923 and 1932 the 24 issues published in Hanover by Kurt Schwitters exhibited progressively coherent, not to say rational, tendencies – Dada was combined with constructivism. A gridless mix of serif and sans serif type in issue 6 of 1923 is, by issue 11 of 1924, exchanged for the distinctive bold rules of De Stijl and by the use of typeweight, colour and symbol to create a strong, contrary vertical movement. The trend had already been confirmed by issue 8/9, which was designed jointly by El Lissitzky and Schwitters.

At the Bauhaus, early flirtations with "capricious" expressionism and the construction of word games were stamped out by Laszló Moholy-Nagy on his arrival in 1923. He defined the aims of the school's typography workshop in stern language: "Typography must be clear communication in its most vivid form. Clarity must be especially stressed, for clarity is the essence of modern printing. Therefore, first of all: *absolute* clarity in all typographical work. Communication ought not to labour under preconceived aesthetic notions. Letters should never be squeezed into an arbitrary shape…like a square. A new typographic language must be created combining elasticity, variety and a fresh approach to the

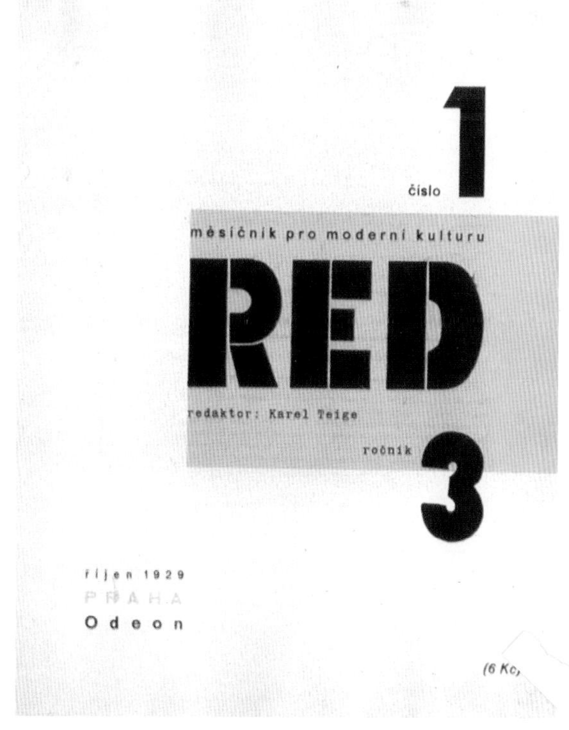

Red

1929

designer Karel Teige

Cover for the Czech "modern culture" magazine Red. Balance is imparted to Teige's typographic construction by the application of contrasting blocks of colour.

materials of printing, a language whose logic depends on the appropriate application of the processes of printing."[9]

The seeds of conflict lie in the double emphasis on *absolute* clarity on the one hand, and the application of "elasticity, variety and a fresh approach" on the other. Rational organization and legibility, and expressive, intuitive work are not mutually exclusive, but therein lies a contradiction that is the primary cause of periodic schism in the graphic design profession, and which appears in exaggerated form in editorial design. Moholy-Nagy's concrete typography for the cover of the international review *i 10* (1927) is a classic example of the use of harmonious space, straight lines and unadorned type to achieve immediate and clear communication of information. In every sense it is a "fresh approach" but it is shorn of emotional meaning. Subjective factors in communication have, by contrast, played a strong role in popular magazine design in the twentieth century.

The Bauhaus legacy can be interpreted narrowly as the creation of a technically "objective" typography through the elimination of serif and black-letter *Fraktur*, ragged right setting, heavy rules as sightlines, the monalphabet, etc., which are merely the minutiae of a formalistic approach to clarity. Tschichold's expression "new typography" can mislead the unwary because its practitioners were concerned not only with type but with the manipulation of diverse design elements – type, photography, colour, symbol, space, and time, in the cinematic manipulation of page sequences – coupled with the exploitation of new production processes. Nor is it a machine fetishism, dumb worship of the straight line at which Moholy-Nagy scoffed. Sant'Elia's assertion is worth repeating: "That real architecture is not, for all that, an arid combination of practicality and utility, but remains art, that is, synthesis and expression." For magazine design, the crucial invention is the graphic synthesis, whereby the magazine becomes a single entity that is more than the sum of its parts.

The theory of integration as a design discipline is primarily El Lissitzky's; the fundamental elements of Malevich's suprematist art – simple geometric forms that are the basic units of composition – are combined with the constructivist sensibility whereby all the elements are "drawn into the design as equally important parts and brought to unity".[10] This "elementarism" came to Germany via El Lissitzky's magazine *Veshch* and the elementarist paintings of Moholy-Nagy, and on to it was grafted selected components of De Stijl, so that: "Space in elementarist art is, indeed, continu-

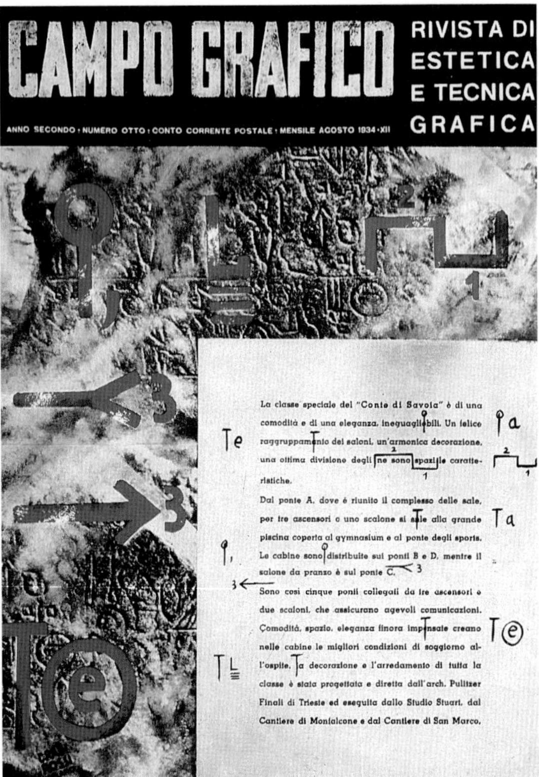

Campo Grafico
vol. 2 no. 8 August 1934
designer Attilio Rossi

Cover montage in three colours – black, blue and red – designed by Attilio Rossi and Carlo Dradi. The designers of Campo Grafico "resorted to every possible optical trick and exploited asymmetry with the fullest freedom and imagination" (Aldo Rossi).

Campo Grafico

vol. 2 no. 12 December 1934

designer Attilio Rossi

Opening page and spread from an exercise in the combination of type and image within asymmetric order. Note the use of a tint of black on the opening page to raise the photograph optically from the page. The photograph is by Antonio Boggeri.

FOTOGRAFIA E TIPOGRAFIA

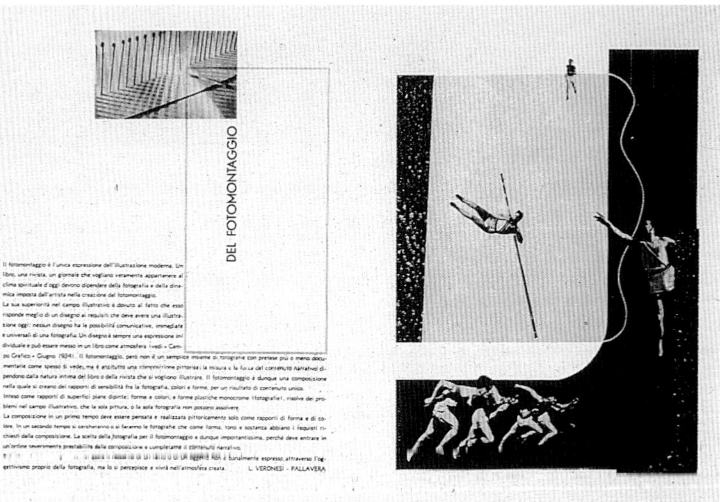

DEL FOTOMONTAGGIO

ous and open, and the work of art is a structure that makes its rectangularity manifest by giving body to its grid-lines and the planes and volumes between them, and this is still true even when the grid, as in some van Doesburg paintings of the mid-Twenties, has been skewed out of the vertical."[11]

The relationships between the elements are those of mass, space, plane, proportion, rhythm. Mass is provided by colour (mainly red and black), by weight of type and rules, and by shape (circle, square, triangle) juxtaposed to create moments of force and equilibrium – relationships which were explored within Tolmer's *Mise en Page*, published in Paris in 1929. Tolmer, a printer, introduced with his book new printing and photographic techniques together with this theory of layout: "the art of layout is an art of balance. It cannot, however, be expressed merely as a mathematical calculation" (although many have tried). Weight and movement can, after all, be implied; they need not be manifest on the page. El Lissitzky extended the volume of space in which he worked to a notional third dimension, experimenting in his paintings with architectural perspective and optical illusion, with the idea of lines of force extending beyond the confines of the page. The idea can be seen in much of the work of Piet Zwart, Ladislav Sutnar (especially in his magazine *Zjieme*) Karel Tiege and by Alexander Rodchenko in *Novi Lef*, the journal of the Left Front of the Arts in Moscow.

The practical implementation of such techniques was demonstrated in design, art and architectural magazines of the period. The new design was exported internationally by the German *Gebrauchsgrafik* magazine and, specifically, to Poland in *Blok*, to Czechoslovakia in *Red* (designed by Tiege) and Sutnar's *Zjieme*, *MA* in Hungary, and rather later within Italy in *Campo Grafico*. In Germany the new typography spread most rapidly from design publications to agitation and propaganda magazines – *Das Neue Russland*, with covers by John Heartfield and Gyorgy Kepes and typography by Paul Urban, *Sowjet-Russland im Bild*, *Sichel und Hammer*, and in its most vibrant form in the sports magazine *Die Arena*. In the young Soviet Union constructivist typography became the norm in many sectors of publishing, used in its purist form in which type was given a double function, as a conveyor of words, and as an expressive building block for the page. This explicitly typographical approach could be found in many of the period's journals: the style is evident in *Architecture* (c. 1923) designed by Alexander Vesnin, in Solomon Telingater's *Revoulutsyonnaya Arkhitektura*, in Mayakovsky and Rodchenko's *Lef* and *Novi Lef*, in *30 days*, designed by Gustav Klusis, and perhaps at its most developed in the theatre weekly *7 dnei MKT* (*Seven days at the Moscow Kamernyi Theatre*). The most active of magazine designers in Moscow in this period was Alexander Rodchenko, who was concerned with the formatting, cover design or photography of numerous publications, including the aforementioned *Lef*, *Sovetskoe kino* (*Soviet Cinema*), *Krasnoe studenchestvo* (the *Red Studentship*), *Sovremennay arkhitektura* (*Contemporary Architecture*), *Za rubezhom* (*Abroad*), *Borba Klassov* (*Class Struggle*), *Smena* (*Shift*), *Literatura i Iskusstvo* (*Literature and Art*), and *Soviet Life*;[12] and from 1933 onwards was photographer/designer with El Lissitzky of *SSSR Na Stroike* (*USSR

De 8 en opbouw

May 1932

designer Paul Schuitema

An example of graphic synthesis achieved through the superimposition of type on type and on photography. A tint of red is utilized as the linking medium between the separate elements.

in Construction), which is examined in more detail in the next chapter.

The popularization of modern design theory was interrupted by the rise of fascism in Europe. In Germany, the avant-garde was viciously suppressed. Heavy-handed monumentalism and heroic realism triumphed in almost all European countries in the period up to and including the Second World War. Switzerland remained as a haven for rationalism, and in Italy the unique *Campo Grafico* experiment, exploiting the peculiar inconsistencies of Italian fascism, provided an essential source of continuity in a country which, today, boasts the finest magazines in the world. The *Campo Grafico* studio and magazine of the same name were founded in Milan in 1933 by a group of printers led by Attilio Rossi. The impact of the magazine within Italy was considerable; its significance lay in the role it adopted as a standard-bearer for modern editorial and advertising design in opposition to fascism's bombastic aesthetic of neoclassical symmetry. Rossi and his collaborators self-consciously explored the relationship between modern art and contemporary editorial design ("True renewal", it was written in an early issue, "is impossible unless the revitalizing influence of modern art and the problems of avant-garde are brought into the field of printing"[13]), and the development of a unity of photography and typography, building upon the basis laid by graphic artists in Germany. Constant experimentation contributed to the very varied layouts of the magazine. *Campo Grafico* provided a foretaste of the development of magazine design in the commercial sphere.

Links Richten

no. 9 1933

designer Paul Schuitema

An expressive, unified and mobile cover for the Dutch worker-writer magazine. It is created from minimal components: three lines of lower-case type, an issue number and a single photograph repeated as a tint.

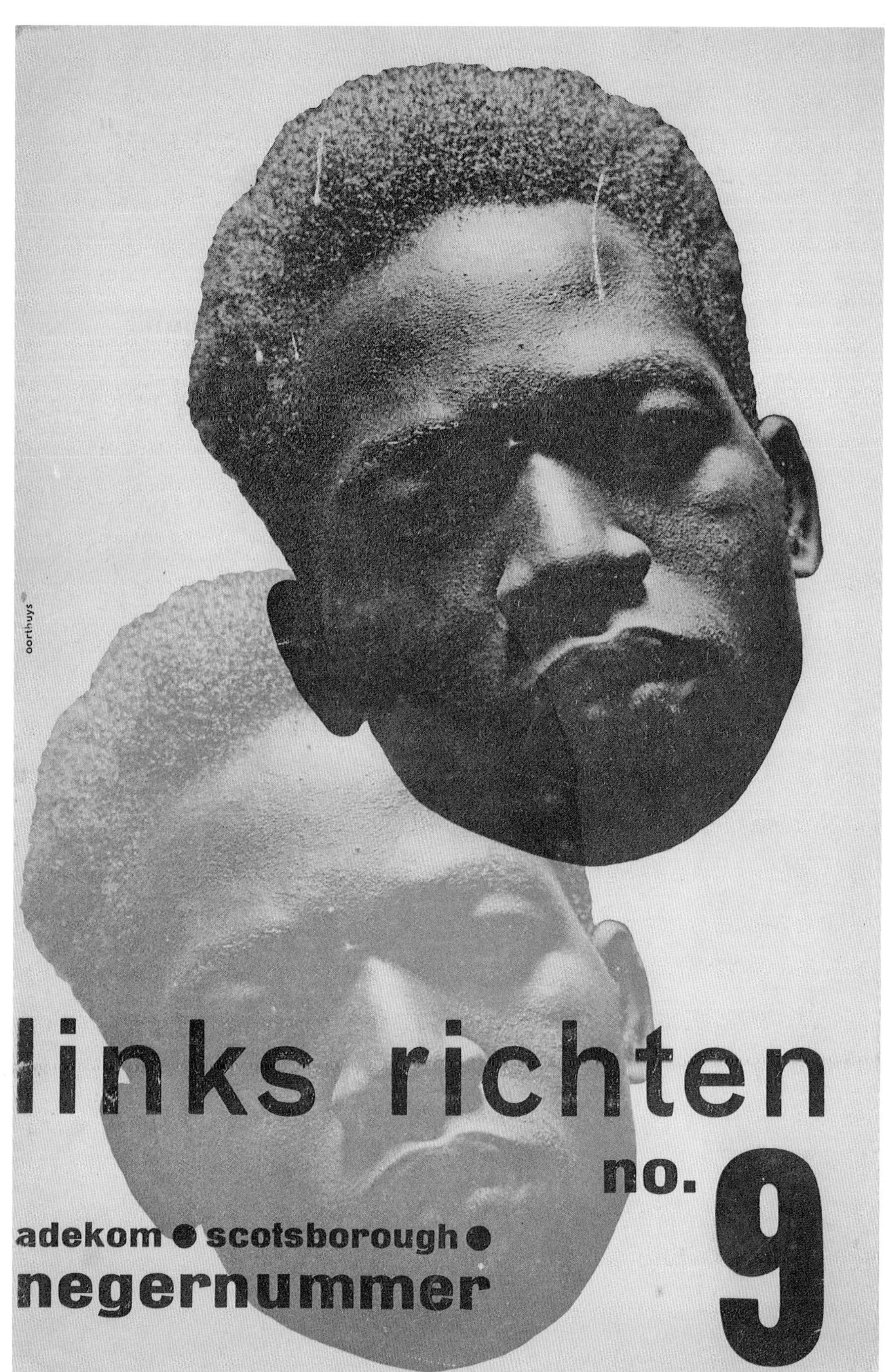

The big picture: photojournalism between the wars

The rapid development of magazine design between the wars can be illustrated emphatically by a comparison of any of the grand old illustrated weeklies with the new, aggressive photojournals: ostentation gave way to purpose. *London Illustrated News*, *L'Illustration*, even *Berliner Illustrierte Zeitung* up until the First World War, had taken reluctantly to photography. *L'Illustration* in 1930 was an extravagant publication which delighted in showing off opulent new colour printing techniques, of the kind which had recently been demonstrated by Tolmer using heavy embossed or metalled papers. *L'Illustration* was anything but plain and functional; it flaunted a decorative, half *belle époche*, half *deco* style, befitting the house magazine of the French plutocracy. This was the old way. Its opposite could be found in the new-style picture magazines in which typography and layout had been simplified to a reductive and austere formula, a formula perfected in the art department of *Life* magazine as "a good, squared-up photograph with a bold, short caption leading into short, crisp text."[1] Decorative treatments were banished, type variation within a story was minimized, bolder headings coupled with brief standfirsts stood alongside the "foursquare" photography, confidently sized to dominate the page.

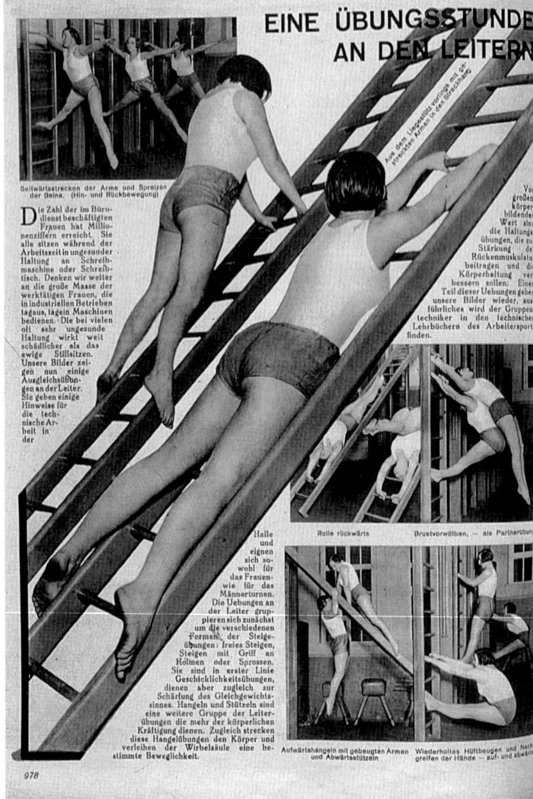

EINE ÜBUNGSSTUNDE AN DEN LEITERN

Seitwärtsstrecken der Arme und Spreizen der Beine. (Hin- und Rückbewegung)

Die Zahl der im Bürodienst beschäftigten Frauen hat Millionenziffern erreicht. Sie alle sitzen während der Arbeitszeit in ungesunder Haltung an Schreibmaschine oder Schreibtisch. Denken wir weiter an die große Masse der werktätigen Frauen, die in industriellen Betrieben tagaus, tagein Maschinen bedienen. Die bei vielen oft sehr ungesunde Haltung wirkt weit schädlicher als das ewige Stillsitzen. Unsere Bilder zeigen nun einige Ausgleichsübungen an der Leiter. Sie geben einige Hinweise für die technische Arbeit in der Halle und eignen sich sowohl für das Frauen- wie für das Männerturnen. Die Uebungen an der Leiter gruppieren sich zunächst um die verschiedenen Formen der Steigeübungen: freies Steigen, Steigen mit Griff an Holmen oder Sprossen. Sie sind in erster Linie Geschicklichkeitsübungen, dienen aber zugleich zur Schärfung des Gleichgewichtssinnes. Hangeln und Stützeln sind eine weitere Gruppe der Leiterübungen die mehr der körperlichen Kräftigung dienen. Zugleich strecken diese Hangelübungen den Körper und verleihen der Wirbelsäule eine bestimmte Beweglichkeit.

Aus dem Liegestütz vorlings mit gestreckten Armen in den Streckhang

Von großem körperbildenden Wert sind die Haltungsübungen, die zur Stärkung der Rückenmuskulatur beitragen und die Körperhaltung verbessern sollen. Einen Teil dieser Uebungen geben unsere Bilder wieder, ausführliches wird der Gruppentechniker in den technischen Lehrbüchern des Arbeitersports finden.

Rolle rückwärts

Brustvorwölben, — als Partnerübung

Aufwärtshangeln mit gebeugten Armen und Abwärtsstützeln

Wiederholtes Hüftbeugen und Nachgreifen der Hände — auf- und abwärts

978

Arbeiter Illustrierte Zeitung
c. 1930
designers
Wieland Herzfeld et al

Sport was a favourite editorial subject in AIZ, and was almost always represented in graphically dynamic fashion. Sharp diagonals, cut-outs and contour setting were commonly used to this end.

It was the invention of the first hand-held 35mm camera – the Leica – by Oskar Barnack in 1923 that provoked such a revolutionary change in attitudes to photography and its role in print. By the end of that decade magazine design had been pushed into a new era in which the continuity of a story was provided by the pictures, not by the text. The photographic sequence was not an original idea, but it was the format which designers naturally adopted when provided with prints made on the new roll-film. The hand-held camera and newly developed fast film enabled photographers to capture spontaneous action, to tell a story with heightened realism and (often literally) from a new angle; the photographer was no longer bound by the tripod and heavy glass plates to grimly staged poses. Magazine stories, once illustrated by pictures from a variety of sources, found their focus in the 35mm roll produced by a single photographer in a consistent style. The page

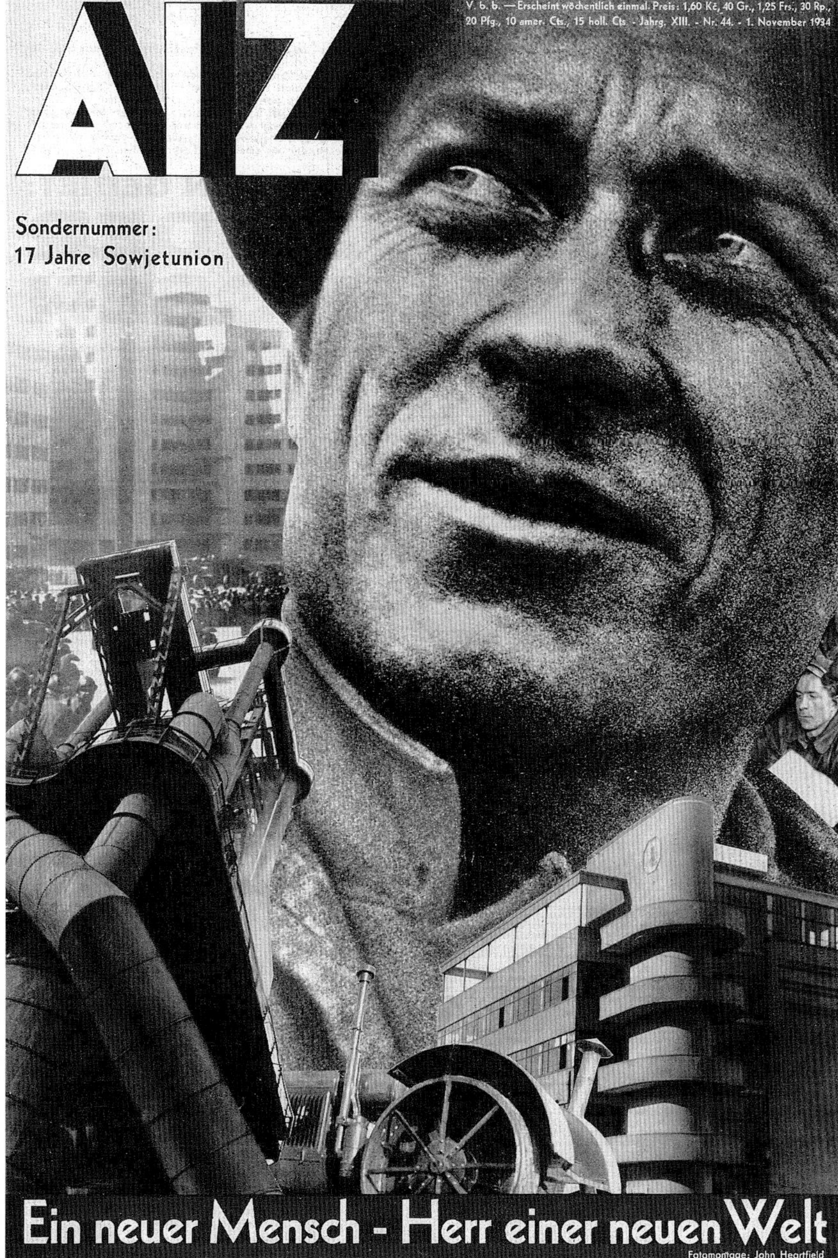

Arbeiter Illustrierte Zeitung
1 November 1934
designer John Heartfield

Cover montage for a special issue celebrating the 17th anniversary of the October revolution.

became a pattern of strikingly juxtaposed images from which its shades, shapes and contrasts were derived, unadorned.

The lessons learnt by the avant-garde were rapidly assimilated by elements of the popular press in Germany and Russia; and rather later, and in more muted form, in France, Britain and the USA. By the outbreak of war in 1939 even *L'Illustration*, impressed by the phenomenal success of the *Life* formula, had donned a severe new uniform within which it competed against the upstart *Match*.[2]

Photography was, as Rodchenko described it, "the new and perfect means to discover the contemporary world of man's science, technology and everyday life."[3] It was also "an indispensable and outstanding means of propaganda"[4] which is why the photojournal came to be regarded as a most potent weapon in a period of harsh political struggle. The progressive left-inclined avant-garde had no monopoly over the new typography, which one contemporary designer described as "a highly effective means of communication" which, in the hands of fascism and the plutocracies, "was being used to spread lies".[5] Modern printing was as usefully employed by Goebbels' *Signal* or Henry Luce's *Life* – an active lobbyist for the cause of American expansionism – as it was in the Soviet five-year plan magazine *SSSR Na Stroike*. There were, nonetheless, profound differences in approach to design which were related directly to political proclivities.

The blueprint for the new pictorial weeklies was drawn by German and Soviet worker photography magazines, primarily *Sov'etskeo Foto, Der Arbeiter Fotograf* and *Arbeiter Illustrierte Zeitung* (or *Workers' Illustrated News* – the title was soon abbreviated to

EIN AJZ-TRAKTOR
FÜR DIE
SOWJET-UNION

Die Internationale Arbeiterhilfe hat zur Unterstützung der sowjetrussischen Wirtschaft zwei große Güter bei Moskau mit über 2000 Hektar Land zur Bewirtschaftung übernommen. Sie hat sich verpflichtet, diese Güter mit den modernsten landwirtschaftlichen Maschinen auszurüsten, sie zu Mustergütern auszubauen und Traktorenstationen zu schaffen, die dazu dienen sollen, das Land der Bauern in der Umgebung der Güter wirtschaftlich zu bearbeiten.

In den nächsten Tagen gehen bereits die ersten Traktoren nach Moskau ab. Zu Beginn der Frühjahrsarbeit im April dieses Jahres sollen im ganzen 40 Traktoren in Tätigkeit sein. Der Ankauf von 40 Traktoren kostet natürlich viel Geld. Die IAH wendet sich deshalb mit einem Aufruf an die Oeffentlichkeit und bittet alle Freunde der Sowjetunion, sie bei der Durchführung dieser Aktion praktisch zu unterstützen. Es bietet sich jedem die Möglichkeit, aktiv bei der Durchführung des Fünfjahrplans mitzuhelfen.

Die AJZ fordert alle ihre Freunde und Leser auf, die Arbeit der IAH durch die Sammlung für einen besonderen

AJZ-Traktor

zu unterstützen, der unseren kämpfenden, aufbauenden Brüdern in der Sowjetunion als Beweis unserer proletarischen Solidarität übergeben wird. Wir werden über die eingehenden Gelder für den AJZ-Traktor in der AJZ quittieren. Zahlungen sind zu richten an Neuer Deutscher Verlag, Willi Münzenberg, Postscheckkonto Berlin Nr. 121770 mit dem Vermerk „AJZ-Traktor". Die Angestellten des Verlags der AJZ eröffnen die Sammlung mit RM 400.—.

Sammellisten, Werbematerial usw. sind von der IAH, Berlin SW 48, Friedrichstr. 235, zu beziehen.

118

Arbeiter Illustrierte Zeitung
c. 1930
designers
Wieland Herzfeld et al

"An AIZ tractor for the Soviet Union". AIZ's designers introduced photomontage, repetition and cinematic sequential picture stories. The magazine was designed collectively, probably under the direction of Muenzenberg, John Heartfield and, on a day-to-day basis, by his brother Wieland Herzfeld.

Arbeiter Illustrierte Zeitung
c. 1934
designer John Heartfield

Right: one of a series of Heartfield montages which in the mid-Thirties appeared on the back cover of each issue of AIZ. This satire on Nazi propaganda minister Goebbels as "der Gesundbeter" or healthgiver, has a more complex composition than usual, but its purpose is clear and its execution seamless.

AIZ). The latter, a communist weekly, was established in 1925 by Willi Muenzenberg,[6] founder of the worker photography movement. *AIZ* was created as a foil to bourgeois counterparts such as *Berliner Illustrierte Zeitung*; Muenzenberg's understanding of the power of the new printing was articulated in an *AIZ* editorial of 1926 thus: "The illustrated magazine is the paper of the future...today the biggest bourgeois publishers announce that in a few months time there will be no German newspapers without illustration, that the illustrated papers will soon achieve the circulation of existing dailies...The bourgeois press photographic agencies create a wealth of pictures to influence the masses with capitalist and bourgeois viewpoints. Pictures from the life of the proletariat are unknown...This gap has to be filled."[7]

AIZ sought to fill that gap by a direct appeal to its readers for photographs – an appeal not intended to encourage amateurism, and which resulted in the successful recruitment and training of a stable of highly professional "worker photographers". From its launch, and after its removal to Czechoslovakia in 1933, from where it was published and distributed clandestinely to Germany until the invasion of 1938, the magazine achieved enormous popularity. At its height in 1931 *AIZ* had a print run of half a million and an international distribution;[8] it spawned similar titles such as *Workers' Illustrated News* (*W-I-N*) in Britain and *links richten*, the Dutch worker-writers' magazine designed by Paul Schuitema.

AIZ epitomized the very rapid development of magazine design between 1925 and 1935. Initially, the appearance of *AIZ* differed little from that of its competitors, with a blackletter masthead and a staid, symmetrical and rather cluttered dogleg page layout. By 1930, under the influence of John Heartfield, the magazine's radical campaigning role had been given graphic expression. *AIZ*'s designers introduced photomontage, repetition, cinematic sequential picture stories in which a page of photographs, hand-drawn lettering and cast type were combined in sequence to tie in a story or polemic. Dramatic contrasts of picture scale, and the use of cut-outs merged with squared-up photographs, completed the highly integrated effect. By 1931, sans serif typography and a simplified, modular grid had been introduced as an anchor for the kaleidoscope of images, which included Heartfield's powerful photomontages used as centrepieces.

John Heartfield worked in Moscow throughout

Dr. GOEBBELS, DER GESUNDBETER

„Die Reichspropagandaleitung der NSDAP hat eine umfassende Versammlungs-Propagandaaktion angeordnet gegen die Miesmacher und Kritikaster, gegen die Gerüchtemacher und Hetzer. Die Versammlungen werden alle erfassen bis in das letzte Dorf hinein, mit jeder Woche in ihrem Tempo stärker, in der Unerbittlichkeit der Forderungen härter, an Durchschlagskraft und Erfolgen alle bisher durchgeführten Aktionen in den Schatten stellend." (Völkischer Beobachter)

„Eben in diesen Tagen schleichen sie umher und tuscheln jedem Willigen oder Harmlosen einen mageren Witz vom »Apotheker Coué« in die Ohren." (Fränkische Tageszeitung)

Fotomontage: John Heartfield

»60 MILLIONEN ANTRETEN ZUM NACHBETEN!«

SSSR Na Stroike

no. 2 1933

designer El Lissitzky

The people, party and army, encapsulated in Red Square as a raking five-pointed star: the montage of cheering faces to the right of the spread opens out as a gatefold.

most of 1931 by invitation of *SSSR Na Stroike*, the magazine in which El Lissitzky, Rodchenko and Nikolai Troshin promoted photomontage to the foundation stone of editorial page layout.[9] As in the pages of *AIZ*, photomontage was used not as mere illustration, but as an integral part of the design such that text and photography had little respect for each other's territory.

The monthly two-colour, oversize magazine was published in four editions (Russian, French, German, and in English under the title *USSR in Construction*) between 1930 and 1941.[10] This was an international platform in print for the social and economic gains of the Soviet people, and a brilliantly constructed publication. Despite its wide international distribution and influence, *SSSR Na Stroike* has rarely figured in Western design histories. This may well be because the magazine thrived in a period which coincided with the leadership of Josef Stalin and, as a result, cannot flatter conventional theses that constructivism had been entirely superseded by a monumental social realism by 1930.

Our major interest in *SSSR Na Stroike* is in its treatment of space and content in a large format, exploiting the great size of the page to produce both intricate montage and bold, tightly cropped photography on a previously unseen scale – so large, in fact, that often it employed double-width gatefold pages – combined with the bare minimum of text. Recurring features were the use of strong diagonals to evoke movement, contrasting close-ups and long-shots in the cinematic manner derived from Eisenstein, and multiple montaged faces, a popular means of expressing the mass appeal of socialism. In both *AIZ* and *SSSR Na Stroike* montage had an overtly political role, on the one hand to emphasize the progressive nature of socialism and, on the other, as in Heartfield's direct political commentaries, to expose the true social relations of capitalist economy. It was this aspect of montage which made the technique unacceptable to Western news magazines, which relied for their authority on an air of superior impartiality. By manipulating photography in a highly subjective way, photomontage undermines the illusion of disinterested and objective truth which is imparted by news photography – the certain expectation that one would not only "see and be amazed" but also "see and be instructed".[11] The intervention of photographer, editor, picture editor and designer between the event and its ultimate reportage is made

SSSR Na Stroike
no. 12 1935
designer Rodchenko
Cover (above) and two spreads from an issue devoted to the Red Army parachute corps. The heroic portrait of a paratrooper (right) is set in a triangular vignette which opens up to create a full diamond across the spread. Opposite is a spread from the same issue, re-worked in three colours and with elaborate paper engineering for a special bound set dedicated to Kliment Voroshilov, Commissar of all the Armies and Navies of all the Russias. Only a hundred or so copies were printed, for distribution to senior Red Army officers and members of the CP Central Committee.

Медникова изучила укладку парашюта. Здесь ты каждой сборкой, каждой складкой, каждым стропом отвечаешь за жизнь человека. Малейшая неточность, незаметная морщинка на шелке, захлестнувшемся за строп, и... тебе уже не разгладить потом морщин горя у десятков людей...

ПРЫЖОК комсомолки КАТИ МЕДНИКОВОЙ был назначен на 4 ОКТЯБРЯ

Уложенный, упакованный в ранец парашют, заряженный на вытяжную шпильку, ждал Катю Медникову на старте.

— Ну, как? — спросил у Медниковой инструктор-комсомолец летчик Балашов.

— Все в порядке, — сказала Катя.

Балашов одел на Катю парашютные ранцы, один сзади, другой на всякий случай спереди, застегнул лямки.

— Ты чего это смеешься? — спросил он.

— А что ж мне плакать...

— Ну, раз смеешься, значит дело пойдет, — сказал Балашов, — садись, завезу.

Подошел врач. Катя отмахнулась. Но врач поймал ее руку и стал считать пульс.

— Пульс немножко учащенный, ровный, хорошего наполнения, — сказал врач.

Катя полезла в самолет. Балашов занял свое место впереди.

...Что-то выхлестнулось за спиной, ее с силой вздернуло кверху, качнуло, все в мире стало ясным, сразу встало на свое место — и земля, и небо, и аэродром внизу. Распахнувшийся большой напруженный зонт закрыл полнеба. И Катя Медникова, смеясь от радости, переполнившей ее, стала спускаться.

ПОТОМ — ЗЕМЛЯ!

SSSR Na Stroike

no. 2 1933

designer El Lissitzky

The designer creates dynamic force through the use of a single, bold, diagonal rule, offset against the angles of both the two upper pictures and the rake of the steering wheel and balanced perfectly, like an exclamation mark, above circular vignettes.

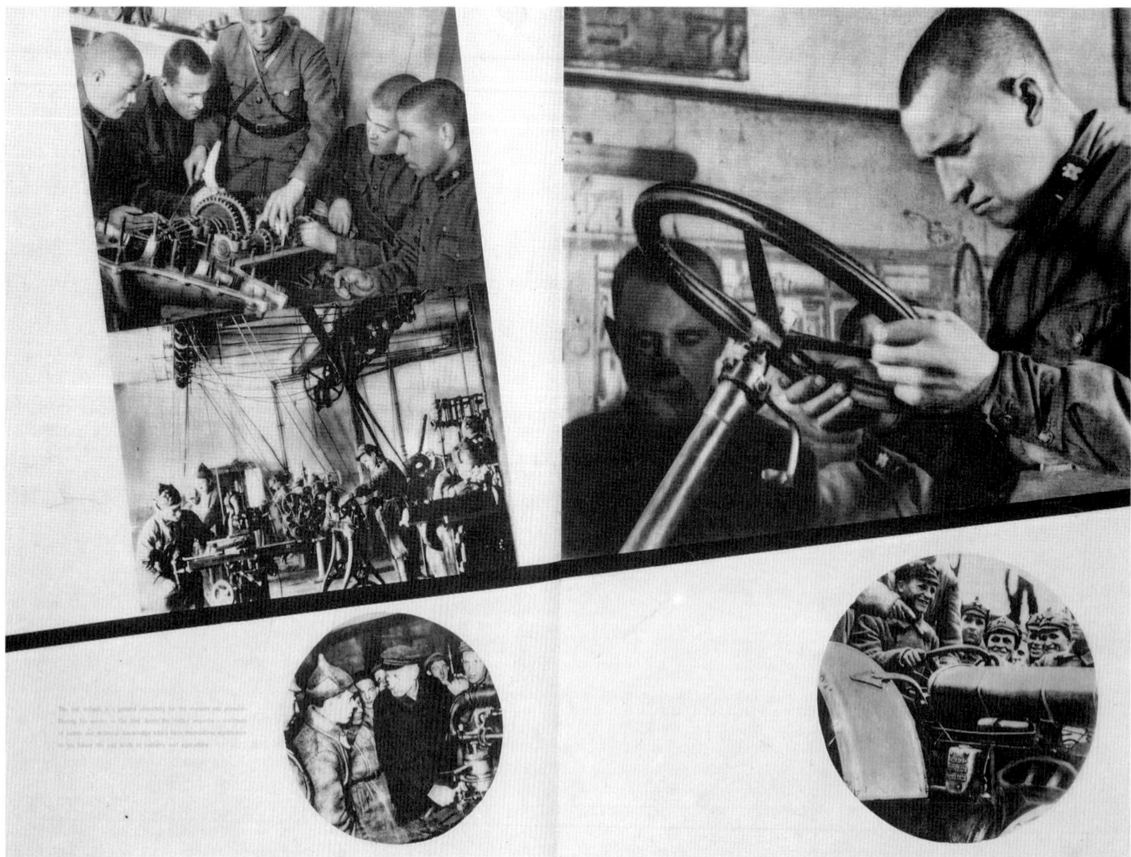

SSSR Na Stroike

no. 9 1933

designers El Lissitzky, Alexander Rodchenko

Constructive montage in SSSR Na Stroike: the dominant image and spatial organisation of photography creates the illusion of linear perspective.

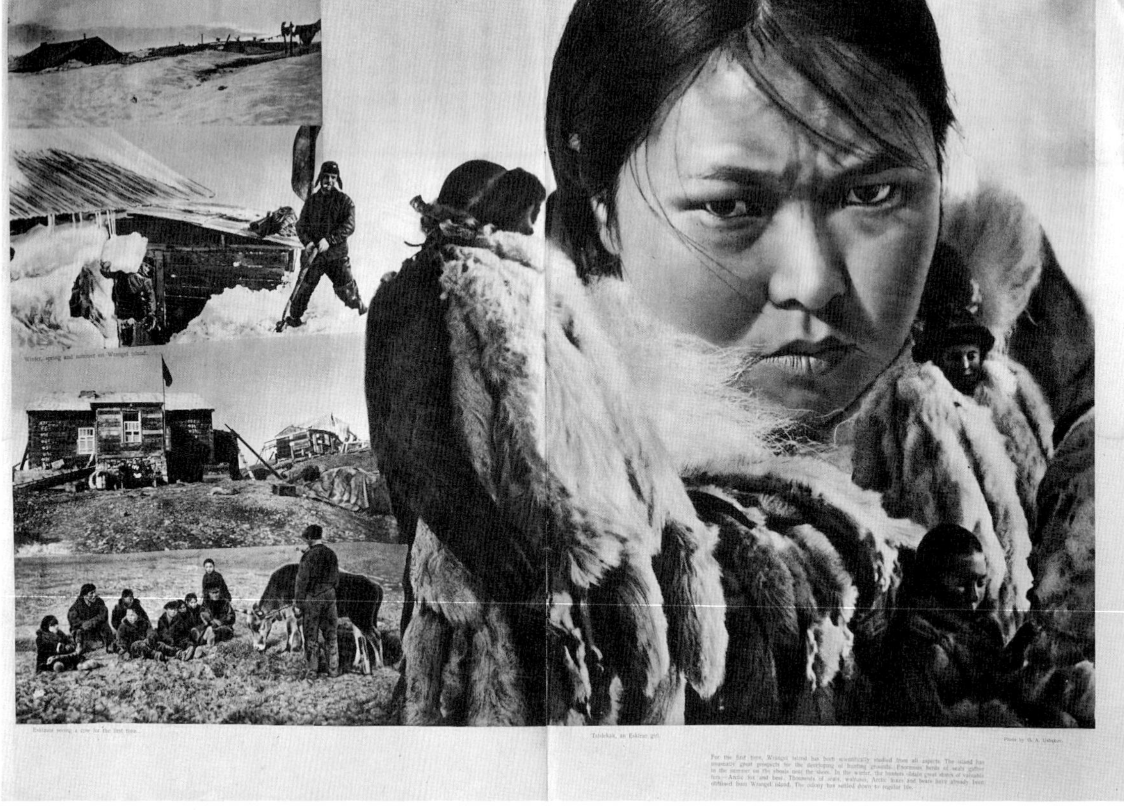

evident by montage, whereas, within a conventional format, the reader is unaware of "the political effect which is achieved by the juxtaposition of several pictures, by captions and accompanying texts." So said Muenzenberg, who continued: "this is the decisive point. In this way a skilful editor can falsify every photograph into its opposite, and can influence the politically naive reader in any way he chooses."[12]

The French *Vu*, founded in 1928 by Lucien Vogel and designed by Alexander Liberman, and the leftist *Regards*, launched three years later, were influenced strongly by *AIZ* and adopted lively forms of montaged layout, but in Britain and America the technique was received with far less enthusiasm. It was significant that the British picture weekly, *Picture Post*, failed to utilize John Heartfield's skill once its first editor, Stephan Lorant, had departed. *Picture Post* stood in the camp of the Popular Front. For Lorant, a Hungarian Jew and refugee from fascism, and Tom Hopkinson, his assistant and successor as editor, "it should be strongly political, 'anti-fascist', in the language of the time."[13] Heartfield, who had escaped to London, was commissioned to design early covers which lampooned Hitler and Chamberlain and, in response to Jewish pogroms, Lorant himself designed a remarkable sequence of photographs of Nazi leaders entitled "Back to the Middle Ages". Hopkinson described these as "photographic cartoons"[14] and restricted his own polemic to astute picture selection and straightforward criticism of certain aspects of the war effort (as a result, the magazine was banned from distribution to troops serving overseas). *Picture Post* "naturalized and domesticated the montage impulse"[15] and, in common with many of the wartime news weeklies, adopted a form of social realism, an heroic view of the working class (numerous covers portrayed soldiers and workers photographed from below – chin shots – to emphasize nobility) and a reformist, campaigning style which nevertheless shied away from asking the fundamental political questions posed by Heartfield's photomontage. Montage was not incorporated into the fabric of the magazine; when it was used it was as illustration or as a cartoon, sharply distinguished from text or news photography.

Two aspects of the German and Russian designers' techniques – picture cropping and rational picture organization – were borrowed more eagerly by publishers in the USA and Britain. The German influence on photojournalism became dominant as more and more journalists, photographers and designers were forced west by fascism. To *Weekly Illustrated* and later *Picture Post*, Lorant co-opted the photographers Felix H. Man and Kurt Hubschmann and of course Bill Brandt. *Life*'s photographic team was built around Alfred Eisenstaedt who, with Thomas McAvoy, Margaret Bourke-White and Peter Stackpole, were to develop *Life*'s particular form of candid camera, a style derived from the technique of Erich Soloman, photographer for *Berliner Illustrierte* who, using his small Leica, was the great exponent of the unselfconscious and often stealthily taken picture.

The Germans brought with them the novel idea that page design was a job for professional designers, not for journalists, and that the most important task was picture selection and positioning. Lorant was a journalist and not a designer, but he nevertheless understood the primacy of pictures. Articles were written to fit the photographs and not the other way around, and usually only after the pages were laid out.[16] There is, however, little evidence of European design sensibilities at *Picture Post*. Its News Gothic was a very English and a very newspaper-oriented response to the new typography. Pictures were meanly sized, rarely cropped effectively, and inefficiently arranged. The magazine flourished through the unerring popular touch of its editors and the verve of its photographer/writer teams.

Whereas *SSSR Na Stroike* was an example of highly integrated visual journalism designed by skilled graphic artists, *Life*, founded in 1936, was largely the product of ex-*Time* journalists (and publisher Henry Luce's ambitious and liquid imagination). Early prototypes of the magazine (provisionally entitled *Dime*) were saved from complete disaster only by the intervention of the German emigré and former editor of *Berliner Illustrierte*, Kurt Korff. Korff taught the inexperienced American editors the difference between good pictures and bad, to look for "a little something more than the content". His emphasis was on realism, frankness. And he drilled home the maxim, still new to news journalism, that a picture's purpose is not to illustrate but to tell a complete story in itself.[17]

The absence of artistic direction in the earliest *Life* dummies was manifestly plain. Paul Hollister, an advertising executive at Macy's, wrote to Luce that he was "appalled" by the look of the dummy. One story had pictures "trimmed into odd shapes as if by a cookie cutter" (this was said to have been laid out

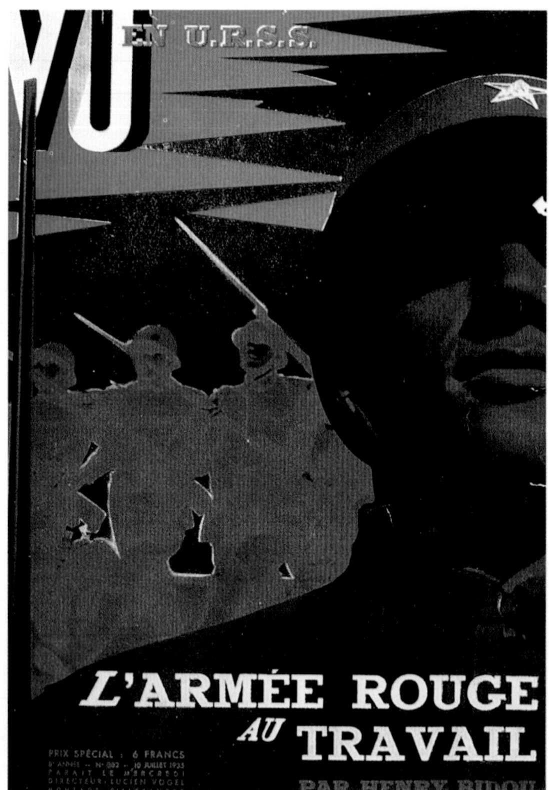

Vu
10 July 1935
designer
Alexander Liberman

A cover montage by Alexander Liberman, "The Red Army at work". Liberman, born in Russia, emigrated to Paris after the revolution where he worked as apprentice to Cassandre and later as art director of this social democratic picture magazine. Vu's distinctive masthead was designed by Cassandre.

by Luce himself). Hollister wrote : "It is inconceivable that even an avowed dress-rehearsal just for 'fun' should have turned out so far short...great God – that a magazine should make even a tentative peek looking like this."[18]

The critique earned Hollister the job of creating *Life*'s first consistent typographic format. "My task", he recalled, "was to make a better pattern of each page, conforming to a total 'basic format' character: to 'sell' each page for itself, each picture within that pattern; to suggest changes of pace; to clean up margins and gutters; to...eliminate sloppy disturbances and tricks from the page."[19] So Hollister summarized the essential principles of magazine formatting which were, by this time, second nature to central European designers and which had already been firmly established in the USA by Dr M. F. Agha at Condé Nast and by T. M. Cleland on Luce's own *Fortune* magazine.[20] *Life* was not remarkable in either design or editorial format, both of which consciously followed European models, in particular those of *Vu*, *Berliner Illustrierte* and *Weekly Illustrated*, which were closely watched by Luce. *Life*'s primary original contribution to magazine design was its brash front page, in which the impact of large paper size was maximized by a single black-and-white bleed picture, making *Life* loom over the *Saturday Evening Post* on the newsstands. The idea of a single picture was proposed by the artist Edward Wilson; with art director Howard Richmond's stark white-out-of-red *Life* slug[21] above a red strapline it became the hallmark of the photojournal, and was emulated the world over.

Life's novelty was its sheer magnitude in terms of budget, staff, resources and circulation. Henry Luce's goal of creating a mass-circulation glossy picture magazine was realized only by investing enormous sums in new printing technology. To produce the magazine on coated paper, in the vast quantities required at great speed, new rotary web-offset presses and flash drying of ink were specially developed at the Chicago printing plant. The palpably superior (and very expensive) paper quality and picture reproduction contributed to *Life*'s 250,000 sellout first issue, at the almost giveaway price of 10 cents a copy. Circulation climbed rapidly to one and then five million, and in 1936 Luce, a victim of his own phenomenal success, was losing $50,000 a week. By the 1940s, when the magazine was at last in profit, its annual editorial budget was a staggering $7 million. Only thus was Luce able to achieve his ambition of "A bigger and better collection of current news photographs than is available in all the current event magazines plus all the Sunday gravure supplements combined." In the *Dime* prospectus, Luce promised: "about 200 photographs with full explanatory captions. *Dime* will seek to advance the art and function of pictorial journalism. It will have its own staff of four or five outstandingly good camera men. It will also be a ready purchaser of the best products of the best freelance camera men. And above all, it will have a constant stream of editorial ideas which, through the various [photographic] agencies, it will seek to translate into significant pictorial achievements."

No European magazine could hope to find the resources to fulfill such grandiose ambitions. *Life*, however, succeeded so completely that it dominated the international market for news photography and earned the title, coined by Luce in 1935, of "The show-book of the world".[22] Muenzenberg's predictions of the ultimate power of photojournalism had come true. The American historian Theodore H. White could say that, by 1940, "magazines had become the dominant political medium of this nation. No greater demonstration of media authority has been exhibited in our time than when three East Coast magazine publishers forced the nomination of

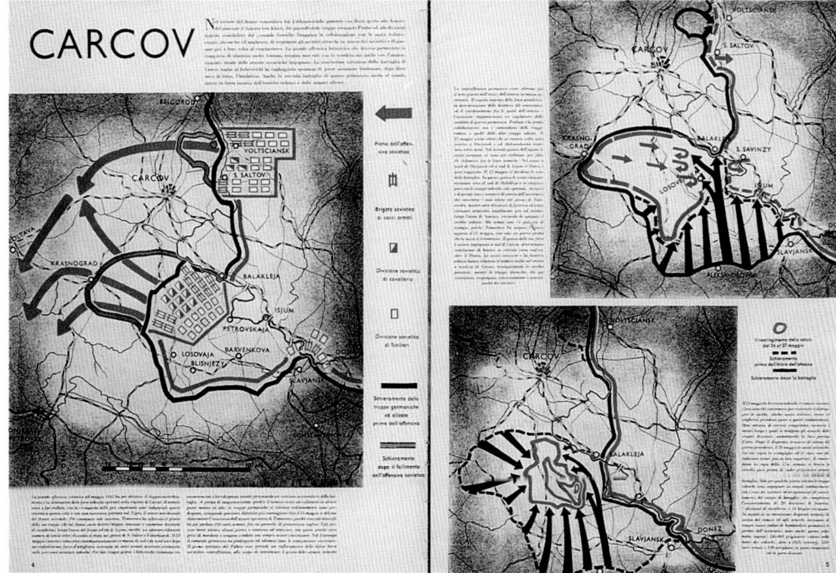

Signal

1 August 1942

Italian edition

designer unknown

Signal was Goebbels' answer to Life and Picture Post. The Fascist propaganda magazine, distributed throughout occupied Europe in several languages, was an object lesson in the application of modern design principles to reactionary ends. With its angry red battle maps and strict geometry it dehumanized conflict. The modular arrangement of surfacing submarine and lurking periscope is a chilling abstraction of the machinery of war.

Life

dummy no. 2, 1936, and issue no. 1, November 1936

designer Paul Hollister et al

Top is a spread from Life's "printed dummy no. 2", which was distributed to advertisers a month before the launch. Carefully designed formats were now seen as a major factor in publishing success. The dummy was designed by Paul Hollister, probably with Kurt Korff. The condensed gothic headline face, which stayed in use for many years, was an effective means of maximizing the word count of heads and minimizing typographic disturbance. There are, however, dissimilarities between the dummy and first issue, which had a less formal picture grid. The spread above is part of a sequence of photographs by Margaret Bourke-White of Montana relief workers; it has a more popular feel than the rigid geometry of the dummy.

Wendell Wilkie on the Republican Party in 1940 – the publishers of *Life* and *Time*, *Look*, and the *Saturday Evening Post*."

The rise of the news picture weeklies is often attributed to the outbreak of war and the important political and social role which such magazines played in the first half of the twentieth century: "A war, any sort of war, is going to be natural promotion for a picture magazine – the history of European illustrated magazines bears this out", wrote Daniel Longwell, who worked on the *Life* launch and became managing editor in 1944.[23] Tom Hopkinson, *Picture Post*'s wartime editor, said: "We argued [prior to launch] that if war came everyone would want war pictures, so the magazine would quickly find a public." Conversely, the fall from grace of the picture magazine is attributed solely to the advent of television news – a decidedly suspect notion. Picture magazines coexisted successfully for many years with the newsreels, and rarely pretended to offer instant news: they were more reflective, even at the height of the war. Only a small section of *Life* was reserved for hard news, and at *Picture Post* the editors decided that: "...for a magazine which is sold ten days after it goes to press, the one thing fatal is to follow news".[24] Indeed, the point was proved by the gravure-printed newspaper colour supplements which successfully reinvented the picture magazine in the 1960s, yet worked to deadlines measured in weeks, rather than days. Only magazines with vast agency and photography networks, such as *Paris Match*, have been able to maintain weekly hard news coverage. Many of the failed attempts to revive photojournals can be attributed to editors and art directors underestimating the complex logistics and great expense of assembling in-house and agency photography to tight deadlines.

The closure of the great picture magazines is attributable to a crisis of faith. They were, in most cases, wedded to a political cause which, if lost, removed the *raison d'être* for publication. *Life* played a cohering role in the creation of the American nation – a country without national newspapers – and in asserting American power internationally once the restraints of isolationism had been removed. The magazine sought to justify US intervention abroad, often in an overtly racist manner (the very first issue carried a feature which described Brazilians as "charming people but incurably lazy" who lost their coffee and rubber interest to "more energetic races"). Henry Luce saw his magazine as a semi-official organ of the US government and while national prestige and self-confidence remained high, so did circulation. It is significant that *Life*'s demise as a weekly magazine in 1972 coincided so closely with the defeats in Vietnam and their debilitating effect on US imperial ambitions. *Life* lost substantial advertising revenues to television, but it had also lost its political role. *Picture Post*, so much a product of the struggle against Hitler, had suffered a similar fate. With the war over and Britain clinging brutally to the last vestiges of its empire, the democratic spirit of the magazine could not be maintained and, soon after Hopkinson's resignation in 1950 in protest against his publisher's self-censorship, the magazine closed.

The political inclinations of photojournals provoked an inevitable moral conflict between art directors and photographers which still reverberates today. In 1947 the Magnum agency was founded by Robert Capa, Henri Cartier-Bresson, David Seymour and George Rodger. This influential collective was established to own and preserve photographers' copyright, and one of its central demands was that the originator should have control over cropping and captions which, the photographers complained, had been used by magazine editors to distort the "truth" told by their pictures. The argument, which undoubtedly stemmed from a real grievance, demonstrated at best idealism and at worst a pretentiousness and arrogance which is misplaced in commercial photographers who possess the ultimate sanction of witholding their work. The strictures Magnum exerted on caption writing have justification where the intention is to maintain an accurate description of the circumstances in which a picture was taken. However, to insist that photographs be uncropped, or cropped only under the eye of the photographer, betrays a naive belief in the objectivity of the art of photography. The argument assumes that the art director's role should be restricted to that of a compiler of images, each in the proportions of 35mm film, and that freedom to interpret, size and mix illustrations – a primary role of the magazine art director – is curtailed. The montage impulse, in which a collective image has supremacy over its individual components, has become an essential ingredient of magazine design and cannot always encompass this requirement. The art of cropping, sizing and combining illustrations and text to communicate a unified narrative, a single thread, is the basis of the photojournalistic technique. The method adopted by the picture weeklies has become universal, fundamentally altering the content and format of all of magazine types.

Picture Post
November 1936
designer Stefan Lorant

A powerful example of pictorial propaganda, designed by Lorant as a respost to fascist pogroms. Lorant's careful choice of hectoring images, headline and text is graphic and agitational; the design is a much more effective and heartfelt combination of words and images than the abstracted representation of fascist uniformity expressed in the Life dummy (opposite, top).

The four guardians of German culture today: they shield its purity from the "contaminated race."

HERMANN GOERING.—*Economic dictator of Germany. Went straight from school to become a fighting pilot in the war. After the war, was inmate of a mental home in Sweden. A Swedish court decided he was not fit to have custody of the children of his first marriage. He once said: "When I hear the word culture, I push back the safety catch of my revolver." First man to think that guns are better than butter.*

JULIUS STREICHER.—*Nazi boss of Franconia, Jew-baiter No. 1. Owner of the notorious "Stuermer." A former schoolmaster who was expelled from his profession. Boasted in a speech: "Accompanied by several other members of the party, I went into Steinruck's cell, and found a miserable object whining and behaving like a schoolboy. I gave him a good thrashing with my whip." Suffers from epileptic fits.*

ADOLF HITLER.—*Chancellor and Führer. A former housepainter, his only education an Austrian elementary school, where he was a dull pupil. Speaks no language but German, writes ungrammatical German, declares that he reads only what he knows will please him to read. Two months ago, said the "terrible sufferings" of the Sudeten Germans could no longer be tolerated by Germany, and would be stopped at the cost of war.*

PAUL GOEBBELS.—*Minister for Propaganda and Enlightenment. Entitled to call himself "doctor," he is one of the few Nazi leaders with a University education. Owes his academic distinctions to studies under Dr. Gundolf, a Jewish professor at Heidelberg University. His wife, a Belgian war refugee, was adopted and brought up by a Jewish family in Berlin. He says all Jews must be eliminated from German life.*

Anti-Jewish signs on a Jewish clothing-shop in Vienna. One on the left says that the owner is on holiday in Dachau concentration camp.

BACK TO THE MIDDLE AGES

A fortnight ago persecution on a scale unknown even in Germany broke out against the Jews. Here is a brief factual record

It was November 7, on which Herschel Grynsban, 17-year-old Polish Jew, shot Vom Rath, Counsellor at the German Embassy in Paris. Vom Rath died in Paris on the afternoon of November 9. Almost simultaneously the German government in Berlin issued the first of its decrees against the Jews, which must have been prepared before Vom Rath died. These ordered all Jewish newspapers to stop publication. All Jewish cultural and educational associations were to be dissolved.

On the same day, two synagogues were burnt down in different parts of Germany, and there was a small demonstration against the Jews in Berlin.

Early in the morning of November 10, after the beer-halls and cafes had closed, bands of young Nazis, acting simultaneously in towns all over Germany, set fire to synagogues, desecrated Jewish religious vestments and books, smashed the windows of Jewish shops, harried, beat and stoned Jewish people in the streets, and began widespread arrests of Jews.

Later that day began the worst pogrom since the Middle Ages. Looting went on all over Germany and Austria. The houses of Jews were broken into, children were dragged from their beds, women were beaten, men arrested and taken to concentration camps. Foreign journalists were prevented, as far as possible, from gathering details, but it is known that in Berlin several Jews were stoned to death. In the provinces, the number must have been higher.

The police did not interfere. The fire brigades turned their hoses only on non-Jewish buildings. All Jews in the streets or in wrecked shops, who were not manhandled, were arrested. In Munich, 10,000 Jews were rounded up and ordered to leave within 48 hours. This order was later rescinded, but not before hundreds of terrified Jews had run into the forests to hide from the mobs. In Vienna and the Sudetenland, Jews were

Continued on page 19

The damage the Jews were called upon to make good—pillaged shops in a Berlin street. Two of the passers-by smile over their destruction.

14 PICTURE POST

PICTURE POST 15

The first age of the art director: Cleland, Agha and Brodovitch

Fortune
December 1932
art editor Eleanor Treacy

Right: the classical symmetry of T. M. Cleland's Fortune format is reflected in this colour rendering by Joseph Urban. According to Cleland, writing in the first issue, "The design of Fortune is based upon its function of presenting a clear and readable text profusely illustrated with pictures, mostly photographic, in a form ample and agreeable to the eye... The size and proportions of the magazine are designed to give scope to its illustrations and text without crowding and margins to its pages which shall be in accord with the best principles of fine bookmaking."

In 1930 the publisher Henry Luce promised that his new *Fortune* magazine would be "as beautiful a magazine as exists in the United States. If possible the undisputed most beautiful".[1] And *Fortune* undoubtedly was – in its various guises until its unfortunate degeneration in the 1970s – one of the most gorgeous magazines ever published. In the format devised by T. M. Cleland the magazine epitomized the best in the American typographic vernacular, and from 1946 under the art direction of Will Burtin and, subsequently, Leo Leonni, it presented a perfect synchrony of European modernism and American exuberance.

Cleland's design was described by Allen Hurlbert as "a milestone because it represented a magazine that unified editorial and visual concepts in its initial presentation".[2] And after 1930 *Fortune* was not alone in this respect. It was in this period, characterized by the increasing professionalism and sophistication of American magazine publishing, that the central editorial role of the art director was established at the three foremost New York publishing houses: at Luce's *Time* Inc.; at Condé Nast, where Mehemed Fehmy Agha introduced a new graphic language to *Vogue* and *Vanity Fair*; and by Alexey Brodovitch at Hearst Magazines' *Harper's Bazaar*.

Luce's emphasis on the appearance of *Fortune* is significant. The magazine was a great gamble, very much a "conceptual" product which flew in the face of conventional wisdom. *Fortune* was a business magazine launched as the depression hit its deepest low. Paradoxically, it celebrated the strength and power of American capital at its hour of crisis; the magazine was directed at the country's elite, and was appropriately and expensively priced at "One

Fortune
February 1932
art editor Eleanor Treacy

Right: Fortune's grandiose cover format was the magazine's sole concession to decorative typography. Conceptual art of the highest quality was commissioned to sit within the trompe l'oeil frame. An appendix to issue number one, February 1930, stated: "The covers are to be a special feature and in place of the 'process' reproductions in half-tone generally employed on periodicals, a design by a distinguished artist will appear each month, which will be made especially for printing in flat colours and which will have the character of an original print." This example is by Paolo Garretto.

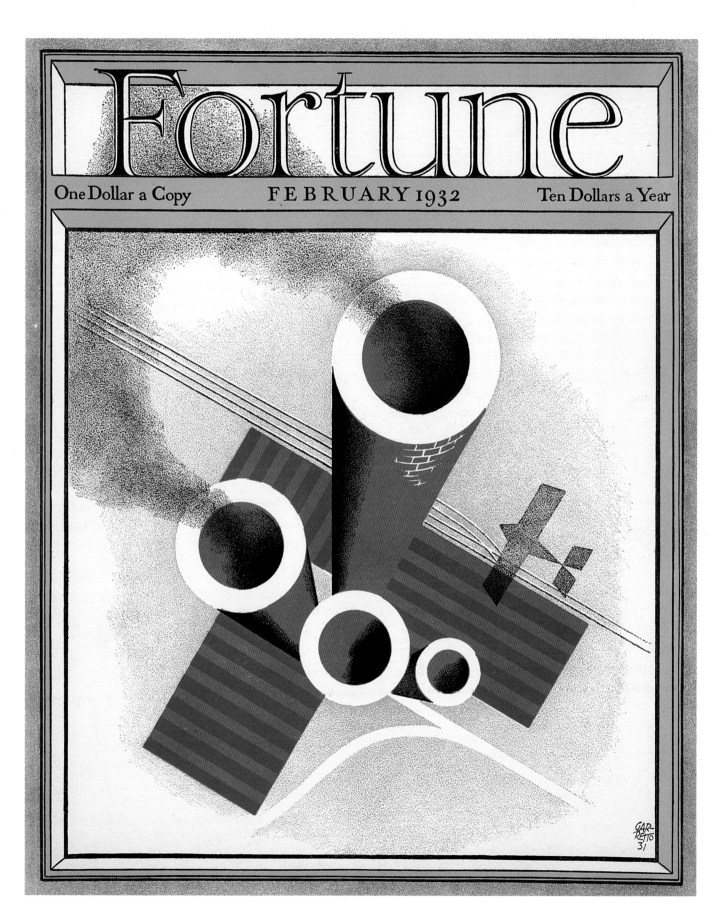

Fortune
One Dollar a Copy
FEBRUARY 1932
Ten Dollars a Year
GAR-
RETTO
31

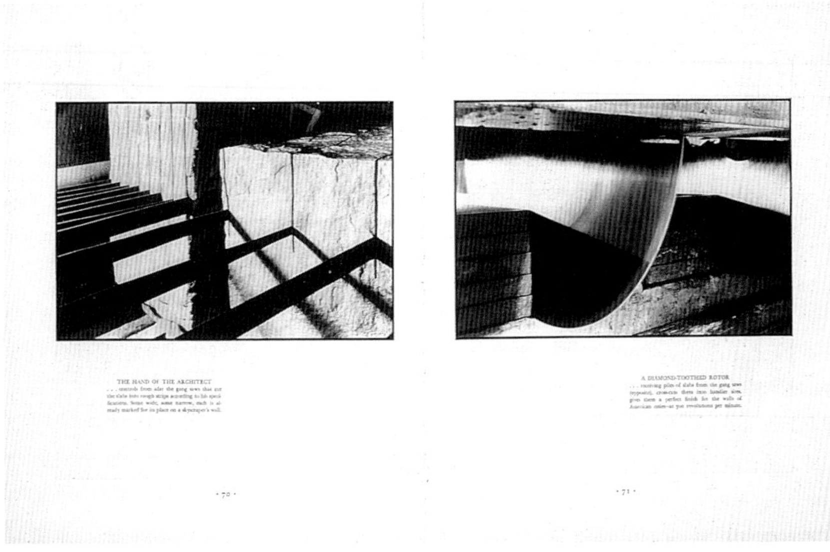

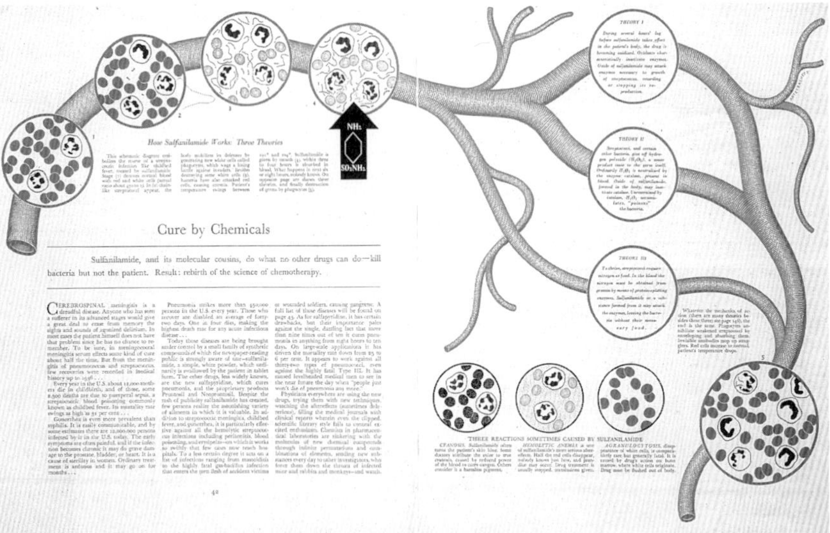

Fortune
September 1931
art director Eleanor Treacy

Top: Fortune specialized in the pictorial celebration of the productive power of American industry. This essay in machine aesthetics by Margaret Bourke-White is presented with simplicity and courage in an acre of white space.

Fortune
September 1939
art director Francis Brennan

Above: an explanation of the action of the drug Sulfanilamide is enhanced by a beautiful and informative scientific diagram. By 1939, when Brennan succeeded Eleanor Treacy, Fortune had an established repertoire of creative map-making skills. Under Brennan's art direction the magazine made further significant advances in the design of information graphics.

Dollar a Copy" (set proudly, in 24pt, on the masthead). Such audacity was expressed in *Fortune*'s physical presence. The paper size was 14 x 11¼ inches and the stock heavy and uncoated. Running to between 160 and 220 pages, the magazine weighed up to 3lb, and was delivered to subscribers in a strikingly designed thick cardboard package: *Fortune* was a magazine to be read from a lectern, not from the lap.

Cleland's design was in the protestant craft tradition: exact, plain and fit for its purpose. The title-piece, fudge and cover illustration were adorned by a *trompe-l'oeil* border, a single concession to decoration. Within, there was no embellishment – there was strict symmetry and economy of type. *Fortune* was printed in letterpress in a cut-glass Baskerville with just three gradations of typesize: for heads, standfirsts, and body text, the latter set solid over three wide columns, occasionally over two. Every photograph was bordered by an imposing black 4pt rule.

If this description conjures up a stark and spartan picture then it is not entirely accurate: the art director who implemented the Cleland format, Eleanor Treacy, commissioned dramatic industrial photography – much of it by Margaret Bourke-White who was a full-time editor at the magazine – generously proportioned to exploit the oversize format. The colour printing, used for both photography and illustration, was superb, with richly saturated hues which took well to the uncoated and thickly textured paper. Colour was used at its best for the lavish pictorial maps and diagrams which were the backbone of *Fortune*'s major features. *Fortune* was an instructive publication, treating its readers' intelligence with the utmost respect. Through its intensively researched editorial the magazine became an encyclopaedia of science, industry, and cultural and political life. And it was the design, which set a new standard in the communication of complex information, which established this solidity of purpose: that is how it "unified editorial and visual concepts".

Fortune prepared the ground for a new style of magazine publishing which presented a coherent mix of related articles. It was carefully targeted at a restricted audience, recognizing the strict divisions of labour and class that had developed in industrial society, and the corresponding variations in reading habits and preferences. The policy was manifest in *Fortune*'s coherent format, which contradicted the practice, current at the time and for a number of years

Manhattan Hackie

The New York taxi business takes in $35,000,000 a year in fares, rolls up over 1,000,000 miles a day. To Harry Faber, Badge 37046, it stinks.

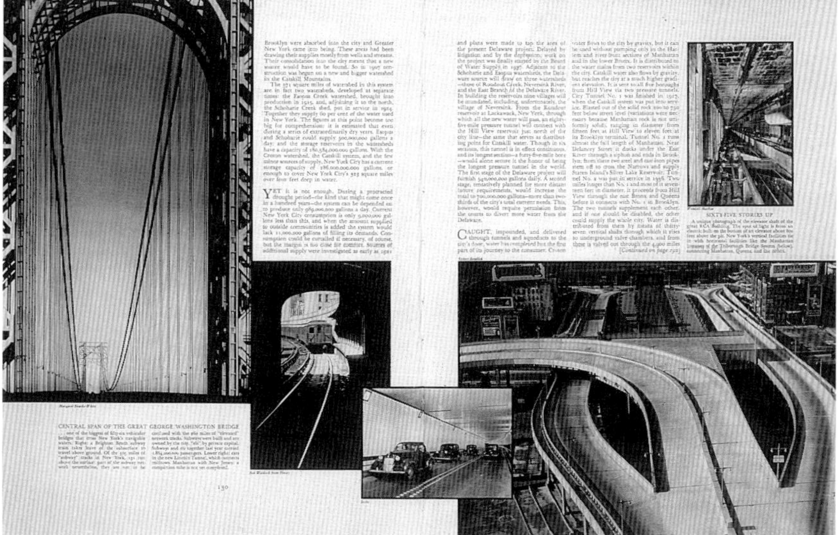

Fortune

July 1939

art director Francis Brennan

Two spreads from a special issue on New York. Top: cab driver Harry Faber photographed by Otto Hagel. Like most Fortune features, this one began with a statistic: "The New York taxi business takes in $35,000,000 a year in fares, rolls up over 1,000,000 miles a day. To Harry Faber, Badge 37046, it stinks." Above: a spread with depth and direction: the vertical stress of the bridge is offset against the horizontal slide of a freeway exit, cutting its way into an adjacent picture of a subway train. Between these is overlaid a fourth image, forcing the perspective towards the reader. The photographers were Margaret Bourke-White, Bob Waldeck, Sozio, Wendell MacRae and Robert Bendick.

after, that every article in a magazine should be presented in a typographically distinctive way. By contrast, Cleland dictated that the same typographical system be used throughout, with the needs of different subject matter provided for by illustration and subtler variations in layout. The opposite approach can be seen in magazines of the period, such as *Match*, which even up until 1940 offered a veritable specimen book of alphabets, with a different type for the heading and standfirst of each article. This old way of working took the word "magazine" at its most literal, eighteenth-century definition, as "a book not willing to stick to one subject only, but rambling all over the lot...a repository of miscellanea". In England, the designer John Farleigh was echoing this backward sentiment, espousing variety without typographic restraint: "A magazine is consciously designed to appear as different on every opening as it can be; that is part of the structure of a magazine...You can have a very formal page immediately followed by a drawing that is spreading, a different arrangement of type, paper of a different colour...The more variety there is, the more exciting is the magazine."[4] In America in 1930, publishers were acutely aware of the new marketing techniques and magazines had become specialist providers of a very particular kind of product; this homogeneity was communicated by systemized design.

Although Cleland and Treacy demonstrated that conventional typography, employed functionally and without superfluous decoration, could meet the new requirements successfully, it was nonetheless axiomatic that the new magazines would employ constructivist methods, and it was propitious that changes in publishing practice coincided with the influx of German and other European exiles to America. In the New World a cultural freedom could be found which compensated for banishment from the Old.

In Europe, the design vanguard had made its first, tentative steps in limited circulation political, art and architecture magazines and, after the closure of the radical design schools, in technical publishing and advertising: Moholy-Nagy was art director of *International Textiles* in the Netherlands before emigrating to Chicago via England; Herbert Matter designed covers for *Foto*, Herbert Bayer worked on *Die Neue Linie* and the Frankfurt typographer, Hans Leistikow, designed local cultural and commercial publications such as *Das Neue Frankfurt* and *Die Form*. By contrast, in the USA, modern principles could be applied to commercial magazines with budgets to fit their size; the price to be paid for the migration to America was that the emigré designers would be working in a comparatively anodyne political environment, in which the strength of their leftist polemic (which in the case of the Germans was anyway more often social democratic than communist) was co-opted by the needs of industry, commerce and above all, fashion. The American graphic design historian Lorraine Wild commented that: "The political and ideological connotations of modern graphic design disappeared with its acceptance by business and industry here. The depoliticized 'futurism' of modern design suited the optimism of the American businessman and the needs of the society at large."[5]

American business became a powerful patron of the new arts. *Fortune*'s cover was a favoured platform for the best of modern European and American illustration. Treacy commissioned covers by Joseph Binder, Diego Rivera, Paolo Garretto, Walter Buehr, Antonio Petrucelli and Roger Duvoisin. Her immediate successor, Frances Brennan, employed Fernand Léger, Edmund Lewandowski and Herbert Bayer, who was to become a regular contributor.

It should be stressed that publishers were not always passive recipients of the European style: they sought it out, and in at least one case prior to the flight from fascism. In 1928 Condé Nast toured Europe in search of a replacement for Heyworth Campbell, the long-serving art editor of American *Vogue*, who was "steeped in the old school of decoration, classical type and dense layout";[6] a replacement who would oversee *Vogue*'s transition from a "Society" to a modern (that is, middle-class) fashion book.

Condé Nast's discovery was Dr Mehemed Fehmy Agha (1898-1978),[7] a former studio chief of Dorlands advertising agency in Paris, and in 1928 employed as chief assistant and layout man at the ailing German *Vogue*. He was selected by Nast for his sense of "order, taste and invention". Agha, from a Russo-Turkish merchant background and a supporter of Kerensky, was by no means a radical but was nonetheless a pragmatic constructivist who declared in 1932 that, "The temple of constructivism is full of treasures and is therefore recommended to the commercial designer for new inspirations."[8] The treasures were to be sacrificed on the altar of consumerism.

As art director of Nast's flagship magazines Agha introduced a rapid succession of technical and artistic innovations which exemplified the modern approach to magazine design. Typography was simplified and systemized; at *Vanity Fair* a variant of Paul Renner's elemental Futura was used throughout for heads, standfirsts and captions, and in the exceptionally refined contents page. Photography was given preference over illustration, and used large. And Agha quickly stripped all extraneous components from the layout: out went column rules, sidebars and any kind of decorative border; margins and gutters were widened. Most importantly, he understood the synergy of design and editorial matter, striving to achieve a tight relationship between words and pictures and excelling in the simple picture story comprised of punning headline, photographic sequence and short captions. This sense of editorial purpose was attainable only where the art director succeeded – as Agha did – in carving out considerable editorial power for himself.

Agha was an iconoclast who understood that headlines could achieve as much impact at the foot of the page as at its head, and that minimal typesizes were maximized by a generous background of white space. He refused to acknowledge the page as a confining and separate entity: he violated the margins with his bleed photographs – a novelty in the United States – and utilized to the full the landscape format offered by the double-page spread. Agha was even capable of taking two related stories across the gutter as a means of combining the pages, where a more literal mind would have allotted each to a separate folio. The effect was achieved with a strong eye for asymmetric balance, and apparently effortlessly, but contemporaries testify to the man's perfectionism which demanded that each spread be re-worked many times before satisfaction was finally achieved.

Agha's work was characterized by powerful understatement and great clarity. *Vanity Fair* shows none of the graphic mannerism of the contemporary *moderne* style, with which he is often associated. He did have a weakness for experimentation with novel forms of photographic layout, experimenting with montage and, less successfully, with the "fan" of sequential action pictures, distributed in overlapping diagonals across the page to mimic movement. Sometimes the technique worked and gave life to the subject; sometimes it created a jarring cacophony.

Photography, and its development in new spheres, was Agha's great enthusiasm: he inspired features on

Vanity Fair

December 1934

art director M. F. Agha

Agha exploits the double-page spread: the montage is allowed to break across the spine and invade the territory of a second article, bringing the two pages together.

Towie, the new form of Contract Bridge

BY WILLIAM J. HUSKE

the new commercial photography in *Vanity Fair* and nurtured an early form of realist "snapshot" fashion photography at *Vogue*. A photographic studio was installed at Condé Nast's offices where Agha, with his chief photographer Edward Steichen, pioneered new lighting and printing effects (including duotones). The quality of photographic reproduction achieved enabled Agha to dispense largely with illustration as the medium for showing new fashion, and in April 1932 *Vogue* was given its first photographic cover, a girl in a bathing suit, by Steichen. For its part, *Vanity Fair* produced galleries of glamorized Hollywood star portraits of pinpoint focus and superb contrast. The art director and his photographers, heavily influenced by contemporary advertising practices, set out to create in their subjects, both animate and inanimate, an image of physical purity and surface brilliance which could only be captured by the technically perfect photograph. They used a chiaroscuro style, with solid blacks offset by luminescent highlights, a form of super-realism which had first entered advertising art as "good salesmanship". That this object fetishism had infiltrated editorial art was consummate proof of the submission of magazines to a consumerist ideal. "Advertising has been boring from within for a long time now", wrote Agha some years later,[9] and it was the current keyword of advertising design in the United States – "elegance" – which best typifies Agha's own work, in which modern techniques were employed in a rational but chastened manner, with none of the dissonance or challenge of the new European typography of the 1920s.

Alexey Brodovitch (1898-1971) was also a Russian, a White who had fought with the counter-revolutionary armies, and fled to Paris where he came into contact with the surrealist and purist movements, and whose graphic skills were first practised on layouts for *Cahiers d'Art* and *Arts et Métiers Graphiques*. Brodovitch emigrated to the United States in 1931 and quickly established a reputation as a teacher of modern graphic techniques at the Museum School of Industrial Art in Philadelphia. He achieved early recognition for his advertising work at the N. W. Ayer agency – painterly productions in the French decorative modern style, which came to the attention of Carmel Snow, the newly appointed editor of *Harper's Bazaar*. Snow was an Agha acolyte: formerly a fashion editor at *Vogue*, she had learnt through her work with Agha and Steichen of the new dramatized fashion photography and was determined that a similar style be introduced at *Harper's*.

The magazine was in transition from a staid and traditional women's magazine to a purveyor of high fashion, literature and art. Snow favoured "the new European style of layouts, which were a complete departure from the static, stilted look of all American magazines at the time". This follower of fashion wanted "more white space and modern typography".[10]

Brodovitch became art director of *Harper's Bazaar* in 1934 and remained in the job for 24 years, becoming through his work and teaching the most influential editorial designer of his time. Most of the techniques used in contemporary magazine design were pioneered or exploited at some time or another by Brodovitch – an undogmatic and instinctive rather than rational designer, who obsessively pursued change and modernity, and whose watchword was "Make it new". He initiated novel styles of fashion photography in a perpetual and unwinnable battle to distinguish editorial from advertising, and presided over the introduction of colour to the magazine interior; despite its novelty, he used colour with considerable maturity and resisted the temptation of excess.

Brodovitch's career spans many variations of mood and style and visibly grows in stature and vitality through to the early 1950s when much of his best work was created. Early influences of abstract expressionism, surrealism and decorative *art moderne* (exemplified by Cassandre's illustrations for *Harper's Bazaar* and Brodovitch's own surrealistic covers) were superseded by minimalist and geometric forms of great beauty and economy. "Elegance" and "good taste" are the bland soubriquets most often applied to Brodovitch's sense of space and type, but the typography is most notable for its precision and lyricism, and the layout for powerful contrasts of scale, colour and movement, imparting a vibrancy and drama which belied – but may well have been provoked by – the very banality of the subject matter with which he often had to work.

Frank Zachary, who co-edited the experimental *Portfolio* magazine with Brodovitch from 1949-51, describes him as "the master designer": "In many ways he created the look of the contemporary magazine. And he created a whole generation of photographers and art directors through his course at the Museum College of Art, through his own courses in New York. Everyone from Irving Penn, Richard Avedon, Henry Wolf and countless others – they're all Brodovitch's offspring."[11]

Brodovitch pioneered impressionistic fashion photography, in which the general style, demeanour – and surroundings – of the model carried as much weight as the clothing she wore. The use of location photography shot with hand-held cameras provided a naturalistic contrast to the dictatorial studio-bound fashion photography of the 1930s. Staged photography with high-contrast spot lighting was superseded by outdoor sequences in which blurred objects implied movement and vitality; technique was secondary to spontaneity; the stark simplicity of colour-field backgrounds was substituted for monumental baroque sets.

The Brodovitch layout technique – which, after all, had the display of fashion and accessories as its primary function – is most easily understood by examining the way in which photography was employed and, above all, the way in which he taught his photographers, notably Richard Avedon and Irving Penn

New Design in Movement –
New Movement in Design:
Starting with the Slay-On Mule

The Crossbarred Sandal
and the Roman-Striped Pump

Harper's Bazaar
March 1954
art director
Alexey Brodovitch
Cinematic pacing in a sequence: the head "New Design in Movement..." is echoed in Lillian Bassman's photograph – fleeing legs (produced by rotating the image through 90 degrees), which re-appear on the subsequent spread. The typography, which follows the contours of the body, is typical of Brodovitch's graceful, ragged style.

Harper's Bazaar

August 1940

art director
Alexey Brodovitch

A photomontaged cover by Herbert Bayer employing a favourite technique of both the designer and the art director: repetition. The gorgeous lip colours are enhanced by the over-exposed image of the face.

Harper's Bazaar

March 1954

art director
Alexey Brodovitch

A classic example of the Brodovitch fashion layout technique. The reflected curvature of the body in the two photographs is used to create a pair of arcs of visual force which meet at an imaginary point below the page. Depth is created by the contrasted scaling of Lillian Bassman's photographs, and note how the eye, invisible in the right hand picture, is also cropped out of the left to ensure that the reader focuses on the body, not the face.

182

LILLIAN BASSMAN

The Mold of the Princesse— Everything Black, and Lacy

FOR THE NARROW PRINCESSE LINE, unbelted and carved to the figure: the famous French "Scandale" girdle, now made in America. Chiffon-weight nylon power net, shaping in at the waist; garters adjust to your length of leg. By Tru Balance. About $13. Lord and Taylor: Jordan Marsh. Wired nylon Alençon lace bra by Edith Lances, about $23. Saks Fifth Avenue; Neiman-Marcus. FOR THE CARVED AND FLARING PRINCESSE (opposite), a strapless mold of the torso in nylon lace: the wired brassiere melting into a smooth curve at the waist, and continuing beyond. Flawless master line for bare-shouldered dresses that cling to an unbelted waist and then break wide *below* the hipbones. By Lily of France. About $25. Altman; I. Magnin; Marshall Field. All nylon by Du Pont.

HARPER'S BAZAAR, MARCH 195

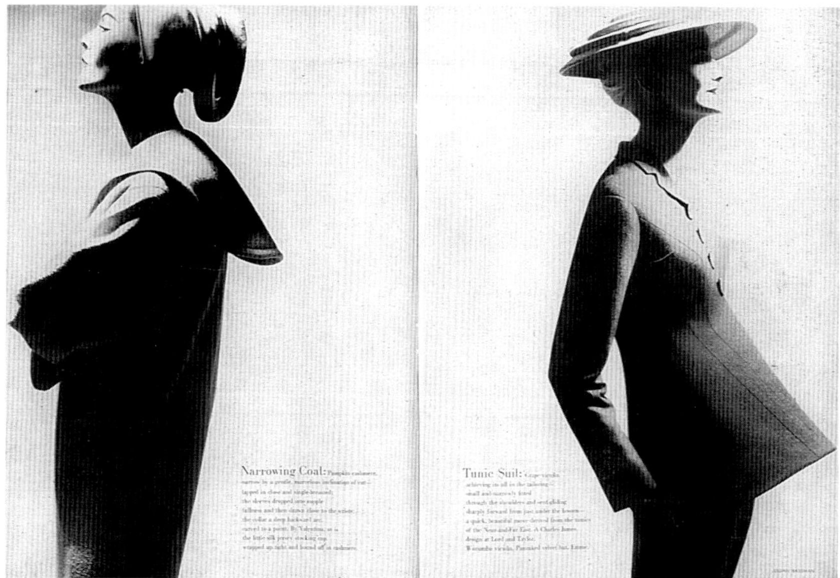

Harper's Bazaar

July 1955

art director
Alexey Brodovitch

By placing the images close to the outer margins, facing outwards, Brodovitch breaks a cardinal rule of layout in order to extend the perceived width of the spread. This is simple reflection about a vertical axis, but turning the back makes a powerful social image. The photographs are by Lillian Bassman.

(then a designer), also Hiro, Lillian Bassman and Herman Landshoff. The photographer was encouraged to design the page in the lens, to use props and movement to create force and balance, and to use plain backgrounds which enabled the designer to bleed the picture across the entire page: caption and heading could then be superimposed to create a seamless bond between type and image.

Typography was restrained and never allowed to grate against illustration; it was used expressively to echo and accentuate the photographic composition. Carefully measured captions drifted around or against the image, often and intentionally set extremely ragged, as if windblown, as a means of merging or breaking the text block into the page.

Brodovitch commanded a fulsome repertoire of graphic devices: repetition; reflection; diagonal and horizontal stress; juxtaposition of animate and inanimate forms; tricks of perception; contrasts of scale, colour and type. *Harper's Bazaar* possessed a linear rhythm which betrays an understanding, rarely appreciated, of pace, in which the reader is offered dramatic highlights, disjunctions, charging and calming of mood. The flow of features was given graphic emphasis. The aristocratic Bodoni, used as the base type throughout Brodovitch's years at the magazine, might suddenly be interrupted by stencil or typewriter faces. Scale would vary dramatically in a single spread, combining large foreground portraits with smaller, detail shots to give strong visual depth to the page. Brodovitch introduced the photographic prop to fashion photography – objects, or display type, which conferred cultural and symbolic references to the clothes, and around which women were draped, disturbingly, as secondary subjects, props themselves. As few other art directors before him, Alexey Brodovitch saw the page as a three-dimensional landscape – with depth as well as height and width – upon which to build with blocks of pictures and words against a reinforcing counterpoint of plain white space.

At the core of his work is a remarkably complete understanding of visual dynamics. Zachary believes that at an early stage in his career Brodovitch received architectural training. "I think the major canon of his philosophy was the spread. He never looked at an open magazine as two separate pages. The spread was the page. He always treated the spread as a unit, and he thought of the spread as an architectural element – as a wall, and the wall was to be pierced, fenestrated with windows, a door, and bricks...he had such an elegant sense of proportion and scale, it was absolutely impeccable."[12]

It is essential to remember that such perfection was probably attainable only thanks to an unprecedented access to photocopying facilities. It is undoubtedly true that the fluency and originality of Brodovitch's later work was greatly assisted by his ability to order as many as ten different sizes of every print, enabling him to experiment with many different page treatments: a process which by its nature encourages a sympathetic yet unconventional use of photography, with varied scale, cut-outs and deft combinations of images and type. This is not to decry Brodovitch's questioning and versatile mind, but designers before him – and many after who operated on smaller budgets – were by comparison working in the dark, forced to trace out enlargements using Grant or Curso projection. It is difficult to exaggerate the influence of photostats on American, and later European, pictorial magazine design. It was an essential tool in the production of *Portfolio*, a magazine which, from its first issue in 1949, was the subject of special discussion sessions at the New York chapter of the American Institute of Graphic Arts and which became the exemplar for a generation of designers. Such was Brodovitch's profligacy with the photostat machine that the expense forced the magazine's closure after only three issues.[13]

Portfolio was Brodovitch's swansong in editorial design. But he left a powerful legacy as a teacher and practitioner of graphic design as a communication art. Both in the development of technique, and through teaching in classrooms and on the job, Brodovitch and Agha had laid the foundations for contemporary magazine design. Many of the great names of what became known as the New York School passed through their hands at one time or another. At Condé Nast, Cipe Pineles, William Golden and Frances Brennan served their apprenticeships under Agha. Agha continued to influence the New York scene in his role as editorial consultant following his departure from *Vogue* in 1943. Numerous designers and photographers, including Lillian Bassman, who art directed *Junior Bazaar* with Brodovitch, Henry Wolf, Art Kane, Irving Penn, Hiro and Richard Avedon attended Brodovitch's design laboratory in Philadelphia, or his workshops at the New York School for Social Research and School of Industrial Arts, New York. In these classes Brodovitch drilled home to his students the virtue of surprise and dramatic contrast, the constant employment of original and lateral thought in the service of communicating content, which became a signature of post-war American graphic design. His frustration, and the undoubted limitation of his work for *Harper's Bazaar*, was the frivolity of the subject matter. Fashion may be the most widely practised living art, but how much value should we place on one more novel means of presenting a new pair of shoes in print? The method was the message, and had to remain an end in itself. Nonetheless, the peripheral nature of Brodovitch's chosen field does not diminish his significance as a powerful contributor to the intuitive and expressionistic editorial art which dominated American design practice throughout the 1960s.

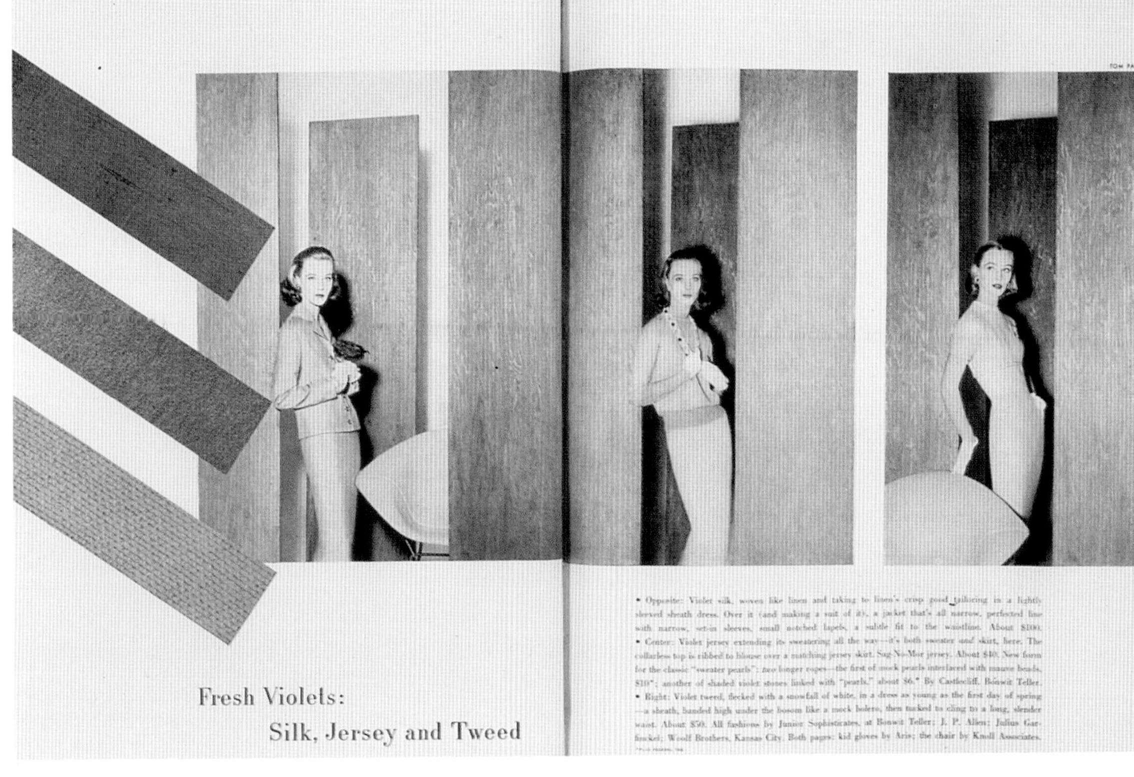

Fresh Violets:
Silk, Jersey and Tweed

• Opposite: Violet silk, woven like linen and taking to linen's crisp good tailoring in a lightly sleeved sheath dress. Over it (and making a suit of it), a jacket that's all narrow, perfected line with narrow, set-in sleeves, small notched lapels, a subtle fit to the waistline. About $100. • Center: Violet jersey extending its sweatering all the way—it's both sweater *and* skirt, here. The collarless top is ribbed to blouse over a matching jersey skirt. Sag-No-Mor jersey. About $40. New form for the classic "sweater pearls": *two* longer ropes—the first of mock pearls interlaced with mauve beads, $10*; another of shaded violet stones linked with "pearls," about $6.* By Castlecliff. Bonwit Teller. • Right: Violet tweed, flecked with a snowfall of white, in a dress as young as the first day of spring—a sheath, banded high under the bosom like a mock bolero, then tucked to cling to a long, slender waist. About $50. All fashions by Junior Sophisticates, at Bonwit Teller; J. P. Allen; Julius Garfinckel; Woolf Brothers, Kansas City. Both pages: kid gloves by Aris; the chair by Knoll Associates.

Harper's Bazaar
c. 1950
art director
Alexey Brodovitch

Three violet swatches in silk, jersey and tweed, a striking example of straightline geometry and subtle use of colour. Brodovitch has resolved the journalistic requirement of illustrating the texture of the cloth with the desire to create an aesthetically pleasing page.

The New York School: 1945-68

The immediate postwar period to the mid-1960s is commonly considered as the golden age of American magazine design: a twenty-year span in which the concentration of talent in New York publishing was unsurpassed, and the prestige, pay and budgets commanded by editorial art directors were at their highest. This view stands scrutiny, even though our hindsight is distorted by recollection of only the best work produced; and even though print and production standards could stand little comparison with those routinely achieved with today's technology.

Designers of this period were distinguished primarily by their positive commitment to information design in the popular press, and were hidebound neither by stylistic fetish nor slavish adherence to the typographic dogma which sometimes encumbered European contemporaries. The self-conscious adaptation to magazines of an integrated and "scientific" design discipline by such mid-century practitioners as Francis Brennan, Will Burtin, Lester Beall, Cipe Pineles and Bradbury Thompson created a powerful tendency in American graphic design, which was reinvigorated in the 1960s in the modular systems favoured by news and picture magazines, such as Allen Hurlbert's *Look* and David Moore's *Amerika*. This lucid journalistic tradition was, however, neither ubiquitous nor lasting. It coexisted with the inspired *haute couture* and seamless art direction of the Brodovitch school; the populism of Liberman and Peck's *Vogue*; the typographic and pictorial flourish of American expressionism; and the home-baked middle-American provincialism of the bulk of magazines published in the Eisenhower years.

As the middle decade turned, art directors continued to demonstrate a spirit of invention measured by a journalistic sensibility. The pre-planned, picture-based page layout pioneered by Brodovitch, which influenced a generation of designers, reached its zenith in the hands of Otto Storch, the great art director of *McCall's*, and his colleague William Cadge at *Redbook*. It was manifest in the oblique visual imagination of Henry Wolf, and in the colourful compositions of Bea Feitler and Ruth Ansell at *Harper's Bazaar*. For a brief period a satisfactory compromise had been reached between inspiration and objectivity. The emphasis, however, was subtly shifting from Burtin's "new discipline" of integration of graphic elements, which retained an abstract constructivist core and was suited to the technical needs of the business press, to a more literal and intuitive reliance on copywriting and figurative rebus techniques derived from advertising arts. This was an entirely new kind of visual journalism. The rebus – the attention-grabbing, punning picture – was coupled with the ideogram, of which Cadge, Herb Lubalin and Henry Wolf were the great exponents. In the words of a European contemporary, a modernist who was by no means unimpressed, these expressionistic designers "were full of ingenious ideas and ready to use any types, motifs, printing techniques, fancy papers, drawn lettering and so on, that suited the job on hand. American typefounders' matrices were dusted off and put to work again; lively alternatives were sought to the left ranging line, which had been the *sine qua non* of the new typography".[1]

In the chaotic American commercial bazaar it was perhaps inevitable, however, that the formal strictures of European typography would give way not only to a dionysian empiricism but, ultimately, to a return to classicist, vernacular and naive ornamentation.

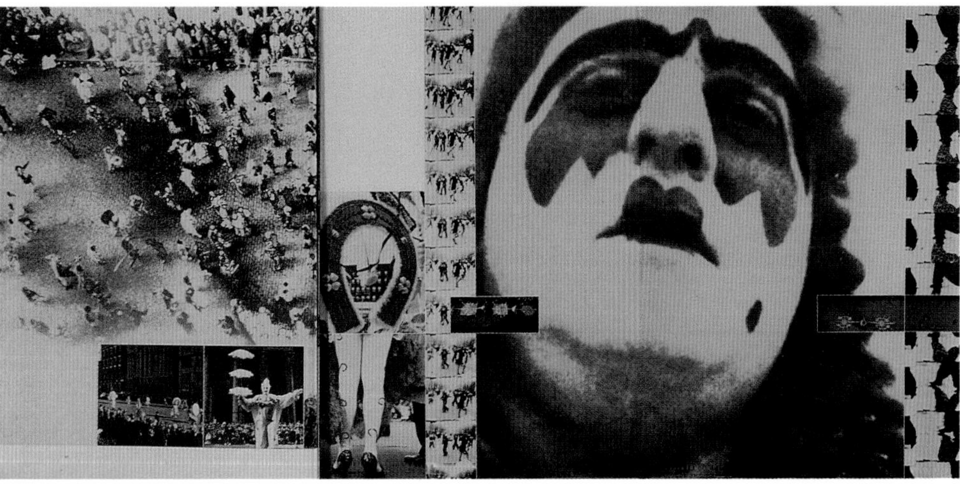

Portfolio
no. 2 1950
art director
Alexey Brodovitch

"The Mummers' Parade": an experiment in cinematic magazine presentation and photographic juxtaposition by Brodovitch, published in Portfolio as a series of opening gatefolds. The photographs were by students of the Philadelphia Museum School of Art.

Although Storch, Wolf and Lubalin had moved beyond the modernist aesthetic, their work solidly embodied content in its form and its style was an appropriate reflection of contemporary culture, whereas the subsequent generation exhibited a strong tendency toward typographic adornment and the disengagement of graphic elements. A creeping process that would eventually lead to a complete break from modernism was set in train. With pop came revivalism, an increasing reliance on decorative, pre-industrial forms, and a preference for the subjective art of illustration at photography's expense. The cultural dominance of consumption over the business of production generated a climate unfavourable to the uniformity of new typography, even in its vigorous local form and despite the stubborn resistance of those orthodox journalist-designers, working mainly on news picture magazines, who used systemized grid-based design derived from Swiss models. This school included Allen Hurlbert and Will Hopkins who created the last word in modular design at *Look*, Bernard Quint at *Life*, and David Moore, who successfully projected a lively contemporary style within a modular asymmetric format for the US Information Agency's *Amerika/America Illustrated*. It was of course these very magazines – the generalists – which first bore the brunt of a cooler economic climate as advertising which could not be pitched at specific income or interest groups was switched to television.

It was economic circumstance as much as the prevailing aesthetic which ultimately broke the modern spirit of American graphic design. By the late 1960s, the abandonment of the advertising graveyard and central editorial well had spread from photojournals to generalist and consumer magazines. The new pagination severely restricted the creative possibilities open to art directors. With the double recessions of 1972 and 1974 advertising revenues were sharply reduced and paper prices spiralled, and the industry suffered a catastrophic loss of confidence. Magazines, chasing maximum circulation at minimum expense, became mean in size and scope. Publishers fell under the influence of marketing professionals and attempted to reduce cover and format design to a base set of common denominators: designers adapted to the superficiality of editorial content by switching their attention from communication to production techniques. Editorial design in the 1970s – not only in the United States, but in Europe, too – descended into a barren period of "over-styled, meticulous conservatism"[2] as typography (often excruciatingly over-wrought) was placed in an opposing role to art direction as the basic discipline of editorial layout.

There were notable exceptions, designers who retained their grip on the ideal of uncomplicated communication of ideas and information: Fred Woodward, whose tremendous feel for photography is evident in the pages of *Texas Monthly*; the visual wit of Tom Gould, art director of *Psychology Today*; Mike Salisbury, who displayed a sure instinct for penetrating editorial design at *West*; and Dugald Sturmer, who on *Ramparts* generated a succession of hard-hitting polemical covers and within, a polished literary typography. This radical trend, with its roots in American expressionism, represented a single strand of continuity with half a century of graphic discovery.

The singularly American brand of modern information design was given its first practical expression

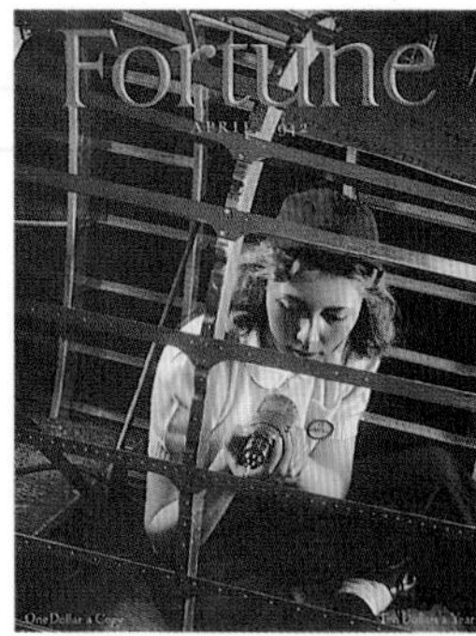

Fortune

April 1942

art editor Francis Brennan

In early 1942 Brennan replaced Fortune's 12-year-old Cleland format with a more flexible typographic scheme. The ornate border was stripped from the cover and, for a two-year period, conceptual cover illustration was replaced by photographic realism, as in this "Rosie the riveter" shot by Dmitri Kessel.

in editorial design at *Fortune* magazine. In 1939 Francis Brennan, who had worked with M. F. Agha at Condé Nast, succeeded Eleanor Treacy as art director. He quickly stripped the old-fashioned ornate border from the cover and in March 1942 replaced the twelve-year-old Cleland format, which had served the magazine so well but was showing distinctly sclerotic symptoms, with a harder-edged and less formal design which reflected *Fortune*'s total commitment to the war effort. Stencil faces, News Gothic and hurried Futura italics embodied the race for war materials production, to which almost the whole of the magazine's editorial content was devoted for four years. As *Fortune* assumed the role of organizer and reporter of the industrial effort, Brennan built on an existing tradition of illustrative charts, diagrams and maps to give visual expression to the performance of "the working front". The one weakness of the old, strictly uniform format, was that it could not impart dramatic visual context; this was remedied by Brennan's substitution of a more varied typographic palette and illustrative and photographic montage.

In late 1945 Will Burtin relaunched *Fortune* on a three-year period of graphic experimentation. Burtin, born and educated in Germany, had served a conventional print apprenticeship before attending evening classes at the Cologne Werkschule, where he embraced the new typography. He later wrote that the classical typographic principles he had first learnt, "applied mainly to the symmetry of classical book titles and book work, and ignored the fact that the kinds of communication had expanded and changed".[3] Once in the United States, Burtin set about formulating a personal design discipline which in many respects exemplified the American experience. His first principle was elementarism: "I attempted to prove my contention that character of a material and its interpretation, illustration, text, technical data, type character, size, page units, colors and shapes, are part of one integrated entity." He then attempted to define his method: "I noticed that the integration of job components toward a dramatic end-product asked for a measure of discipline difficult to define. If followed sternly, it resulted in rigid, mechanical design. But arbitrary disregard of this or that facet left the principal design work to instinct, a powerful, but nontheless unreliable basis. Yet instinct and creative urge put to work at the proper place seemed to be

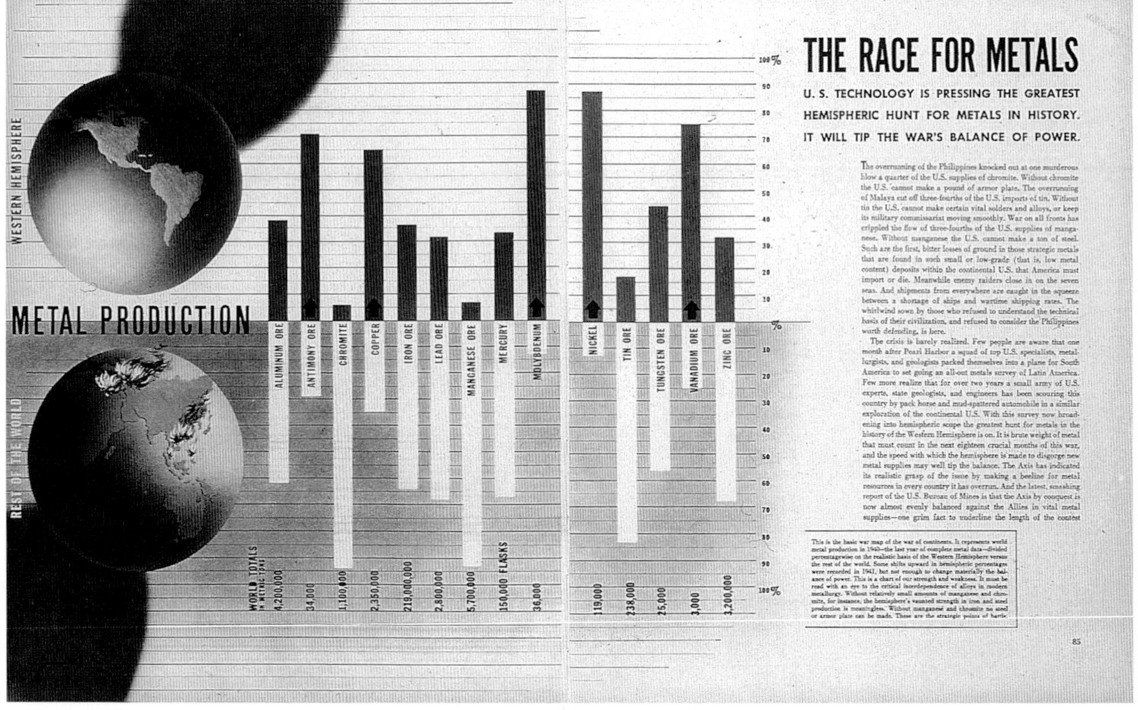

THE RACE FOR METALS

U. S. TECHNOLOGY IS PRESSING THE GREATEST HEMISPHERIC HUNT FOR METALS IN HISTORY. IT WILL TIP THE WAR'S BALANCE OF POWER.

The overrunning of the Philippines knocked out at one murderous blow a quarter of the U.S. supplies of chromite. Without chromite the U.S. cannot make a pound of armor plate. The overrunning of Malaya cut off three-fourths of the U.S. imports of tin. Without tin the U.S. cannot make certain vital solders and alloys, or keep its military commissariat moving smoothly. War on all fronts has crippled the flow of three-fourths of the U.S. supplies of manganese. Without manganese the U.S. cannot make a ton of steel. Such are the first, bitter losses of ground in those strategic metals that are found in such small or low-grade (that is, low metal content) deposits within the continental U.S. that America must import or die. Meanwhile enemy raiders close in on the seven seas. And shipments from everywhere are caught in the squeeze between a shortage of ships and wartime shipping rates. The whirlwind sown by those who refused to understand the technical basis of their civilization, and refused to consider the Philippines worth defending, is here.

The crisis is barely realized. Few people are aware that one month after Pearl Harbor a squad of top U.S. specialists, metallurgists, and geologists packed themselves into a plane for South America to set going an all-out metals survey of Latin America. Few more realize that for over two years a small army of U.S. experts, state geologists, and engineers has been scouring this country by pack horse and mud-spattered automobile in a similar exploration of the continental U.S. With this survey now broadening into hemispheric scope the greatest hunt for metals in the history of the Western Hemisphere is on. It is brute weight of metal that must count in the next eighteen crucial months of this war, and the speed with which the hemisphere is made to disgorge new metal supplies may well tip the balance. The Axis has indicated its realistic grasp of the issue by making a beeline for metal resources in every country it has overrun. And the latest, smashing report of the U.S. Bureau of Mines is that the Axis by conquest is now almost evenly balanced against the Allies in vital metal supplies—one grim fact to underline the length of the contest

This is the basic war map of the war of continents. It represents world metal production in 1940—the last year of complete metal data—divided percentagewise on the realistic basis of the Western Hemisphere versus the rest of the world. Some shifts upward in hemispheric percentages were recorded in 1941, but not enough to change materially the balance of power. This is a chart of our strength and weakness. It must be read with an eye to the critical interdependence of alloys in modern metallurgy. Without relatively small amounts of manganese and chromite, for instance, the hemisphere's vaunted strength in iron and steel production is meaningless. Without manganese and chromite no steel or armor plate can be made. These are the strategic points of battle.

85

Fortune

March 1942

art editor Francis Brennan

A simple bar chart is transformed by designer Herbert Bayer into a graphic, three-dimensional image of urgency and conflict.

Fortune

October 1943

art director Peter Piening

The Fortune cover was a ready source of work for European immigrants of the modern school. Peter Piening (art director 1943-45) and Will Burtin commissioned abstract and conceptual art from Sutnar, Lidov, Lewandowski and Bayer. This design, built around a photogram, is by Herbert Matter. It illustrates a major feature on the ball-bearing industry.

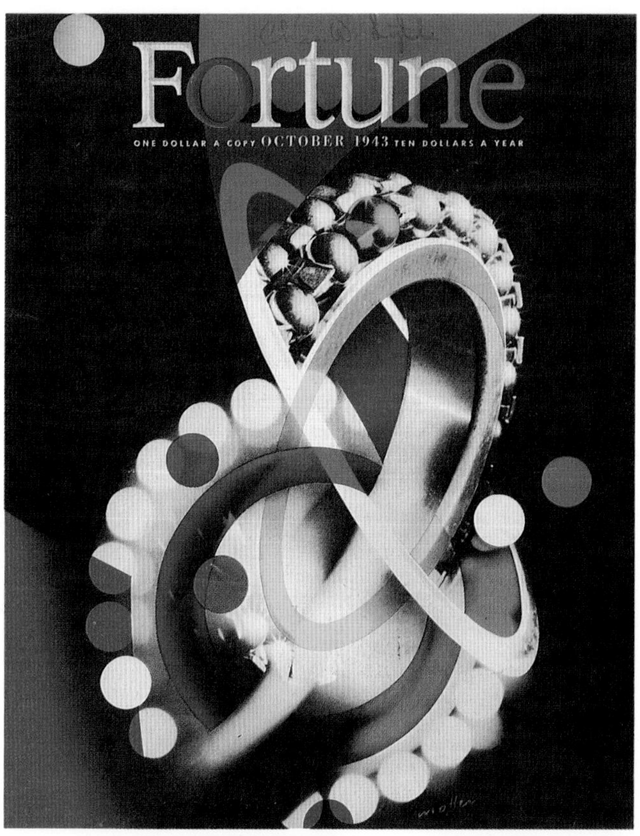

Fortune

December 1946

art director Will Burtin

Right: jewelled sunburst cover by Alvin Lustig, incorporating a photograph by Rouben Samberg.

Fortune

July 1963

art director Walter Allner

Far right: after Burtin's departure from Fortune, Leo Leonni introduced a cooler, rationalist typographic format within a modular layout arrangement. Both Leonni and Walter Allner (art director 1960-71) retained the tradition of conceptual cover art begun by Cleland in 1930. This riveted Fortune 500 cover by Ivan Chermayeff and Thomas Geismar is accurately described as "sturdy" in the magazine's credit page.

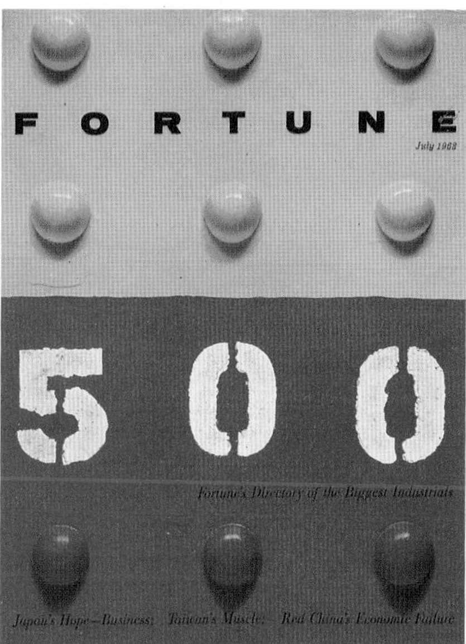

Fortune

July 1946

designer and art director
Will Burtin

Burtin was a master communicator of complex scientific ideas. This chart, in which the logic of the argument is beautifully expressed in its graphic presentation, connects antibiotic moulds and crystals with the disease-carrying bacteria which they destroy (squared-up, right).

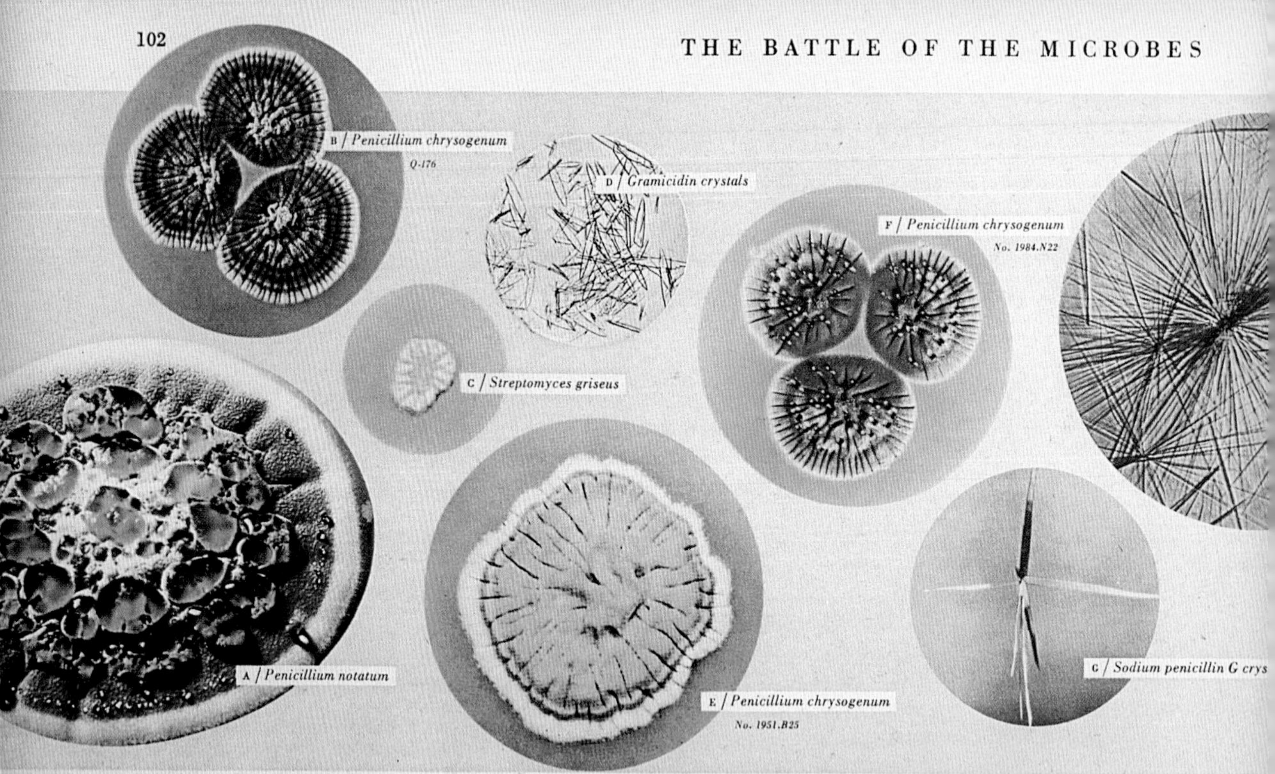

ANTIBIOTICS VS. BACTERIA Into some of the most ancient strongholds of disease, the antibiotics (shown both in producing-molds and in pure crystals above) are driving deep new salients. Though a number of dread diseases—cancer, malaria, virus infections—still hold out stubbornly against treatment, many deadly bacteria (photographed both in culture and in body tissues at right) have capitulated to one or another of the new drugs. With the development of new antibiotics, and with increased knowledge of existing ones, more ground will be gained.

yielded the unheard-of amount of 400 to 500 units of penicillin per cubic centimeter. Researchers at the University of Wisconsin further bombarded samples of the X-rayed strain of *Penicillium chrysogenum* with ultraviolet rays. When they prepared a culture of the surviving spores, it was discovered that one of the new irradiated strains, Q-176, yielded roughly 1,000 units of penicillin per cubic centimeter—more than four times the yield of No. 832. At this news, the entire industry took notice. A higher-yielding mold meant not only greater unit production, but lower unit cost. By the close of 1945 most of the large penicillin producers had shifted to the use of Q-176, and yearly output had shot to over 7,000 billion units worth $60 million.

Yet even this phenomenal total was insufficient. Despite the fact that the WPB had removed penicillin from allocation in the fall of 1945, releasing unprecedented quantities of the drug for civilian use, demand showed no signs of diminishing. The use of penicillin by hospitals and private doctors had become so widespread that last fall, when a shortage of corn-steep liquor and other factors caused a slump in production, the situation was viewed as a serious hazard to public health. Sharp criticism was directed toward producers who diverted penicillin for consumers from the cheap (roughly $1 per 100,000 units) injectable form to the high-cost oral form, which requires five times as much of the drug (at about $6 per 500,000 units) to produce the necessary concentration in the blood stream.* On top of domestic requirements came urgent demands from abroad. (In a single month the value of penicillin exports was about five and one-half times that of *all* drugs and medicines exported by the U.S. during an average month in 1938.)

Last January, to ensure fair distribution, the CPA put penicillin back on allocation. During the next few months production began to climb; hospitals and drugstores reported a rise in penicillin stocks. By the end of winter, domestic demand for the drug subsided, and sorely needed supplies were released in larger quantities for export. New dosage forms—troches, ointments, and sprays—appeared. Though potential demand was still estimated to be three times the available supply, the industry felt that its major penicillin problem—production—had been overcome at last.

"Most promising . . ."

Until early in 1945 the wonders of penicillin held the public mind firmly entranced. Most people cherished the belief that in penicillin—and in the somewhat less fashionable sulfonamides—protection was to be had against almost all forms of disease, with the possible exception of cancer. Actually, this was far from true. Beyond the reach of both drugs were such ancient scourges as tuberculosis, bubonic plague, tularemia, typhoid

**During its comparatively slow passage from the digestive tract into the blood stream, penicillin is subjected to the inactivating influence of gastric juices and various intestinal bacteria.*

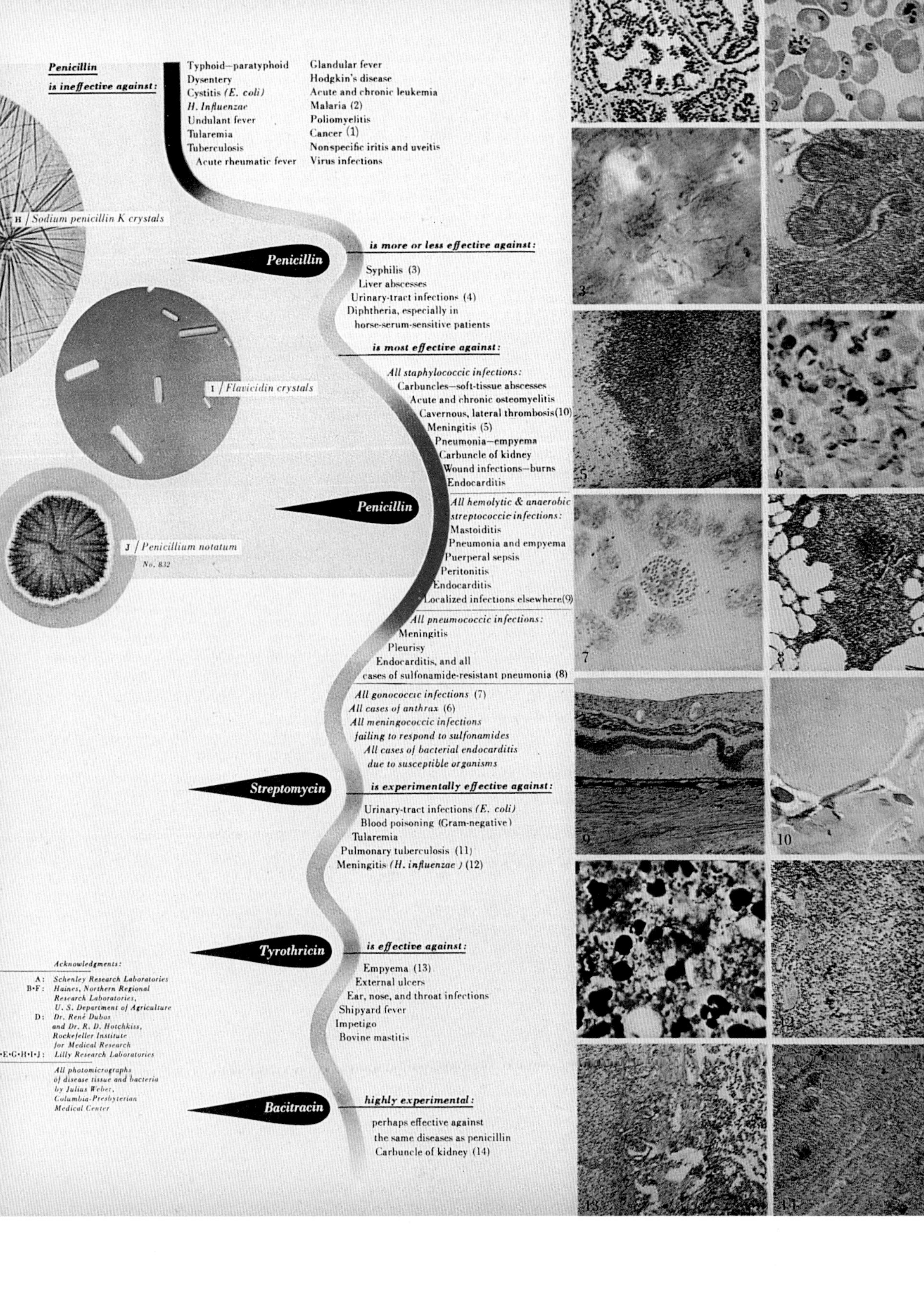

Acknowledgments:
A: *Schenley Research Laboratories*
B·F: *Haines, Northern Regional Research Laboratories, U. S. Department of Agriculture*
D: *Dr. René Dubos and Dr. R. D. Hotchkiss, Rockefeller Institute for Medical Research*
C·E·G·H·I·J: *Lilly Research Laboratories*
All photomicrographs of disease tissue and bacteria by Julius Weber, Columbia-Presbyterian Medical Center

Fortune
February 1946
art director Will Burtin

An example of "natural discipline" in graphic design: this illustration, cleverly integrated with the text and designed as a pseudo-chart by Lester Beall, is an exuberant evocation of technological strength.

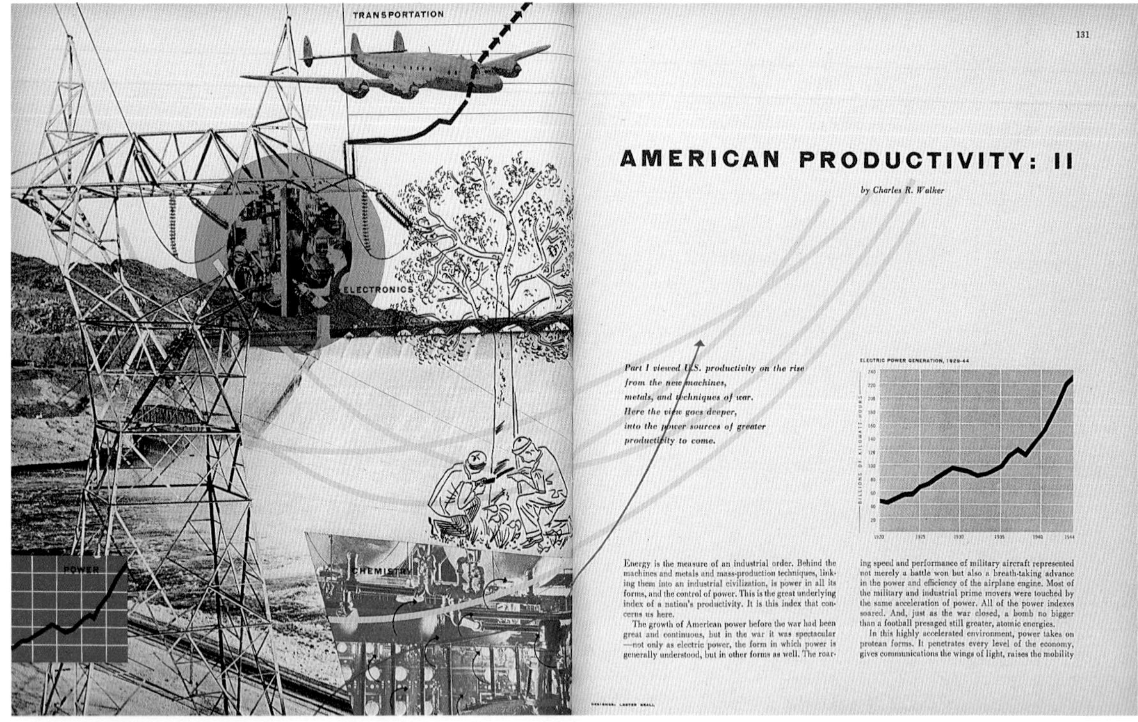

AMERICAN PRODUCTIVITY: II

by Charles R. Walker

Part I viewed U.S. productivity on the rise from the new machines, metals, and techniques of war. Here the view goes deeper, into the power sources of greater productivity to come.

Energy is the measure of an industrial order. Behind the machines and metals and mass-production techniques, linking them into an industrial civilization, is power in all its forms, and the control of power. This is the great underlying index of a nation's productivity. It is this index that concerns us here.

The growth of American power before the war had been great and continuous, but in the war it was spectacular —not only as electric power, the form in which power is generally understood, but in other forms as well. The roaring speed and performance of military aircraft represented not merely a battle won but also a breath-taking advance in the power and efficiency of the airplane engine. Most of the military and industrial prime movers were touched by the same acceleration of power. All of the power indexes soared. And, just as the war closed, a bomb no bigger than a football presaged still greater, atomic energies.

In this highly accelerated environment, power takes on protean forms. It penetrates every level of the economy, gives communications the wings of light, raises the mobility

DESIGNER: LESTER BEALL

Fortune
November 1948
art director Will Burtin

Entitled "The American Bazaar: a picture gallery of the chief activities of Americans – selling things to one another", this portfolio piece by Burtin was a celebration of popular advertising art which ran over 14 wildly coloured pages. Its themes, "Assault on the Senses" and "The Aural Nerve", are more than adequately expressed in the composition.

Eternal Female

The greatest symbol in American advertising was, is, and always will be the face of a beautiful woman; it is used to sell everything except municipal bonds and steam locomotives. Any other aspect of a woman is almost as good, as these examples show (the kiss is The Woman in Action). Popular magazines are one long procession of pretty girls, including both front and back covers. Bettina Bolegard, the Conover model *(below)*, who is thirty, married, with an eight-year-old son, has been for almost a decade one of the best-known Unknown Faces in the U.S. Most American men see her picture more frequently than the faces of their wives, for her range is from "goddess stuff" to "young-matron-with-recipes stuff." An even greater influence on American mores is *Vogue*'s famous Carl Erickson ("Eric"), the supreme fashion artist, whose classic 1930 cover (on opposite page) is still soigné seventeen years later. Bolegard, Eric, and the fact that women are supposed to control the American purse strings are reasons why the U.S. advertising scene is predominantly feminine.

most necessary implements. The need for more tests to develop a sort of natural discipline was indicated."[4]

Burtin, in this measured heresy, had discovered the Achilles heel of "objective" typography: its inflexibility when applied according to a narrow criterion of legibility or functionality. "Both groups [traditional and modern]", he continued, "based their appraisal on pre-conceived values. Neither the industry catalogue set in German black-letter nor the bible set in Futura were appropriate." Burtin was no dogmatist, and in this respect it is significant that he felt no imperative to replace the flattering Baskerville body text of *Fortune* with a modern serif. The same face was retained for standfirsts – set, according to the current fashion, in loosely spaced capitals.

The "natural discipline" which Burtin opposed to machinistic typography is an ill-defined idea, whereby "individual job requirements led quite naturally to their own visual expression". What, we may ask, is "natural"? The answer can be found in the pages of *Fortune* and of *Scope*, the Upjohn Company pharmaceutical magazine which Burtin designed after leaving *Fortune* in Spring 1949: it is the typographically rich, colourful and often entertaining constructions which incorporated cultural context – a democratic, populist culture – in the direction and logic of their visual language. This was the hallmark of modern American design in the mid-century, and its application can be seen most clearly, perhaps, in Burtin's portfolio piece for the November 1947 issue of *Fortune*, entitled "The American Bazaar".

At both *Fortune* and *Scope* Burtin concentrated his mind on the problem of communicating complex scientific and economic information. His solutions combine visual clarity with high drama. Drawing on his own knowledge of montage and photograms and on the superb technical draftsmanship of the *Fortune* art department, he created both flat and three-dimensional – squared off and amorphous – flow charts, tables, maps and exploded mechanical diagrams which are notable for their remarkable use of simple formal elements and colour. Colour, line, curves, squares, circles, were used to link ideas and images with a superb eye for both the composition and function of the diagram. Similar techniques were employed in conceptual illustration and were used regularly on *Fortune* covers, in which photography and illustration were combined to communicate an impressionistic summary of the month's major theme.

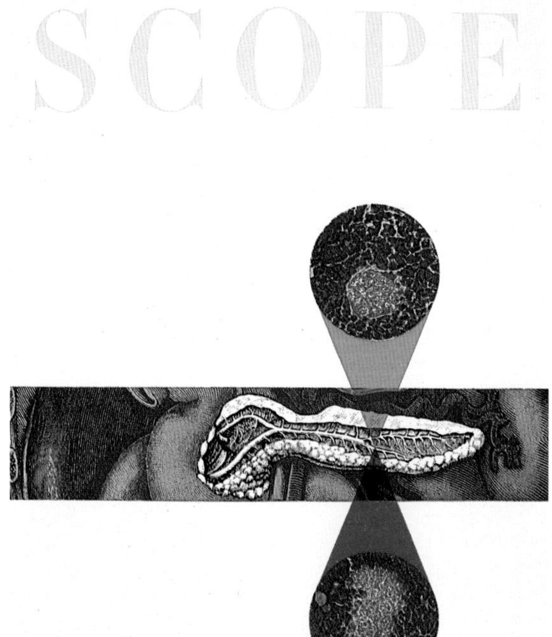

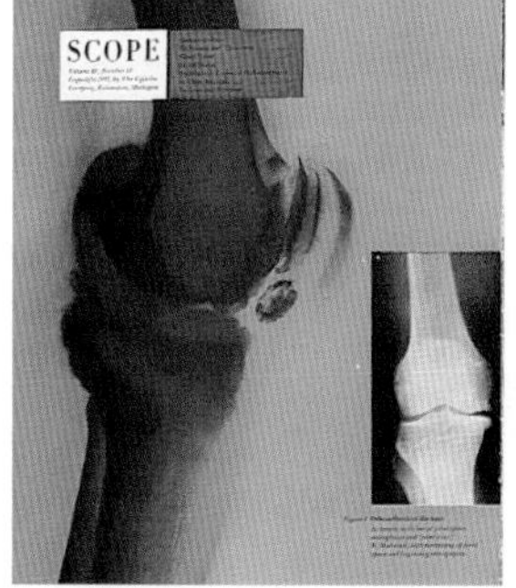

Scope
vol. 5 no. 1 1957 and
vol. 4 no. 12 1957
art director Will Burtin

At the pharmaceutical magazine Scope, Burtin continued to develop his method of integrating image and text, creating abstract compositions from combinations of modern scientific photography and early medical illustration. The startling images were measured by an economical, asymmetric typographic scheme with no contrasts of type weight, giving a very quiet, uniform tone appropriate to the needs of a scientific journal.

For this purpose Burtin commissioned a roll-call of what were the finest European and American designers and illustrators: Herbert Bayer, Edmund Lewandowski, Alvin Lustig, E. McKnight Kauffer, Ladislav Sutnar, George Giusti, Herbert Matter and, most notably, Lester Beall.

Beall's relationship with Burtin began at *Fortune* and continued at the Upjohn Company's *Scope*, which Beall had designed since 1944 and on which the two men collaborated from 1949. Beall, an accomplished technician, clearly shared Burtin's design philosophy, and showed a marvellous fluency – a "naturalism" – in his constructive patterns, contrived from photography, type, old woodcuts, lithographs and drawings, overlaid by an electric sense of colour.

Together, Burtin and Beall exerted a considerable influence on the business press (Beall was also responsible for the design of *Red Cross* magazine and Abbott Laboratories' *What's New;* Burtin for *Architectural Forum*), effectively re-educating a generation of clients and peers in the possibilities of graphic design. The two were in the vanguard of a succession of adventurous designers working in trade and technical publications: George Elliot, art director of the splendid *Jewellery* and *Spot* magazines; D. B. Ruther on *Modern Packaging*; Leo Leonni, who took over art direction of *Fortune* from Burtin; Peter Bradford at *Industrial Design*; and Romaldo Giurgola and Roberto Mango, joint art directors of *Interiors* magazine, are the outstanding examples. The sheer joy of their work for a technocratic business community which, in its devotion to productivity, was then "less biased by narrow interpretations of tradition",[5] could have no greater contrast than the pompous, pinstripe design of so many business publications today.

Bradbury Thompson undertook a separate but closely related experiment in editorial design at the aptly titled *Westvaco Inspirations for Printers*, the promotional magazine of the paper manufacturer Westvaco Corporation. Over 23 years (from 1938-62) and with an audience of 35,000 members of the graphic arts community in the United States, Thompson gave virtuoso demonstrations of the dynamics of typography, layout and print.

Thompson had the great advantage of being his own editor, with what he called his own "graphics laboratory",[6] a substantial print budget, although very little cash for commissioning. These circumstances shaped the magazine, in which Thompson indulged his interest in semantic typography against a background of collage created from found images and process colours.

In his earlier work Thompson repeated images in the four process inks to create movement in a manner reminiscent of the futurists. Organic blocks of colour gave coherence and balance to often intricate, but always tightly controlled compositions built from type, photography, and engravings extracted from Diderot's *Encyclopédie*. The same technique, in which the block or line served as a fulcrum in asymmetric layout, was used by Burtin and Beall and can be traced, via Kepes, Sutnar, Moholy-Nagy and El Lissitzky, to Malevich's suprematist spatial studies. The difference was merely in the replacement of geometric shapes by the biomorphic – Thompson was a fan of Miró.

Perhaps Thompson's most enduring influence on American editorial design was his treatment of type, which he used as an alliterative and illustrative communication tool. Type created movement, mood, volume, scene; it followed abruptly changing sightlines; its shapes an integral component of layout. "Type as toy",[7] as Thompson spoke of his work, became a

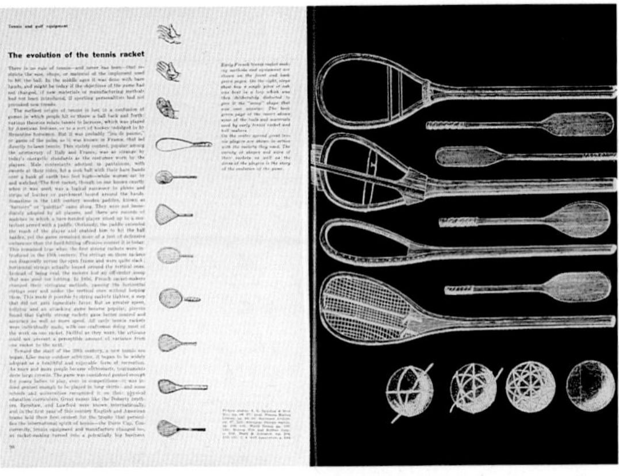

Industrial Design
August 1956
art director
Martin Rosenzweig

Alvin Lustig's styling of Industrial Design (1955) was typical of the adventurous style of the American business press. Here, Rosenzweig uses the format as a canvas for a perfectly composed exercise in visual journalism.

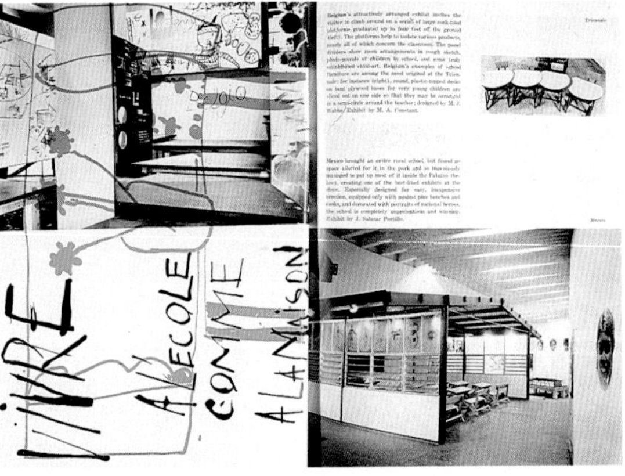

Industrial Design
September 1960
art director Peter Bradford

Bradford introduced to Industrial Design a kind of humanistic rationalism. He tempered the rigorous geometric grid of the page with expressive splashes of colour; in this example, a naive painting and hand marks overprint a feature on school architecture.

Mademoiselle

February 1953

art director
Bradbury Thompson

Below: Mademoiselle possessed a striking regularity of line, type and composition. The cover gains its strength from the cleverly placed diagonal cross in the background of Stephen Colhoun's photographic composition.

The sweater suit

Left: A fitted Botany worsted bouclé cardigan, bound in worsted flannel, buttoned into shape over a flannel skirt. By Moordale, $59.95. Lord & Taylor; M. M. Cohn, Little Rock

First suits

The right-size box

Left: Perfect for you who are not-so-tall, a double-breasted worsted tweed box suit, straight as a streak. A Whitleyette, $49.95. Bloomingdale's; Woodward & Lothrop, Washington

Jersey . . . jeweled

Right: A white-beaded collar on Heller checked worsted jersey. By Miss Mayfair, $55. The May Co., Los Angeles. Below: The hat, a mushroom of straw, by Debway, $5.95. Bonwit Teller, New York

Stephen Colhoun

118

Slouch suit, ensembled

Right: Gray wool flannel, one long curve from shoulder to hem. It's lined in striped rayon taffeta to match the blouse. By Arlene Norman. $55. Henri Bendel; Woodward & Lothrop, Washington

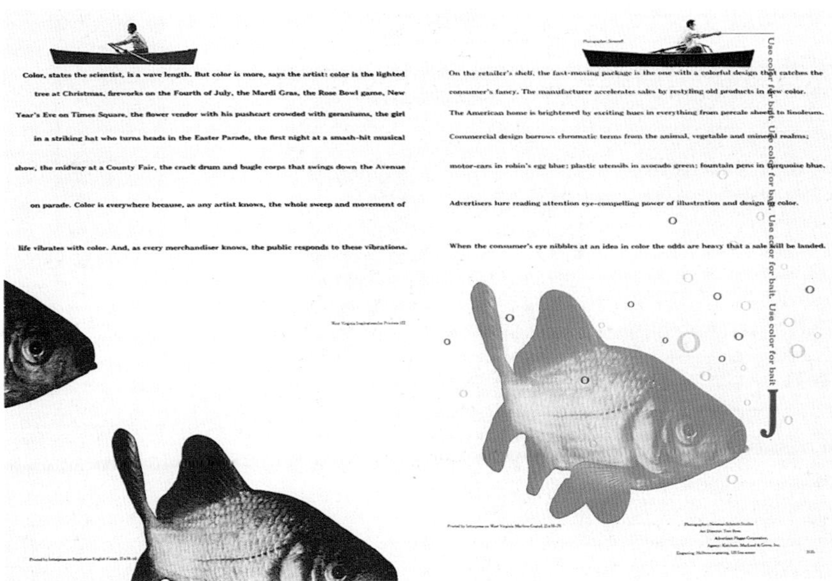

Color, states the scientist, is a wave length. But color is more, says the artist: color is the lighted tree at Christmas, fireworks on the Fourth of July, the Mardi Gras, the Rose Bowl game, New Year's Eve on Times Square, the flower vendor with his pushcart crowded with geraniums, the girl in a striking hat who turns heads in the Easter Parade, the first night at a smash-hit musical show, the midway at a County Fair, the crack drum and bugle corps that swings down the Avenue on parade. Color is everywhere because, as any artist knows, the whole sweep and movement of life vibrates with color. And, as every merchandiser knows, the public responds to these vibrations.

On the retailer's shelf, the fast-moving package is the one with a colorful design that catches the consumer's fancy. The manufacturer accelerates sales by restyling old products in new color. The American home is brightened by exciting hues in everything from percale sheets to linoleum. Commercial design borrows chromatic terms from the animal, vegetable and mineral realms; motor-cars in robin's egg blue; plastic utensils in avocado green; fountain pens in turquoise blue. Advertisers lure reading attention eye-compelling power of illustration and design in color. When the consumer's eye nibbles at an idea in color the odds are heavy that a sale will be landed.

Use color for bait. Use color for bait. Use color for bait. Use color for bait

Above: the fashion sequences in Mademoiselle were arranged on a horizontal grid splitting the page in two, with squared-off pictures floating left-to-right between the margins. This cleverly art-directed spread is given graphic power by the geometric backdrop against which the model is photographed.

Mademoiselle

February 1953

art director
Bradbury Thompson

Westvaco Inspirations

1949

art director
Bradbury Thompson

Westvaco Inspirations, a promotional magazine for the Westvaco Paper Corp., was used by its art director Bradbury Thompson as a laboratory for experiment in print and design. His montages of found images and figurative typography influenced a generation of American designers.

fundamental weapon in the American designers' armoury, wielded as concrete expression of content. In Thompson's hands it was a lake, a railway track, a sneeze, a primitive mask; in like manner, William Cadge would allude to nuclear fallout, Otto Storch to the sag of a mattress, Henry Wolf to the light of a streetlamp, and Herb Lubalin, who baptised this approach "The American school of graphic expressionism",[8] would make type jump through hoops, crash, collide, whisper and scream in his contorted ligatures and architectonic constructions.

Also apparent in Thompson's work is a strong affinity with modern art, which was a common component of his pictorial essays for *Westvaco Inspirations* and a feature of illustration for the teenage fashion magazine *Mademoiselle*, which Thompson art directed from 1945-59. Painting, he said, inspired "new directions in typographic expression through exploration of the painter's work, an art which traditionally affords greater freedom of expression and less restraints on time than one's own."[9] This was a fairly common preoccupation. American editorial designers, most notably Agha, Brodovitch, Burtin and Hurlbert, closely followed the development of the optical arts and sciences, in studies in representation, composition, the dynamics of light, and the psychology of perception. Contemporary art, architecture, and the three-dimensional design disciplines informed their work directly, and not as a set of second-hand principles derived from the German and Russian graphic experiments of the early part of the century.

This interest was indulged in the non-commercial prototypes, such as Thompson's *Inspirations* and Brodovitch's *Portfolio*, and was applied practically in commercial magazines. *Portfolio* was not only a design workshop in which Brodovitch played with type and the placement and juxtaposition of photography, it also assumed a didactic role, introducing the reader to contemporary illustration and industrial design, to graphic symbol, modern art and crafts, and to traditional calligraphy and advertising typography, which Brodovitch clearly believed could counteract the "deficiencies" of functional modernism. In *Portfolio* he betrays his ambivalence towards modern graphic design, which he accuses, in its utilitarian form, of lacking expression: "Rarely is the printed page considered a medium of plastic invention. Its design has become standardized; a machine-like element devoid of feeling and aesthetic significance. This is a cause for regret for the variety of forms possible when typography and calligraphy are creatively

129

Upper Left
ORDINARY LIPSTICK
CHANGES COLOR
UNDER INCANDESCENT LIGHT

This lipstick appeared red-orange when it was applied. The light has drained away the red, leaving only unbecoming orange.

Upper Right
MILKMAID'S RED CURRANT
KEEPS ITS CLEAR TRUE SHADE
UNDER INCANDESCENT LIGHT

This shade, becoming to all types, stays the same as when applied.

Lower Left
ORDINARY LIPSTICK
CHANGES COLOR
UNDER FLUORESCENT LIGHT

This lipstick appeared bluish red when applied. The light has drained away the red, leaving only unbecoming purple.

Lower Right
MILKMAID'S RED CURRANT
KEEPS ITS CLEAR TRUE SHADE
UNDER FLUORESCENT LIGHT

This shade, becoming to all types, stays the same as when applied.

A Lipstick
Which Keeps Its Color
Under Most Lights

It's Milkmaid's new Red Currant and it's revolutionary. If you'll think back, you'll realize that only once in every decade or so does a *truly* important cosmetic development turn up. Nail polish was a gigantic one. Cake make-up was another.

Now Milkmaid has achieved what cosmetic chemists have long struggled for, and women have long hoped for: a formula to lick the problem of lipstick colors which look different under different lights.

The trouble—and it really *was* a trouble, was this: color changes with light. Your lipstick has no will of its own—chameleonlike, it changes shade at every chance gleam that happens to shine upon it. And in the course of a day and night, there's simply no telling *how* many gleams, and kinds of gleams, will shed their mischief upon you.

You start out, say, under the incandescent light at your dressing table. Then you step into the daylight—yellowish if it's sunny, greyish if it's drizzling. Off you go to the office, where the lights are probably white fluorescent unless you happen to work in a factory or designing room—when they're probably bluish. When you go out to dine in the (Continued on page 170)

Glamour
November 1945
art director Cipe Pineles

After working at Vanity Fair and Vogue with M. F. Agha, Cipe Pineles became art director of Glamour in 1945. This was a unique opportunity. War employment had given women increased social and economic power, and this was reflected in the editorial and design of young women's magazines such as Glamour, Junior Bazaar and Mademoiselle. Pineles gave Glamour a strong journalistic flavour, applying the discipline of information design to features on work and social issues, as well as fashion. The photographs in this example are by Joffé.

Junior Bazaar
April 1946
art director
Alexey Brodovitch
designer Lillian Bassman

Primary colour and militaristic type marked out Junior Bazaar from its sophisticated parent.

used approaches that of abstract painting."[10]

Brodovitch was perhaps echoing Burtin's "naturalism", but if anything contradicts his view it is Thompson's *Mademoiselle* – an exemplar of functional design applied to a popular women's magazine. Thompson's arrangement of fashion photography was based on a grid of two squares, fixed vertically one above the other, floating both left and right on the horizontal axis. Where he departed from this system it was, usually, to explore compositions of rectangular picture blocks, set flush together in varied scales and proportions. For masthead, coverlines and headlines, he used a single condensed sans serif Gothic with a Modern[11] serif for body text. *Mademoiselle* therefore had a striking regularity of line, type and composition which, it could be argued, was inappropriate in a teenage magazine. The structural uniformity was, however, offset by intelligent art direction of photography, vibrant colour, the simplicity and strength of visual dynamics – horizontal, vertical and diagonal elements which the designer incorporated in both layout and photographic backgrounds – and by the typographic inventiveness which Thompson imported from *Inspirations*.

In the late 1940s the technocratic efficiency of *Mademoiselle* must have been a startling contrast to its competitors, and it would certainly not have been out of place twenty years later; it was, nonetheless, no more uncompromisingly modern than Brodovitch and Lillian Bassman's *Harper's* spinoff, *Junior Bazaar*, which first appeared in 1946. *Junior Bazaar*, which was pitched at only a slightly younger readership than *Mademoiselle*, was a radical if short-lived publishing experiment. The cover telegraphed a new role for women: primary-coloured montaged covers and militaristic stencil type for the masthead; inside, the rakish, constructivist design, bold graphic symbols and energetic photoplay bespoke activity and initiative. This was not what little girls had been told they were made of. In early 1947, however, in a changed political and social climate – war work forgotten and domesticism reinstated – *Junior Bazaar* was incorporated back into *Harper's*. With this, and the departure of Lillian Bassman, it lost its vigour, sinking back into the coiffured and comparatively passive elegance of its parent.

In the 1950s and early 1960s, and well beyond their respective tenures at Condé Nast and Hearst Magazines, M. F. Agha and Alexey Brodovitch continued to exert a powerful influence over the design of consumer magazines, while Alexander Liberman formed a third part of this dominant triumvirate. A

Vogue
15 September 1957
art director
Alexander Liberman

Liberman became art director of Vogue in March 1943. In the 1950s and '60s the combination of Liberman, art editor Priscilla Peck and photographer Irving Penn evolved into one of the most creative partnerships in American magazine publishing. As editorial director, Liberman took Vogue into the mass market, introducing a popular, punchy style of layout characterized by montage and Penn's startling close-up "stoppers".

How to look like a beauty
continued

covers grey hair if she hates it; *or* she has a pastel tint put over it (gold, blue, platinum, a hint of pink) to make it the prettiest shade of grey imaginable; or she has streaks of her own original hair-colouring dyed into her grey hair to give it definite line and character. She will risk a new coiffure, and if she has trouble managing it herself, between settings, she asks the hairdresser to let her brush and comb it in his presence so that he can coach her to keep the pattern he has set. And she has a better chance for keeping the pattern—no matter what the weather conditions—now that she can use a hair-spray to reinforce her brush and comb.

The woman who needs to look like a beauty has heard that a professional make-up can diminish unfavoured features, highlight the best; that, in fact, it could give her a *new* face. But how? She finds out; sometimes she discovers that make-up artists who guide photographers' models or transform actresses for the theatre or for television, are available to teach their magic to non-professional women. And every cosmetic company that maintains beauty salons will give excellent personal advice on colours and techniques; or will give transforming make-ups on appointment. If she *wants* to be changed, by make-up, she seeks professional make-up help.

If her complexion is not satisfactory, she learns the creams and lotions for her needs—and their routine and timing. The woman who wants to look like a beauty doesn't just *buy* products—she uses them consistently, faithfully, intelligently. Even the very advanced, and highly beneficial formulae of today are no over-night miracles (a hormone cream, for instance, should be used daily for a month, before results are judged). She learns that basic skin-care is a basic necessity, should be as habitual as toothbrushing. And she learns that its slow, but sure, effect can be heightened quickly for galas by special treatments, of which the surest is usually a professional facial and make-up; or, failing that, a masque at home.

She knows, without being lectured, that taking on overweight is beauty-suicide; and she knows, more than most women, that the satisfaction of slipping into a small-size dress is infinitely greater than the satisfaction of sipping in a chocolate-malted. She diets when she has to, as a matter of course, and she exercises habitually; she knows that slenderness is not enough for a figure, it must also be flexible, graceful, and if she can not exercise, she explores the new machines that exercise for her, toning specific muscles.

And most of all she learns not to be rigid in her ideas of beauty. If she is forty, she knows that she does not look exactly as she did at twenty, simply older. Therefore she decides to look different, which is exciting, because it is new—and what is new is *(Continued on page 160)*

Green-eyed beauty

This page: Possible to the blue-eyed, brown-eyed, and hazel-eyed now, something of the green-eyed beauty's sparkle, it seems. This new eye-shadow formula is based on green with flecks of silver. And while no blue-eyed woman is suddenly going to be emerald-eyed because of it, almost every cosmetic-maker now plans some version of this colour; its chemistry makes *any* eye-colour seem more brilliant. The perfect "neutral," the first such in eye make-up, it's an answer to a not-too-made-up-looking eye make-up for day. This version, by Coty; others, page 180.

Beauty—highlighted

Facing page: This is beauty—with gloss added in one of the newest ways around. To fingernails made up in a muted-red shade, an overlay of spun gold has been added. It's Juliette Marglen's new Cellini Gold, applied here over her Rousseau Rouge nail glacé (same red that makes the glossy oval lipstick). The Marglen lipstick, nail glacé, and Cellini Gold, all at Saks Fifth Avenue. Diamond and ruby-striped ring from Cartier.

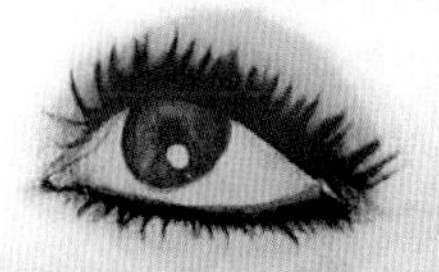

Vogue

15 April 1957

art director
Alexander Liberman

As editorial director of all Condé Nast publications, Liberman took a journalistic approach to the commercialization of Vogue. He pursued dramatic effect and rubbished aesthetic pretension. A well developed sense of incongruity was combined with intuitive layouts, sometimes intentionally crude, always bold. The technique was designed to present high fashion in a popular format. The juxtaposition of $5,000 haute couture with affordable department store fashion was reflected graphically in the combination of classical serifs and aggressive modern sans serif within one headline, and by the brimful, montaged and torn paper layouts in the front of book and feature sections. This visual rush was punctuated by powerfully magnified images in the beauty section, all eyes, lips and fingers (right, photographed by Irving Penn and William Klein). Liberman proved his skill as a graphic designer through his Vogue covers of the 1950s which brilliantly conveyed the spirit of fashion. He would, however, perhaps prefer to be regarded not as a designer but as an editorial director with a publisher's pragmatic eye for circulation. In this respect he vigorously separated his attempts to popularize fine art through Vogue editorial from the practice of design and photography which, in the bourgeois manner, he appeared to regard as separate from and beneath "high" art.

WILLIAM KLEIN

Beauty notes from all over

Opposite: From bottles with a new label, nail glacés in almost every shade of red you'd be likely to meet in fashion this year. Source of the colours themselves: reds that might have been used by famous painters. For instance, striking the B note at far left, a thumb dressed in Rembrandt Ruby. Continuing along the chord: Mondrian Coral; Degas Mauve; Lautrec Orange (added brilliance on this finger: a swirl of diamonds backed with gold, by Cartier); and on the A-flat, Cézanne Cerise. All these, by Juliette Marglen. Saks Fifth Avenue. *This page:* From an elegantly slender oval golden tube, a creamy new lipstick with excellent staying powers. This, also by Juliette Marglen, and in the same red mutations as the nail glacé. At Saks Fifth Avenue. From a king-size package, news to keep any lipstick prettier when it's working and you're smoking: a filter-tip cigarette (i.e., it's non-tobacco-shedding). The one above, a Kent.

PENN

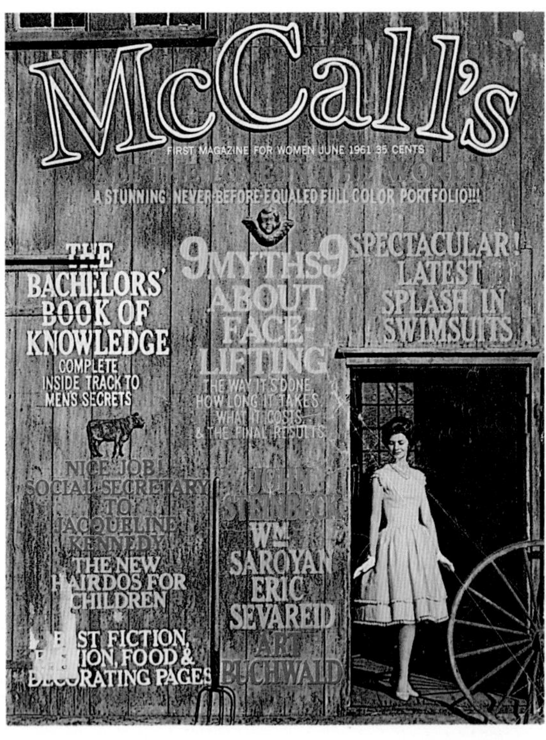

McCall's

June 1961

art director Otto Storch

A very literal engagement of type and image. Close examination of the cover reveals that most of the text was printed – not painted – over the barn door, but the effect remains the same. The photograph is by Onofrio Paccione.

family tree of their protégés – and their protégés' protégés – would by 1964 account for the art directors of a large sector of American publishing. It was Agha who secured Thompson's appointment at Street & Smith Publications' *Mademoiselle;* Agha's assistant from *Vanity Fair* days, Cipe Pineles, was the accomplished art director of Triangle's *Seventeen*, and subsequently Street & Smith's *Charm* magazine. Art Kane, the photographer who had attended Brodovitch's classes, took over from Pineles at *Seventeen,* where he was followed by Marvin Israel, who in turn succeeded Henry Wolf at *Harper's Bazaar.* Wolf, of course, had also studied at Brodovitch's proverbial knee, as had Otto Storch who, on the master's recommendation, had resigned his restrictive job at Dell Publishing, later to transform *McCall's.* The continuity of design method was as unbroken as that of personnel: common features were a precisely shaped typography, and the bonding of type and image through staged full-bleed photography – often accompanied by the visual metaphor or pun that so concisely transmitted editorial ideas. The plastic organization which Brodovitch and Agha had introduced to commercial magazine design – repetition, reflection, contrast of scale to produce linear perspective, diagonal axis construction – was employed with enthusiasm. There was no apparent allegiance to sans serif typography: "Modern" (Didoni) and Latin serifs were generally preferred, with certain notable exceptions.[12]

There was no better practitioner of the new visual journalism than Otto Storch. He became art director of *McCall's* in 1953 when the magazine was losing sales and stayed there until 1967. At first Storch could make little impact on this women's food, fashion, fiction and features magazine, but when Herbert Mayes was appointed editor some five years later the art director was given *carte blanche* to re-examine the whole graphic approach. The combination proved an outstanding success. By the mid-1960s, circulation had risen to 8,500,000.[13]

From the remarkable pictorial format that developed it is clear that Storch had a dominant influence over editorial content. He exerted such control through absolute implementation of the self-evident axiom that a designer must a) have a complete understanding of editorial, and b) provide photographers and illustrators with the most detailed brief possible. The spread, in *McCall's,* was planned in detail long before galley, prints, paste and scissors were picked up by the layout artist. Storch wrote: "To my mind, there are two moments in the preparation of material for a magazine that are of supreme importance to the art director, and indeed determine the ultimate success or failure of his work. The first is the preliminary editorial conference that outlines the material to be

McCall's

date unknown

art director Otto Storch

At McCall's, planning and a clear visualization of story presentation were the axioms of art direction. This brilliant example of figurative typography working hand in hand with photography has three preconceived design elements: the striking reversal of colour in Allen and Diane Arbus's two photographs; the kicked and falling typography, which imparts the action and creates a total unity between text and image; and the coup de grace, the model's direct stare at the headline.

"A FOOL FOR A FATHER"

my life with Ed Wynn, by Keenan Wynn

On July 12, 1958, I reached the age of forty-two, having appeared in a hundred and seven plays and more than ninety movies. Chances were I'd passed the halfway mark of my life; yet here I was, trying to be some sort of artist in an art form of little consequence. From the time I climbed out of bed, it turned out to be a day for brooding.

"I think," I said at dinner, "that I should have done something else with my life."

"Like what?" asked Sharley, who is my wife.

"I don't know. I've no training except for the job I'm in."

"Well, you ran that car agency once."

"That was more of a hobby," I said.

"Anyway, you'd miss the excitement and everything."

"Honey, there's this wonderful thing about actors. Heroic and exciting as they try to be, they really don't amount to much."

Sharley, who is twenty-five, is a straightforward girl. She said, "You make me so mad sometimes! Look at everything you've achieved. You ought to take pride in that."

I stopped to think. I tried to make a list of achievements in my head, forgetting nothing.

I had achieved, as the result of an accident, a silver plug embedded by surgeons in my skull. I have been credited in some circles with having lizard blood, because of the speed with which I recovered from assorted hurts and broken bones suffered in the pursuit of pleasure.

I had a nodding acquaintance with internal-combustion engines, whether in sports cars, aircraft, motorcycles, or powerboats.

Creating an acting role was something I could do without too much trouble: acting, in fact, was probably a little too easy for the good of my soul.

I'd made friendships with a gratifying number of people and had managed to keep the friendship of my first wife, Evie, and my good friend she married, Van Johnson.

I had achieved two sons by Evie and two daughters by my wife, Sharley, to whom I am most satisfactorily married.

And that just about covered it. At forty-two, it seemed I hadn't discovered yet where I was going. The reasons weren't difficult to find. You could trace them back to an upbringing best described as irregular.

God knows I've no patience with self-pity. But it was very clear to me that I had grown up both early and late. I realized I grew up late in wanting to prove courage and rebellion in racing boats and motor continued on page 131

A CONDENSATION FROM THE BOOK TO BE PUBLISHED LATER THIS YEAR BY DOUBLEDAY & COMPANY

McCall's

August 1959

art director Otto Storch

Storch regularly built layouts around a single bleed picture which doubled as illustration and background texture. This photograph is the perfect amplification for the headline and shows careful forethought in the provision of clear space for the text. The photographer was Culver Service.

Redbook

date unknown

art director William Cadge

Cadge worked closely with Storch and employed similar methods. Here, out of a single word of type, he creates a memorable and telling image, with recourse to neither photography nor illustration.

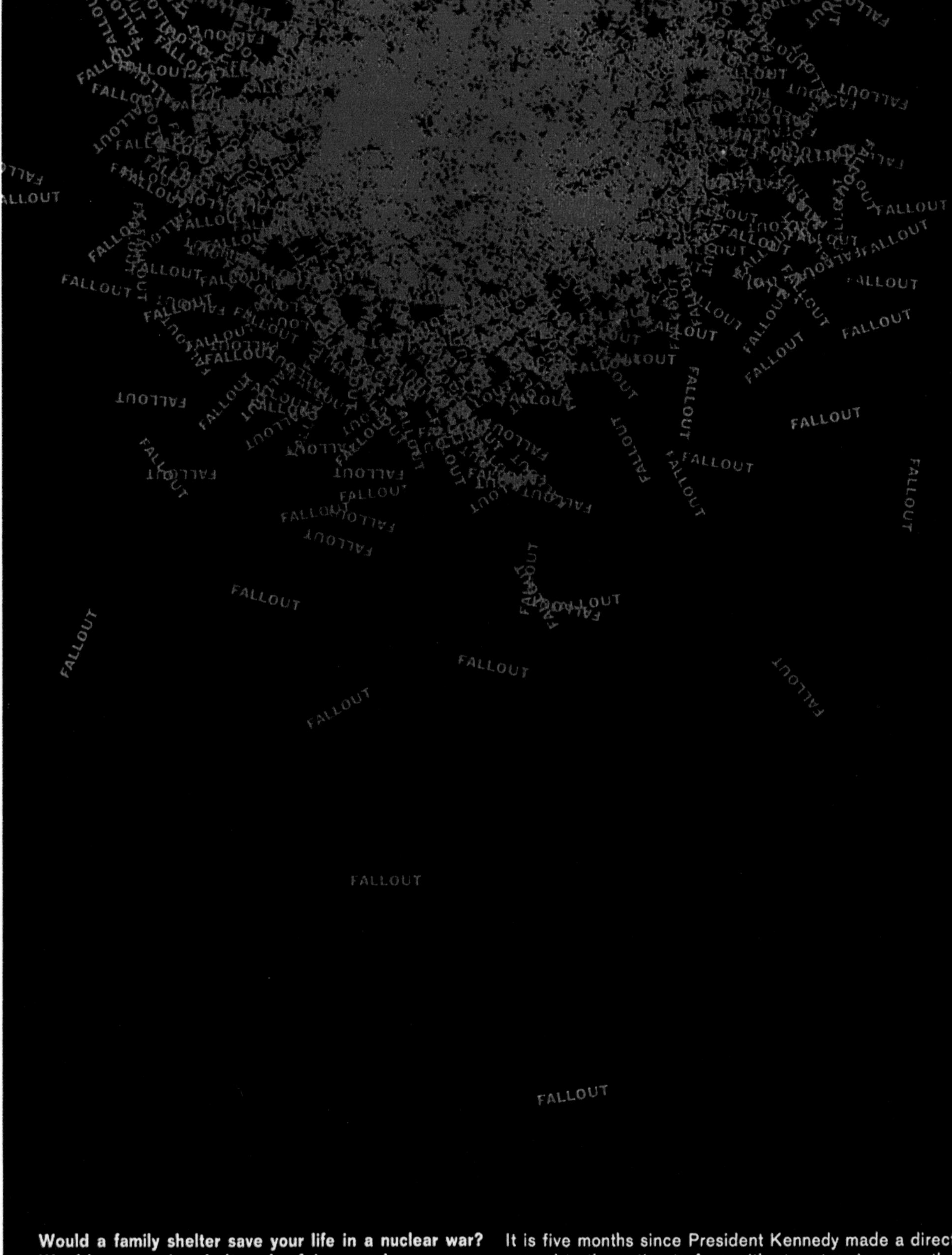

Would a family shelter save your life in a nuclear war? Would community shelters be fairer—and save more people? Or are shelters themselves a threat to peace? This report provides no final answers but it does present vital facts that have generally been ignored. And it brings into sharp focus the questions that every American must keep asking in the coming months / by Walter Goodman

It is five months since President Kennedy made a direct appeal to the nation to face with utmost seriousness the Berlin crisis and to be prepared for the possibility of nuclear war. In the course of his speech last July 25th he promised "to let every citizen know what steps he can take to protect his family in case of attack."

In the weeks following the President's speech most Amer-

FALLOUT

FALLOUT

FALLOUT

FALLOUT

FALLOUT

THE TRUTH ABOUT FALLOUT SHELTERS

icans found themselves wondering how, if at all, they could prepare for the holocaust of 20th-century war. The best kind of preparation seemed to be the construction of shelters against radioactive fallout. But what, exactly, was a shelter? How practical was it? How expensive? Should the homeowner build one himself? Or would the government launch a program of community shelters?

The confusion was not lessened by the fact that much of the information the Federal Government issued was piecemeal, inadequate and contradictory. Statements from public and private institutions, television and radio reports and continually changing advice from all sections of the country's press did little to clarify the situation.

And finally the confusion was compounded by commercial

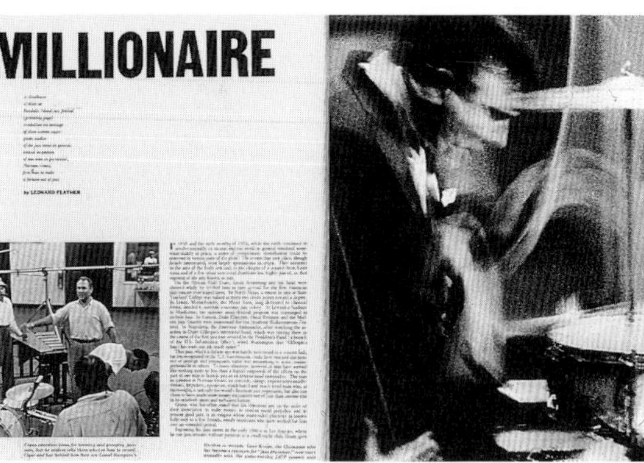

Esquire
January 1957
art director Henry Wolf

A novel opening to a 16-page study of jazz artists. Wolf wraps the headline around the turn page to build up to the dramatic first spread, imparting modular clarity by matching the column height to the picture depth.

presented and the thinking behind it...The second decisive moment is concerned with my instructions to the photographer, illustrator and layout men...planning is vital. They want, just as I want, to have a clear visualization of what they are going to accomplish *before* they start."[14]

The typical *modus operandi* was to superimpose copy on a carefully composed full-bleed photograph, which provided both a narrative image and background texture; a Storch speciality was to blow up small objects or details into a double-page spread – and this was an over-size magazine. Often the type was included within the photograph itself, that is, rubdown or hand-lettered type was placed on the object in the most literal union of word and image. "We are a picture-minded country", said Storch,[15] and his pictures were instantly comprehensible cartoons which telegraphed either an impression, or a blunt and unambiguous disclosure, of the editorial message. The contrast of subtlety and brute force was most emphatic in Storch's picture essays, usually shot by *McCall's* staff photographer Onofrio Paccione, in which a short piece of prose introduced pages of emotive pictures captioned by lines of poetry. This was very much "conceptual" editorial, unselfconcious art without rational content.

Type also became illustration, as concrete poetry. Storch would knock it out of place, squash it or squeeze it, or kick it around to make a point. And this was a feature of Storch's work which his assistant William Cadge was to develop to remarkable effect when given his own magazine, the *McCall's* stablemate *Redbook*. Cadge commanded the art direction of *Redbook* throughout the 1960s – this was a time when long tenures were the rule rather than the exception – and although his name tends to be overshadowed by Storch, he showed an equal grasp of typography and its application as plain text or within pictorial layouts. Most notable were Cadge's powerful montaged fashion spreads, and his novel presentation of food – potentially the dullest and most demanding task asked of an editorial designer – which he enlivened with still-life compositions shot from over-head to emphasize unusual forms.

A third key participant in this "editorial design revolution"[16] of the late 1950s and early 1960s was that idiosyncratic trickster, Henry Wolf, art director of *Esquire* from 1952-58,[17] art director of *Harper's Bazaar* from 1958-61, and of *Show* magazine from 1961-64. Wolf is not an easy man to assess, because he spread both his imagination and his artis-

Harper's Bazaar
February 1959
art director Henry Wolf

The composition incorporates elegant contrasts of hard blacks and soft colour, straight lines and curves. The image is explained by the copy, which is trite fashion-speak saved by Wolf's setting it as a poem. The photograph is by Ynoncancio.

Show
February 1963
art director Henry Wolf

Wolf's sensitivity to the graphic unity of text and image is evident in the lowering of headline to the level of the hand in Irving Penn's portrait. The eye is directed from image to title and the image's verticality is reflected in the layout.

Show

April 1963

art director Henry Wolf

Below: Wolf's covers for Show were masterpieces of pop art. This cover, "Too many Kennedys?", employed two of his favourite techniques – the manipulation of symbol and repetition.

Esquire

July 1958

art director Henry Wolf

Right: the Americanization of Paris – a lesser mind would have stuck the Stars and Stripes atop the Eiffel Tower. Wolf's solution is witty and more direct. The photographer was Ben Somoroff.

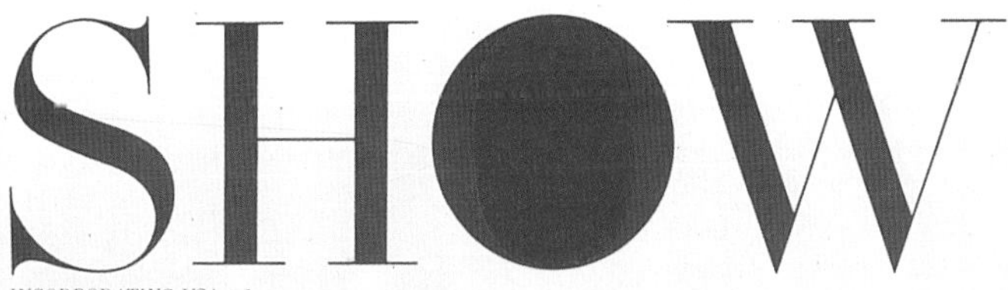

SHOW
INCORPORATING USA • 1
THE MAGAZINE OF THE ARTS
75 CENTS
APRIL 1963
TOO MANY KENNEDYS? by ALISTAIR COOKE

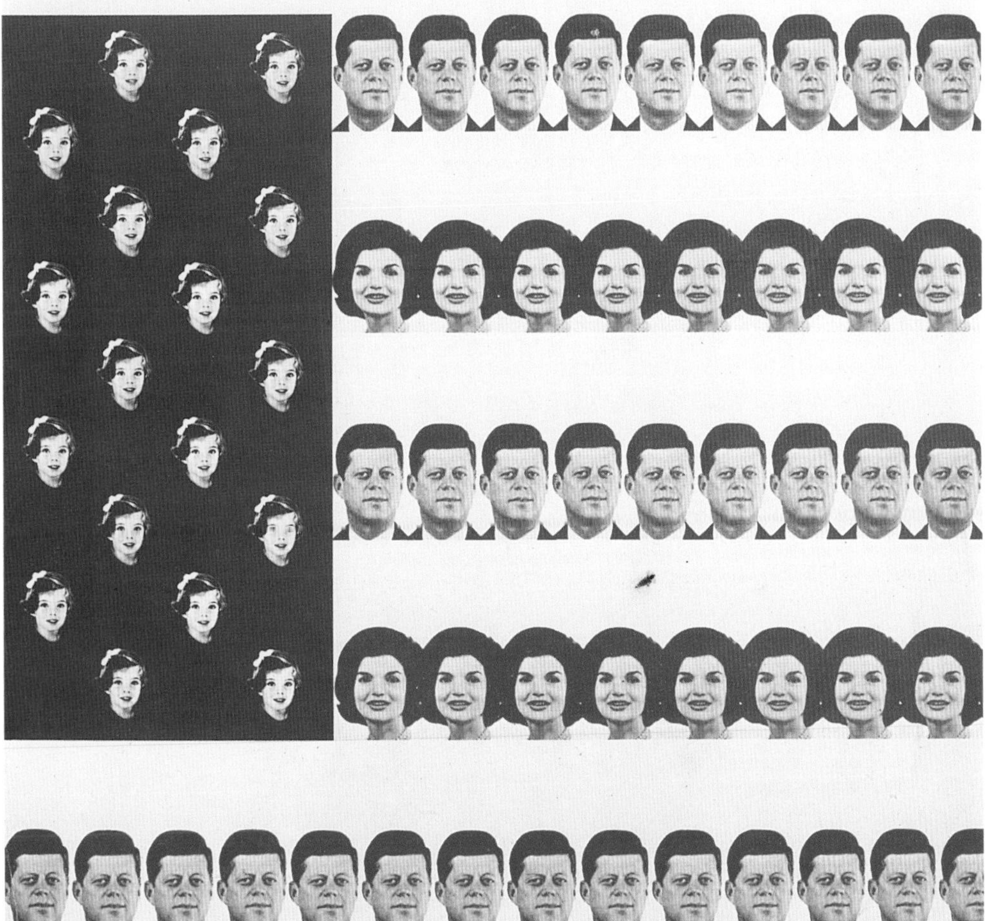

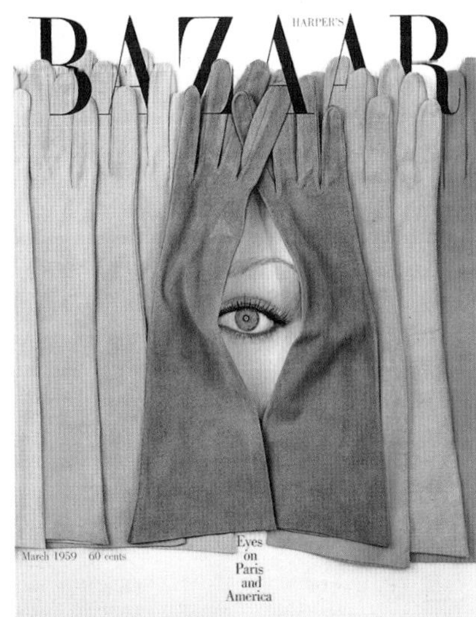

Harper's Bazaar

March 1959

photographer Ben Rose

art director Henry Wolf

A riveting and almost disturbing image. The dominant eye peering from Ben Rose's photograph scrutinizes the reader. Masking out elements of the logotype creates the effect of interlocking with the fingers, unifying the image within three dimensions.

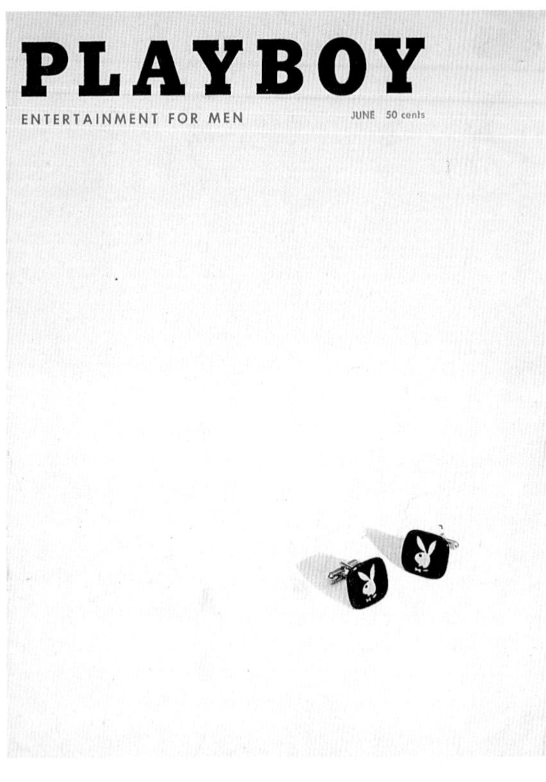

Playboy
June 1957
art director Art Paul

Playboy was as well known for its enigmatic and punning covers as for its centrefolds. Art Paul utilized collage, montage, illustration, newsprint and, occasionally, photographs of partially clad women, turning cover design into a monthly game of spot the Playboy rabbit. This issue is his most extreme example of understatement. The cufflinks are given not one word of explanation, not a single coverline – a daring and yet successful policy from a magazine relying heavily on newsstand sales.

tic interests so widely. He epitomizes the easy, if discriminating, receptivity of designers of the time, ready to use any idea or graphic tool "that suited the job in hand". There is no better analysis of Wolf's method than that which can be extracted from the contents list of his own book, *Visual Thinking.*[18] The chapter headings include: Unexpected combinations; Strange perspective; Repetition; Motion; Manipulated symbols; Scale; Type as design; Color; Collage; Improbable settings; Roundabout ways of telling a story. This was a well stocked toolbox. The last in the list is perhaps the most telling. Wolf, who began – and will end – his career in advertising, used the descriptive imagery of selling to sell magazines; the cock-eyed, left-brain hieroglyphics and enigmatic jokes which he first introduced for the covers of *Esquire*, the most notorious of which is perhaps "The Americanization of Paris", which featured an "Instant Vin Rouge" sachet dropping into a wine glass. This cover, although it was one of the last in a long line for *Esquire*, shows an ill-thought colour sense. In this period Wolf's execution was quite often not up to the initial idea; the magazine had an incoherent and interrupted flow which was a symptom of Wolf's overriding interest in the initial spread that was not maintained throughout a piece: pages of unbroken columns of unleaded text would follow the first graphic flood. "That", according to Wolf, "was always a trade-off, otherwise I'd never get a spread. Editorial meetings were like an auction house and there was great competition for space."[19]

A further contribution to the variety, and the discontinuity, of the magazine was the range of papers used – coated, uncoated, cartridge sections, even a kind of wrapping paper on at least one occasion. This was partly the designer's preference, partly necessity, for *Esquire* was printed by all three print methods: gravure, letterpress and offset. There was also an incongruous mix of illustration: contemporary monochrome lino-cuts appeared back-to-back with old-fashioned colour renderings. Headline type was a hotch-potch of numerous gothic serifs, old style italics and romans;[20] again, partly a reflection of Wolf's immaturity, mainly a function of the slight eccentricities and literary quality of *Esquire*'s editorial.

But at *Harper's Bazaar* Wolf was able to prove unequivocally his status as the premier art director of his time. He was lucky to be handed the world's best fashion and portrait photographers on a plate – Avedon, Hiro, Bassman, Horst, Derujinsky, Leiter, and Ben Rose whom Wolf took with him from *Esquire* – but that cannot account for the quite outstanding quality and visual inventiveness of the photography under Wolf's stewardship. He out-Brodovitched Brodovitch.

Covers were adventures in surrealism and charming typographic chicanery. In the editorial well, the subtle monochrome photography was displayed with a marvellous tranquillity and lightness of touch. Wolf had learned the skill of rhythmic pagination from Brodovitch, switching in and out of soft greyscales and harsh blacks, from blown-up detail to small head-to-toe shots. His typographic format was simplified to give minimum variation, and a speciality was made of the small, quiet headline, highlighted only by the white space surrounding it. The one item missing was Brodovitch's graceful ragged captions; Wolf used perfect rectangles, justified columns of type always carefully cast off to ensure a full last line.

Show was a more personal project where Wolf could indulge his love of the arts and, as its first art director, develop a more personal typography. He continued his radical experiments in "left brain" cover design to emerge as an accomplished conceptual artist in his own right. The *Show* covers combine a Magritte-like surrealism with the repetitive and consumerist iconography of pop art.

This new "magazine for the arts" covered a wide range of subject matter but nevertheless had a fairly homogenous typographic format, based on a Didot variant remarkably similar to that which Wolf had left behind at *Harper's Bazaar*. A restrained selection of alternative faces provided limited thematic variation; most commonly used was a heavy condensed grot to which the Viennese Wolf, like his European contemporaries, had graduated. Wolf made a change from the *Esquire* days by imposing on himself the restriction of a grid, in two, three and four columns for different editorial sections. An innovation (in America) was the use of vertical and horizontal 8pt rules to highlight headlines and running heads. The new typography was making a brief comeback.

In the early 1960s European design ideas were again exerting some influence across the Atlantic. In other graphic disciplines, particularly corporate design, the international style was becoming dominant. In editorial design, Willy Fleckhaus's *Twen*, in particular, had been received with great interest. Herb Lubalin's daring redesign of the *Saturday Evening Post* in 1961, which reintroduced bold grotesques and banner headlines, had made a considerable impact in American design circles. Also in 1961 *Life* gained a new art director in Bernard Quint, who tidied up the magazine's tendency towards fussy typography, replaced the dated Tudor Gothic heads with elegant neo-grot italics, and introduced bigger and more tightly arranged pictures on a modular format. At *Look*, the picture weekly which had always played second fiddle to *Life*, Allen Hurlbert was quietly evolving a clean modular format on a cast iron three-column grid, on which he made a play with architectural constructions of squared-off photography and with the typographic contrast between heavy condensed serif headings and ultra-light standfirsts. This was a typographic style which required sensitive printing; its use was coincidental with the considerable improvements made in long-run print quality in the early 1960s. *Look* was printed by its own patented gravure method called Lookchromatic which, when used with blade-coated papers, enabled a lot of ink to be laid down in an even, deep etch of high fidelity. For the first time the designers could use large areas of black and tightly spaced heavy type – as had Fleckhaus on *Twen*.

The *Look* format did not reach full maturity until 1968. In the early 1960s Hurlbert tended to use single bleed photos across the page against plain blocks of three-column serif body text. Multiple picture placement was relatively untidy and symmetrical, with only occasional forays into the varied geometrical constructions and dramatic cropping that would become his hallmark.

In 1966 Hurlbert was joined by an assistant, Will Hopkins, a Cranbrook graduate and self-confessed "disciple of Müller-Brockman" who had worked with Fleckhaus for the previous two years. Hopkins introduced to *Look* the twelve-part grid with nine vertical divisions which Fleckhaus employed at *Twen*. Hopkins was primarily interested in how a column of type related to the 35mm format, which worked out at 2 x 5 units or 4 x 10 units of the grid, portrait or landscape. The mathematical grid allowed wide variation in column width and "...while relating each

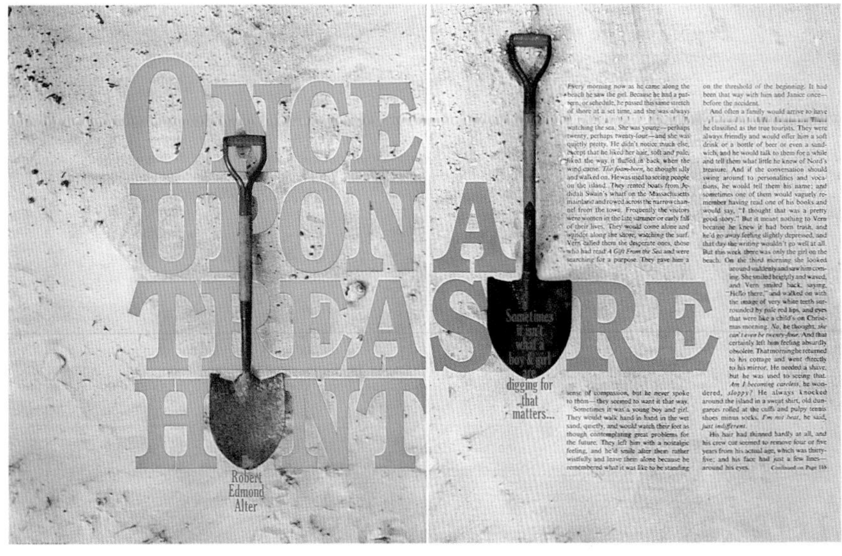

Saturday Evening Post
16 September 1961
designer Herb Lubalin
art editor Kenneth Stuart

Lubalin was commissioned by the Post as consultant designer "to keep in step with the times". He introduced meticulously spaced extra condensed grots and, as in this characteristic example of Lubalin trompe l'oeil, his pictorial three-dimensional typo/photographic constructions.

individual spread to the overall format...creates an almost endless group of design options".[21] It was effective for two-, three-, four- or six-column makeup and a vast array of picture sizes and placements.

Look represented a radical change in American design sensibility, a reassertion of the scientific method in a culture which had come to prefer individual expression. But Hurlbert was not formalist in his approach and had an unerring editorial touch. In 1968 he consciously moved the magazine into new territory, into the arts and popular culture; towards politics and with less emphasis on sport and leisure. It suited the time, and certain special issues stand out as first-rate examples of timely pictorial journalism: The Sound and Fury in the Arts; The Sixties issue; the Beatles photographs by Avedon; Hurlbert's New York special; Hopkins' The Blacks and the Whites issue, and a superb Herman Hesse feature with photographs by Will McBride.

If *Look* was the most extreme example of Apollonian modernism in American magazine design (barring Massimo Vignelli's work for *Industrial Design* and *Skyline*), David Moore's design for *Amerika* was its final and most complete manifestation.[22] *Amerika (America Illustrated)* was published by the US Information Agency in various languages for distribution to the eastern bloc. It was the summit of two decades of discovery in editorial design: in typography, in illustration, in modular design, in graphic expression. Within a typographic format originated by Herb Lubalin, Moore combined the layered art direction pioneered by Storch with the narrative vision of a Henry Wolf, and a sensitivity to picture cropping and placement equal to Hurlbert. This was a triumphant final fling. *Amerika* was the last of the great generalist, large-format magazines.

America Illustrated
July 1969 (Polish edition)
art director David Moore

Cover, by George Giusti, and two spreads from an issue on the American cinema. The headline face, which varied each month but was always set tight, after Lubalin, is in this case an Egyptian. The bold over-size dates in the spread (above right) provide body, tone and unity. The combination of justified and ragged text and varied column widths is unusually successful: it divides the page into three. A set of stills (right) is arranged on a four-column, 35mm-proportion grid, creating a three-dimensional effect by mixing red tints with half-tones.

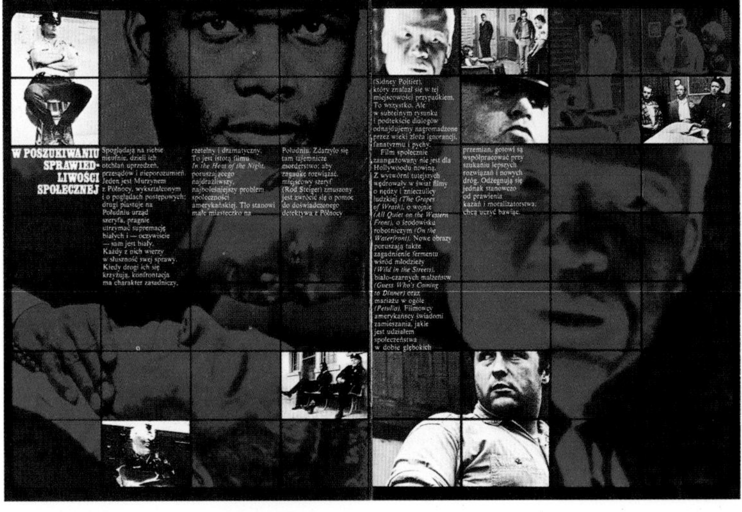

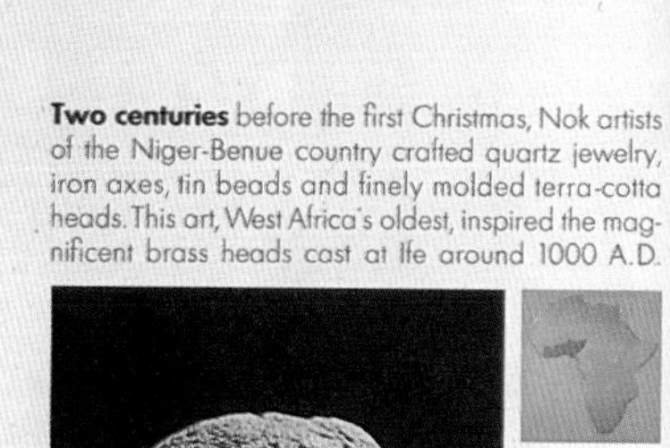

Look

7 January 1969

art director Will Hopkins

Top: Hopkins' imposing use of photography elicits a strong response. Here he has used a macro lens shot with narrow depth of field at full page size, cropping in to the reflective axis of the head. Equilibrium is created by placing the eye of the bust, to which the reader is drawn, to the left of the spine. The layout revolves around a pivot provided by the map. The photographer was Joel Baldwin.

Look

28 June 1966

art director Allen Hurlburt

Above: during his long tenure as art director of Look, from 1952 to 1968, Allen Hurlburt developed a highly educated and rationalist system of layout based on modularity and asymmetric order. This subtle example of the interplay of words and pictures is from a Look special issue on California. Hurlburt's page design was clean and, in this case, serene. However, it is not immediately obvious why these simple layouts are so successful. The impressionistic photography, by Paul Fusco and Art Kane, is of course the most important contribution. But the immaculate presentation within wide margins, the small, cleverly inset headlines and, above all, the reflection of the levels of the coffee pot in two bastard widths of type, are the essential details that resolve these two spreads so beautifully.

The new rationalists: a European revival

Domus
May 1963
editor Giò Ponti

Domus, founded in 1928 by the architect Giò Ponti, has throughout its history been a sanctuary for fine architectural photography and modern design. This remarkable cover is a photographic study of form in furniture by Charles Eames.

The rapid evolution of American editorial design in the two decades from 1939 went unseen and unmatched by Europeans. In Europe, recovery from six years of war had been painstakingly slow; the publishing business lacked human, economic and technical resources, and, more importantly, the markets and advertisers that would pay for them. Magazine publishing was dominated by pulp weeklies churning out escapist fiction. All editorial design was constrained by the need to conserve paper and so artistry was measured by the ability to pack the page; the generosity, the colour and space of American design were neither appropriate nor attainable. It was not until the post-war boom took a full hold in the late 1950s that working European designers, inspired by such magazines as *Fortune, Harper's Bazaar, Esquire* and *McCall's,* awoke to the new American expressionism.

But first, Europe had to rediscover its heritage. Although the 1950s was a period of entrenchment and conservatism in commercial publishing, it coincided with an intense debate in the educational institutes of Basel, Zurich and Ulm, which was resolved at the end of the decade in a reassertion of frugal, ascetic modernism. The dominant influence was initially Swiss typographic orthodoxy. Switzerland had survived as a reservoir of rational design exerting great influence in the immediate post-war period, on the Italians through Max Huber, and on the Germans, Dutch and, more belatedly, the English, through the work and writings of Hans Finsler, Armin Hofman, Josef Müller-Brockmann, and Karl Gerstner.[1]

As in the 1920s, this modern revival entered editorial design via architectural, cultural and design publications: in Italy, *Domus* and *Urbanistica*; in England, *Art and Industry, Architectural Review, Architectural Design* and *Design*; in Switzerland, *Werk, Du, Neue Grafik* and *Typographische Monatsblatter.* Company and trade magazines also gave designers the licence to experiment free from commercial constraints, and early examples of systematized design theory can be seen in the Swiss pharmaceutical magazines; in England, in F. H. K. Henrion's work for the Weidenfeld & Nicolson magazine *Contact* and Derek Cousin's *Fusion*; in Holland, in Otto Truemann's designs for *Rayon Revue* and Ton Raateland's layouts for the Philips promotional magazine *Range*. It was, however, in newsstand publishing that the great flowering of European talent emerged in 1959, successfully combining elements of Swiss typographic theory with the visual wit and intuitive, empirical approach of the Americans. Although heavily influenced by Swiss rationalism, its "universal" typography and systematized grids, this generation of magazine designers could not afford to be inhibited by immutable rules which outweighed emotional and subjective responses; it was to the Americans, pre-eminent in magazine design, that art directors looked for their inspiration. Three European magazines are outstanding in this respect both as prototypes for a decade of magazine design, and as natural hybrids of the Swiss and American tendencies: they were *Elle, Twen,* and *Town* designed by, respectively, Peter Knapp, Willy Fleckhaus and Tom Wolsey – a Swiss (a disorderly Swiss), a German, and an Englishman of German extraction.

That the last of these magazines should be English, and was the most uncompromisingly modern and bellicose in its approach to type and space, deserves some explanation. The country had a poverty of tradi-

Du
November 1959
designer Roland Schenk

Cover of the Swiss arts journal Du, designed by Roland Schenk who later worked with Willy Fleckhaus at the German publishing house Marthens, at Quick, and at Neue Review.

Schenk moved on to England, working as art director of Town and then Management Today (see page 152). His characteristic tectonic typography and bold constructivist layout are already apparent in the cover of this special issue on the photography of August Sander.

tion in pictorial magazine design and an apparently unshakable attachment to classical form, yet in the decade following *About Town*'s relaunch in 1959[2] London generated an unsurpassed range of original and inventive periodicals, which benefited from a rare receptivity to external influences and a recognition that magazine design was a journalistic exercise: neither advertising nor the peddling of dry information.

In England, what little had been assimilated of modern design in the inter-war period was distorted, sweetened, to suit the country's provincial petit-bourgeois taste. The English had a strong tradition of craft printing and of poster illustration, which tended to stifle and overwhelm the nascent practice of "industrial" or "commercial" art. Resources were concentrated in the powerful national newspaper industry, where a secure relationship was enjoyed between journalism and design, and typography had been revolutionized by men of the stature of Morison and Hutt. This success was, however, often at the expense of magazine publishing, which had failed to recover from an embargo on staff, paper and print enforced during the war years. The long-lasting impact of the war and subsequent austerity programmes are thrown into focus by the simple fact that *Radio Times*, the biggest-selling magazine in the country, did not resume colour printing of covers until 1964. After the closure of *Picture Post* English magazine publishers could boast only a ragbag of titilating weeklies, purveyors of handy hints for hobbyists, "county" magazines for the upper classes, and anaemic and elitist fashion books. There were two mass circulation women's weeklies of some merit, *Woman* and *Woman's Own*, printed in colour gravure; English *Vogue* and

Typographische Monatsblatter

January 1961

editor Rudolf Hostettler

According to Swiss orthodoxy, type had a functional role. There was to be no ornament or arbitrary composition. Lettering was unpretentious, i.e. sans serif. Uniformity was sought through the application of grid systems which brought the elements of the page together in a formal relationship. Here, the basic elements of the grid are two wide measures for text, one narrow measure for captions and illustration, reflected across the spine, with a further horizontal division fixing depth of body text. These divisions are a geometric function of the page, and create a harmonious proportion.

378

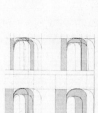

monde
monde

Neue Grafik
New Graphic Design
Graphisme actuel

2

New Graphic Design

July 1959

designed by Richard Lohse, J. Muller-Brockman, Hans Neuburg, Carlo Vivarelli

A classic example of Swiss exactitude.

werk

Januar 1961	48. Jahrgang Heft 1	England
		Inhalt
Seiten 1–4	Verfasser: Pierre Bussat, Architekt BSA/SIA, Genf	Die Industrialisierung des Bauens in England
Seiten 5–8	Verfasser: Michael John Keyte, Architekt	Stand und Ziele des «CLASP»
Seite 9		Bauforschung in England
Seiten 10–12	Verfasser: Bruce Martin, Architekt, Little Hadham, Hertfordshire	Das Wesen der Normung und die britischen Normen
Seite 13	Verfasser: Mark Hartland Thomas, Architekt, London	Modular-Koordination
Seiten 14–16	Architekten: Bruce Martin und Derek John Weate, London	Laborgebäude für die British Standards Institution in Hemel Hempstead
Seiten 17–24	Verfasser: Anthony Penfold und Anthony Travis, Architekten, London	Stadt- und Landplanung im Nachkriegs-England
Seiten 25–29	Verfasser: Dr. Josef Paul Hodin, Bibliothekar des Institute of Contemporary Arts, London	Englische Skulptur seit Moore
Seiten 30–32	Verfasser: Robert Melville, Kunstschriftsteller, London	Der Maler Francis Bacon
Seiten 33–36	Verfasser: Kenneth Garland, Graphiker, London	Die britische Werbegraphik
		WERK-Chronik
Seite 1*		Bauchronik
Seite 3*		Hinweise
Seite 3*		Der kleine Kommentar
Seite 4*		Der Ausschnitt
Seite 5*		Wettbewerbe
Seite 11*		Verbände
Seite 15*		Hochschulen
Seite 16*		Kunstpreise und Stipendien
Seite 16*		Ausstellungen
Seite 24*		Bücher
Seite 26*		Formgebung in der Industrie
	Redaktion Architektur	**Benedikt Huber, Arch. BSA/SIA, Minervastraße 33, Zürich**
	Redaktion Bildende Kunst und Redaktionssekretariat	**Dr. Heinz Keller, Meisenstraße 1, Winterthur Telephon (052) 2 22 56**
	Mitarbeiter in der Schweiz	Frédéric Brugger, Arch. BSA, Lausanne; Dr. Lucius Burckhardt, Basel; Pierre Bussat, Arch. BSA, Genf; Dr. Hans Curjel, Zürich; Niklaus Morgenthaler, Architekt, Bern; Dr. Maria Netter, Basel; Prof. Alfred Roth, Arch. BSA, Zürich; Dr. Willy Rotzler, Zürich; Hans Schenker, Arch. SIA, Buchs bei Aarau; Dolf Schnebli, Arch. SIA, Agno, Tessin
	Mitarbeiter im Ausland	Hendrik Hartsuyker, Architekt, Amsterdam; Dr. Franz Roh, München; François Stahly, Paris
	Herausgeber	BSA Bund Schweizer Architekten
	Verbände	Offizielles Organ des Bundes Schweizer Architekten Offizielles Organ des Schweizerischen Werkbundes Offizielles Organ des Schweizerischen Kunstvereins
	Druck, Verlag, Administration, Inseratenverwaltung	**Buchdruckerei Winterthur AG, Winterthur, Schweiz, Technikumstr. 83, Tel. (052) 2 22 52, Postcheck VIII b 58**

Werk

January 1961

designer Heinz Keller

Contents page of Werk, the Swiss art and architecture magazine, laid out to a grid devised by Karl Gerstner.

The Architectural Review
September/October 1969
designer Bill Slack

The Architectural Review, designed by Bill Slack from 1960-90, was one of the major intellectual outlets for modern design in Britain. The magazine included Nikolaus Pevsner on its editorial board and Reyner Banham and Ian Nairn on its staff. Its idiosyncratic editorial policy, which emphasised themes and concepts rather than individual works, was reflected in Slack's varied design solutions. AR changed its logotype from one issue to the next, and often sported no name at all. This cover illustrates the second "Manplan" issue, a survey of the built and technological environment.

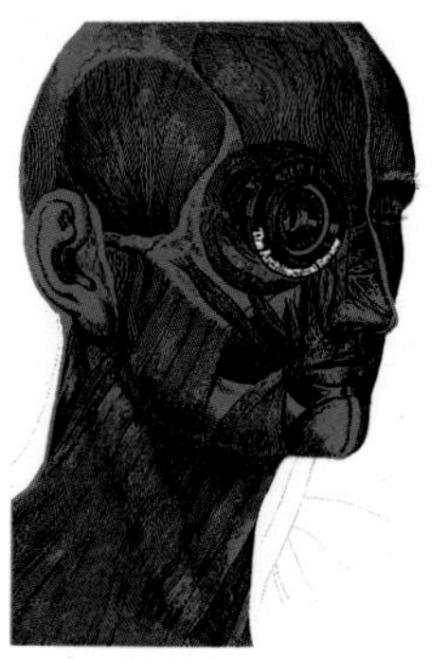

Harper's Bazaar, of course, both a fraction of the size of the American editions; and the excellent journals *New Statesman, The Spectator* and *The Economist* – which followed literary values and were, accordingly, set in bookish type. This was not an environment in which compelling or original magazine design could flourish.

The general tenor of English magazine design in the mid-century is sounded in Allen Hutt's definitive study of newspaper typography, *Newspaper Design*.[3] In a short commentary on magazine design – "the synthesis of artistic and typographic mastery" – Hutt expresses an attitude indicative of the period: for its recourse to American sources; for its strong emphasis on journals and news tabloid format magazines; and above all for its limiting view of the function of magazine display typography as a provider of decorative "thematic variation". For this purpose Hutt offers an embarrassing admixture of over-elaborate "fancy" scripts and display faces of Victorian and Edwardian provenance. The development of a unified typographic format is unconsidered.

Hutt's choice of type reflected the economic and technological resources of English magazine publishing, as well as an obsolete typographic sensibility (which is not apparent in his newspaper work). High speed web-offset had only recently been introduced to the country. Most of the four thousand commercial periodicals published in 1960 were printed letterpress – which, because of the expense and difficulty of block-making, inhibited the combination of type and pictures – or in photogravure. The soft contrast of the latter eroded the definition of bold sans serifs. Modern grotesques and the "rational" types favoured on the Continent and in America were in any case not readily available in England. At almost precisely the time that Hutt was writing, Tom Wolsey was making his way to Switzerland to purchase the Haas Grotesque, unobtainable in London, which he would use as headline face for *About Town*.

The immaturity of graphic design and the relatively subservient position of the art director were symptomatic of the divorce of English art from the European mainstream, and of the primacy of literary journalism in publishing. Both factors stemmed from the dominance in English culture of the middle and upper middle class: its classical – as opposed to humanist – education system; its distrust of the polemical ambitions of modern design; its affection for the exclusivity and uniqueness of fine art and equivalent

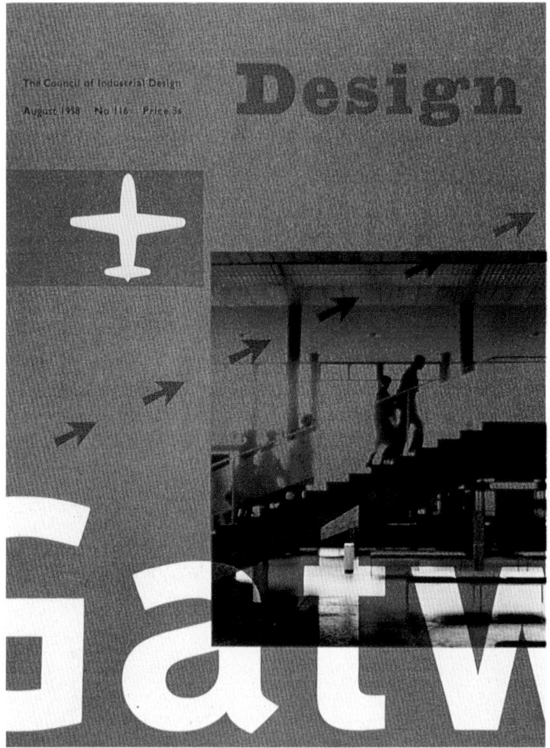

Design
August 1958, February 1962
art director Ken Garland

Ken Garland's manifesto, "Structure and substance", was a plea for a common visual language which combined "the exuberance of the Americans with the orderliness of the Swiss." His art direction of Design put these principles into practice, through the combination of ordered grids and unorthodox typography, overlaid by vibrant colour tints.

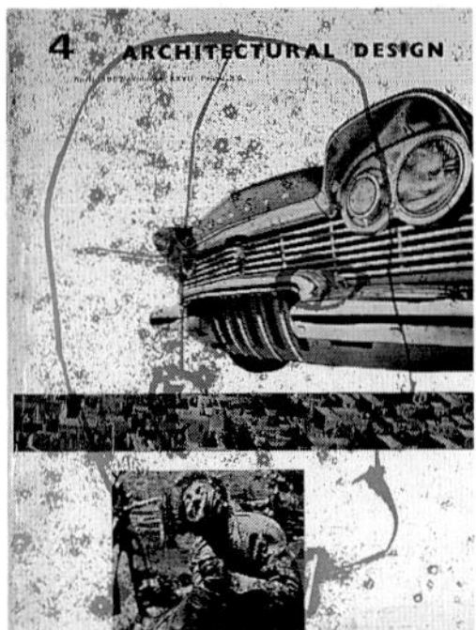

Architectural Design
April 1957
designer Theo Crosby

Architectural Design was in the vanguard of the post-war modern movement in British magazine design. Crosby's covers featured abstracted geometric compositions built from overprinted process colours or, as in this example, a montage of found images.

hostility to popular, mass-produced media; these sentiments, together with the absence of a left-wing socialist party and the anti-intellectual prejudice of the social democratic Labour movement, could not be reconciled to a modernist philosophy of unified art and design. In English society the arts were clearly defined and knew their place. Literature, painting and sculpture were "high" artistic pursuits: photography and design were the province of the artisan. England was not so much cursed with a "literary" rather than a "visual" sensibility; rather, the two were to be kept separate. It was an attitude which Paul Nash described as English art's "one crippling weakness – the lack of structural purpose", a sense of "immunity from the responsibility of design".[4] The English, quite unwilling to accept the German response to their own Arts and Crafts Movement – "the cold, bony finger of the Bauhaus" – took refuge behind their smug neo-georgian façades.[5]

The combining or synthesizing discipline of graphic design was, accordingly, technically underdeveloped and disorganized. However, a minority of intelligent designers were responding to austerity by making necessity the mother of invention. In the 1940s at *Art and Industry,* Robert Harling had overcome wartime restrictions by using clever type combinations, stock picture blocks and solid blocks and tints of colour to produce graphically rich layouts – a technique remarkably similar to that being used at the same time on the opposite side of the Atlantic by Bradbury Thompson on *Westvaco Inspirations.* Trichromatics and the Solotone and Colotone processes imported from the United States were to become a popular means, in advertising and editorial art, of compensating for the lack of four-colour print and their use clearly dates work of the period. F. H. K. Henrion was another firm advocate of maximizing limited resources: he "was very keen on design for production – using colour overlays, very cheaply".[6] Denied the luxury of four-colour printing, he created a rather folksy kaleidoscope of two-dimensional block and tint overlays for both the *Contact* magazines and for *The Compleat Imbiber,* a magazine promoting the inebriate benefits of Gilbey's gin.

The *Imbiber* was produced between 1956 and 1957 with the assistance of Henrion's students at the Royal College of Art. It was from this school, and the Central School of Arts, that the core of the new avant-garde were to emerge.[7] This informal movement, which cut its teeth on periodical design, paralleled and was associated with The Independent Group, a contemporaneous clique of architects, artists and critics, with which the new generation of graphic designers shared a fierce idealism, a belief in design for communication – not decoration – and a contempt for English parochialism. They included Theo Crosby, technical editor and designer of *Architectural Design*; Kenneth Garland, art director of *Design* from 1955 to 1964 and the chief polemicist of his generation; Brian Grimbly, who took over from Garland at *Design*; Max Maxwell and Derek Birdsall, who in the early and mid-1960s worked on numerous fashion and generalist magazines. From a more commercial background in advertising and editorial design came Tom Wolsey and Mark Boxer. Their work was typified by the use of modern sans and slab serif typography,

Go!
January 1961
art director Mark Boxer
art editor Angus Hamilton

Go! was a briefly successful upmarket holiday magazine from Stevens Press. It made up for a tight budget by using stock shots and treating type as illustration. The result was extremely effective.

About Town
September 1961
art director Tom Wolsey

The face of anger: through the simple expedients of a coarse grain screen, an impetuous splash of pink and an angry orange background, Tom Wolsey turns this dramatic portrait of Chita Rivera by Terence Donovan into the most memorable of covers. The logotype was not shortened to Town until 1962.

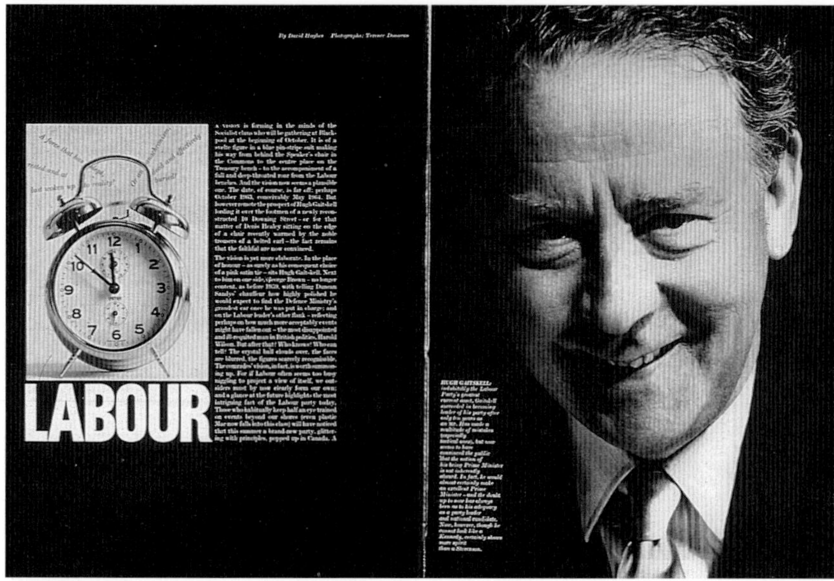

About Town
September 1961
art director Tom Wolsey

Top: more graphic anger – the semantic clash of type in harsh Haas Grotesque combines with the scratched pen style of illustrator Sydney King to create an unmistakeable atmosphere. At Town, King and Roger Law revived a fine English tradition of caustic and aggressive illustration.

Town
October 1961
art director Tom Wolsey

Above: a graphic representation of the question "Will Labour wake up?" in which the type over the clock becomes a noisy ideogram in a tight-fitting arrangement of head, body copy and photograph. The portrait of Hugh Gaitskell by Terence Donovan is atypically flattering.

experimentation with and adaptation of Swiss grid systems, open asymmetric layouts, generously sized photography, in the use of flat tints and duotones to provide colour and, above all, by an overriding emphasis on the leading editorial role of the art director and the necessity for a strict continuity of format. Garland wrote in 1960: "Consistency and continuity of style are more decisive in magazines than in any other form of graphic design, and there should be frequent reference to precedents as well as forward planning. There is some correspondence between the design of a periodical and that of a film, since turning over a sequence of pages is similar to scanning a sequence of film frames in the cinema." To this method he opposed that of the designer, who "contents himself with peripheral activities such as pretty vignettes and decorative headings. This view of the layout man as decorator is probably the reason why there are so few popular interest magazines of visual merit in this country".[8]

Garland and Crosby, in particular, were attracted to the Neue Grafik; to Swiss models of typographic exactitude such as the architectural magazine *Werk*, composed in point-perfect precision by Heinz Keller to a grid system devised by Karl Gerstner, to the technocratic efficiency of *Paris Match*, and to rarer American examples of formal, modular design: primarily, Allen Hurlbert's *Look*, and *Industrial Design*, styled in 1954 by Alvin Lustig.[9] This was a natural appropriation of a form suited to the geometry of architectural magazines, but one slightly at odds with the new abundance. Garland, acknowledging the limitations of Swiss dogmatism, issued a plea in his essay "Structure and Substance" for a common visual language which combined "the exuberance of the Americans with the orderliness of the Swiss".[10] This was to be the theme for the first half of the 1960s: the overthrow of the too-structured letterpress mentality and a celebration of wealth. No longer was the quality of design to be measured by the poverty of circumstances under which it was created.

Concluding his essay, Garland insisted that designers be "properly accepted as responsible executives in the operation of applying a form to the essential message to be transmitted. They must be given enough responsibility to allow them to conduct experiments in the same way that industrial research scientists can."

This was a unique proposition in English magazine publishing. That the art editor did indeed achieve

"... don't know if I'm really beautiful. I believe I'm strange looking. I've got a young girl's head, woman's body." Without having seen much of her but nude shoulders at the Royal Command, and two films not on general release here, **Claudia Cardinale** is beginning to impress us. Soon, after the appropriate period of denial and mortification, English audiences, reduced to an acme of discrimination, will have their chance to lose themselves in at least some of her personalities – virgin in *Senilita* (old age), vagrant in *The Girl with the Suitcase* (both coming this summer) and the social-climbing coquette Angelica in *The Leopard*, now filming.

Act innocent

She is 22, and has lived most of her life in Tunis, where she was born of Italian parents. The unreal world of acting did not interest her. At 17, while still at school, there came a declaration to the effect that she was 'The Most Beautiful Italian Girl in Tunis'. Venice, during the film festival, was the prize. While there, the flattery and envy changed into something positive; a producer offered a long-term contract. Claudia was surprised, refused it, and went home. Later, upon being approached by Unitalia Films, she agreed to go to Rome, pass a screen test, and attend the cinema school. A month later she was back home in Tunis.

One year passed. Then Vides Films attacked and won the day. Together with her family she moved to a villa outside Rome. Immediately the cameras moved in and her career (the word is justified) began.

Since then seventeen films have been made. A lot, yes; too many the cynics and pessimists will say, pointing out those which are unquestionably trash. They will be quite wrong. Because she is both young and untrained; a state of being which is immensely conducive to learning, and because, after seeing several of her films, I have no qualms in saying that already she has demonstrated one of two things. Either she *has* learned a great deal, or the nature of her acting ability is so much a part of her character that she cannot be taught, and can only develop from within. In either case, a very fortunate treat is in store for cinema battered movie-goers in this country. Two of her most interesting films to

Town
June 1962
art director Tom Wolsey

Top: a brooding opening to a feature on Claudia Cardinale – the deep black and powerful economy of the inset headline are typical Wolsey touches. The photograph is by Terence Donovan.

Town
December 1962
art director Tom Wolsey

Above: Wolsey used white space in the same way as he used black. The headline and body text are put to work with Mel Calman's illustration to make a cohesive and immediately comprehensible spread.

such stature was due largely to a firm kick in the industry's backside delivered by two new publishing houses: Cornmarket, run by Michael Heseltine and Clive Labovitch, and Stevens Press. Mark Boxer, art director of *Queen* and later *Go!*, testified that he had found, in Jocelyn Stevens, "an art director's essential requirement – a boss who was young, enthusiastic, and who had a real feeling for exciting layouts".[11] The regime at Cornmarket was equally beneficent. At *Man About Town*, a title purchased and resuscitated by Cornmarket in 1959, Tom Wolsey's inventive typography, bold layout, and sensitivity to subject matter was to mark a significant turning point in English magazine design.

Tom Wolsey was born in Aachen, Germany, in 1929, and was sent at an early age to school in England. Wolsey studied at Leeds College of Art and began his working life at Crawfords advertising agency, where he fell under the uninhibitive influence of creative director Ashley Havinden.[12] He joined Cornmarket in 1960 and proceeded to effect a rapid transformation of *Man About Town* – as it was then called, a quarterly "clothes dummy" for the tailoring trade – which became, under editors Clive Labovitch and Nicholas Tomalin, a general interest men's magazine with a strong line in sarcasm and an unerringly intelligent, if sardonic wit: a style reflected in a design in which Wolsey combined emotion and energy with strong visual coherence.

This direct style was at odds with the rectitude of Wolsey's compatriots yet, like *Town*, it came to typify the age. The art director was reacting against what he called the "fey, effete, good taste of English design".[13] "I wanted to produce something that was interesting to look at and would stop people in their tracks – would make them think twice about some aspect of society." In this he was supremely successful. Photography and illustration was actively agitational, rather than passively descriptive; layout had a tectonic strength rarely seen in English magazines; the covers exhibited alternate pictures of passionate anger, calm, joy, pathos, and occasional excursions into the surreal. The cover was surmounted by an elemental masthead which, bleeding off three edges of the page, utilised the simple geometric shapes of the four letters of the title in a manner that was then novel and is now a commonplace.[14]

Wolsey's ability to shift quickly up or down a gear is evident in the pace of *Town*, which was carefully paginated to provide contrasting pictorial and typo-

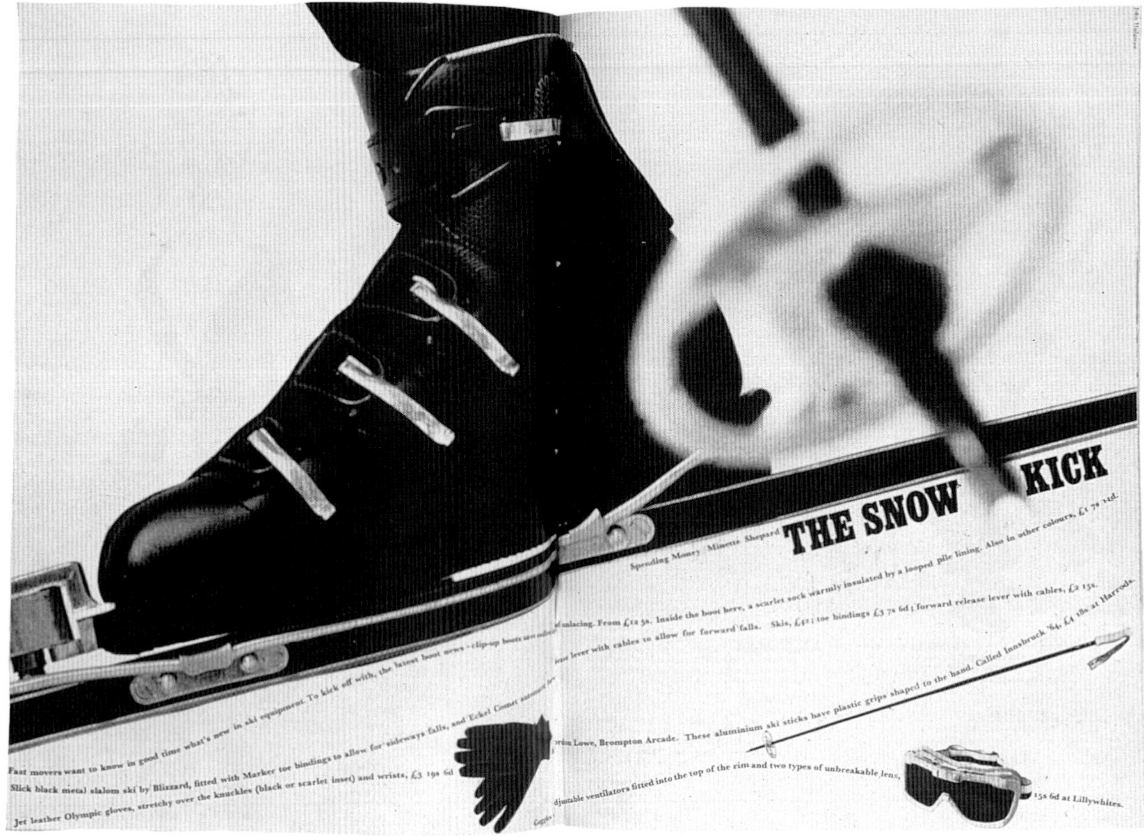

Queen
23 October 1963
art director Tom Wolsey

Wolsey was art director of Queen from July 1963 to July 1964. The technique and style remained much the same as Town, with contrasts of aggression and serenity mirrored in the versatile combination of bold heads and graceful body text and, in this example, by evocatively undulating lines of type supporting a life-size ski boot. The photographer was John Hedgecoe.

graphic layouts. His competence as a typographer and information designer can be seen in the clarity of contents page and tabular material, and in the communication of style and subject through the irreverent, semantic typography of heads and standfirsts. Headlines were Haas Grotesque, used with Modern, "a nice English face to contrast with it", and to these were added occasional old-fashioned display types to add variety and surprise. On the three magazines on which he worked full-time – *Town*, *Topic*, and *Queen* – this typographical scheme was hardly varied, its limitations overcome by the versatility with which it was employed. Where Wolsey played with type, it was always as a function of meaning. His visual tricks are reminiscent of Henry Wolf's work, not always with Wolf's unrivalled lateral wit, but executed with equal subtlety and perhaps greater consistency and technical strength.

Town was a tightly designed, unified product. Production quality was superb; this is evident in the high contrasts and dense blacks – a hallmark of the designer's style – obtained in print. *Town* was printed letterpress, yet the layout has a freedom one expects only of lithography – an achievement made all the more remarkable because Wolsey had no access to photocopying and had to rely on a "Lucy".[15] He also dispensed with the systematized order of a grid, yet his intuitive picture placement was unerringly well balanced, never over-complicated. The quality of photography, too, was of the highest. Wolsey, with a budget of only 15 guineas a page, commissioned the best of an upcoming and then unknown generation of photographers: Bill Klein, John Bulmer, Terence Donovan, Brian Duffy, John Donaldson and Don McCullin, and by allowing considerable freedom of interpretation he nurtured their individual styles. As the magazine gained readership and revenue, a few established talents, including Bill Brandt and Art Kane, were employed.

Wolsey also contributed to a more forceful magazine design by pioneering the new mode of illustration, characterized by the heavy dark wood- or lino-cut and violent scratched pen styles of Roger Law, Sidney King and John Sewell. Homely, narrative magazine illustration was, at least for the next decade, consigned to the patronizing ghetto of housewives' weeklies.

Elle was a women's weekly to which no such indictment applied. Founded in 1945, *Elle* was always resolutely modernist in outlook, intellectually and visually the most advanced women's magazine of its day, with none of the shy delicacy or moral passivity of its competitors. The magazine's style and philosophy were reflected in the appointment in 1959 of the Swiss artist, Peter Knapp, as art director. He took the magazine into the 1960s with a raw and punchy style that shattered conventional notions of the appropriate "look" of a women's magazine. *Elle* in 1960 had much in common with Wolsey's *Town*, despite the fact that the magazines shared neither nationality, readership, or frequency of publication. Knapp commissioned aggressive expressionist illustration, used bold, "masculine" type – Helvetica and heavy com-

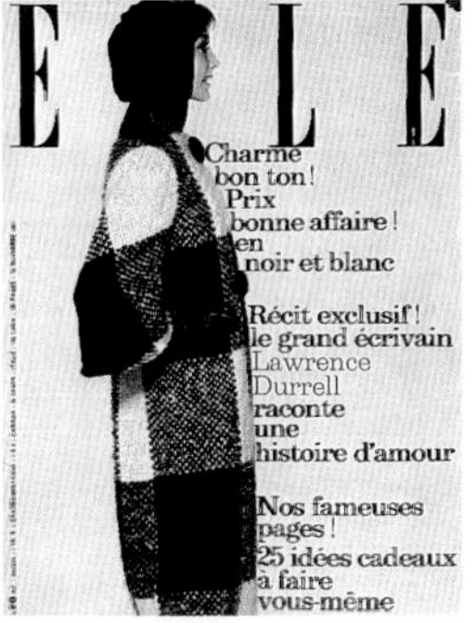

Elle
10 November 1961
art director Peter Knapp

The art director rarely passed up the opportunity to obliterate at least one of the letters of the distinctive Elle masthead. The scheme focuses on the heavily pregnant cover lines, one of which is subtly picked out in red.

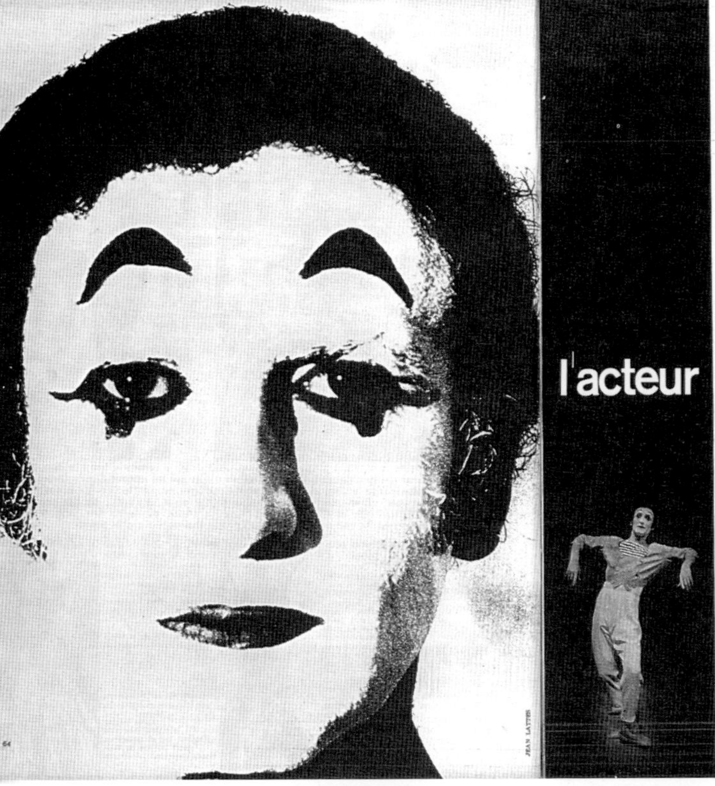

A Lille, à Reims, à Metz, Jean-Jacques Delacroix a suivi cet étrange muet qui depuis 15 ans fascine les foules du monde entier, mais que torture le drame des génies incompris : le mime Marceau.

l'acteur le plus seul

Un jeune homme de vingt ans, fou de théâtre, découvre dans l'horreur qu'il a une voix de gorge, qu'il ne « passe pas la rampe ». Mais il est fou d'orgueil aussi, il veut avoir raison tout de suite, il refuse de livrer le combat douteux de l'apprentissage et des cours de diction. Et il a en outre des motifs très personnels de se défier des mots. Cette voix sourde, enchaînée, indique peut-être qu'il entretient avec ses semblables des rapports difficiles, qu'il doit, s'il veut communiquer, se déprendre des prestiges de la parole, ce piège égalitaire : la parole, décide-t-il, n'est pas mon langage. Il choisit le silence : il occupera la scène, il la peuplera, chaque soir, avec son corps, il forgera autour de lui un univers de significations, mais il se taira. Cette résolution héroïque, il la prend en un temps où le discours est roi, où la parole seule, diffusée, amplifiée, multipliée à l'infini, appelle la parole, où le silence a tort. Mais jamais le jeune homme ne faiblira : le plus solitaire des destins fut ainsi scellé, le mime Marceau était né. Depuis 1946, il n'a pas prononcé un mot sur une scène.
Pourtant il a tenu la scène plus qu'aucun acteur vivant, pratiquement sans interruption depuis quinze ans. Investi par décision souveraine, du mandat de ressusciter la pantomime au cœur du XXe siècle, il est à lui-même son propre auteur et son propre metteur en scène. Il n'est jamais en quête de rôles. Marcel Marceau, c'est d'abord, dans cette profession saisonnière, le miracle du plein emploi : si vous ne trouvez pas son nom dans les théâtres parisiens, soyez sûr de le découvrir à l'affiche d'un opéra de province ou plus loin encore, à Jérusalem, Bombay, New York, Tokyo ou Montréal. Au box-office des globe-trotters, des grandes tournées mondiales, ce silencieux occupe la première place, avec une confortable avance sur Jean Vilar et les tonnerres du T.N.P. A New York, en 1955, avant que le miaulement sidéral du premier Spoutnik n'ait stupéfié l'Amé-

Elle
10 November 1961
art director Peter Knapp

A study in black-and-white: this layout is built around extreme contrasts – of tone, of form, and of scale – which create a perfectly resolved design as well as a visual comment on Marceau and his art. The detachment of the word "seul" (alone) in the headline is the final detail. The photographer was Jean Lattes.

Elle
29 March 1963
art director Peter Knapp

Dynamism and continuity are created by skewing the grid throughout this fashion sequence, and on the opening spread by pushing the headline through the bleed. The photographs are typical of Knapp's lively and spontaneous location work.

Twen
October 1959
art director Willy Fleckhaus

Below: Fleckhaus employs surrealist repetition to create a penetrating cover design. The trumpet under the logo was a symbol repeated throughout the magazine to identify editorial matter.

pressed grotesques – in an angular layout. This was in the spirit of the new decade but, by comparison with Knapp, Wolsey had been restrained, for Knapp was a precursor of punk, a kitchen-sink primitive two decades ahead of his time. He would introduce elements of disorder to create immediacy. His typography was roughly cut, in the manner of Saul Bass. He blew up hand-drawn and typewriter faces, and used type degenerated by repeated photocopying; headlines were slanted, or were swished and curled through photographic deformation; type sizes were mixed within a single word, in torn paper titles and fabric collage. Knapp's fashion photography was of the new breed, unsnobbish, approachable, of laughing rather than pouting faces. He placed models in incongruous surroundings and would skew pictures off the perpendicular, sometimes cropping violently into heads to draw attention to the clothes.

Both the photography and layout of *Elle* were of a consistently high standard – much of the photography by Knapp himself – and as a rule it was preconceived as an integral part of the layout. Despite its "untidy" and variegated forms, the magazine always retained its internal coherence and geometric harmony. Knapp would, for example, sustain the continuity of a fashion sequence by imposing the same grid throughout – although that grid may have consisted of nothing more than a single notional oblique line. If *Elle* suffered, it was in the poor quality of its colour printing. But the layered and carefully wrought chaos of the pages was a *tour de force*, a remarkable achievement in a weekly which was made possible by an art department, at fourteen strong, of American dimensions.[16] In 1966 Knapp, like so many art directors at that time, moved on to concentrate on photography and teaching. But he remained a profound influence on French magazine publishing as his former art staff migrated throughout the industry.

Twen, when it made its appearance in 1959, had a cathartic effect on international magazine design. It was a prototype "youth" magazine (the title an abbreviation of twenty), founded by a group of young journalists and photographers for the *Halfstrong* – the first postwar generation of German teenagers. *Twen's* editorial policy was confused, a provocative and sometimes lightweight mixture of sex, art, travel, sport, politics – anything went. But it could be understood only as a set of poetic visual images from the otherworldly eye of its art director, Willy Fleckhaus. In *Twen*, photography was used not as illustration, but as revelation, a vision of the world from hitherto unseen angles, of disembodied features, of bizarre contrasts and impossible situations, designed to shock. Fleckhaus, the *de facto* editor, had invented a new form of journalism which, in its combination of words and pictures, replaced everyday reality with a spiritual or emotional *reportage*.

The magazine's outstanding feature was the unusual exploitation of photography, around which its layouts and story treatments were constructed. Fleckhaus has been described by the American designer Will Hopkins, who was for two years an art assistant at *Twen*, as "the super cropper",[17] for he had no respect for the conventions of photographic usage. The Americans on the staff called him a "Monday morning quarterbacker", a second guesser who would scour the world's press for images which he would reproduce in radically different ways, subverting the original intention, altering composition to achieve maximum emotional impact, slicing off the forehead to emphasise the eyes or massively enlarging facial detail. He had the ability to make an apparently banal image sing; and thus the apocryphal Fleckhaus-ism is, "You can run a good picture large or small. You can only run a bad picture large", and, "an unusable photo – larger still".[18] This cavalier approach to copyright and the individual's art did not

Twen
June 1969
art director Willy Fleckhaus

Right: Fleckhaus used the contents page to make a pictorial comment on the month's editorial content – in this case, a feature on changing attitudes to the female form. The page has clarity, and is given additional graphic force by the issue number, the bold figure "6".

6

60 Die Formen der Frau sind wandelbar wie der Geschmack der Männer. Warum stellten Kunst und Mode niemals die Frauen so dar, wie sie wirklich waren? Unsere große Untersuchung über die heimlichen Wunschbilder

3 Wählen Sie jetzt schon die nächste Regierung

6 Mit Kommune und ihr Leben zu acht: Warum Deutschlands schönste Kommunardin nichts vom Leben zu zweit hält

15 Wer macht die Liebe kaputt? Ein Mann steht Rede und Antwort

18 Karriere machen — aber wie? Start zur großen Aktion „Weiterbildung mit twen"

24 Hallucinations Die twen-Platte des Monats

32 Apo-Opa-Lotto Das twen-Spiel, das Generationen spielend an einen Tisch bringt

38 Witze

40 Leserbriefe

42 Der Computer gewann für twen 3417 Mark Wir untersuchten zehn Gewinnsysteme fürs Roulette

48 Willkommen im Affenhaus oder wie Billy der Poet die Selbstmord-Hosteß deflorierte Kurzgeschichte von Kurt Vonnegut

70 Ein Elefant mit Talent Wolfgang Schneider — die Ideologie eines Einzelgängers

72 Warum Richard Lindner Maschinenfrauen malt

77 Bei einem Mörder zu Besuch Das atemberaubende Abenteuer eines Unterwasserfotografen

84 Ehe auf Probe Wie man auch ohne Trauschein zusammenleben kann

86 twen-Autoquitäten-Salon Nr. 2

92 John Lennon und Yoko Ono: Der Frieden, der aus dem Bett kommt

98 twen-Mode: Großstadtblumen — die neuen Citykleider Die roten Schuhe

104 Der Zwang, ein freier Mensch zu sein twen-Interview mit Professor Herbert Marcuse

113 Lehrer im Kreuzfeuer zwischen Schule und Eltern twen-Report über Sex und Schule — dritter Teil

122 Iron Butterfly: Ball Vier Antitypen machen eine Antimusik

127 twen-Magazin Neue Gedichte von H. C. Artmann Das „Bread and Puppet-Theatre" (New York) bei der Experimenta III in Frankfurt „Accident" — der neue Film von Joseph Losey

138 Ein Seesack für 14 Tage Das brauchen Sie für eine twen-Cliquen-Reise unter Segeln

152 Sterne und Zitronen

Titelfoto: Guido Mangold

Will McBride

Dieser Junge auf dem Bild rechts heißt David Heinemann. Er ist ein Kind noch, knapp 15 erst, aber er ist ein Prophet. So lernte ich ihn kennen: ein hübscher Junge mit langen Haaren, der auf der Straße schwerverständliches Zeug vor sich hin redete. Mit sanfter High-Fidelity-Stimme sprach er Versfetzen. Er sprach von einer neuen Welt, die käme, voller Liebe und so. Er kam mir vor wie ein Jesus Christus, der sich in die Welt von 1969 verirrt hat. Also ein bißchen lächerlich. Aber dann bemerkte ich, daß seine Gedanken lange in meinem Gehirn hingen, wie zarte Töne elektrischer Gitarren. Dann dachte ich: Den müßte man sich öfter anhören; es würde einem verbitterten Gottlosen wie mir sicher guttun. Später traf ich ihn wieder, und ich ließ mich von ihm überreden, ihm in das Musical „Haare" zu folgen, wo er auftritt, spielt und singt. So hörte ich mir die Psychodelic-Predigt an, elektronisch lautstark, Beat-bitterness auf lieb. Es war wirklich eine Predigt. Ich lernte die Texte auswendig und wurde ein anderer Mensch. Ich schrie meine Frau und meine Kinder nicht mehr an; ich war auf einmal nett zu meinen Mitarbeitern; und die Fotomodelle, die 'rein- und 'rausströmten aus meinem Atelier, die habe ich nicht mehr beschimpft, wenn sie falsche Bewegungen machten; ich habe sie umarmt und geküßt. Für mich ist das Bühnenstück „Haare" wie eine Religion. Und ich finde, alle Leute sollten davon wissen. Deswegen habe ich es fotografiert, deswegen habe ich die frohe Botschaft aufgeschrieben.

DIE PROPHETEN

Die Jungen und Mädchen, die in dem Hippie-Musical „Haare" in München auf der Bühne tanzen, singen und lieben — spielen sie wirklich sich selbst? Der amerikanische Fotograf Will McBride, der seit zehn Jahren in München Wohnsitz, Familie und Atelier hat, lebte einige Wochen lang mit ihnen zusammen. Er will mit ihnen sogar auf Tournee gehen. Hier berichtet er von seiner Begegnung mit den Jungen und Mädchen von „Hair". „Es war", so schreibt Will McBride, „eine Begegnung, die mein Leben veränderte . . ."

„David Heinemann, wie heißt das Lied, das du in ‚Haare' singst?"
„Es heißt: O mein Gott, der alles sieht, schau, was hier mit uns geschieht, nicht länger an! Wie sie noch wagen, mit uralten Lügen um soviel Schönheit uns zu betrügen! Die Welt, die sie verbau'n, erben einmal wir — Kriege brechen sie vom Zaun, sterben dürfen wir!"
„David, warum hast du die Rolle angenommen?"
„Es macht Spaß. Es ist eine hübsche Nebenbeschäftigung."
„Also ist es dir eigentlich wurscht?"
„Überhaupt nicht."
„Kriegst du viel Geld bei ‚Haare'?"
„Nein. Nicht viel. Aber ich brauch' kein Geld."
„Wie lange gehst du noch zur Schule?"
„Noch vier Jahre. Und nach dem Abitur mach' ich erst mal Kriegsdienstverweigerer."
„Hast du schon mal Streit gehabt mit jemandem?"
„Ja. In einem Lokal. Da war ein Bauarbeiter, der sagte zu mir, ich soll mir die Haare schneiden lassen, und er wollte mich verprügeln."
„Was hast du da gemacht?"
„Ich hab' ihm ein Bier gekauft, da war er wieder lieb . . ."

Twen
February 1969
art director Willy Fleckhaus

The contrast between small and big picture, the extra-wide and extra-narrow columns of type and tight headline arrangements were all hallmarks of the Fleckhaus technique. The tiny margins admit no room for error, whereas the standfirst is allowed to hang above an ocean of white space. The main photograph is by Will McBride.

result in ostracism – anything but. Fleckhaus successfully commissioned the world's greatest photographers (foremost among them Will McBride) who, reputedly, he would direct with dictatorial exactitude to realise his conception for a page.

The architecture of Fleckhaus's layout was extraordinarily simple, with rarely more than four elements – typically, one large and one small picture, one heading, one narrow block of copy – with an emphatic tonal quality of solid blacks and whites or livid colour, perfectly reproduced by high-quality black-and-white gravure and colour offset printing. Type was used constructively, as bricks in a wall, with typestyles from two narrow bands at each end of the spectrum: Haas Grotesques, and the extra bold Ehrhardt which he would later employ at the *Frankfurter Allgemeine Zeitung* magazine. In the later period at *Twen*, his hallmark would be the heavy black border around a double-page spread, asymmetrical, with one side wider to accommodate the caption, and with rounded corners: in other words, exactly like a television screen. This idiosyncrasy was adopted by many designers in Britain and the United States, including David Hillman at *Nova*, and Will Hopkins at *Look*. *Nova*, in its design technique and defiant editorial, was in part an English manifestation of *Twen*.

Fleckhaus was always carefully watched by his peers. He changed forever the rules of photographic treatment and encouraged confident, unembellished editorial design. He made a considerable if transient impact on German publishing, where in the post-war period strong, simple layout was unknown and sheer visual noise substituted for direct communication. Fleckhaus was not, however, a journalistic art director in the conventional sense, even though he started his career as a journalist and never trained formally as a designer. He was a self-indulgent designer who refused to adapt to conventional editorial constraints or readers' expectations. In both his visual style and personal relations he was provocative, he abhorred complacency and prejudice. Fleckhaus ultimately became the victim of his own power at *Twen*: a power manifested in the regular sacking of editors and, by 1970, a tendency to whimsical eccentricity.

Twen

July 1969

art director Willy Fleckhaus

Opening to a "concept" fashion feature: using photography as symbol – hands in prayer – the size of the main picture is again emphasised by contrast with small pictures which, with the type hanging below them, are allowed to drop to irregular heights. The letters of the wall-like head are divided by a scalpel's thickness. The photographer was Tassilo Trost.

AFRICA NOVA

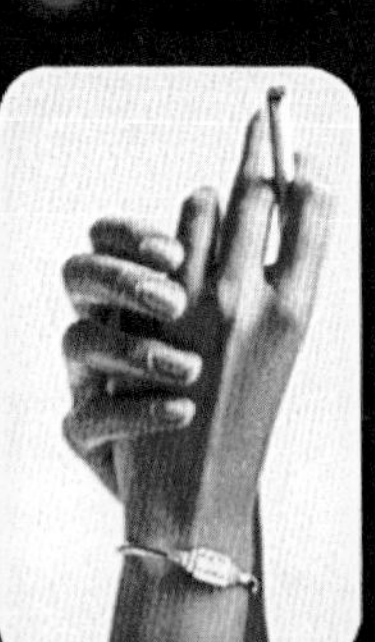

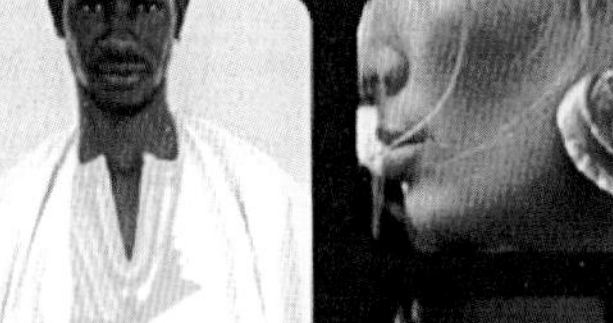

Schwarz ist schön. Diese Hände flehen nicht und drohen nicht. Sie zeigen sich in ihrer selbstbewußten Stärke. John Blain (Foto oben) will die alte Kunst und Kultur seines Heimatlandes Gambia nach Europa bringen. „Africa Nova" heißt die Gesellschaft, die er in Gambia gegründet hat. Für twen öffnete er seine Schatztruhe mit kostbaren, handgestickten Stoffen, gebatikten Kleidern und dem Schmuck seiner Heimat.

Gambia, der kleinste unabhängige Staat Afrikas, begleitete sein Erwachen mit dem Import europäischer Zivilisation. Heute importiert Europa afrikanische Kultur. Junge Europäer entdecken inmitten der lieblosen, perfektionierten Massenproduktion die Schönheit afrikanischen Kunsthandwerks. Dieser Armreif (oben) ist nur ein Beispiel wie das bestickte Häuptlingskleid.

Schwarze oder weiße Haut – alle Mädchen dieser Welt schmücken sich. Jane (oben) trägt die goldenen Ohrringe mit dem gleichen Stolz durch München wie Maruanda (unten) auf dem Eingeborenenmarkt in Gambia. Die Mandigo-Ohrringe werden heute wie vor Jahrhunderten mit den gleichen Werkzeugen nach einem uralten Blattmotiv von den einheimischen Goldschmieden gearbeitet.

So selbstverständlich fährt ein afrikanisches Kleid durch den deutschen Großstadtverkehr. Es ist gebatikt und an Hals und Ärmeln bestickt. Die Designer solcher Kleider haben noch nie etwas von Mode gehört. Wie ihre Väter hokken sie vor der Tür und nähen und sticken die traditionellen Stammesgewänder. twen entdeckte, wie harmonisch sie sich in die europäische Zivilisation fügen.

twen-Fotograf Tassilo Trost hat eine ganz besondere Beziehung zum schwarzen Kontinent. Er lebte vier Jahre in Afrika und ernährte sich vom Tauschhandel. In München beobachtete er die Afrika-Kleider mit seiner Kamera und zeigt auf den nächsten Seiten, in welch überraschendem Einverständnis sich das Stilgefühl zweier Kontinente begegnet.

Fleckhaus was fired that year, and shortly afterwards the magazine closed. He turned to book design and teaching and it was to be ten years before he again worked as an editorial art director, at the magazine supplement of the newspaper *Frankfurter Allgemeine Zeitung*.

FAZ Magazin was a very beautiful publication. Again, simply constructed, but with greater tranquillity than the boisterous *Twen*. The magazine's editor stipulated a very different brief: "The intellectual weight of the newspaper had to be reflected, and it had to supplement and enrich it with news and other aspects of reality as well."[19] With a quite different design problem and a more stringent journalistic role, Fleckhaus employed a great deal of classical imagery, traditional typestyles, and tended towards illustration rather than photography. In fact he did with illustration what he had done with photography at *Twen*, presenting it in "new and daring formulations",[20] creating novel combinations of text and image, daring in their apparent artlessness, again, with maximum picture size and minimum text hung in narrow columns from a field of white space. This tradition is maintained today by the art director Hans-Georg Pospischil, who succeeded on Fleckhaus's death in 1983. *FAZ* remains a showcase of remarkable images.

The impact of Fleckhaus's work on his contemporaries is difficult to underestimate. In Europe and America copies of *Twen*, with its rich blacks and poster-sized photography, were ripped up to make dummies for new projects; few designers working in the 1960s will not admit a debt to its designer. The English, caught up in their own home-grown pop culture and a fashion boom on which magazines could feed, were most receptive to *Twen's* radical visual style. From 1963, under Max Maxwell (who was also a photographic contributor to *Twen*) and Tom Wolsey, *Queen* magazine showed an equally confident use of photography – of which there was quality and quantity from the lenses of the new generation of Hedgecoe, Bailey, Donaldson, Bulmer and Donovan. Wolsey, who transferred to *Queen* from *Town* in 1964,[21] provided the additional touch of his dashing typography. His assistant at *Queen* was David King, who with Michael Rand would be the driving force behind the didactic and polemical editorial style of the new *Sunday Times Magazine*.

These were years in which the rapid expansion of magazine publishing in London coincided with a remarkable crop of graphic talent – the fruit of a transformation in design education. In 1960 the Commercial Art course at the London School of Printing had been renamed, significantly and with some ostentation, Graphic and Typographical Design, and was re-staffed by new and younger tutors including Derek Birdsall and Richard Hollis. David Hillman and David King graduated from this course in 1961 and 1962. At the West of England College of Art a school of design was established in the European multi-disciplinary tradition[22] with a graphics course run by Richard Hollis, recently returned from working with Peter Knapp at *Elle*. Hollis emphasized experimentation in basic printing techniques and maximum employment of graphic tools. Hollis's participation was short-lived but among his students was Terry Jones, whose "instant design", born of silk screen experiments and owing much to the ideas of Peter Knapp, would become the most original force in English magazine design in the 1970s and 1980s.

Das ist der neue Mensch

Eine Vision von Will McBride

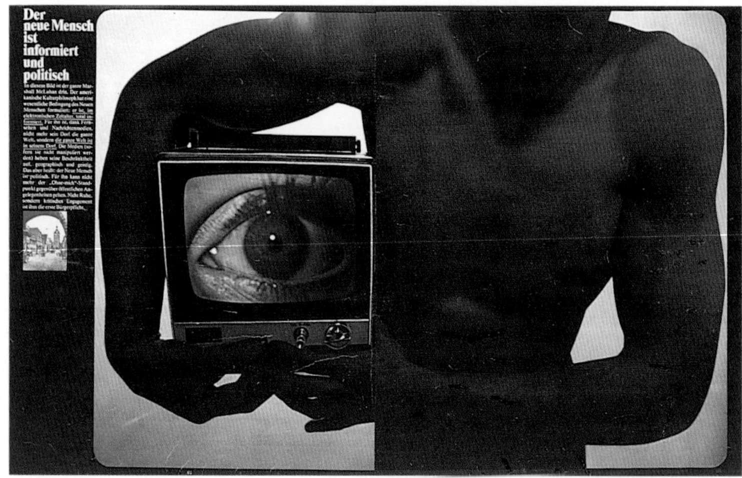

Der neue Mensch ist informiert und politisch

Twen
May 1970
art director Willy Fleckhaus

Introductory page and spread from a 13-page photo-feature by Will McBride on that perennial editorial obsession, "the new man." Fleckhaus and McBride combined to create photography as revelation, in which the text supported images notable either for their absurd incongruity or sheer normality, twisted by a vicious crop or close-up. Again, in this example, the impact of the main photograph is emphasised by the contrast of a smaller picture in the narrow text column. The asymmetric introductory page, with customized headline cemented a millimetre above two columns of body text into which a sub-head has been squeezed, exemplifies Fleckhaus's precisely constructed typography.

By 1966 the editorial transformation of British magazines was to all intents and purposes complete. What had occurred, initiated by *Town* and *Queen* was a fundamental shift in journalistic values from the literary to the visual. Stories were conceived at the earliest stage as mutually reinforcing combinations of text and pictures, as a conceptual narrative, in which the designer had achieved the status of Cassandre's "telegraph operator", quickening and clarifying the communication of information. The art director was introduced at the beginning of the editorial process rather than at its end, acting as initiator of editorial instead of superficial decorator.

This was a design-led revolution which was impelled by novel social and technical conditions: colour printing was now cheap; there was a new respect for illustrative photography – as opposed to straight news reportage; and the visual impact of television undoubtedly played a part; but perhaps the two most important factors were the editorial freedom provided by the new Sunday newspaper supplements, and the politicization of women's magazines where the designer had traditionally retained a more powerful position. Art direction was extended from fashion stories to general features on art and sexual, social and economic politics. *Queen*, and even English *Vogue*, pushed this process forwards: *Queen* under the editorship of Beatrice Miller (who in 1965 moved to *Vogue* and initiated radical changes in editorial[23]), and *Queen* under the art direction, and subsequent editorial control, of the Italian Willie Landels, who took the magazine into a new era of pop typography and illustration. *Nova*, however, was the magazine that made the most of its explorations into conceptual editorial.

Nova, edited by Dennis Hackett and art directed by Harry Peccinotti, was founded in 1965 as a radical women's monthly; radical both by political and editorial inclination, for *Nova* was a women's magazine conceived like a men's general interest magazine, with only the horoscope and fashion-well as immediate clues to its readership. Editorial was an entertaining and intellectual mix of sex (lots of it), health, politics, fashion, travel writing, art, an eclectic selection of excellently written offbeat features and photographically inspired editorial ideas. Cover design expressed the new philosophy, replacing witless face and body shots with photographic epigrams in the American expressionist mould. This editorial aberration was a mighty success, and the magazine

Nova

January 1966

art director Harry Peccinotti

A cover and opening spread for a feature on racism and racist immigration law. Like the article, the presentation was confrontational, forcing a question on the reader through dominating text and Clive Arrowsmith's blurred, over-blown photograph.

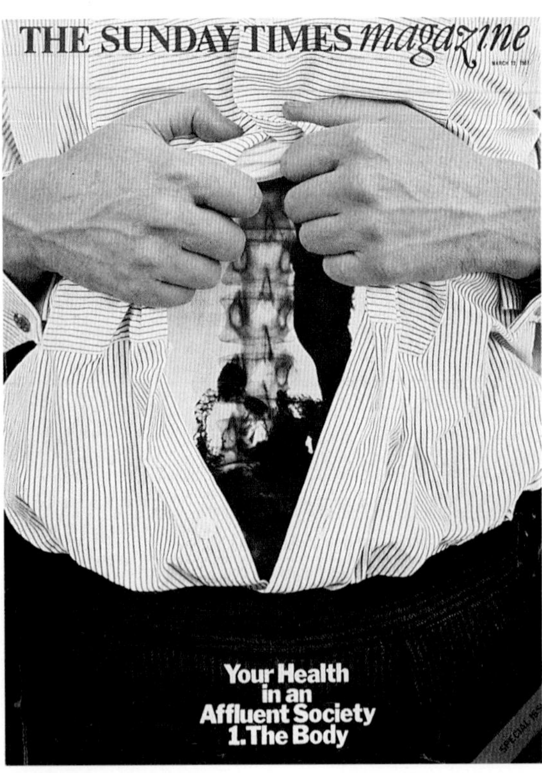

The Sunday Times Magazine
12 March 1967
art editor David King
art director Michael Rand
The Sunday Times Magazine was sold with the newspaper, and not on its cover alone. Nevertheless, its poster-like covers demonstrated a perfect understanding of the tastes and neuroses of its middle-class readership.

rapidly achieved a circulation of over 150,000.[24]

Peccinotti, an accomplished photographer, used pictures big and in unconventional combinations, in cracked-mirror repeated images and fenestrated matrices of multiple photographs. He cropped aggressively, in fashion sequences adopting a style similar to Ansell and Feitler at *Harper's Bazaar*, using the angularity of the human body, shot against white and tightly cropped, to create expressively mobile layouts. Current fashion dictated bright fluorescent colours, reproduced in excellent colour photogravure on high-quality coated papers.

Peccinotti's typography was unconventional, yet effective. He swopped between sturdy axial symmetry and lighter, asymmetric spreads built on a grid with deep top margin to create space. The Windsor headlines, a rounded, pop serif, were placed in striking tombstones above unbroken columns of Times and Helvetica body text. Long standfirsts were built as half-page height walls of 30pt Times which positively forbade the reader to ignore them.

Peccinotti, who resigned in 1967, was followed by a succession of designers, including Bill Fallover and Derek Birdsall (both brief occupants) and, from 1969, David Hillman, who continued to develop conceptual editorial based, in the *Twen* manner, around clever combinations of images and copywriting, but always with the backbone of substantial and well-written feature articles of up to 5,000 words.

While *Nova* prospered, the ex-newspaper designer Michael Rand had built for himself a working brief of equal and surpassing freedom at *The Sunday Times Magazine* which, following its launch by Mark Boxer in 1962, had by the mid-1960s established a new and exciting genre of magazine publishing. Implicit in the idea of the newspaper supplement was a wide-ranging editorial vision, which would both build on the newspaper's content and introduce entirely new features which the paper could not provide. "Colour supplement" was a good name. It added colour and supplemented the rush of news with more considered ideas. What was most notable in *The Sunday Times Magazine* was that it provided space; space in which photographers, writers and designers could excel and create instructive literary and pictorial features; and, of course, space for the advertisers.

The advertising opportunities guaranteed by a million-plus, up-market circulation generated massive revenues and, as a consequence, an editorial budget unprecedented in English magazine publishing. This, together with two visually literate editors in Godfrey Smith and Magnus Linklater, gave Rand the opportunity to make *The Sunday Times Magazine* the premier newspaper supplement in the world – in an editorial format which was flattered by imitation throughout Europe and the United States.

With Rand as art director and David King as art editor, *The Sunday Times Magazine* became a veritable encyclopaedia of images and ideas. Editorial possibilities were limited only by the imagination of its editors and the stomach of its readership – the educated English middle class, sections of which, by 1966, were veering sharply to the left. World affairs, social issues, history, health, technology, art and design, fashion and sport were given meticulously considered and often entertaining treatment. Neither Rand, nor King, were over-concerned with the design aesthetic or typographic virtuosity, except in that it facilitated their mission to explain and educate. King explained that he was "never interested in the design for its own sake", that "layout is very boring unless it can make the content jump". The colour supplement, he said, "enabled me to develop from being just a designer to creating visual features".[25]

This pragmatic approach led naturally to the adoption of communication techniques derived from con-

The Sunday Times Magazine
24 March 1968
art editor David King
art director Michael Rand

Headlined on the cover "Old Glory: young blood," this photographic record of the Tet offensive was one of a series of bloody and uncompromising war reports by Don McCullin, from Vietnam, Cambodia, Biafra and Beirut.

THIS IS HOW IT IS

Photographs and commentary by Donald McCullin

This is Donald McCullin's photographic report on a bunch of young American Marines engaged in a bloody confrontation with the Viet Cong. His own words describe what is happening in his pictures:

"This big Negro was doing what they call hand-to-hand fighting. Both sides were dug in and lobbing grenades at each other. Unfortunately on this occasion the Marines were short of grenades. We were trying to advance along the earthwork top of the Citadel wall of Hué and the grenades were being passed up the line of dug-in men one at a time. Naturally there had to be a pause in supply at some stage. When this happened the Viet Cong popped up and hurled a grenade. I'd just taken this picture before it happened . . . the grenade landed short but it wounded the GI in the hand.

"I spent 11 days with the Americans fighting their way into the Citadel. What worried me about this whole battle was the fact that there were so few mature soldiers with the Marine platoons. The captain back at the command post was only 24 and the average age of the platoons going out to storm the Viet Cong positions was only 20. There seemed a great need among the young men for leadership.

"The most impressive thing was the accuracy of the American shelling. Their ships out at sea were hitting the streets right in front of our positions. And shells from an army base 16 miles away were landing 200 yards ahead of us.

"Something I found very moving was the way the Negroes and the Whites have developed this uncanny kind of relationship while they're fighting together. They cook each other's food and drink out of each other's canteens. It's strange. A kind of love. It's not that the Whites go out of their way to be nice to the Negroes – rather the other way round. I got the feeling it was a kind of protectiveness on the part of the Negroes. I think it's something to do with the fact that for the first time they find themselves in a situation where they're all equal and they're accepted.

"The general attitude of the ordinary American soldier in Vietnam has changed a lot since I was with them two years ago. Then they were confident about the war and felt sure they had a right to be there. Now they have their doubts."

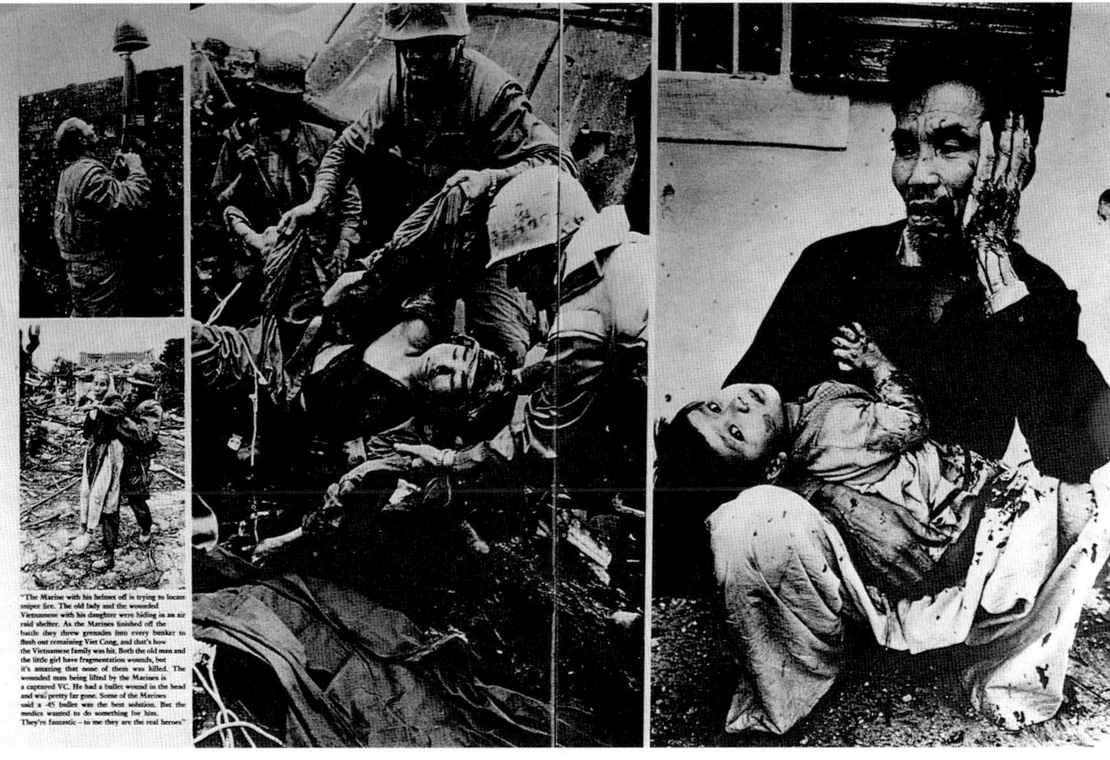

"The Marine with his helmet off is trying to locate sniper fire. The old lady and the wounded Vietnamese with his daughter were hiding in an air raid shelter. As the Marines finished off the battle they threw grenades into every bunker to flush out remaining Viet Cong, and that's how the Vietnamese family was hit. Both the old man and the little girl have fragmentation wounds, but it's amazing that none of them was killed. The wounded man being lifted by the Marines is a captured VC. He had a bullet wound in the head and was pretty far gone. Some of the Marines said a ·45 bullet was the best solution. But the medics wanted to do something for him. They're fantastic – to me they are the real heroes"

The Sunday Times Magazine
22 August 1968
art editor David King
art director Michael Rand

The Czech leader Alexander Dubcek as Gulliver in Lilliput, a photomontage by David King after John Heartfield.

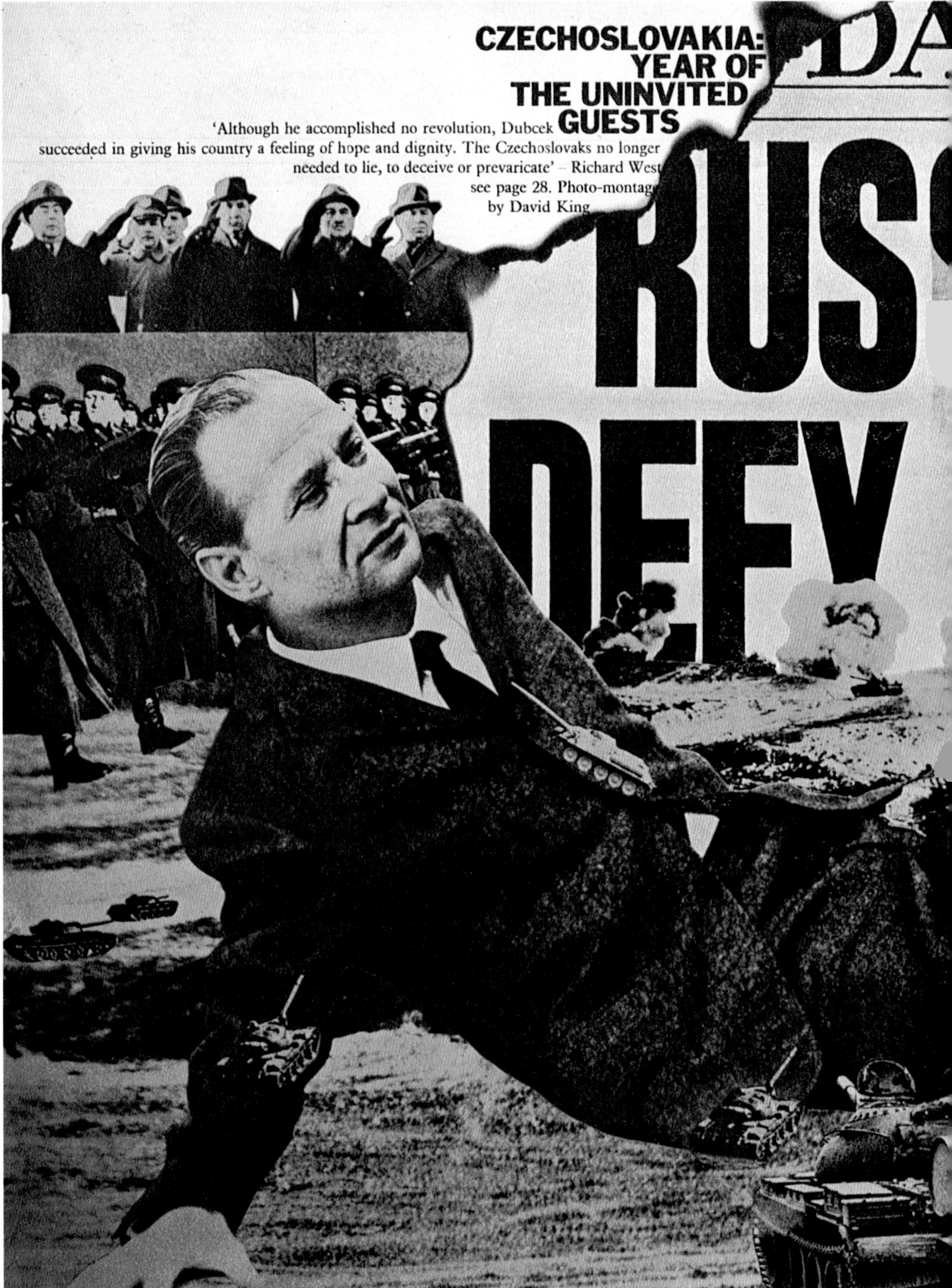
CZECHOSLOVAKIA: YEAR OF THE UNINVITED GUESTS
'Although he accomplished no revolution, Dubcek succeeded in giving his country a feeling of hope and dignity. The Czechoslovaks no longer needed to lie, to deceive or prevaricate' – Richard West see page 28. Photo-montage by David King
RUS
DEFY

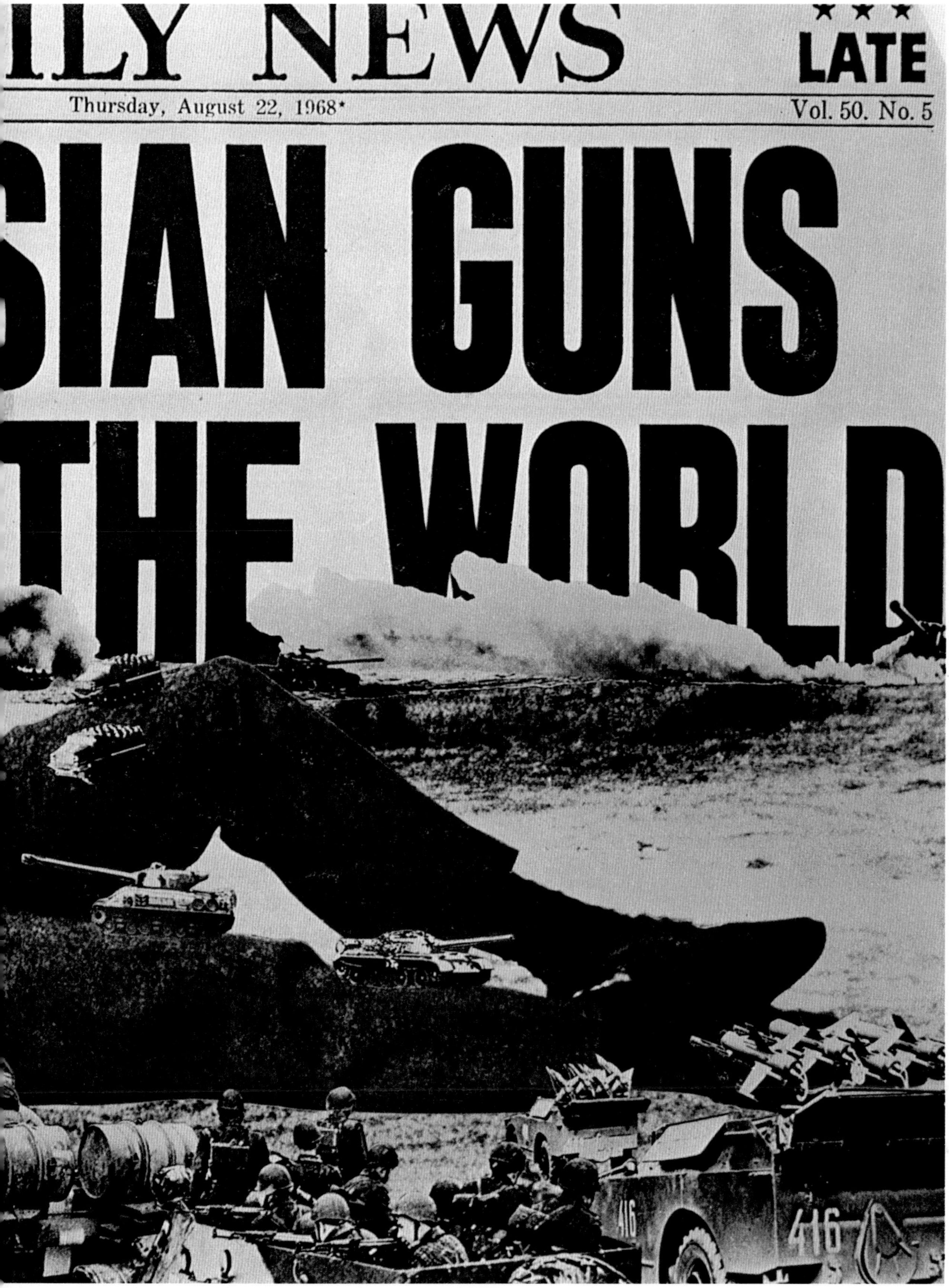

ILY NEWS

★★★ LATE

Thursday, August 22, 1968*

Vol. 50. No. 5

SIAN GUNS

THE WORLD

In October 1935, after the Long March, Mao's Red Army finally reached Yenan in Shensi province. Of the 90,000 men who started only 8000 remained, despite the fact that reinforcements had joined the march along the way. In Yenan the three Communist leaders above, Chou En-lai (left), Mao (centre) and General Chu Teh, defended themselves against the attacks of Chiang Kai-shek for 10 years, built and administered a primitive Communist society, and were soon joined by revolutionary armies from other parts of central China
Above: Mao the eternal scholar also has a fine hand for calligraphy. During the years his Red army was quartered in Yenan he pored over his books, often reading and writing by candlelight throughout the night
Contrary to custom, Mao has had four wives: first a village girl chosen by his parents; then Yang Kai-hui, executed by the Nationalists in 1930; then Ho Tzu-chen (below right) who endured the Long March with him. Finally, with Tzu-chen away in the Soviet Union getting medical treatment, he married Chiang Ching, the film actress (two pictures below left), who has had increasing influence in the Party
Mao was the political leader, Chu Teh the field commander. Above, they discuss tactics in the war against Chiang. The youthful idealism of 1923 (right) was now tempered by experience

The Sunday Times Magazine
March 1969
art director Michael Rand
art editor David King

The Sunday Times Magazine's forte was comprehensively researched visual journalism. Its didactic urge was given full rein in blockbuster specials: "A Dictionary of the Russian Revolution" and, running over many issues, "Makers of the Twentieth Century". This landscape spread is from a pictorial biography of Mao Tse Tung, presented in typically encyclopaedic style with its Edwardian contoured type and oval vignettes.

temporary advertising – big pictures accompanied by succinct snaps of cleverly written copy (of which the "America Hurrah!" issue of 1968 was a classic example). The message was simple and direct; the commitment to journalism and concern for public education paramount. News analysis – always a central feature – was carefully constructed of layered components which simplified the digestion of information: the headlines posed a question, answered by combinations of short texts, captioned photographs, charts and illustrative diagrams. The effect was of a saturated information pack that could be browsed through or studied at length.

Although the magazine carried these deliberately treated news stories it was never primarily a news magazine or photojournal. *The Sunday Times Magazine* of the 1960s and early 1970s is most celebrated as the vehicle for Don McCullin's searing photographic reports from Biafra, Vietnam and Cambodia, but it could not and did not compete with *Paris Match:* it was printed colourgravure and had a six-week lead time; instead of immediacy the magazine offered a reflective and generous presentation, devoting half a dozen spreads and more to McCullin's photographs which it printed in four-colour process to give the richest, deepest black-and-white reproduction.

McCullin's "Old glory young blood" special on Vietnam was a highpoint in the magazine's early history. The story won a Design & Art Direction Gold Award but was allowed through by management only after much debate of the "did readers want to look at this material over Sunday breakfast?" variety. This question would arise again and again, but until 1975 the editors kept the magazine on a campaigning course which paralleled its parent newspaper. 1968 was notable for features on Lenin, Mao and the 1917 revolution. King entertained his interest in Russian constructivism and the work of John Heartfield, producing both conventional montage and silk screened collage (created in twelve colour; printed in four), and for the blockbuster historical specials such as "Makers of the Twentieth Century", he developed an idiosyncratic style of layout which matched the didactic editorial, a pastiche, in heavy Egyptians and oval-framed portraits, of the Edwardian illustrated dictionary. The aggressive, agitational stance of the magazine was expressed in the poison-pen humour of Ralph Steadman's illustrations and the satirical puppet "sculptures" of Fluck and

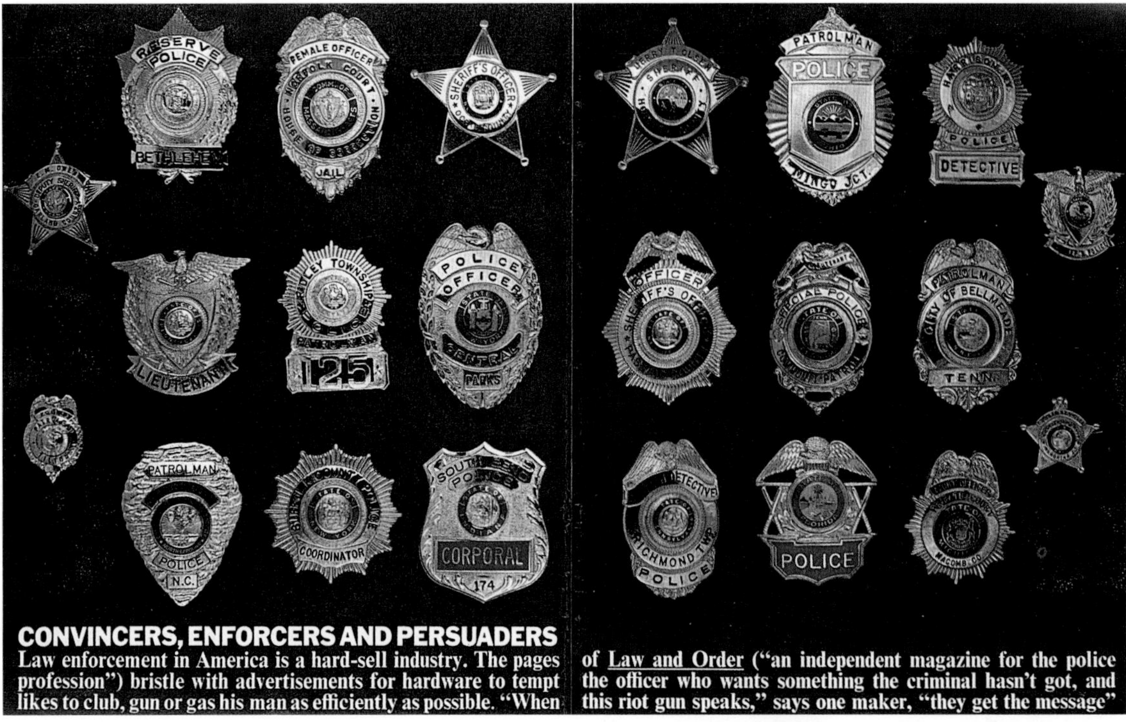
CONVINCERS, ENFORCERS AND PERSUADERS

Law enforcement in America is a hard-sell industry. The pages of Law and Order ("an independent magazine for the police profession") bristle with advertisements for hardware to tempt the officer who wants something the criminal hasn't got, and likes to club, gun or gas his man as efficiently as possible. "When this riot gun speaks," says one maker, "they get the message"

The Sunday Times Magazine
c. 1967
art director Michael Rand
art editor David King

A second example of the pictorial treatment of suitable subject matter. This story on the regalia and machinery of law enforcement agencies was inspired by advertisements in Law and Order magazine. The presentation is beautifully simple: a short, intriguing headline and two slugs of crisp caption copy.

Law; it was measured by well written coverage of gardening, travel and sports.

It was, however, the lighter editorial which came to dominate the magazine. With the departure of Linklater from the editor's chair in 1975, those who questioned the value of feeding readers harsh reality for breakfast gained the ascendancy. *The Sunday Times Magazine* turned its perspective inwards, to that editorial muesli of "leisure and home" and to the palatable and marketable consumerism of "Lifestyle". But whatever it was to become, in its first decade of existence *The Sunday Times* had mastered a novel and demanding form of editorial which was almost limitless in scope, and therefore required the most varied forms of visual expression: from the rigours of information design to photojournalism and conceptual graphics. The format was followed and taken forward at the *New York Times* and *Boston Globe*, in Italy by the *Corriera della Sera* supplement *Sette Giorni*, and in England at *The Observer, The Sunday Telegraph* (adroitly designed by Geoff Axbey), and the *News of the World* magazine *Sunday*, the latter a unique example of the well-designed downmarket supplement, by ex-*Sunday Times* design assistant Clive Crook. The most intriguing aspect of the evolution of the newspaper magazine supplement, however, was its impact on newspaper design. For the first time in the history of graphic design, magazines were influencing, not emulating, another medium. Newspapers, in a process that began on broadsheet weekend reviews and graduated to the main news sections, rapidly increased their visual content and expressive imagery. This was done under the direct influence of magazine designers, including Michael Rand and David Hillman at *The Sunday Times Weekend Review*,[26] Willy Fleckhaus, who produced supplements for *Die Welt*, ex-*Stern* designer Conrad Boch at *Publik*, and former *Radio Times* designer David Driver who became design director of *The Times Saturday Review*.[27] Thus the process had come full circle, and the revolution in pictorial magazine design of the 1960s had created a corresponding upheaval in newspapers a decade later. In the 1970s, however, magazines would once again suffer cruelly from the deprivations of recession and the damaging ingress of advertising into editorial. The large commercial publishers withdrew budgets and withheld editorial control from journalists and designers, and a monopoly on inventive magazine design was passed to small independent publishers and the radical press.

1968 and after: underground and up again

IT

19 June 1972

designer Mick Farren

Angela Davis as ticking bomb, simply and powerfully executed in flat process colour.

The magazine publishing industry was hit hard by successive economic slumps in 1972 and 1974, which diminished consumption and thereby advertising revenues, and sent paper prices spiralling upwards. The way in which these events deflated the optimism of the previous decade was quite remarkable, although in America in the latter part of the 1960s design and editorial had already become noticeably more conservative. *Nova* and *Twen*, the quintessential 1960s magazines, were natural victims of this new and harsher decade. *Nova* became the incredible shrinking magazine, progressively reducing its size from the original 32.5 x 25cm (13 x 10in) to under A4 (letter) size, and then to A5, becoming nothing better than a pamphlet. The magazine lost its editorial direction in a foolhardy attempt to compete with the pragmatic commercialism of *Cosmopolitan* and in 1975 it collapsed. This experience was extreme but not untypical of the times. In Europe and America magazines shrivelled or died. *Twen* folded early, in 1970; *Town* had already succumbed, and *The Sunday Times Magazine* turned from campaigning to consumerism. *Esquire, Fortune, Holiday, Vogue* and *Harper's Bazaar* all reduced the size and weight of paper,[1] and a generation of readers and designers grew up believing that magazines were mean little pocket-sized things. In a collective loss of faith these once great magazines limited their editorial vision and turned to the mass market for survival. *Vogue* joined the rush for circulation and dived straight downmarket, wearing the gaudy trappings of multiple cover lines, clashing coloured panels, brash typography and crammed pages of small pictures. This magazine turned its back on the elegant conceit of its past, not recovering its poise until a belated response was made to the graphic strength of the new US edition of *Elle*, when Derek Ungless was appointed *Vogue* art director in late 1988. At Condé Nast, editorial director Alexander Liberman had in the intervening years never allowed aesthetic principles to interfere with the dictats of commercialism. Everything was second guessed, yet his position was no different from that of publishers in almost all of the major houses as the creative freedom of both editors and art directors was reined in by marketing and advertising constraints. The urge to survive created a deadening homogeneity in mainstream magazine design.

Which is not to say that this was a dull period in magazine design: on the contrary, it was a decade of radical change in both editorial content and design. In Europe and America a fundamental break was made with the past as almost an entire generation of art directors moved on into other areas of design.[2] The new intake, however, found that the "underground", and later the independent, press were the most welcoming to ideas. In commercial publishing, with only a very few exceptions, ideas had become anathema.

The underground press already had a long history – anti-establishment publications in politics and the arts were hardly new – but they had tended to adopt the newspaper or pamphlet format rather than that of the illustrated magazine.[3] The post-war underground press in the developed world was born in the 1960s, beginning in the UK with *Private Eye* in 1964, perhaps best described as the satirical organ of the anarchist wing of British toryism (if that is not too much of an oxymoron), and in America with the political monthly *Ramparts*, and *The San Francisco Oracle*, a panegyric to the drug culture. *OZ* was launched in London in 1967 by Richard Neville and Martin Sharp,[4] as a kind of proto-hippy *Private Eye*, but it was to become much

Oz

no. 6 1968

designer Jon Goodchild

The Other Scenes issue was published at the height of Oz's psychedelic phase. Colour as a graphic element was still a novelty in European magazines, especially when used in this way as textured underlay. The copy is legible, but only just.

Oz

no. 16 1969

designer Martin Sharp

The Magic Theatre issue was entirely composed of collage culled from newspapers, comics and art books. Throughout its existence the impoverished Oz relied on "free" art for illustration.

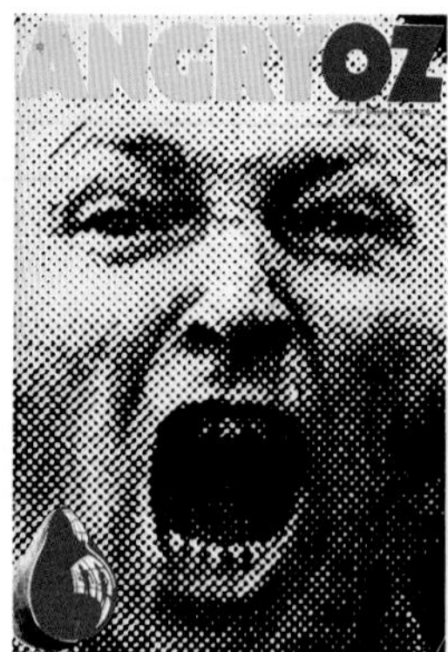

Oz

no. 37 September 1971

designer Pearce Marchbank

Blown-up half-tone had long been used by modernists as an expression of aggression. This cover of the "Angry" issue was one of a pair, with the back cover illustrated in a contrasting 1940s cheesecake style by Peter Brookes.

more than that. *OZ*, which at first assumed the guise of a psychedelic illustrated comic,[5] very rapidly evolved an inconsistent but nonetheless remarkable iconography which subverted every convention of graphic communication. Its novel use of print technology, collage and footloose typography was to have a positive and enduring influence on graphic design in Britain. *OZ* was not only genuinely inventive but also showed an understanding of purpose and historical context. The kitchen sink politics of such magazines as *OZ*, *IT*,[6] the short-lived *Ink* and leftist *7 days*, and the French communist weekly *rouge*, was reflected in an impossibly eclectic jumble of styles, but out of this mash evolved a fresh and exhilarating attitude to design for print which opened the way for punk and neo-modernist forms and re-integrated art with design.

The underground press was founded on an idea, and on a production process. The idea was that anyone could produce a magazine with which to cock a snook at the establishment (but not so hard that it fell); the production process was offset litho and the IBM golfball. Web and sheetfed offset printing had made few inroads in English magazine publishing, in which letterpress and gravure were the dominant print form until the early 1970s, but it was the clever exploitation of this technology that was primarily responsible for the unique colour sensibility and graphic virtuosity of the underground magazines.

OZ was designed by Jon Goodchild from 1967 to 1970, when he left for the USA to work on *Rolling Stone*. Martin Sharp and David Wills, together with dozens of itinerant and often uncredited contributors, were also involved in illustration and design, which is one explanation for the magazine's ramshackle collection of styles: for this was "the artroom as theatre of experiment".[7] In their desire to create jarring visual shock and gratuitously to disrupt convention these designers stumbled, as much by accident as design, on original graphic forms; they also concocted self-confessed "appalling messes, typographical horrors, pages that were so dense they were illegible".[8] Such disasters were the price of ambitious, low-budget printshop experiments in colour and background texture. "So many of the *OZ* innovations occurred as a result of getting the [printers] interested in doing something that they would never be able to do again. We used colour washes, silver ink, gold ink...it wasn't as illegible as people remember."[9] Colour as a graphic element was still a novelty in European magazines, especially when used in this way as textured underlay, and as a dynamic or decorative component.

In their use of coloured text, the rainbow effect of split-fountain inking,[10] multiple passes through single colour presses, in the decorative borders and florid and fantastic art, *OZ* in particular was undoubtedly influenced strongly by earlier American counterparts such as the *Oracle* and John Wilcock's *East Village Other*; indeed, Wilcock co-edited one issue of *OZ*. However, they also showed an acute awareness of the political function of collage, which was used at first shambolically (and as an expression of contempt for copyright); and in later issues with precision and to inci-

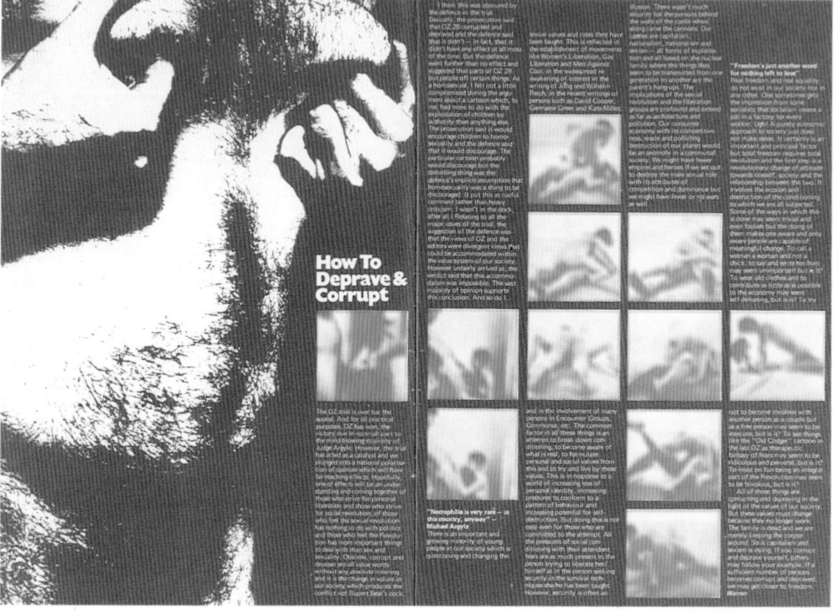
How To Deprave & Corrupt

Oz

no. 37 September 1971

designer Pearce Marchbank

Maximization of limited colour resources in a striking, modular design. The layout builds on contrast of image size and irregular column height, in a development of the techniques used at Twen by Fleckhaus. The images are stills from an Andy Warhol film.

Ramparts
May 1968
art director Dugald Stermer

Right: "The American flag as redesigned in 1901 by Mark Twain." For this double issue of Ramparts, the image was wrapped around the spine, with the logotype on what would normally have been the back cover.

sive effect. *OZ* and *IT* incorporated the visual imagery of abstract expressionism, op art and pop. There are clear references to the work of the European-influenced English designers of the 1940s and 1950s, and even, although it seems an absurd contradiction, to the international style – suitably distorted. The art of *OZ* was by no means naive, not always childish; on the contrary it was designed by knowing artists of some calibre, including Sharpe, Wills, Richard Adams, Jim Anderson, the illustrator Peter Brookes, Pearce Marchbank[11] – who had previously worked on the rigorously modernist *Architectural Design* – and Barney Bubbles.[12] Ultimately, in attempting to establish an aesthetic strategy which adapted earlier forms to their own situation, they came inevitably to adopt the language of opposition.

As a loose political movement the "underground" was, on both sides of the Atlantic, based around hippy psychedelia, drug culture and music on the one hand, and in the radical democratic movement which arose in 1968 on the other. From 1972 the two trends tended to diverge. This split was reflected in graphic style. The relatively air-headed and nostalgic music press favoured American-flavoured pop and psychedelic art and *art nouveau* revivalism, in which illustration assumed a new importance, as did the comic book cartoon (in France the *bandes dessinées* was, as ever, the dominant format), and this competed with aggressive expressionism, blown-up halftone, collage and photomontage "snare-pictures"[13] – used in the more overtly political publications; this was the product of an indigenous Euro-centric art school movement. In the later issues of *OZ* these opposing styles can be seen within the same magazine, with elaborate decorative borders on one spread competing with strictly modular arrangements – nonetheless vibrantly coloured – on another.

The use of photomontage and a raw, unfinished typographic style was confined to Europe. In the USA in the period immediately preceding 1970 experimental "indulgence" tended to be equated with disrespect for content, and an austere simplicity was in vogue. American radicals had no comparable nonconformist graphic tradition on which to draw and tended to be more conservative, and there was in the US a less well defined separation between the mainstream and independent press, which from the beginning had been founded on a strictly commercial basis. This was very much a transitional period in which designers searched for new, but not too unfamiliar forms of visual

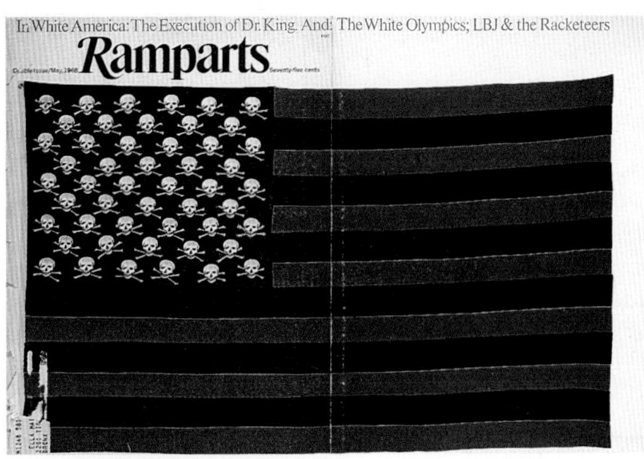

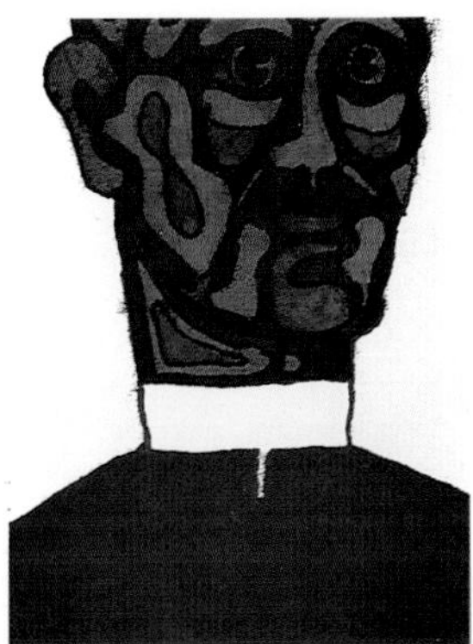

Ramparts
April 1966
art director Dugald Stermer

At this radical monthly, Dugald Stermer implemented a conservative typographic regime, with embellishment restricted to finely cut drop capitals and square-bracketed subheads. Ramparts' bold illustration, muted but intelligent use of colour, and close attention to the quality of print and paper encouraged a new appreciation of craft principles, especially in the more literary magazines. The illustration was by Ken Harshfield.

Fact

November/December 1966

art director Herb Lubalin

In the early 1960s Lubalin was the doyen of the American typographic expressionists and he made an art out of the integration of type with photography. However, he also established a tradition of finely crafted typography derived from book design, which is clearly apparent in this cover, a carefully cast-off essay in Goudy Old Style bold, and in the symmetrically arranged Times Roman head, byline, standfirst and body copy of the spread. The illustrations are by James Grashow.

fact: $1.25 VOLUME THREE ISSUE SIX

Paul Goodman says, "I don't give a rap who killed Jack Kennedy." Harry Golden: "Senator Kennedy told me, 'The family is satisfied there was this one fellow.' He couldn't even mention Oswald's name!" Dwight Macdonald: "If I had to say yes or no to Oswald's sole guilt, I'd still say yes." Melvin Belli: "The real villain in this piece is that latter-day King Farouk, J. Edgar Hoover." Mark Lane: "I myself don't see any evidence that President Johnson was the assassin." Other comments by Allen Ginsberg, Arthur Miller, Al Capp, Cleveland Amory, John Updike, Theodore Bikel, Marya Mannes, Gordon Allport, and many others.

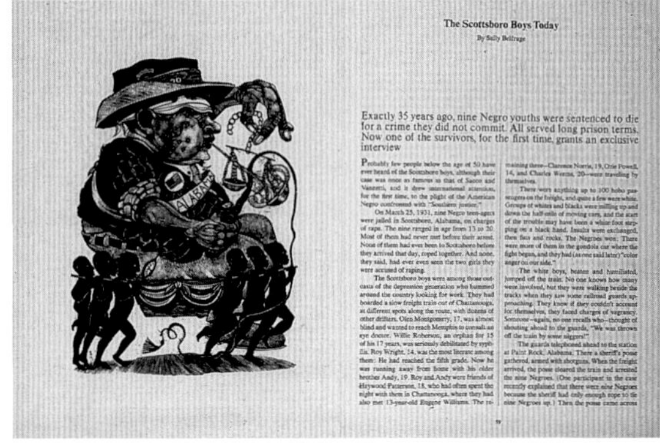

The Scottsboro Boys Today

By Sally Belfrage

Exactly 35 years ago, nine Negro youths were sentenced to die for a crime they did not commit. All served long prison terms. Now one of the survivors, for the first time, grants an exclusive interview

Tom Wesselman is (with Warhol, Oldenburg, Lichtenstein, Rosenquist, and Dine) one of the half-dozen American Pop artists whose work seems likely to survive the vagaries of present and future fashion. His brilliant, sensual style and concentration on erotic subject matter, so shocking a few years ago, already have taken on a remarkably "classic" look. Certainly he has done much to reinstate the nude as a subject for serious modern art. And his lush, Matisse-derived color-forms, infused with Pop literalism, have helped establish a uniquely American way of painting that is at once formal, figurative, and plain fun. Wesselman's paintings are about pleasure. They are feasts of color, sunlight, flesh, and undulating form that you can almost taste and feel as well as see. They are about all kinds of pleasure, not just sex—though they do mostly contain nudes or parts of nudes (breasts, feet, or lips dangling suggestive cigarettes). An orange or a pillow in an interior can be as much a source of delight as a nipple outlined against the sky. Above all, these paintings are innocent. Wesselman resents the charge, occasionally made, that his nudes are modeled after "girlie magazines," with the implication that they are somehow tawdry and pornographic. "As if," he says, "perfectly respectable women, wives or girl friends, never spread their legs or stick their tongues out at their men." Which is what his works do at their viewers—cheerfully proffer themselves for delectation, and teasingly indicate that it's just a game, after all. The name of the game is painting.

TOM WESSELMAN: PLEASURE PAINTER

Avant Garde

November 1968

art director Herb Lubalin

In contrast to Fact, Lubalin's design of Avant Garde was full of typographic variation, with no two headlines in the same style. This highly wrought construction is typical of his approach to type design: a customized slab serif hybrid of his own ITC Machine face, in a tightly butted and ligatured configuration.

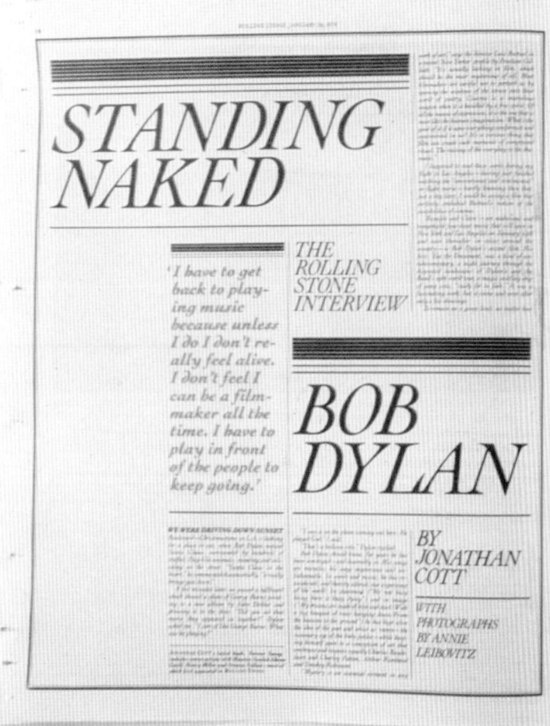
STANDING NAKED

'I have to get back to playing music because unless I do I don't really feel alive. I don't feel I can be a filmmaker all the time. I have to play in front of the people to keep going.'

THE ROLLING STONE INTERVIEW

BOB DYLAN

BY JONATHAN COTT

WITH PHOTOGRAPHS BY ANNIE LEIBOVITZ

Rolling Stone

c. 1975

art director Roger Black

An archetypal Rolling Stone spread of the mid-Seventies, with a full-page portrait by staff photographer Annie Leibovitz separated by the gutter from an elaborate construction of serif italics bedecked by scotch and column rules. Traditional type forms were revived and designers reverted to type as the foundation of layout.

expression. Modernism in America had almost always been put to the service of corporate wealth and was therefore too closely associated with the status quo. Instead, designers combined the (wild) western tradition – symmetrically set wood-blocks, early industrial typeforms, shaded and ornamental slab serifs – with the American expressionist style. This is most apparent in Mike Salisbury's treatments for the *Los Angeles Times* supplement *West*, which combined typographic precision with strong art direction, and in Fred Woodward's *Texas Monthly* and in his later work for *Rolling Stone*. Dugald Sturmer's impassive format for the radical political monthly *Ramparts* (from c. 1966-70) pre-dated this approach: classical, symmetrical typography, enlightened patronage of illustration in a wide variety of styles (realist, expressionist, caricature and Regency lampoon), and strictly limited use of photography; but for the covers, the designer employed aggressive visual and typographic polemic. Stermer steered clear of the frivolity of pop, unlike Bea Feitler, who after leaving her partnership with Ruth Ansell at *Harper's Bazaar* in 1970 had moved to the very different *Ms*, a vibrant feminist magazine with – typically – more polish, more colour, and a bigger budget than its British equivalent *Spare Rib*.

Psychedelic art and the revival of pre-modern styles had a strong but transient effect worldwide, informing the typography and illustration of publications as diverse as *Look, Playboy, Lui, Queen, Nova, Redbook, Esquire* and *Vogue*, and even business magazines such as Crookes' Laboratories *New Doctor*, designed by John McConnell. In illustration, which gained a new popularity, this movement was very largely instigated by the Push Pin Studio, which had initiated an easily accessible and rather homely illustrative form which superseded the dark social realism of Ben Shahn and others. The Push Pin style, created by Seymour Chwast, Ed Sorel and Milton Glaser, used the flat perspective and vibrant colours of pop within a pastiche of the whole gamut of nineteenth- and twentieth-century decorative styles, be it Victorian commercial vernacular, pre-Raphaelite, *art nouveau* or *deco*, and although it produced some powerful conceptual images this was very much the acceptable face of the so-called counter-culture, executed with flat-toned precision.

Although this style dated as rapidly as the images from which it borrowed, the formal, type-led approach has shown remarkable tenacity, and is evident in much of contemporary American magazine design. The elevation of production values to new levels of perfection, and a creeping craft sensibility of quality finishing and prudence, led unerringly to what Allen Hurlbert described – as early as 1971 – as "a new formalism in magazine graphics". This was characterized by "fewer bleed photographs; a new emphasis on symmetrical balance; more type-rules, borders, and occasional ornament; revival letter forms from the periods of Biedermeier to the Bauhaus; more carefully composed photographs; and formal, often decorative, illustrations [of the kind described above]".[14]

In America in 1970 the new conservatism was, paradoxically, at its strongest in the independent press. *Rolling Stone* magazine, which at the time of its launch in 1967 was strictly speaking a foldover tabloid newspaper, was crowned with a shaded, scrolled ornamental logotype. The magazine, which started out as a left-field music publication, had by 1973 achieved a 500,000 worldwide circulation and was thoroughly inculcated into the music establishment; it personified the embrace of youth culture by big business. Its American vernacular adequately expressed the style of the blue jean generation, and, when alternated with the Morisonian type of English newspapers, it reflected its underlying conservatism too. According to Roger Black, a former art director of the magazine, "The rock-and-roll tabloid in 1967 embraced Times [New Roman] Bold as an antidote to the psychedelia of the underground press."[15] A succession of art directors, including Salisbury, Black, Mary Shanahan, Stephen Doyle, and an ex-*Radio Times* design assistant from England, Derek Ungless, emphasized typographic design over art direction, and continued to do so when the paper changed to magazine format. Roger Black recalled that, "feature headline 'spec' became a game: a new typeface for every story, preferably one that the other art directors could not guess… Lettering artists retouched phototype, and the paste-ups were done to hot-metal standards".

Thus there was a reversion to the treatment of type as provider of thematic variation and a breakdown of the unity of type and image. This is apparent in Milton Glaser's 1978 re-design for *Esquire*, and more so in the subsequent elaborate typographic format initiated on the magazine by Robert Priest (also a graduate of *Radio Times*) in 1980. *Esquire* makes an interesting case study of shifting fashions in American magazine design in the 1970s. The magazine was reduced to letter size (American A4) in 1975 and for a brief period in 1978 went fortnightly. Michael Gross, the art director preceding Glaser's intervention, stressed simplicity and "under-design" in a format which allowed less white space, and promoted *Esquire* as a "show-case for photography",[16] while removing illustration. This was the age of custom-designed type, and a new slab-serif

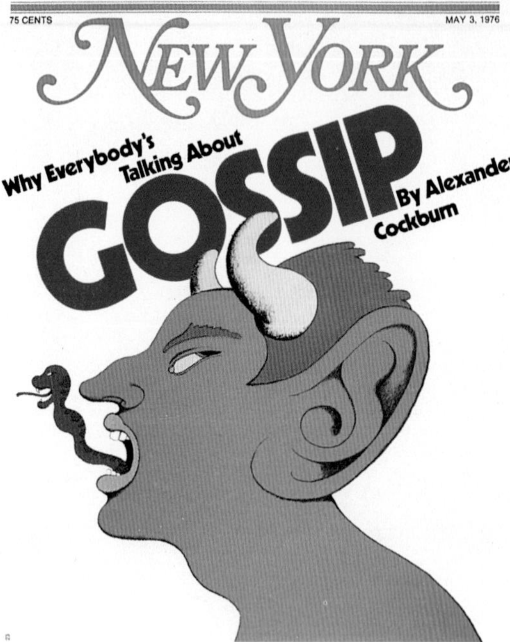

New York
3 May 1975
design director
Milton Glaser
art director Walter Bernard
Cover illustration by Seymour Chwast in the flat tones and rounded forms of the Pushpin style.

New York

Seven Days of Killing

By Peter Hellman

"… It was a week when almost everybody hated to be in New York…"

The first victim was a loner, a bum named Sydney who was found stabbed twice in the chest on a bad corner in Williamsburg. That was a few minutes into the morning of Friday, July 14. At the same moment, on Staten Island, Milagros Rodriguez awoke to find a man beating her husband on the head with a chair leg. The man took $50 from her pocketbook on the dresser and fled. Wilson Rodriguez died a day later. The next killing wasn't until five in the afternoon. In the middle of an argument at 165 Lenox Avenue in Harlem, Josephine Lataillaof stabbed Alice Marshall fatally in the back and head. Two and a half hours later, twelve blocks away on 125th Street, Clemmon Pettway Jr. picked up a kitchen knife during another argument and killed his father, Clemmon Pettway Sr.

That Friday began a week of a record 58 slayings in New York City. It came after two weeks of rainy, muggy days. As much rain fell in the first half of July as normally falls in an average whole month of July. On Thursday the 13th a record three inches fell. Then the heat set in. Heat and humidity. Each day the temperature hung in the high 80s or low 90s. At night the heat sometimes let up a little but the humidity kept the air dank. On Monday night at 10:10 Con Ed blacked out Bay Ridge, Sunset Park and other sections of Brooklyn. Later in the week, on Thursday, New Yorkers consumed an unprecedented 2.4 billion gallons of water, compared with 1.4 billion on a normal hot summer day. It was a week when almost everybody hated to be in New York.

Of course, the city gets horrible stretches of weather every summer, sometimes worse than this one. Yet this week's record 58 killings were not a surprise to the police. They know the city is experiencing a rising homicide rate: 1,466 homicides last year, up from 1,117 in 1970, 746 in 1967, 314 in 1957. For the first six months of this year the rate is up another 20 per cent. Peak summer weeks in the last few years have often run to 40 murders. It was only a question of when the right weather would shoot the total up over 50. In fact, for the ten-day period ending July 23, the Chief Medical Examiner recorded 74 homicides—three less than occurred all last year in London, a city of a size comparable to ours. "The sad fact is," says Detective James Ray, who works in Harlem, "we have very little regard for human life here, and we seem to be getting less all the time."

At 12:45 on Saturday morning, July 15, Charles Diaz walked into his room at the Franklin Arms Hotel in Brooklyn and found Elijah Jones robbing it. Jones came at Diaz swinging a pipe. Diaz replied by slitting open Jones's right side with a knife he says was on the night table. Jones ran out in the street and fell down dying. Five minutes later, at the Lincoln Houses project on upper Madison Avenue in Manhattan, Nathanial Watkins tried to rob an off-duty state correction officer named Lawrence Brockington, who emptied his pistol into

NOTE: *Although the weapons shown here are not the actual ones used in each homicide, they have been supplied by the Police Department as characteristic of such weapons.*

FRIDAY, JULY 14, 1972

Time: 12:30 a.m.
Victim: Sydney (last name unknown)
Place: Northwest corner Flushing & Throop Aves., Bklyn.
Weapon: Knife

Time: 12:58 a.m.
Victim: Wilson Louis Rodriguez
Place: 514 Richmond Terrace, S.I.
Weapon: Wooden club

Time: 5:00 p.m.
Victim: Alice Marshall
Place: 165 Lenox Ave.
Weapon: Knife

Time: 7:30 p.m.
Victim: Clemmon Pettway Sr.
Place: 430 West 125th St.
Weapon: Kitchen knife

Time: Unknown
Victim: Lawrence Brown
Place: Unknown
Weapon: Knife

Time: Unknown
Victim: Charles Samuel
Place: Unknown
Weapon: Knife

Time: Unknown
Victim: Roger Harrel
Place: Unknown
Weapon: Knife

SATURDAY, JULY 15, 1972

Time: 12:45 a.m.
Victim: Elijah Jones Jr.
Place: Franklin Arms Hotel, Bklyn.
Weapon: Knife

24 NEW YORK

Photographed by Matthew Klein

New York
28 August 1972
design director
Milton Glaser
art director Walter Bernard
The editorial story supplemented by deceptively simple graphic imagery was a regular feature of New York. The typographic format was very regular, based on the forceful contrast between slab serif heads and the (then) ubiquitous Times Roman standfirst. Overlaid on this was the paraphernalia of raised capitals, column rules, vertical rules and scotch-ruled running heads. The layout was rigidly symmetrical throughout the magazine. The photographs here were by Matthew Klein.

Esquire

March 1983

art director Robert Priest

Priest belongs to the school of typographer-designers. The headline face is custom cut for use at banner sizes. The two pages of the spread are separated out by box rules, although the positioning of the beautiful extended capital "C" in relation to the photograph serves to re-integrate the pages. The picture is by Brian Griffin, staged with his usual technical virtuosity.

NOTHING AROUND CAT CAY IS FASTER THAN BLUEFIN TUNA—EXCEPT FOR MASTER CAPTAIN GARY STUVE.

ESQUIRE/MARCH 1983 64

THE SPORTING LIFE

The Million-Dollar Fish Hunt

Competitors in the Cat Cay Tuna Tournament spend vast fortunes in pursuit of a quarry that has all but disappeared

by *Fred Waitzkin*

Cat Cay is an island of sea-blown fragrances, beating sun, pleasant salutations, fine wines, and French cuisine—the trappings of privilege and unlimited wealth. The few dozen millionaire retreats here are sequestered within groves of imported plants and trees, manicured by congenial Bahamian gardeners to effect a wild and untouched lushness. Doors are never locked on Cat Cay—the only intruders are flocks of wild turkeys. Vanderbilts and Phippses stroll dreamy, palm-shaded pathways between luxurious homes, and Bebe Rebozo strides the golf course beside his tanned and carefree guest Richard Nixon, without a bodyguard in sight.

Once a year this tranquil island sixty miles east of Miami becomes the base for the most violent and highly specialized of all big-game fishing. Each spring, pods of Atlantic bluefin tuna migrate across the calm Gulf of Mexico past the Riding Rocks and push north along the Bimini chain like fleets of small submarines. As the mammoth fish near Cat Cay, high-powered, custom-built sport-fishing boats cross the Gulf Stream to rendezvous with the boat owners—some of the wealthiest men in the world, who fly from distant places in private jets, seaplanes, and helicopters to compete against one another for five days in the Cat Cay Tuna Tournament. Many of them consider Cat Cay the crowning jewel in a Grand Prix circuit of big-game fishing. For these super-rich boat owners, the year is a succession of tournaments—a fervent, global pursuit of huge migrating fish. In July you'll find them trolling the fifty-fathom drop-off north of Tortola in the Virgin Islands for blue marlin. In August there is broadbill swordfishing off Nantucket. In the fall the men jet to Australia to live for weeks aboard opulent yachts a hundred miles from port and fish in the afternoon for thousand-pound black marlin, within view of the breaking Great Barrier Reef. They are stateside again in time to catch the sailfish run off Palm Beach in January and February.

Whenever possible, these peripatetic sportsmen prefer to fish with their own crews on their own boats, which takes planning and tremendous amounts of money. (Aside from an original outlay of, say, $750,000 for boat and tackle, operating expenses may come to $10,000 for a week of fishing.) One boat owner who enjoys fishing for striped marlin in the Pacific arranges for his boat to be towed thousands of miles from Florida through the Panama Canal by a 112-foot yacht. Another boat owner sent his million-dollar sport-fishing boat

Fred Waitzkin is a fiction writer and journalist who lives and writes in New York City.

65 ESQUIRE/MARCH 1983

Esquire

August 1980

art director Robert Priest

Given the multiplicity of typographic elements in this spread it is surprisingly successful; its cohesion is achieved largely through the continuation of the steps of Blair Drawson's triptych into the standfirst. Each component of the layout is squared off by hairline rules; there are some seven or eight gradations of type in script, roman and italic, all capitals, small capitals, and upper and lower case. In the construction and catholic selection of type Priest utilized the capabilities of phototypesetting to the full.

LOVE LETTERS *from* OLYMPUS

by RONALD STEEL

Walter Lippmann was the godhead of American journalism, correct in public manner, incisive in judgment, firm in moral purpose. In his late forties, he fell deeply in love with the wife of his best friend.

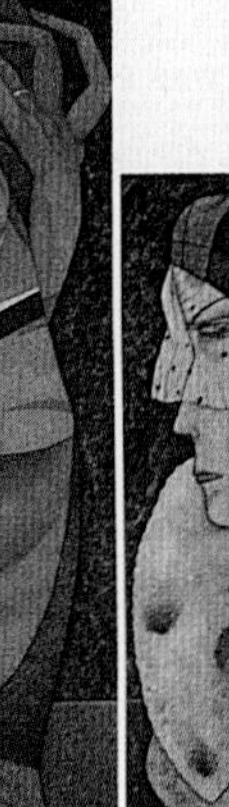

WALTER LIPPMANN (1889–1974) was without doubt the nation's greatest journalist. His was, as the critic Van Wyck Brooks once said, the "most brilliant career ever devoted in America to political writing." Lippmann began his career in the halcyon days before the First World War, when human progress seemed unlimited and inevitable, when poets danced in the squares and science promised a life of leisure and abundance for all. He ended it with the trauma of Vietnam, the shame of Watergate, and the panic of rioters running through the streets. His career spanned a century during which the American empire was born, matured, and began to founder—a time that some have called, first boastfully, then wistfully, the American Century.

As a small boy in the 1890s, Walter Lippmann shook hands with President McKinley, was formally presented to Admiral Dewey, and rapturously cheered Theodore Roosevelt on his return from San Juan Hill. He studied at Harvard with George Santayana, took tea with William James, worked as a legman for Lincoln Steffens, debated socialism with Bernard Shaw and H. G. Wells; he was in Belgium when the Germans invaded and in the House of Commons when Britain declared war in 1914. For a time he worshiped Theodore Roosevelt, and when he was twenty-five TR pronounced him "the most brilliant young man of his age in all the United States." He was a founder of *The New Republic* and one of the movers and shakers who sounded the trumpet for a cultural and social revolution in America before World War I. He became the éminence grise to Woodrow Wilson's own alter ego, Colonel House, and he was a key member of the secret organization that produced the territorial portion of the Fourteen Points.

Ronald Steel is the author of Pax Americana *and writes frequently on American politics. His latest book, from which this article is excerpted, is* Walter Lippmann and the American Century, *forthcoming from Atlantic–Little, Brown.*

Enthusiastically supporting the war to make the world safe for democracy, Lippmann bitterly denounced the peace that within a generation spawned an even more terrible conflict. He became editor of the greatest newspaper of its day, Pulitzer's *World*, the voice of America's liberal conscience. High in a tower above Park Row, protected from telephones and reporters by a shield of secretaries, he penned for more than nine years the biting editorials that first made him a national figure. None of these editorials were signed, and few are remembered today; but for the devoted readers of the *World*, they bore their own special stamp.

INDEED, LIPPMANN WAS anything but anonymous. When he traveled, as he did in great style for a part of every year, he conferred with heads of state. Often they sought him out, eager for the privilege of being interviewed by a man who commanded so many faithful and influential readers. As a colleague once said, his was "the name that opened every door." On a trip to Greece in the mid-1950s, for example, he jotted in his private engagement book: "Saw the King, the prime minister, etc.—the usual people." For him, they were a part of the common run. Eschewing scoops and scorning planted leaks, which he thought unworthy of a serious commentator, he ruminated on the meaning of events in a column that was required reading in every chancellery, foreign office, and editorial room.

For nearly forty years, his syndicated column appeared in the leading newspapers of the United States and the world. When he went into semiretirement in 1967, it was as though an institution had suddenly ceased to exist. Three generations had been led through the maze of political affairs by Walter Lippmann. He was not always right, and he was not universally popular. His rare gaffes—such as his early dismissal of Franklin D. Roosevelt as a well-meaning playboy—were memorable. His occasional enmities—such as his bitter feud with Lyndon Johnson over the Vietnam War—were monumental.

Readers turned to Lippmann not for solutions but for dispassionate analysis. He had a marvelous ability to simplify the complex. His extraordinary success sprang from two qualities: a mind that could plunge through the miasma of contention to grasp the

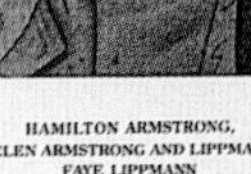

HAMILTON ARMSTRONG, HELEN ARMSTRONG AND LIPPMANN, FAYE LIPPMANN

ESQUIRE/AUGUST 1980 50 51 ESQUIRE/AUGUST 1980

THURSDAY tv

BBC1

5.15 pm: Apollo docks with Soyuz over Germany. 6.02 pm: Slayton opens hatch 1 and begins first of four crew transfers. 8.18 pm: as the spacecraft is passing over Soviet Territory, Stafford opens hatch 3 to the Soyuz orbital module, and exchanges initial greetings with Leonov and Kubasov. Then he and Slayton transfer to Soyuz, where they have a meal and begin joint experiments. 10.30 pm: Stafford and Slayton return to the docking module

Spacefood
The US Astronauts planned their own food for each 'eat period' before the mission started. This is tonight's meal (left) for Command Module Pilot Brand, who remains in the CM while the others are in the Soyuz eating from the selection of food available in the Soviet spacecraft which includes Shchi (Cabbage Soup), Kharcho (Georgian Soup), Tongue, Rye Bread, Honey Cakes, Prunes, Nuts, Cottage Cheese, Blackcurrant Conserve with Cream, Tea, Sweets, Chilled Water. All these items are eaten directly from tubes and tins, and can be heated if necessary

*Mixed with hot water from the CM water gun and kneaded in their plastic wraps until ready to eat

FEATURE P4

1.0 pm Llangollen 1975
International Musical Eisteddfod
(First shown on BBC Wales)

1.30 Ragtime
with MAGGIE HENDERSON and FRED HARRIS
(Repeat)

1.45 News
Weatherman MICHAEL FISH
1.53 Closedown
3.58 Regional News (exc London)

4.0 Play School
A programme for children under 5
(Shown on BBC2 at 11.0 am)

4.25 Pixie and Dixie and Yogi Bear
Two cartoons
(Repeat)

BBC1 Variations

4.40 *New series* **Newsround Extra**
John Craven and the *Newsround* team begin a series of special news reports. *The End of the Space Race?*
With only minutes to go to the planned moment of link-up between Soyuz and Apollo, space correspondent REG TURNILL in America, and JOHN CRAVEN in the *Newsround* studio, present a live report on the background to this historic meeting in space.
Why did Russia and America decide to co-operate instead of competing with each other? What is the future for space travel now?

5.5 Apollo/Soyuz
The Docking
Live coverage of the tensest minutes of the Apollo/Soyuz Mission as the two spacecraft inch towards a meeting 138 miles above Europe. The docking is more than the connection of two objects in space. It represents the merging of two technologies into a single living space for five men.
Presented by **James Burke**

5.40 Sir Prancelot
(Repeat)

5.45 National News
with Richard Whitmore
Weatherman

6.0 Nationwide
Look North, South Today
Look East, Midlands Today
Points West, Spotlight South West
News, interviews and analysis from your region tonight, including local weather

6.45 A Question of Sport
Questionmaster **David Vine** featuring 50 years of world sporting action
Henry Cooper and **Cliff Morgan** return to captain two teams of sporting celebrities who will be puzzling over faces, places and voices from the history of sport.
Guests this week include
Ann Jones, Brian Barnes
Brian Brinkley, Barry Richards

7.15 Top of the Pops
Discs, stars and the news from this week's Top Thirty
Introduced by **Dave Lee Travis**
TOP OF THE POPS ORCHESTRA
Musical director JOHNNY PEARSON
PAN'S PEOPLE

7.50 Apollo/Soyuz
'Privyet, Alexei'
'Greetings to you, too, Tom'
The climax of the ten-day Mission as astronauts TOM STAFFORD and DEKE SLAYTON swing open the last hatch in the Docking Module and reach out to greet Soviet cosmonauts ALEXEI LEONOV and VALERI KUBASOV.
James Burke introduces the live coverage with the aid of a full-scale replica of the docked spacecraft.

The political detail is filled in by film interviews with senior administrators of both programmes.
Dr James C. Fletcher (NASA) and **Prof Boris Petrov** (Chairman of the Intercosmos Committee of the Soviet Academy of Sciences) explain how this once unthinkable event came not only to be thinkable but a necessary part of the Nixon-Kosygin détente agreement.

TELEVISION FOR 17 JULY

Radio Times

12 July 1975

art director David Driver

Peter Brookes' and Nigel Holmes' technical charts and diagrams were the perfect complement to the BBC's informative programme-making. David Driver insisted on a high degree of accuracy from the illustrators and this was combined with a popular style reminiscent of English comic illustration of the 1950s. In this example, one page of a week's television listings focusing on the Soyuz/ Apollo spacecraft linkup, the illustration is tied to the programme information through graphic symbols. Holmes later reinvigorated the chart-making department at Time magazine.

headline face was specially designed by Pelegrini & Kaestle. Glaser gave type further prominence, opting for serifs rather than the butch Egyptian, with a more complex three-deck headline, credit and standfirst; the page design was "more rigorously structured"[17] in three columns, and busier. There were more, smaller pictures in a format suited to the fortnightly which *Esquire* had become, with a corresponding increase in news content. Robert Priest's design was much more ornate, approaching the style of what we now call the post-modern magazine. Photography was superseded by illustration, which Priest commissioned with skill, employing many English illustrators he had known from the *Radio Times*. However, each element of the page was rigorously separated out, squared off and boxed by column rules. Typography was fussy with scotch and split rules, drop caps, small caps, indefinite articles in headlines picked out in script, emboldened first lines, and body text set in dog-legs around quotes. Over the next four years the typographic constructions in Century Old Style and Modern became ever more elaborate.

Milton Glaser and Walter Bernard are the best known exponents of this boxed, over-ruled style although this hardly characterizes their recent work which is less formal. However in numerous re-designs for news-oriented magazines, and for magazines which had reduced in size and increased periodicity, this was their dominant method of working. The design systems they evolved were pragmatic, stressing altered reading habits and the necessity to design for production, and this tended to lead towards two-dimensional, rectangular layout – practical but lacking in dynamic force. Glaser's *New York*, for example, was designed according to an assumed attention span of seven minutes, which, he said, "coincided exactly with the interval between television commercials during most TV programmes. So we designed *New York* to be read by somebody with that temperament, for the television generation. It had constant interruptions – headlines, subheads on every page, everything was designed for easy access."[18]

Both before and after they teamed up in 1983 to form WBMG, Glaser and Bernard dominated magazine design in the 1970s and early 1980s as hired design and editorial consultants to a vast number of magazines in the USA and Europe. Bernard was assistant art director of *Esquire*, art director of *Time*, and redesigned *Adweek*, *Atlantic Monthly* and *Fortune*. Glaser was design director of *Village Voice*, founder and designer of *New York* magazine (from 1968), redesigned *Esquire* and *Paris Match*; as WBMG the two restyled *Jardin des Modes*, *L'Europeo*, *New West*, *L'Express*, *Manhattan Inc.*, *Channels*, *Washington Post Magazine*, *Lire*, etc. Their style was watched and copied relentlessly, especially by business, trade and state magazines (the latter often emulated *New York* down to the last typographical detail). Both in Europe and America this was ultimately deeply damaging, as magazines became bound by a formulaic tyranny of

Design

January 1984

designer Keith Ablitt

When he reformatted Design in 1983, Keith Ablitt exploited the technology to minimize the number of typesizes required to direct the reader around the page. Emphasis was given by reversing type out of black or underlining, rather than by changing size or weight. Captions were identified by a solid rectangular dingbat. Ablitt also drew up a grid which related screen area to pre-set codes, enabling layout instructions to be transmitted by telephone.

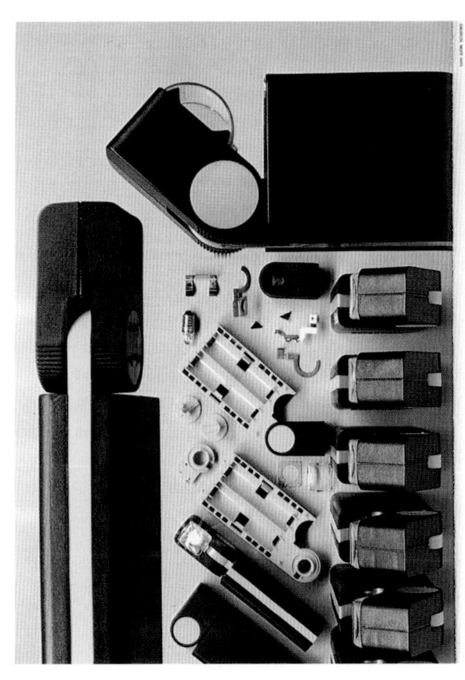

Design management The development of the flip-top Durabeam torch had its hitches. But the product is a success, financially, functionally and aesthetically. How was this achieved? Jane Lott reports

Flip-top torch

'You couldn't get a better brief.' John Drane of BIB, the designers of the flip-top Durabeam torch, which is proving to be a best seller just nine months after its launch, is unstinting in [illegible] break a new product: the client.

In this case the client was Duracell UK and the brief written by Bob Winstone, the company's marketing manager. Duracell has rapidly become established in the battery market in Europe from its US base, taking something like 25 per cent of available consumer cash with its expensive, long-lasting and well-promoted little bundles of alkaline cells. Winstone wanted to diversify somewhat, starting with a product that would show there was more to the European wing of the company than batteries, but which would aid the company by being battery-powered.

A torch? Winstone did not want to use the connotation-carrying word and so limit imaginative thinking. Instead his brief – sent to three design consultants after consultation with Michael Bungay, Duracell's advertising agency – asked for a 'battery-operated light source', in three sizes. The name of Durabeam had been selected. Other requirements were that the device should be of good quality construction, be free-standing when put down and have a directional beam.

There were non-functional requirements too: Winstone 'wanted to go out on a limb', to escape what he perceived as the staid, old-fashioned, reliable but unprogressive image of other UK torch manufacturers. Therefore, the new device was to be associated, through its imagery, with the shiny Duracell 'modern technological style and presence', as the marketing department put it. And the price was to be high, 'but not prohibitive'.

Duracell manufactures batteries in Crawley, Sussex, and in Belgium. But it is primarly a sales and marketing organisation, with no other products, and certainly not equipped to run a consumer product launch. It wanted both design and manufacturing supervision from its selected design consultancy. On the other hand, Winstone was not going simply to hand the project over. 'I felt it was very much my responsibility', he explains.

Why does Drane consider the brief such a good one? 'Because it was specific, yet open; it invited clear ideas. Most briefs have to be untangled before you can start.' Most managers, he adds, don't do their homework to prepare a thorough briefing document. For example, Winstone not only did not say that he wanted a torch, he also did not say specifically that he wanted the device to be free-standing. Instead, he observed in the brief that a problem with torches is they are not free-standing. How the designers he approached interpreted the oblique point would obviously help in selecting the final one to carry out the job.

BIB responded not with a specific design but with a eight-page document detailing the 10 phases through which it steered jobs, from initial concept to managing the first stage of production, and added a general presentation of previous work. 'BIB didn't understand the brief any better than other consultancies,' says Winstone, 'but their approach was very organised, very structured, and their previous work was good.'

When BIB proposed a choice of concepts in the autumn of 1980, with sketches and simple block models, Winstone and the project team that had been set up (it included Duracell's European quality assurance manager and European engineering manager, along with Winstone and BIB) immediately took to the flip-top device, 'even though we hadn't exactly figured out the way it would work', as Drane put it.

This meant that an element of the unknown, even rashness, had now entered the design process. Duracell removed some of it by market researching the proposal, in case simple, cheap cylindrical torches proved to be unassailable. The public turned out to be sophisticated enough to prefer the flip-top torch to others tested by a huge majority, and gave a clue about price too: roundabout £3 for a pocket version, about £4 for a medium-sized one. The reassurance was welcome, since Winstone had by now persuaded Duracell Europe to invest the £70 000 or so needed for design development.

In February 1981, BIB was given the go-ahead. Duracell wanted the product ready for market testing by October of that year, a data BIB thought impossible to achieve. Winstone thinks that Duracell's inexperience in handling consumer product manufacture 'meant a lot of mistakes' – an exaggerated view of the problems actually encountered.

For example, the materials in which the phosphorbronze sliding contacts (they cause the light to come on when the torch is opened) were plated, nickel and tin, turned out to be incompatible at three volts. To discover this and change the plating accordingly, as well as sorting out precise details of the plastics moulding to the high standard demanded by Duracell, took nine more months than had been allowed. A Kent company, Insulators, had been selected to make the mouldings and assemble the torches because of its high quality control standards and the reputation of work it did for Black & Decker. In the course of devising the black abs and yellow acetal mouldings, Drane produced several details that have now been patented: the positive ratchet action in the head of the torch and the spring ears concealed inside the head's round acetal hinge, for example.

Bob Winstone, remembers Drane, chaired virtually every single meeting and recorded detailed points about production – 'not the sort of thing marketing people usually do'. It must surely have been this close concern with the torch which gives the product its compulsive charm. Its purity of line is qualified by a brash adaptation of the Duracell house colours, but since this produces vivid colour symbolism of the nature of the torch, it is hard to complain.

The public certainly thought so: after a well-orchestrated launch (which achieved, if by the skin of its teeth, the set date of autumn 1982 – 70 per cent of all torch sales take place in the winter four months of the year) sales were almost bang on target. Half a million torches needed to be sold. The reason that only 450 000 made it across the counter was a shortfall in production; there was never a chance to stockpile the pocket size while the ... six weeks late on delivery (the largest size had been postponed). Insufficient time had been allowed to get production flowing smoothly. Now production is normal but, says Winstone, 'we could have sold a lot more torches during that period'.

On the other hand, he acknowledges that Duracell is the sort of company that 'fixes a date and in order to meet it, solves problems as we go along, rather than waiting till everything is perfect but missing the sales boat'. He also feels that at the end of the day 'BIB provided us with an extremely innovative design, and I'd be happy to look for that from BIB again'.

Armed with this success, Duracell wants more. A lantern-sized product will follow, and there may be other, non-lighting, projects. Will they be managed differently? 'We would want to get very much closer to a manufacturer from the start,' says Winstone, 'and we would like that manufacturer to be closer to our product area so it could make a stronger input.'

As well as the design development costs for the Durabeam there were capital costs of £130–£140 000 and higher marketing costs. With the product now earning in the region of £90 000 a month, the Durabeam will clearly have little problem paying for itself. If there were technical problems it was at least partly because of the innovative nature of the design: in the end they were not too hard to sort out. The point is that an exciting design was clearly sought and carefully pursued, and that it is a welcome, as well as a profitable, addition to the world of products.

Externally, the addictive flip-top Durabeam is a deceptively simple compact block. The kit of complex acetyl and electrical parts that are its components – partly shown here – fits together as snugly as any three-dimensional puzzle

Photography by Howard Kingsnorth

City Limits
February 1983
designer David King

David King's interest in constructivist typography developed through researches at The Sunday Times. At the London listings magazine City Limits he applied the constructivist dynamic to cover and layout design. In this cover, the "war of words" has become just that, with a plethora of cover lines skewed off grid, bold rule underlines and a crowd of full and half faces inserted into the type.

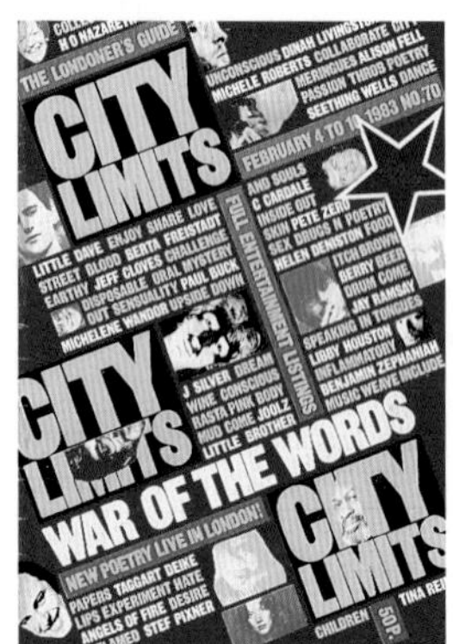

column rules and boring rectangles which may have been well suited to the news format but were hardly appropriate to each and every feature magazine.

In America, by the late 1970s, magazine design was dominated by fusspot typography and flat graphic construction; magazines lacked spontaneity and intensity. In Europe, likewise, before 1980 there were precious few sparks of inventiveness, with a very few outstanding exceptions. All that remained in the wake of the almost complete collapse of the British underground press[19] in 1973 were a few campaigning local magazines, including the *New Edinburgh Review*, *Manchester Review*, and foremost among them, *Time Out*. The London listings magazine was a direct descendant of the underground; its proprietor, Tony Elliott, had been a street seller of *OZ* (and like most of his colleagues, a putative capitalist), and its designer, Pearce Marchbank, a contributor to *OZ* and art director of *Friends*. Marchbank redesigned *Time Out* in 1970 and remained as art director until 1972, whereupon he continued to direct cover design for some years. Although notable for the tight typography of its listing pages the magazine is best remembered for those covers, which were a rare European example of the seamless fusion of words and images in the punning, expressionist mould. Marchbank was equally at home with staged photography, collage, illustration and purely typographic treatments; they were an object lesson in the cover as poster, simply and powerfully executed, and often to extremely tight deadlines.

Also in London, Terry Jones singlehandedly upheld the montage tradition during his tenure at *Vanity Fair* (1970-71) and British *Vogue* (1972-77). At Condé Nast, he developed the rough, spontaneous style based on print production techniques – montage, stencil, naive calligraphy – that later evolved as "instant-design". Full-colour montage of varied scale fashion photography gave strong depth of perspective and representation of movement – but it was phenomenally expensive. Jones had the gall to blow up a Polaroid SX70 test shot by Toscani for the cover of *Vogue*,[20] and the graphic look was so strong that eventually advertisers began to complain. Keith Ablitt, who had worked with Jones at *Vogue*, later became art director at *Design* (in 1978) which he invigorated in the modernist style established by Garland and Grimbley, and his predecessor Peter Baistow. However, on reformatting the magazine in 1983 Ablitt made a conscious departure from *Design*'s rationalist tradition, replacing the various weights of Univers used for text, standfirsts and heads with its antithesis – Century Schoolbook – which in the heads and running heads was reversed out of black to give emphasis. The new face, chosen as "everyman's letter", for its "familiar, immediate, and un-

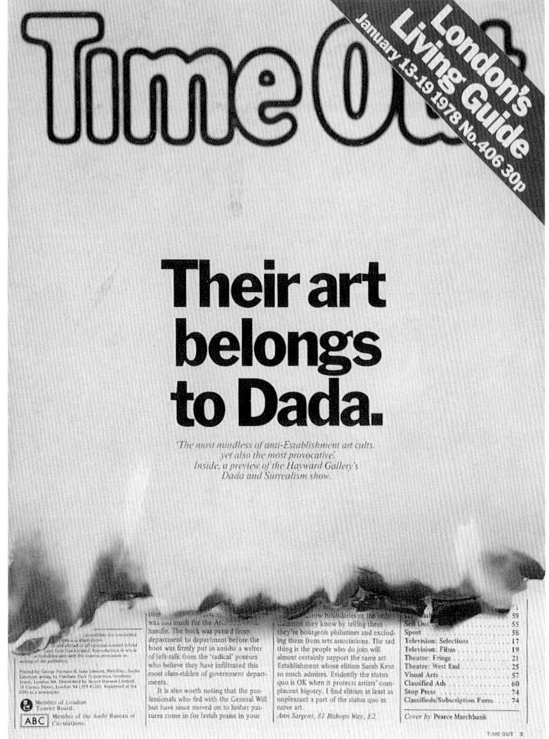

Time Out
13-19 January 1978
designer Pearce Marchbank

A fine example of lateral problem-solving used to telegraph an oblique editorial subject. Charged with publicizing a review of a major exhibition of Dada and surrealism, Pearce Marchbank commits a Dada act on the cover. Below the "burnt" area is an exact facsimile of the contents list on the turn page. Given that Time Out was a weekly and the contents page is the last to be passed for press, the production problems involved in such a feat can only be imagined.

intimidating" form, signified the destruction of one shibboleth of modernist dogma.[21]

Throughout this decade the *Radio Times*, designed by David Driver,[22] provided another rare thread of continuity with the moral didacticism of the 1960s, with an unrivalled commitment to public education and information which echoed the priorities of the BBC at that time. In what was to all intents and purposes a mere TV listings magazine (but also the top selling magazine in the UK) Driver, with illustrators Nigel Holmes[23] and Peter Brookes, broke new ground in information graphics; he also commissioned fine illustration and caricature from Frank Bellamy, Richard Draper, Russell Mills, Fluck & Law, Ralph Steadman and Adrian George – some of the names which Robert Priest took with him to *Esquire*.

In continental Europe, too, the publishing industry had been weakened, if not so severely as in England. There were positive developments at the German *Stern*, art directed by Wolfgang Behnken from 1971 to the time of writing, making him one of the longest-serving art directors in international publishing, and at the French Filipacchi group, under the creative direction of Regis Pagniez and Jean Demachy. Very much in the Fleckhaus mould, Behnken's *Stern* was politically and graphically aggressive, an exemplar of pictorial information design. It combined memorable if exhibitionist covers in the best traditions of yellow journalism, with dynamic layout built using the widest spectrum of graphic techniques. The art direction was extremely well thought out for a weekly magazine. Filipacchi's *Lui* and *Photo* tended towards a simpler graphic approach which relied on the quality of illustration and photography by the likes of Giacobetti and Toscani, together with a dramatic primary colour sense typical of the French style.

The Netherlands, which had a relatively small commercial market was, nevertheless, blessed by a very lively cultural scene which encouraged experimentation in a period in which designers elsewhere were bound by publishers' fears of failure. The country also possessed a strong and unbroken tradition of radical and nonconformist modernism. A small underground press was established in Amsterdam in the late 1960s, with Willem de Ridder's eclectic and ever-changing *Aloha*, the psychedelic *Hitweek*, and the hand-tinted and revivalist *Hollands Diep*; the latter two both large format, both designed by Anton Beeke. *Avenue*, the Amsterdam events magazine, was (and remains) notable for its inspired cover design. Piet Schreuders' covers for the cultural magazine and comic book combination *Furore* (1975-82) were something of a pastiche of early twentieth-century styles, but very knowingly executed. Overall, Dutch graphic design in

Vogue (UK)
January 1977
art director Terry Jones

Terry Jones' improvised design technique, using stencils, graph paper and montage, had an air of inspired spontaneity. This was a popular adaptation of modernism, working in opposition to the crafted perfectionism of contemporary designers striving to revive traditional typestyles.

Stern

no. 15 1973

art director Wolfgang Behnken

Below: Stern's lurid covers were an important contributor to the magazine's massive circulation. Behnken used seamless montage and staged photography to create bizarre images, relying especially on the power of sex to sell. This is one of his simpler ideas: Willy Brandt transfomed into Karl Marx by a garish lick of paint.

the 1970s was intellectually well in advance of the English and Americans. While English designers were struggling in 1980 and afterwards for a basic grasp of early modern design history, often superficially re-learning and re-applying the old discoveries, the Dutch demonstrated a mature understanding of constructivism and the principles and function of plastic dynamism. The arresting graphic synthesis achieved by the Wild Plakken group (Rob Schroder, Lies Ros, Frank Beekers) in the cinema magazine *Skrien* (1977-85) serves to emphasize this point. It preceded Neville Brody's earliest magazine work – which is broadly comparable – by some five years, but with its narrow Dutch audience this magazine was in the wrong place at the wrong time and, much is the pity, had no influence whatsoever on graphic design outside Holland.

These magazines were exceptions. The charmless mass of trade and consumer publications was under too strong pressure from advertising and budgets to attract design talent – if it was wanted – and most of the old school had departed editorial work. Modernist discipline, which might have minimized the effects of this plague of mediocrity, had tended to break down under the weight of revivalism, while the new photo- and digital-typesetting systems were promoting the distortion and misuse of type by inexperienced designers. Some kind of simplifying and renewing force was required. And fortunately, along came punk.

Punk was an artistic, social and quasi-political movement which emerged from English art schools in 1976 and 1977. Without digging too deeply into its philosophical and demographic roots it is sufficient to say that it was autarkic, nihilistic and individualistic – all fairly conventional petit-bourgeois characteristics. Punk was primarily an expression of contempt for the previous generation which, promising so much, had capitulated politically and (worse?) allowed the appropriation of radical culture by corporate business. Correspondingly, it was an attempt to wrest individual control. There has been some discussion as to whether punk was a political or art movement: if the former it had no enduring significance whatsoever, although some elements looked to the Situationist International, and others became involved in movements against unemployment and racism; as the latter, it was iconoclastic and provocative, and successfully destroyed the complacency manifest in music, fashion and the graphic arts. However, if we consider punk as a consumer movement it was supremely successful. Ultimately, punk was packaged for consumption as easily as the hippies had been, and magazines such as *The Face* – "the best-dressed magazine" – played an integral part

Stern

c. 1972

art director Wolfgang Behnken

Right: this feature opening is very much in the German school of studied vulgarity: grotesque and salacious art after Bosch; an opening quotation as big as a headline, set very tight in the Erhardt extra bold popularized by Fleckhaus.

Papst Paul VI. am 15. November 1972:

»Wir alle stehen unter einer finsteren Herrschaft, der des Teufels, des Fürsten dieser Welt, des Feindes Nummer eins. Dieses dunkle und beunruhigende Wesen gibt es wirklich«

Der Teufel lebt, die Hölle ist wieder offen. Ein finsteres Wesen, so weiß der Papst, schleicht durch diese Welt. Es könne uns im Jenseits schlimme Qualen bereiten. Nicht nur der Papst, Herr über 600 Millionen katholische Christen, malt wieder den Teufel an die Wand. Englands Staatskirche will offizielle Geisterbeschwörer ausbilden. In Italien, Frankreich und Deutschland mehren sich Berichte über Teufelsaustreibungen. In Amerika wuchern Satanssekten. Okkultes, Magisches, Dämonisches fasziniert Millionen, rührt an geheimen Ängsten, spült verschüttete Phantasien ans Licht. Stürzt unsere Welt wieder zurück ins Mittelalter?

Das heutige Gesicht des Teufels wird geprägt von Sex, Rauschgift und Alkohol – sagt der Papst

Der Teufel kommt wieder!

Skrien

October/November 1982

designers
Wild Plakken group

Cover montage by Beekers, Ros and Schroder as a graphic representation of film noir.

Skrien

November 1978

designers
Wild Plakken group

A political, typographic and pictorial sense inherited from the constructivists was an important strand in Dutch graphic design, and was promoted by the teaching of Jan van Toorn at the Rietveld Academy, where Skrien designers Frank Beekers, Lies Ros and Rob Schroder studied. These two spreads from the avant-garde cinema magazine show a mature appreciation of the visual dynamic of constructivism. The same structure, but not always the same substance, was popularized in British music magazines after 1982.

JORIS IVENS

Bert Hogenkamp

'Onderwijs de mensen niet te veel over me, laat ze zelf ontdekken wie J. I. is. — Geen raadsels, maar respecteer hun intelligentie, gevoeligheid — de tentoonstelling is als het ware een dialoog met de 'bezoeker' — alsof ze een goede documentaire film ervaren. (...) Laat de intensiteit, de integriteit, de consequentheid zien wanneer je leeft naar je eigen geweten'. Een fragment uit een brief die Joris Ivens schreef aan de samenstellers van de grote tentoonstelling die gedurende de maand november, ter gelegenheid van Ivens' tachtigste verjaardag, in het Filmmuseum te zien is. Bert Hogenkamp was één van die samenstellers. Hieronder doet hij verslag van zijn ervaringen.

Een mooie julimorgen. In een hotel in Amsterdam-Zuid heb ik een afspraak met Joris Ivens om te praten over het boek over de Borinage-film dat ik met Henri Storck aan het voorbereiden ben. Joris vindt het prima wat we doen. Hij is even enthousiast over Storcks grote vondst, de complete fotocollectie van Willy Kessels, als ikzelf. We praten over militaire dienst; ik ben net afgezwaaid. We komen tot de ontdekking dat we allebei in Ede gelegerd geweest zijn. Ivens bij de veldartillerie, zo'n kleine zestig jaar geleden, en ik bij de luchtdoelartillerie. Ivens vertelt over de tentoonstelling over zijn werk die men bij het Filmmuseum aan het voorbereiden is, en waar hij speciaal voor naar Nederland gekomen is. Ook is hij erg blij met het project van een groep studenten en docenten uit Leiden die van plan zijn het Ivens-archief te gaan ordenen. Hij vraagt me of ik meer weet over een film die hij eind jaren twintig in Drente gemaakt had. Met Leo van Lakerveld en Han Pieck. We gaan naar het Vondelpark, het gebouw van het Nederlands Filmmuseum. Ivens laat me een foto uit 'Het Leven' zien: met zijn Kinamo-camera filmt hij een groepje kinderen. Uiterst rechts in beeld is de hoed en de hand van een andere man te zien. Ik beloof in wat kranten en tijdschriften te duiken om meer gegevens over de Drente-film te vinden. Een paar dagen later ben ik terug in het Filmmuseum, met een stapeltje

New Sounds New Styles
7 January 1982
art director Malcolm Garrett

A return to the roots of modern graphic design re-applied to late twentieth-century music and style. This spread receives its graphic strength from the bold rules and strong verticals – including the headline with its mismatched type – and is given cohesion by the rectangular and circular tints. The attention of the eye is forced from the headline to the hand symbol at the centre of the spread.

in this process by establishing a superficial currency of style, dressed up as a marketable commodity.

In graphic design punk resumed the explorations which had tentatively begun in the underground press and were abruptly curtailed in 1972. The word punk, however, defines a very short period in which the primary concern was self reliance, and therefore the celebration of graphic forms which required little or no production equipment – through the replacement of metal or photo-set type with handmarks, stencil and typewriter, and unstructured layout together with the use of found images removed from their conventional context and subverted to a new purpose. This was the modus operandi of the home-made fanzines, such as *Sniffin' Glue, Situation,* and *48 Thrills*, which embodied the autarkic philosophy of punk. A renewed intellectual interest in Dada and the symbolism of pop art satisfied both material and ideological preoccupations, and provoked further interest in early modern design, which was expressed by the first post-punk graduates to enter commercial publishing, initially in the music industry in record cover design – and immediately afterwards in magazines, where designers strove to break free of the self-imposed limits which elsewhere in this book are called the "letterpress mentality". The stylistic impulse of punk served to promote experiment in integrated and free forms of layout, with colour and with new printing techniques. All of the components of production required to do that were now firmly established in commercial publishing: i.e., phototypesetting, drum digital scanners, and web-offset lithography.

Smash Hits, the teenage music magazine launched in 1978, was the first to exploit the new taste for vivid graphic imagery. The magazine's successful and highly fragmented editorial formula (in 1990 it was the tenth biggest-selling magazine in the UK) was adapted in the 1980s by its publisher Emap Metro to a succession of popular youth publications, including *Just 17, Looks* and *More*. These magazines were just as quick to grasp the new availablity of colour and varied typographic form. *Smash Hits'* founding editor, Nick Logan, independently launched *The Face* as a more sophisticated alternative in 1980, with which he intended to address all aspects of youth culture (as reduced on the masthead to the formula "music, movies, style"). The initial design, by Steve Bush, was fairly crude, lively, and otherwise unremarkable except for the powerful geometric logotype on the cover. *New Sounds New Styles*, launched against *The Face* by the publisher of *Smash Hits*, and designed in the second half of its two-year life by Malcolm Garrett, was aggressively over-designed by comparison.

Neville Brody joined *The Face* in 1981. His intitial work for the magazine is most notable for its freshness born of complete absence of prejudice, and for its painterly style. Brody developed a system of symbolic reference to express the continuity of the magazine, and rediscovered the value of plastic form and texture as a means of creating graphic unity. Type was used with great imagination and, again, without respect for conventional methods of construction; it was put to work as an integral design component and as vehicle for meaning. In Brody's first two years with *The Face* the typography was also characterized by mismatching of faces within words to provide unexpected emphasis and, undoubtedly, as a stylistic evocation of nonconformism. As the design evolved, the spontaneity generated by Brody's naive typography and colourful composition diminished; all that remained of the unifying texture were highly abstracted graphic symbols. Some of the fussiness of detail was removed to create mannered and comparatively minimal layout, and an increasing emphasis was placed on the structural composition of Brody's geometric typography.

In the later period less successful experiments were conducted in headline-sized standfirsts of regular and small capitals, braced in a dog-leg around body copy, in which the synthesis of graphic elements tended to break down. However, Brody's constant investigations into the possible combinations of magazine type hierarchies yielded some elegant and very practical solutions to the problem of leading the eye around the page. As the editorial matured, so did its design, and in many respects this was a magazine that grew up with its first readers who, like the art director, then graduated to *Arena*.

Brody is best considered as a graphic designer and

The Face

August 1983

art director Neville Brody

Below: Joseph Beuys was a subject well suited to Brody's intelligent application of symbol and reference. The structure and narrative form of the spread take their cue from the main picture; this is split, reflecting a major theme of Beuys' art – the wound – and the blackboard scribbles are repeated in Beuys' Hauptstrom symbol, reproduced at the top left. The mixed headline of bold and regular type is bled into the turn page to provide continuity, a technique first used by Will Burtin and Henry Wolf and re-invented by Brody.

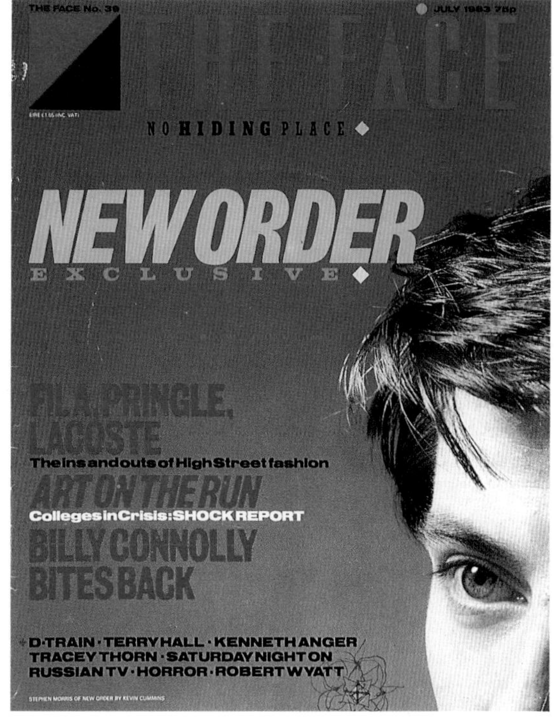

The Face

July 1983

art director Neville Brody

Above: a severe and unlikely crop and warm colour create a memorable cover. The heavy italic of the cover lines pushes the face to the right. The photographer was Kevin Cummins.

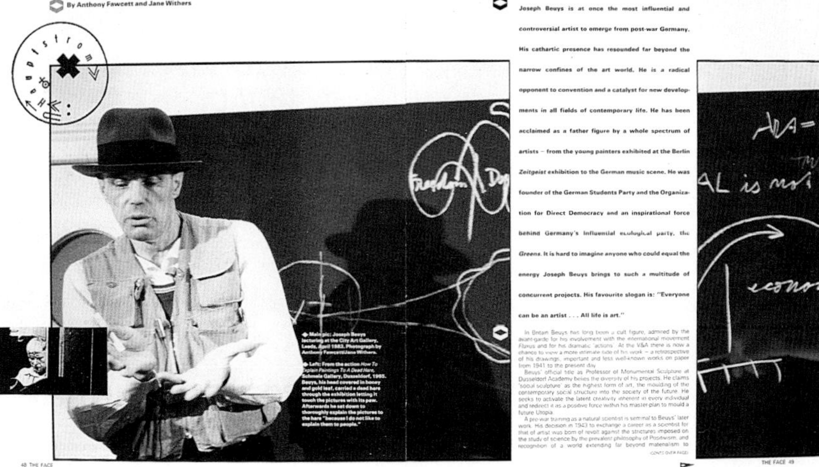

BEUYS+ ADVENTURES

By Anthony Fawcett and Jane Withers

Joseph Beuys is at once the most influential and controversial artist to emerge from post-war Germany. His cathartic presence has resounded far beyond the narrow confines of the art world. He is a radical opponent to convention and a catalyst for new developments in all fields of contemporary life. He has been acclaimed as a father figure by a whole spectrum of artists – from the young painters exhibited at the Berlin *Zeitgeist* exhibition to the German music scene. He was founder of the German Students Party and the Organization for Direct Democracy and an inspirational force behind Germany's influential ecological party, the *Greens*. It is hard to imagine anyone who could equal the energy Joseph Beuys brings to such a multitude of concurrent projects. His favourite slogan is: "Everyone can be an artist . . . All life is art."

In Britain Beuys has long been a cult figure, admired by the avant-garde for his involvement with the international movement *Fluxus* and for his dramatic 'actions'. At the V&A there is now a chance to view a more intimate side of his work – a retrospective of his drawings, important and less well-known works on paper from 1941 to the present day.

Beuys' official title as Professor of Monumental Sculpture at Dusseldorf Academy belies the diversity of his projects. He claims 'social sculpture' as the highest form of art, the moulding of the contemporary social structure into the society of the future. He seeks to activate the latent creativity inherent in every individual and redirect it as a positive force within his master-plan to mould a future Utopia.

A pre-war training as a natural scientist is seminal to Beuys' later work. His decision in 1943 to exchange a career as a scientist for that of artist was born of revolt against the strictures imposed on the study of science by the prevalent philosophy of Positivism, and recognition of a world extending far beyond materialism to

(CONT'D OVER PAGE)

◆ Main pic: Joseph Beuys lecturing at the City Art Gallery, Leeds, April 1983. Photograph by Anthony Fawcett/Jane Withers.

◆ Left: From the action *How To Explain Paintings To A Dead Hare*, Schmela Gallery, Dusseldorf, 1965. Beuys, his head covered in honey and gold leaf, carried a dead hare through the exhibition letting it touch the pictures with its paw. Afterwards he sat down to thoroughly explain the pictures to the hare "because I do not like to explain them to people."

48 THE FACE

THE FACE 49

The Face

May 1985

art director Neville Brody

Right: as Brody's typographic treatments became more elaborate, a more formal separation of text and image evolved. However, the intensity of Nick Knight's portrait of Morrissey is doubled by cropping along the axis of reflection.

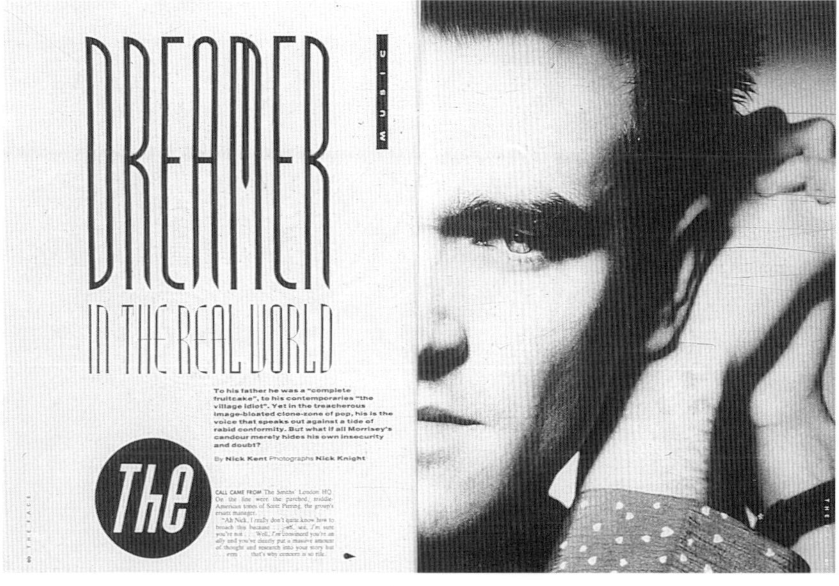

MUSIC

DREAMER

IN THE REAL WORLD

To his father he was a "complete fruitcake", to his contemporaries "the village idiot". Yet in the treacherous image-bloated clone-zone of pop, his is the voice that speaks out against a tide of rabid conformity. But what if all Morrisey's candour merely hides his own insecurity and doubt?

By **Nick Kent** Photographs **Nick Knight**

The CALL CAME FROM The Smiths' London HQ. On the line were the parched, middle-American tones of Scott Piering, the group's ersatz manager.

not as a typographer *per se*. The typography of *The Face* was highly stylized and by necessity transient – perhaps too transient, as its designer became over-concerned with the inevitable plagiarism of his work. Similar typographic treatments given to *New Socialist* and *City Limits* were singularly inappropriate (although Brody's covers for *City Limits* are amongst his best work). Brody's method, and the lively changes and contrasts of his *mise en page* are of much greater interest. His most important contribution to magazine design was made on *The Face* because at this magazine he was able to think, with great care and without cynicism, about the way in which magazines work, and he encouraged other designers to take exactly the same approach: to be uninhibited by convention, and to temper practicality with intuition. Brody, with the sympathetic understanding of his editor, used to the full the opportunity magazines provide to the experimentalist, to the designer who can think in terms of the interplay of words and images. It is interesting that he fell on many design solutions which he regarded as novel, but which had in fact been introduced by American designers in the 1950s only to be discarded in more barren years. This is the best testimony to the utility of his design method.

i-D was a more direct inheritor of the principles of punk. Its art director, Terry Jones, exercised a radical design philosophy within a similar publishing environment; that is, at an editorial-led magazine with a small budget and the confidence to disregard the normal rules of publishing behaviour. In this case, however, the art director also had complete editorial control. There are dangers inherent in such a position – the temptation to aesthetic excess and absence of content – but if *i-D* was occasionally over-extravagant, it was rarely without substance. Despite appearances, *i-D* was composed with a self-discipline born of utility and Jones' predilection for self-reliance, which matched his natural vivacity.

For most of Jones' career he had worked as a fashion magazine art director, at British *Vogue*, German *Vogue*, *Vogue Pelle*, and *Donna*; the latter a first attempt at "anti-fashion", founded in opposition to haute couture with a group of photographers and stylists led by Flavio Luccini. *i-D*, which began life in 1980 as a document of street fashion, would take this approach to its logical conclusion: treating fashion as photo-journalism, presented in landscape format to reflect the panorama of the street in the page. Throughout most of its ten years of existence the magazine has, remarkably, managed to retain its freshness and remain true to its founding principles.

Jones describes his design discipline as "instant design": a layered, saturated "mash" of colour and type, with an apparent randomness which belies the rigour of its execution – this is one of its many contradictions. As Jones admits, "Instant-design is a lie: it is never instant".[24] It does, however, give the impression of spontaneity and freshness. The constraints imposed on the design process are speed of working and, sometimes, self-imposed restrictions which are used to force through new ideas. The governing force is maximum utilization of print resources at minimum cost, and the technical process is celebrated and exposed to view. At the core of instant design is a set of production tools – print effects, photocopy, video, digital effects, hand-marks and typewriter text – which are used to create new graphic forms (to do which, to paraphrase Jean Mohr, you must discard old techniques) and to impart immediacy to the page. This perpetual search for new methods is exemplified in the original colour print effects achieved through masking, overlays, and manipulation of images on digital scanners.

Although fundamentally a technical approach

i-D
no. 6 1981
designer Moira Bogue
art director Terry Jones

The first 13 issues of i-D were in a landscape format ideally suited to its content. The harshly cut montage and panoramic width of this spread is packed with the energy and adrenalin of the dance floor. The photographer was James Palmer.

i-D

March 1985

designers Carol Thompson and Eamonn McCabe

art director Terry Jones

Video stills were used by Terry Jones to provide a sense of speed and the unexpected. Interesting textures and colour effects arise. This cover combines computer type and type distorted by photocopier, screaming face and of course the i-D wink, a feature of every cover after issue 5.

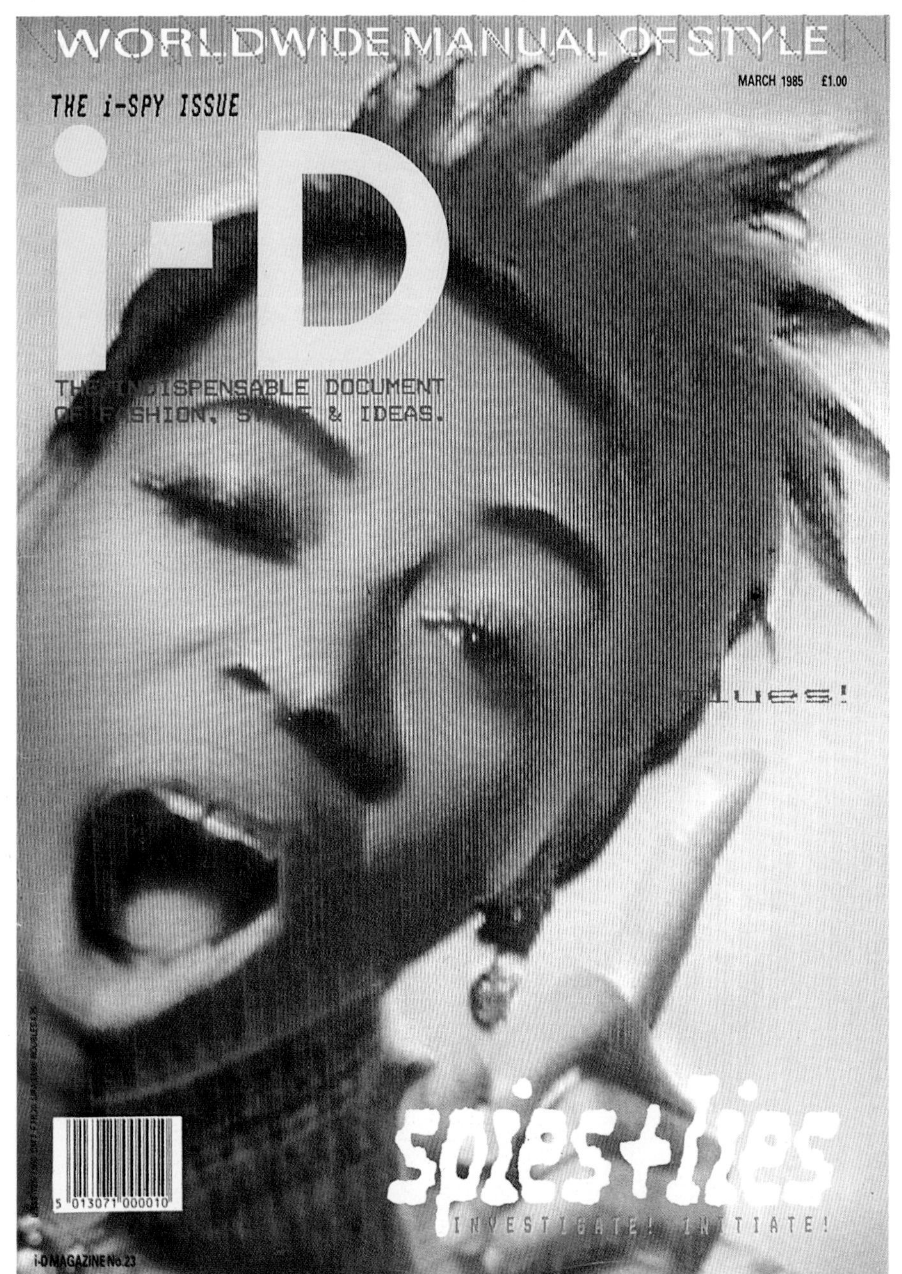

which incorporates both structural and applied decoration, instant design is nonetheless a problem-solving method with a form dictated largely by content and according to the assumption that the brain is capable of rapidly assimilating a massive quantity of visual information. Jones "cannot work without problems" which have to be resolved within a predetermined framework, yet he disfavours "the concept of perfection, because it implies completeness".[25] He is, therefore, completely at odds with the pursuit of typographic purity which obsessed magazine designers on the opposite side of the Atlantic. Jones belongs to the art director tradition which the American school of designer-as-typographer has discarded, working with ideas rather than with type, breaking the rules of taste and technique, and valuing ambiguity over clarity, through wordplay and the wilful maltreatment of photography, and the creation of a sensory banquet of type overlayed on type, coloured text, register-shift, moiré patterns, fluorescence. Only through a virtuoso understanding of the craft of printing could such liberties be taken, together with that most important characteristic of the art director, the ability to exploit talent. In the first decade of *i-D's* existence Jones nurtured a remarkable collection of creative artists, including the designers Stephen Male, Moira Bogue, Robin Derrick and Rod Clark, fashion stylist Simon Foxton, and photographers Nick Knight and Marc Lebon.

In retrospect, and given the moribund state of the great mass of English, European and American design in 1980, it is hardly surprising that *i-D* and *The Face* had such a cathartic impact on editorial and graphic formats. *i-D* made a genuine attempt to return control over fashion to those who wore it – in contrast to *Vogue's* rather shallow "democratic" protestations; and *The Face* successfully cohered its idiosyncratic editorial content within a highly original and fundamentally utilitarian graphic format. Both magazines made a substantial contribution to the technique and aesthetics of page design, and were in many respects the first commercial manifestation of graphic experiments which had proceeded outside mainstream publishing in the previous decade. *i-D* and *The Face* set the agenda for editorial design and concept for what was to become the most important sector of magazine publishing in the 1980s – youth and "style".

A parallel development in independent publishing was the re-introduction of large-format magazines, the "culturetabs", as Steven Heller has called them,[26] in A3 format and larger, with the common denominator of

Fetish

Fall 1980, Spring 1981

designers Jane Kosstrin and David Sterling

This large-format quarterly for collectors of kitsch was a succession of beautifully designed montaged pages. Its free-form, three-dimensional layouts had none of the typographic fetishism or rigid classical structures of contemporaneous American publications.

editorial devoted to miscellaneous cultural concepts, art and architecture. Andy Warhol's *Interview* was perhaps the prototype but, launched in 1970 just as every other magazine was reducing its size, it was hardly representative of the trend. *Interview* was followed by *City of San Francisco* (1975); *Wet* – the delightfully subtitled "magazine for gourmet bathers" (1976); *Hard Werken*, launched by the Rotterdam-based design group of the same name[27] (1979-81); *Fetish* (1980-81) published and designed from New York by two Cranbrook Academy graduates, Jane Kosstrin and David Stirling, and devoted to kitsch and the mythology of objects; the architectural magazines *NATO* (London, 1984), *Blueprint* (London, 1983) and *Metropolis* (NY, 1981); and *Emigre* (1985), published, edited and designed by Emigré Graphics of Berkeley, and devoted primarily to photography, typography and graphic design.

Most of these products (*Blueprint* and *Metropolis* excepted) were purely experimental, produced by, and for, graphic designers. The poster-sized format provided the space for research into novel forms of typography and layout, mainly in the areas of unstructured type, interlocking and floating grids, collage and applied decoration, which have since percolated in diluted form into commercial design. These magazines also popularized the large format by demonstrating its suitability for highly visual editorial and photographic reproduction, and it has become the favoured size for numerous "lifestyle" and "city" magazines, including *LA Style* (1986), *Equator* (San Francisco, 1986-87), *Paper* (New York), *Westuff* (Florence), and by trade fashion publications such as *W*, Comme des Garcons' *Sixth Sense* and *Nadir* (both Japanese), and the big daddy of them all, the A2-sized *Manipulator* (Germany).

Not all of these magazines have successfully utilized the wide expanse of double A3 spreads, which creates problems for the designer who fails to adjust the sense of scale. There is a tendency to suffer from a surfeit of air, producing slack layouts with over-width columns and undersized headlines. *Blueprint* was and is the notable exception, confidently using the broad expanse of its pages to exhibit architectural and portrait photography, as well as illustration, to powerful effect. Its design was also prominent in the early 1980s as a rare adherent to the international style, with a highly organized format, based on a 4/5/8 column grid, which, with its heavy vertical rules and gothic headline face, was strongly reminiscent of Vignelli's

Hard Werken

no. 5 1980, no. 8 1981

designers Willem Kars, Rick Vermeulen, Gerrard Hadders et al

This A3 format, Rotterdam-based cultural magazine attacked the formal conventions of craft typography, using "ugly" hand-drawn, degenerated and typewriter faces. Its layout was painterly and studiously "unprofessional", without apparent structure. Hand-marks were slapped on the page and pictures scrawled over and sealed by painted outlines.

Nato (Narrative Architecture Today)
no. 3 1985
designer Rod Clarke
Collaged cover of Nato representing the retrievalist architecture of Nigel Coates' Unit 10 at the Architectural Association, London, for which this large-format magazine acted as a periodical manifesto.

work for *Skyline* and *Industrial Design*. This format, devised by Simon Esterson, had the inherent discipline and simplicity necessary for this size of page. There was a satisfactory balance between the white space provided by vertical half-width caption columns and the solid architecture of body text supporting bold headlines which were used in up to 50mm and even 100mm cap heights.

The US edition of *Elle*, launched to immediate success in 1985, was a further homage to the power and drama which could be extracted from a direct modernist format. *Elle*, designed and directed by Regiz Pagniez, signified the return of strong graphic values to commercial publishing. Its primary colour, contrasting bold and ultra-light Futura heads, and its dynamic silhouetted and full-bleed photography, took their cue from the style created by Bea Feitler and Ruth Ansell at *Harper's Bazaar* in the 1960s. At a stroke this vibrant new magazine exposed the philistine confusion and lack of direction of almost the entire spectrum of women's magazines then published out of New York: the small pictures, the clashing coloured panels, the uneducated "loud" typography which Pagniez dismissed as nothing better than extraneous "frou frou".

The development of magazine design since 1985 flows directly from the learning process of the previous fifteen years. The divergence of European and American experience since 1968 results from quite dissimilar reactions to crises which snapped the continuity of design development. The causes were both general, and specific to the industry: the cultural and political climate was inimical to rationalism; in the 1970s the magazine industry faced its greatest economic test this century, and was forced to rationalize its marketing and editorial strategies; and in design and production, working methods and disciplines had to be readjusted to new technologies. The way in which these problems were addressed depended on both national and social characteristics – which have only recently been weakened by the growing internationalization of publishing. In almost all cases the dominant response was a return to the roots, as a base on which to rebuild. In Britain, the reviving forces were punk and a renewed interest in both anarchic and technocratic modernism, although there was an equally powerful reaction which leant towards classicism and fine bookish typography – witness *The Independent Magazine* and *The World of Interiors*. In Italy, where the publishing industry was only minimally distressed, there was a less convulsive transition: Condé Nast in Milan, for example, was

FIVE EASY PIECES

THE LEADING MAGAZINE OF ARCHITECTURE AND DESIGN/SEPTEMBER 1986/NUMBER 30 £1·50

BLUEPRINT

MILAN FAIR
PREVIEW: NEW
DESIGNS FROM
MARIO BOTTA
ALDO ROSSI
RICHARD SAPPER
AT HOME WITH
MIAMI VICE
JOSEPH'S
LATEST SHOP

ETTORE
SOTTSASS
AND MILAN'S
NEW MOOD

Blueprint

February 1985, September 1986

art director Simon Esterson

Blueprint's format was appropriately scaled to its A3 size. The discipline of a versatile grid was combined with boldly sized photography and headlines. This spread echoes the engineering of Ralph Ball's furniture, illustrated in the main photograph by Phil Sayer. The symmetrical layout of the right-hand page hangs from the two captions, economically set in half-width columns which provide air as well as structural support. The cover is in the magazine's distinctive tradition of moody portraits. Steve Speller's lighting of Ettore Sottsass's brooding, heavily lidded eyes pulls the face off the page and around a solid wall of cover lines.

able to retain high production and design standards throughout the 1970s and 1980s (Salvatore Gregorietti's work for *Casa Vogue* is the outstanding example), and the larger publishing groups such as Mondadori, Espresso and Nuove ERI Edizioni retained strong individual identities. Editorial design in France was perhaps most severely debilitated by the drop in technical standards prompted by the introduction of phototypesetting, and there was a marked failure to reach new visual solutions independently. The warped typography of the style magazines *Globe* and *Perfect* has only recently been improved. *Actuel's* bad, brash typography was, however, the perfect partner for its sensationalist photography. The discordant typography and layout of *Paris Match* bears no comparison to its clear vision of the 1960s. News magazines have largely borrowed their formats from *Business Week* and *Newsweek*, and French *Elle* has lost much of its sparkle (and its design team – to *Madame Figaro*). *Madame Figaro, Glamour* (designed by an Englishman, Robin Derrick), *Lire* (format by Glaser and Bernard), *Elle Decoration* and *Marie Claire* are amongst a number of honourable exceptions.

In America, as we have seen, rigorous professionalism was the instinctive defence against the bad taste of rampant commercialism. As the industry recovered its poise, classical and vernacular typography and typographic embellishment spread from the underground and independent press into mainstream publishing. The European designers' reawakened interest in pop art, constructivism and montage, with its radical political undertones, was not reciprocated within the USA. Punk re-emerged in muted form in the Californian New Wave, and in the East, Cranbrook Academy built strong links and shared interests with the Dutch neo-modernists. This strand, however, remains in the academic sphere and has not been of great significance beyond the experimental "culturetabs". The vast majority of US publishing is now wedded to the post-modern style, which grew out of the neo-classical typographic sensibility and the capabilities of new technology. It was also admirably suited to the stylistic conceits of the prosperous middle classes, now fed by a booming consumer and style sector. The early protagonists, *Rolling Stone, LA Style* and *Spy*, have been joined by *Esquire, New York, Wigwam, Egg, Metropolitan Home, Smart,* and – as a final seal of approval – that former pillar of American modernism, *Industrial Design* (now renamed *International Design*). The style is sometimes too winsome, distractingly overwrought or mere appliqué, but in the main it represents a positive development because it has revived experiment in graphic – rather than typographic – ideas, and has promoted a new appreciation of structural decoration and multi-layered design. The school has rapidly won its adherents in Europe, particularly in Spain and Italy, where *El Europeo* and *King* are fine examples of decorative eclecticism. Yet although the dominant contemporary trend is post-modernism – the urge to humanize, to decorate, to exercise typographic whim – this co-exists with a continued strand of functionalist severity. Perhaps severity is too strong a word – directness is a better antonym to the circularity of post-modern style. Modernism is, however, much stronger in Europe than America, and we can see its continued endurance in a diverse range of magazines and in many countries: in Italy, in *Domus, Gap Casa,* and even in a teenage fashion magazine like *Cento Cose*; in Germany in *Tempo* and *Apart*; in Britain in *Blueprint, Arena* and *Management Today*. In 1990, although recession looms once more, magazine publishing and design has emerged from a most difficult period with a richness of content, form and style which is worthy of its inheritance.

Part two

New magazine design

Journalism and art

Magazine design is a relatively diffuse creative process to which no immutable principles can be applied, because there is no common problem which confronts the designer of every kind of magazine. As a medium the magazine is ephemeral, a luxury (whereas the newspaper is a staple), in which technical rigour may coexist with artistic abstraction, and which has no definite visual form. There is, therefore, no consistent standard of judgement for "correct" design, and problems of production and communication cannot always be measured from the standpoint of narrow functionalism. For most magazine designers, for most of the time, the journalistic imperative is dominant. That is, maximum exploitation of resources and materials to the end of clear communication – to tell a story – to a closely defined readership; a problem which is overcome at the most basic level by a formalized design structure. Such structures, "magazine formats", can however take numerous and subtle forms, and both within and without this scaffolding the synthesis of type and image offers a range of possibilities limited only by the clear rectangle of the page; there are, moreover, conditions in which oblique and irrational methods of communication can be justified, occasions when even legibility may be sacrificed to art. That is to stress the possibilities, the potential for freedom which has given the magazine its unrivalled position as a medium for graphic experiment; such freedoms exist, naturally enough, within the bounds of technical constraints and editorial intention and should be exercised in harmony, and not in contradiction, with those obligations.

In a print medium, in which editorial content can range from timetables to poetry and from fiction to hard news, the general design problem has to be described in the loosest possible terms. Numerous attempts have been made to define a "magazine" (at least one already in this book), and usually by attacking the Arabic root of the word – as a storehouse. Etymology is not, however, particularly useful in this respect. Any permanent cultural medium is a storehouse of knowledge. The intellectual purview of the magazine has become so wide, and printing technology so sophisticated, that the form of its visual presentation is under no general technical or aesthetic constraint other than those determined by its familiar bound paper package. So unless or until electronics supersedes the paper magazine entirely, we should perhaps limit our definition to physical properties, those of mass and time. Simply, a magazine is floppier than a book and stiffer than a newspaper; it has greater periodicity than a book (which has none) and less than a newspaper, and it has a hybrid structure of serial and parallel reading patterns. We could even make the rule that the intellectual rigour required of a magazine and its reader also lies somewhere between the two – but it would be broken much too often. What matters is not the level, but the proximity of the intellectual relationship between a magazine and its readership; a complex relationship which, through its editing and design, the magazine leads and nurtures. This is a general principle to which we shall return, for it is perhaps the most effective guide to the problems confronted and opportunities available to the magazine designer.

In all editorial media the designer's primary role is to communicate and express content: to act as a catalyst of comprehension in the interaction between message and reader. The word message, as opposed to writer, is used here advisedly because of the pictorial quality of magazines. Many kinds of magazine rely on a visual journalism which is created out of the interaction between writer, photographer, editor and designer, such that in certain circumstances the responsibility of the magazine designer is raised to that of author and instigator, not mere interpreter, so creating the new role of designer-journalist.

The prototype of this breed, the art director Dr M. F. Agha, made the same point and with characteristic cynicism he turned it on its head: the art director, he wrote, "is the autocrat of the drawing table, with authority restricted only by the requirements of teamwork, research findings, editorial policies, client's preferences, reader's mental age and publisher's niece.... He is the first cousin of the movie director, and like the movie director, he plans, coordinates and rehearses, but does not perform; at least not in public."[1]

And this is by no means an exhaustive list of perfidious issues which texture the final product. Advertising requirements, marketing assumptions, budget, paper, print and composition methods, and of course readers' expectations and prejudices, clamour for attention. Where an art director succeeds in becoming an equal partner in the editorial oligarchy, this does not mean that the natural laws of publishing become extinct.

These circumstances shape the form of a magazine. Budget determines the extent of colour and lavishness of photography and illustration, and the resources in terms of time and staff that can be given to all aspects of editorial production. Print method determines deadlines, and to an extent, typography. Advertising requirements influence pagination. Received marketing wisdom informs cover design. And lastly, and by no means least, the nature of the material and the readership govern visual expression.

Within those constraints, and by maximizing the resources available, the designer is assigned to communicate the message according to the strictures of functionalism; that is, "in as simple, direct, orderly and effective a manner as possible...and to this end he ought to be continuously on guard against the wish to 'express himself' aesthetically at the expense of the message.... The main objective of too many designers seems to be to show how 'creative' they are rather than to act as the technically trained presenters of messages they are engaged to be".[2]

This is a truism of the not very helpful kind constantly reiterated in reproaching "typographic trickery" and "the designer ego", and in itself it is quite meaningless. It is unquestionable that simplicity is, generally, the most effective approach, and more so that petty individualism has a destructive effect. But this ascetic mandate from the pen of Robert Harling has an emphasis which is inappropriate to the art of magazine design.

Harling's remarks, significantly, were directed towards newspaper designers, and they reflect the severe technical demands of newspaper design and in that respect carry weight. (But here too, the narcosis of tradition is as dangerous as creative excess.) Magazines, however, fulfil more nebulous cultural functions than the transmission of hard news: they are entertaining, reassuring, they are social bonds for disparate individuals with common interests, they are fickle champions of fashion and consumption, and they demand a rich language of vision. Magazines thrive not on predictability, but on surprise. Must they always be ordered and direct, never enigmatic, never obtuse? The designer's skill is in using the tools available – type, colour, texture and image – to amplify, relate, or simply present a story, and to maintain interest. Whether those tools are used extravagantly or quietly, emotionally or objectively, to create order or disorder, to address the

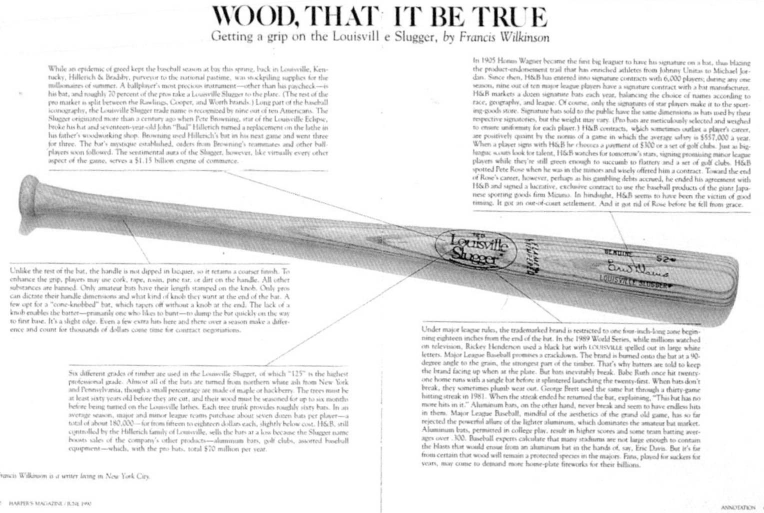

A N N O T A T I O N

WOOD, THAT IT BE TRUE

Getting a grip on the Louisvill e Slugger, *by Francis Wilkinson*

Unlike the rest of the bat, the handle is not dipped in lacquer, so it retains a coarser finish. To enhance the grip, players may use cork, tape, rosin, pine tar, or dirt on the handle. All other substances are banned. Only amateur bats have their length stamped on the knob. Only pros can dictate their handle dimensions and what kind of knob they want at the end of the bat. A few opt for a "cone-knobbed" bat, which tapers off without a knob at the end. The lack of a knob enables the batter—primarily one who likes to bunt—to dump the bat quickly on the way to first base. It's a slight edge. Even a few extra hits here and there over a season make a difference and count for thousands of dollars come time for contract negotiations.

Under major league rules, the trademarked brand is restricted to one four-inch-long zone beginning eighteen inches from the end of the bat. In the 1989 World Series, while millions watched on television, Rickey Henderson used a black bat with LOUISVILLE spelled out in large white letters. Major League Baseball promises a crackdown. The brand is burned onto the bat at a 90-degree angle to the grain, the strongest part of the timber. That's why batters are told to keep the brand facing up when at the plate. But bats inevitably break. Babe Ruth once hit twenty-one home runs with a single bat before it splintered launching the twenty-first. When bats don't break, they sometimes plumb wear out. George Brett used the same bat through a thirty-game hitting streak in 1981. When the streak ended he returned the bat, explaining, "This bat has no more hits in it." Aluminum bats, on the other hand, never break and seem to have endless hits in them. Major League Baseball, mindful of the aesthetics of the grand old game, has so far rejected the powerful allure of the lighter aluminum, which dominates the amateur bat market. Aluminum bats, permitted in college play, result in higher scores and some team batting averages over .300. Baseball experts calculate that many stadiums are not large enough to contain the blasts that would ensue from an aluminum bat in the hands of, say, Eric Davis. But it's far from certain that wood will remain a protected species in the majors. Fans, played for suckers for years, may come to demand more home-plate fireworks for their billions.

Six different grades of timber are used in the Louisville Slugger, of which "125" is the highest professional grade. Almost all of the bats are turned from northern white ash from New York and Pennsylvania, though a small percentage are made of maple or hackberry. The trees must be at least sixty years old before they are cut, and their wood must be seasoned for up to six months before being turned on the Louisville lathes. Each tree trunk provides roughly sixty bats. In an average season, major and minor league teams purchase about seven dozen bats per player—a total of about 180,000—for from fifteen to eighteen dollars each, slightly below cost. H&B, still controlled by the Hillerich family of Louisville, sells the bats at a loss because the Slugger name boosts sales of the company's other products—aluminum bats, golf clubs, assorted baseball equipment—which, with the pro bats, total $70 million per year.

Francis Wilkinson is a writer living in New York City.

60 HARPER'S MAGAZINE / JUNE 1990

ANNOTATION 61

What ever happened to Mary Jo Kopechne's five girlfriends who had the good fortune *not* to drive off with Ted Kennedy? See page 37. Why has there never been a best-seller or a movie or even a television docudrama about Chappaquiddick? See page 40. In the age of Everythingscam and Whatevergate, how, after 18 years, can the Chappaquiddick cover-up remain so airtight? Good question. And why won't anybody publish an impressive new investigative book that for once gets a Kennedy cousin and Chappaquiddick witness *on the record* about the incident? Read this article.

CHAPPAQUIDDICK

The Unsold Story

BY TAD FRIEND

EARLY IN THE MORNING of July 19, 1969, after attending an intimate party of male political cronies and female political aides, Senator Edward Kennedy drove his Oldsmobile off Chappaquiddick Island's Dyke Bridge and into Poucha Pond. His passenger, Mary Jo Kopechne, drowned.

This is not exactly news. Most of us recall that after a considerable public rumpus, Senator Kennedy took the extraordinary step of going on television to explain–altogether unconvincingly–this latest Kennedy tragedy.

Kennedy pleaded guilty to leaving the scene of an accident after causing personal injury and later promised to consider resigning his Senate seat (*Nahhhh*, he evidently decided, instead going on to win reelection three times).

After receiving a two-month suspended sentence, he clammed up. And so did everyone else in a position to fill in some of the blanks–the five women at the party who did not drown in Ted Kennedy's car, the five men at the party who did not swim away from a submerged Oldsmobile and then lie about it. So the inquiries have blundered along without Kennedy's help, or the help of his loyal friends at the party. And so, naturally, strange Chappaquiddick theories abound: Kennedy was driving; Kennedy wasn't driving; Kennedy murdered Kopechne because she was pregnant with his child, and jumped out of the moving car in the nick of time; and so on.

What is news–or should be–is that Joe Gargan, a cousin of Kennedy's who spent much of that fatal evening with the senator, finally did unburden himself of his Chappaquid-

Harpers' (USA)
June 1990
art director Deborah Rust

Top: a literary magazine that understands the meaning of visual journalism: Harpers' records the history and mythology of the Louisville Slugger in a pictorial analysis of the bat's component parts.

Spy (USA)
November 1987
art director Alex Isley

Above: first-class editing, inspired design and humour make this typographic opening to a seven-page article superior to any photographic treatment. The headline as visual pun powerfully expresses its subject and the diminishing type draws the reader into the feature like a magnet.

conscious or subconscious mind, is not a point at issue. The measure of success is – simply – does the result obstruct or assist the communication of the message?

The relationship with the reader is rarely so simple that what is technically direct or ordered is necessarily the most effective means of communication. If this was so we would fall rapidly into a minimum of formulaic constructions based on the three essential components of the page – heading, text, and illustration – just as "too many" designers do, and just as Brodovitch was moved to complain that, "Rarely is the printed page considered a medium of plastic invention. Its design has become standardized; a machine-like element devoid of feeling and aesthetic significance."[3] Allen Hutt provided a well balanced formulation which puts technical competence in its proper context, as a means to an end but not as the end itself, writing that, "Design and make-up of magazines...demand a synthesis of artistic and typographic mastery. On that basis, and only on that basis, it is both possible and desirable to show some audacity, to be experimental."[4]

The problem is one of reconciling objective technical conditions and the disciplines of information design with the expression of humour, emotion, aesthetic values, and so on. An assumption that these aims are mutually exclusive, that order and simplicity are desirable, that "creativity" or "aesthetic expression" may be inimical to communication, creates a double jeopardy. Firstly, as we shall see, no useful critique of contemporary magazine design can afford to use the imposition of order within conventional geometries as its main benchmark. And secondly, the magazine designer is rather more than a "technically trained presenter of messages". Unintelligent and capricious expression may indeed interfere with the message – any fool can set 8pt type over 40 picas – but the sacrifice of expression to narrow technical criteria tends to imply the exclusion of the designer from participation in the creation of the message, if not its interpretation.

The quality of order, simplicity and directness required in page design depends entirely on the kind of magazine in question. To take an example from one end of the spectrum, the news weekly, the functionality of the design is paramount: the news magazine requires a systematized format which facilitates rapid production to tight deadlines, and a typographic hierarchy appropriate to news values. The designer, therefore, must adopt a problem solving approach which resolves the contradiction between the urgency and thirst for space of a news magazine and the need to

Madame Figaro (France)
15 September 1989
art director
Martin Schmollgruber
photographer Pierre Berdoy

Schmollgruber builds graphic narrative out of mundane subject matter – a feature on moisturizing cream products. By splitting the torso from one spread to the next, the art director has created a dramatic cinematic sequence. The headlines and body text move like pistons up and down the column rules.

handhold the reader through a clearly ordered sequence of stories. Here, the tension between literary and pictorial values is self-evident, in that text may have to be sacrificed to orderliness, or to visual illustration, whereas few writers are prepared to see their work cut even if brevity is the price to pay for attractive or explicit presentation. Roger Black's reformatting of *Newsweek* in 1985 is a case in point: text space was cut by 10 per cent to allow room for clearer graphic signposting – bigger headlines, subheads and sidebars – and some longer features. The result was that the writers were "enraged", and circulation increased by half a million.[5] By contrast, the review *The New Yorker* – a self-conscious anachronism of antediluvian typography – lets text run to expiration and makes no allowance for diminished powers of concentration. That is its prerogative: it is an avowedly literary magazine.

Although the news magazine is an extreme example, and other magazine types have equally stringent, if different, material requirements, it is a useful example because its very orderliness raises the question – what is order? Classical order (*The New Yorker*) or asymmetric modularity (*Newsweek* and *Time*)? And how rigid must it be? The American genre of news weekly, in fact, operates within the narrowest conceivable band of design parameters. The internal formats of *Time, Newsweek* and *Business Week* are to the layman barely distinguishable from each other, each with an unshakeable attachment to the dictatorship of delineating column rules and scotch-ruled sidebars, and between them there is the tiniest variation in paper, size, and typography. This indicates clearly that the design of such magazines is very tightly defined by operational demands; it also indicates a rather slavish conventionality, for this is by no means an "optimum" format. The Europeans – even close equivalents such as the austere *Economist, L'Express* and *Der Spiegel* – are noticeably less retentive, and the picture-based weeklies such as *Stern* and *Paris Match*, in which priorities are reversed with features at the front and news analysis at the back, use an open-faced format closer to the popular "people" and "scandale" magazines, such as *Quick, Bunte* and *Panorama*. Even the news format is not cast in stone.

The point is illustrated by a comparison of *New York* and *Spy* magazines (this time monthlies) in which the dissimilarity of editorial approach is clearly exposed by the relative (but not actual) chaos of the latter. *New York* is ordered – and thoroughly ruled in the conventional sense and in spite of its rather extravagant typography. *Spy*, on the other hand, offers a multiplicity of texts, signs and images over variable grids; it addresses the reader on numerous levels and is neither "simple", nor direct in the conventional sense. But *Spy* is nonetheless a carefully unified product of visual and literary journalism, driven by a clear conceptual logic. It is capricious. It is stylized. But it is also indisputably ordered on its own terms – and has been an outstanding publishing success.

By limiting our appreciation of appropriate design to "an innate sense of orderliness" (Harling again), we are forced into an obsolete and crude understanding of the tasks of the magazine designer which discounts the process of initiating and commissioning editorial, a "craft"-based approach against which Gropius could be wheeled in: "whereas building is merely a matter of methods and materials", he wrote, "architecture implies the mastery of space".[6] Superficial functionalism leads us to dogmatic and earthbound formulations of what formats are suitable to different types of magazine, when we should have learnt from Burtin over 40 years ago that a business magazine can have fabulous aesthetic ambitions while retaining the integrity of its editorial and the trust of its readers. The most significant feature of the new magazine design in Europe, Japan and the United States has been the introduction of a new "disorder" and a resurgence of experimentation in multi-layered collage, parallel texts, iconoclastic typography, and novel combinations of page components, and forms of decoration, which are, nonetheless, put to work in the graphic scheme – all of which, according to convention, may constitute "bad" design.

If there is a "new magazine design", however, it is only because there are new cultural and editorial criteria and new production methods. And here we should not allow ourselves to be diverted by the usual quantity of shallow typographic pastiche which exists alongside the useful; this merely confuses the issue. Unconventional, "a-functional" forms can be justified by circumstance and are impelled by changed cultural and material conditions.

The new magazine design is grounded in four conditions: the liberation of designers from certain material constraints by new pre-press technologies; the influence of television on readers' expectations and habits of perception; the establishment of new, generalist editorial products which do not conform to traditional publishing notions; and the enhancement and consolidation of the designers' position in the editorial process, as both initiator and communicator of ideas, and as a constructor of thematic structure, which has resulted from all three of the above. A decade of high economic growth has been an additional encouragement to experimentation and innovation.

These are observable if by no means universal trends, of which the influence of digital composition is the most discernable throughout the industry. Desktop publishing and digital scanning technologies have had a dual effect. On the one hand, they have given the designer greater control over the production process and, in particular, over the manipulation of type and image – this issue is considered in greater detail in pages 224 – 31. And on the other, they have reduced the cost of magazine production to the extent that new editorial concepts from independent publishers have become economic. We have seen, as a result, an apparently contradictory process, in which a revival of the generalist magazine has occured simultaneously with an acceleration in the historical process of diversification into specialist small-circulation sectors.

The re-emergence of editorial-led magazines which do not fit conventional marketing categories is a welcome development after the defensive conformism of the 1970s. The vitality of independent and underground publications, combined with the comparative wealth of the 1980s, undoubtedly weakened the influence of marketing professionals and the preference for the low common denominator of mediocrity which is their constant companion – a fact which has become most apparent in the defeat of the eyes-three-inches-apart-staring-at-the-reader-and-no-monochrome-please school of cover design at *Vogue* and 99 per cent of all women's fashion magazines. The big publishing houses of course retain their commitment to very precise demographic targetting of editorial products; it is rarely from this source that innovation springs and, indeed, the internationalization of magazine publishing, whereby national editions are produced locally or transmitted from the home country by satellite, has encouraged homogeneity. Thankfully, however, a little variety of attack has crept back since 1985.

More importantly, a select group of generalist – mainly men's – magazines have thrived on the basis of original and broad-ranging writing and photography rather than on the precision of their marketing pitch, and they reflect a realignment and blurring of the boundary between work and leisure. The best examples are *Arena, Tempo, Actuel, King, Equator, Emois* and *El Europeo,* and we could also include *Spy* and even *Vanity Fair* in this category. In Japan, the target-

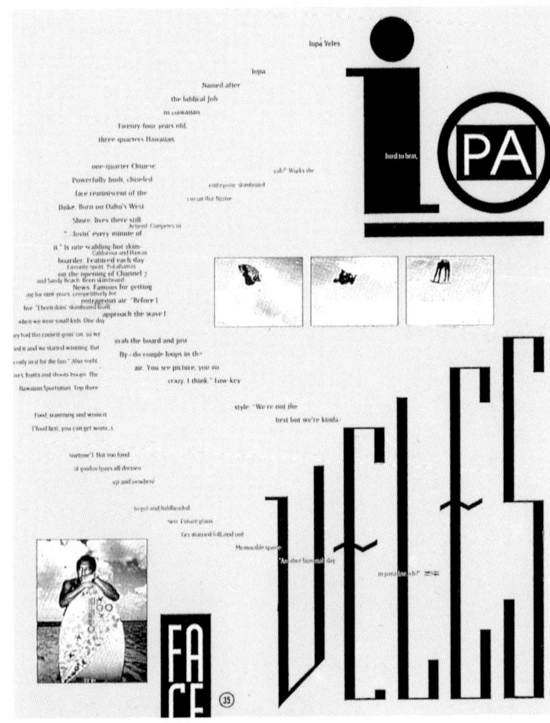

Beach Culture (USA)
Spring 1990
art director David Carson

A highly subjective approach to page layout. The aesthetic establishes mood: type supports the narrative. In this profile of Hawaiian surfer Iopa Veles, David Carson's lyrical typographic construction echoes the shape and shadow of a skimboard. The text, although offset right to left, is surprisingly easy to read and takes on the character of poetry.

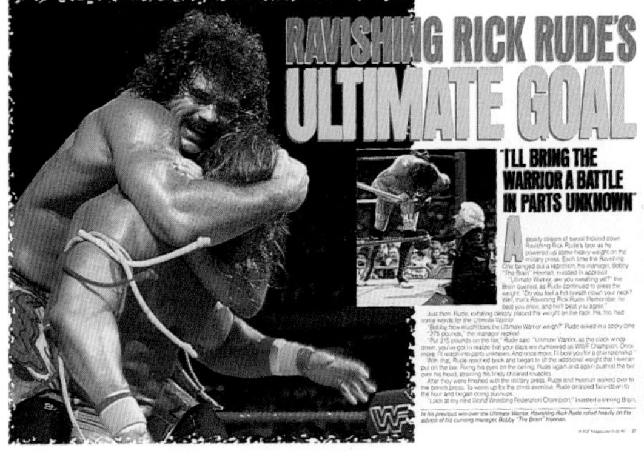
RAVISHING RICK RUDE'S ULTIMATE GOAL

'I'LL BRING THE WARRIOR A BATTLE IN PARTS UNKNOWN'

Wrestling Federation Magazine (USA)
July 1990
art director Susan Fox
photographer Tom Buchanan

A conventional layout given unconventional treatment. Lurid colours, brash headlines and jagged decorative borders defy the norms of graphic taste.

ting of magazines through conceptual ideas instead of specific subject matter has given rise to new story structures and correspondingly unusual visual treatments. The most intriguing example is the curiously named *Money Economy & Time*, which can be explained only as meandering around the circumference of peoples' working lives, a magazine which succeeds in gelling an unlikely combination of poetic illustrated essays with economic analysis, consumer articles and travel in a format in which visual images predominate. *Edge* and *Mr*, two fashion magazines, accompany clothes spreads with incongruously sonorous articles on business. *Switch*, the self-styled "seek and find magazine", is an interview magazine centred loosely in the arts, which has subtly shifted the format by giving up to half of each issue to a single story, and is therefore able to couple in-depth interviews with extensive photographic essays and subsidiary articles, thus successfully re-inventing itself each month. Magazines such as *Interview* and *French Glamour*, in which advertising has crept back to either side of an editorial well, have given art directors a clear opportunity to develop strong visual themes which can run through the length of an issue.

Some specialist magazines have given themselves more liberal definitions, using a fixed focus on specific cultural groupings to create the freedom to explore outside their declared subject area. This is particularly true of those magazines which have their roots in popular youth culture: *The Face* is not just a music magazine; *i-D* is not just a fashion magazine; *Beach Culture* locates itself in the vicarious sensual pleasures of Valley children and geographically within a band of sand between Zuma and Laguna beaches. So the fragmentation of life is reflected in magazines and their art. Highly specialized publications have adopted equally individualistic and provocative visual presentation – and sometimes in spite of restrictive budgets. Certain titles stand out: in music, *Straight No Chaser, Wire* and *Pati Pati*; in sport, *Transworld Skateboarding*; in the arts and design, *Picadia, Items, Metropolis, Apart, Interview* and *Avenue*; in literature, *Lire* and *Diver*; the business magazine *Management Today*; and in fashion, *Vogue Italia, Looks, X-Men* and *Piacere Rakan*.

None of these examples is an "uncommercial" magazine or a pure experiment in graphic virtuosity, and most fit securely within the mainstream of publishing. What they do have in common is an inventive approach to both content and design. Some have confounded expectations and conflict with the norms of public taste, and are therefore, by definition, "difficult" rather than "simple", "challenging" rather than "direct", and sometimes raw-edged and disordered. All combine varying qualities of drama, aesthetic purity, structural coherence, clarity of form and type, and richness of texture.

The following chapters focus on current developments in magazine typography and design: on innovations in cover design, on editorial structures and typographic formulations, photography and illustration, on the mechanics of layout – in floating and interlocking grids, non-linear geometries and parallel texts, collage and colour. The integration of these elements is a function of the complex relationship between the editorial, technical and aesthetic priorities which together create the "look" of a magazine.

Vogue

Fabien Baron's art direction of Italian Vogue is strong and distinctive. The magazine's visual identity is created out of rigidly consistent use of type, colour, illustration and photography (also see page 214). Colour is employed very sparingly: black and metallic inks are relieved by reds and blues saturated by black, and occasionally contrasted by lively oranges and greens. Only one illustrator – the immediately recognisable Mats Gustafson – is ever used. The art director's treatment of type, however, is his most idiosyncratic feature. Baron uses type primarily as a constructive graphic device which communicates at the visual rather than literary level. It echoes and takes on the form of opposing images. Thus the curving serifs of the page-high "i" (page 134) mimic the curving eyeline and lash in the close-cropped portrait of Isabella Rosellini; the angles of a headline set in Franklin Gothic Extra Condensed (right) echo the triangular "pure lines" of the sculpture; and the contorted shape of the body (above right) is matched by type set square with vertical heading. This extreme formalism creates a beautifully integrated visual aesthetic which, in spite of its appearance, cannot be reconciled with conventional modernism – it triumphs over legibility. Vogue is, however, a fashion magazine and words are chosen to attack instinct, not reason: in this case the approach is entirely justified. Baron uses the freedom provided by an editorial well devoid of advertising to build a cinematic narrative of emotive visual images. An immaculate compositional sense is married to an acute sensitivity to subject matter.

Vogue (Italy)
June 1989
art director Fabien Baron
photographer
Barry McKinley

Vogue (Italy)
September 1989
art director Fabien Baron
photographers
Stefano Spedicato,
John Zimmerman/Pignotti

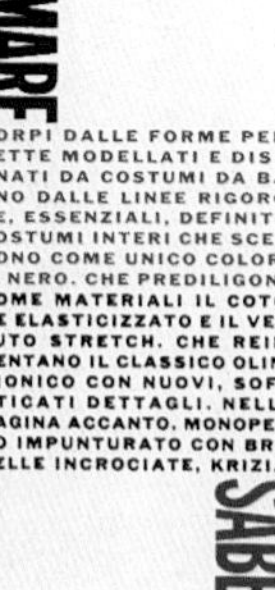

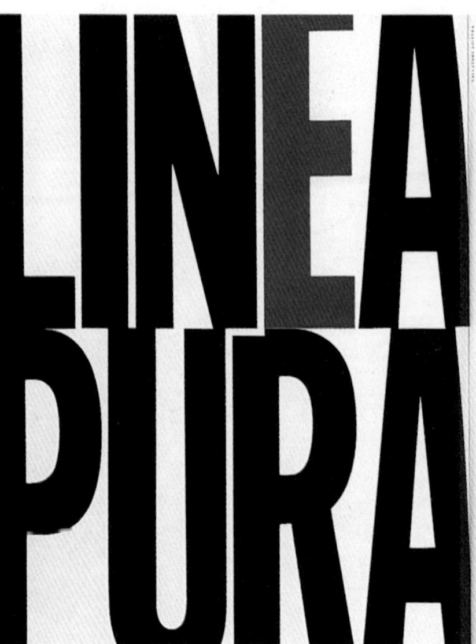

Vogue Speciale (Italy)
March 1989
art director Fabien Baron
photograher
Salvatore Licitra

Non un protagonista solitario, ma un danzatore coreografo capace di dividere il suo talento con altri talenti. Una carriera segnata da incontr[illegible] «eccellenti», ad esempio il lungo, intens[illegible] soda-lizio che ha legato **Nureiev** a Marg[illegible] **Fonteyn** o le collaborazioni con un'altra «grande [illegible] come Carla **Fracci**. Nomi-leggenda uniti qui a Luc[illegible] **Savignano** in una fotografia che appare emblematica e riassuntiva di un pezzo di storia del balletto. Con Nureiev e intorno a lui si sono realizzati spettacoli che costituiscono un'autentica svolta nel panorama del '900.

Vogue (Italy)
September 1989
art director Fabien Baron
photographer Steven Meisel

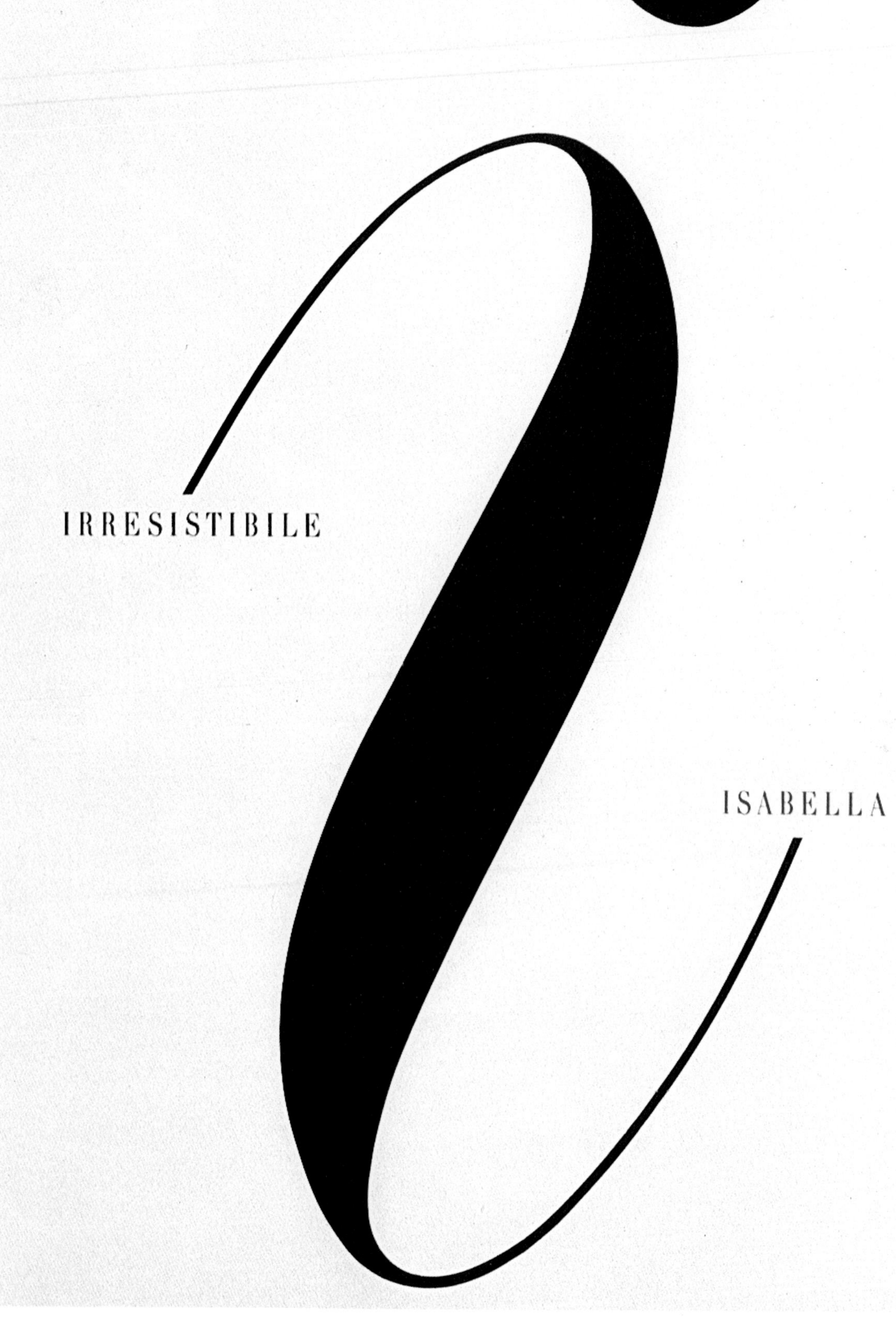

Interview

Interview promotes the artist as "star": it profiles personalities in the fine and popular arts by combining photographic essays with interviews. The anatomy of this simple editorial formula is laid bare by art director Fabien Baron's daring handling of structure. Each of the elements of an article are sternly separated out, page by page. The Bobby Brown feature (right) is a typical example of the technique. The headline fills a full page of the first spread; facing it is a headshot in profile, and following it three more full-page pictures selected to produce dramatic variations of scale and posture. The text, led by two pull-out quotes, is not introduced until the third spread. Thus Baron forces the reader to unfold the story a page at a time, breaking the convention of showing all of the elements of a feature – headline, pictures, text – in a single opening spread. Along the way he creates visual surprise and answers, one by one, Interview's two essential questions: what does this person look like? What do they have to say? This method, which is not economical with space, requires sensitive pacing and a high degree of control over editorial content. His work is marked by bold use of type and space, but equally important to editorial content – rather than appearance – are the portfolios (e.g. facing page, on the rose) commissioned from artists and photographers, which in each issue provide a thematic visual glue between features. This domineering art direction is sometimes to the detriment of literary material but through it Baron has forged a powerfully coherent magazine.

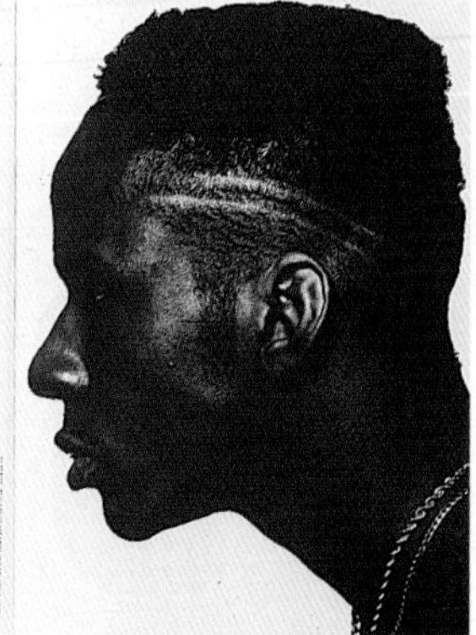

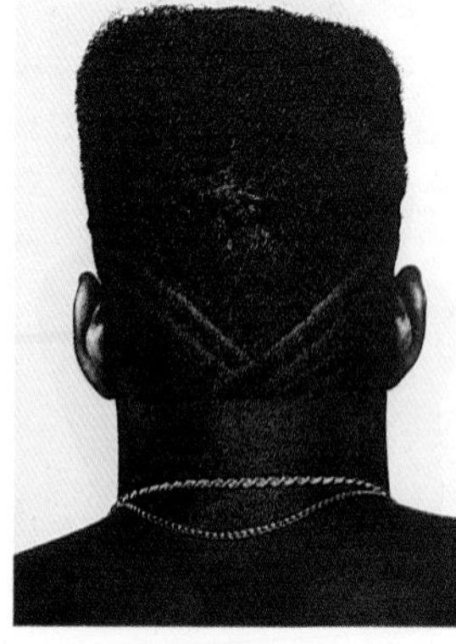

"When I meet someone for the first time, I always look at their shoes. If the shoes are neat, it says this person takes care of himself. I'm one person who can't go out of the house with a pair of dirty shoes."

Interview (USA)

April 1990

creative director Fabien Baron

photographer Albert Watson

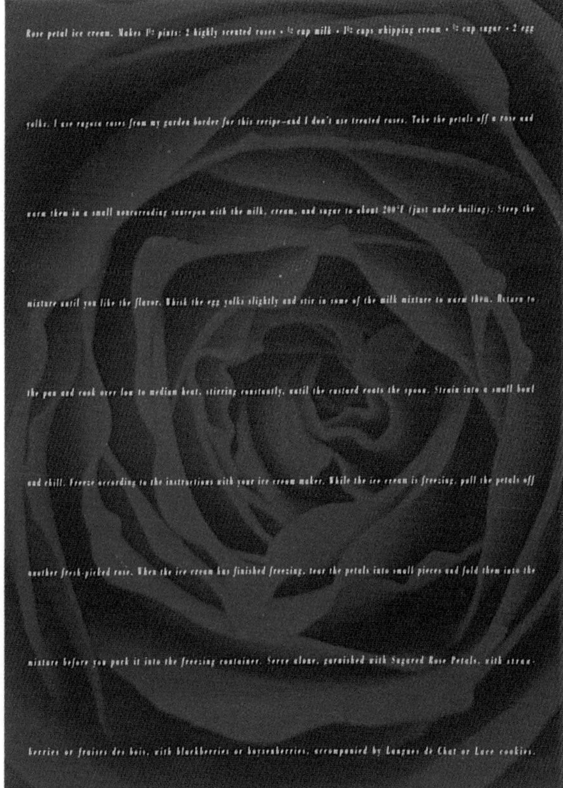

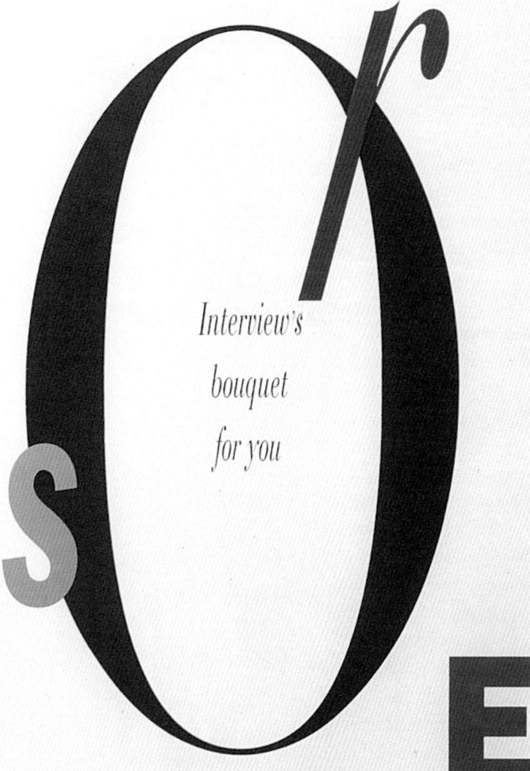

Interview (USA)

February 1990

creative director
Fabien Baron

photographers
Sarah Charlesworth,
Bill Steele

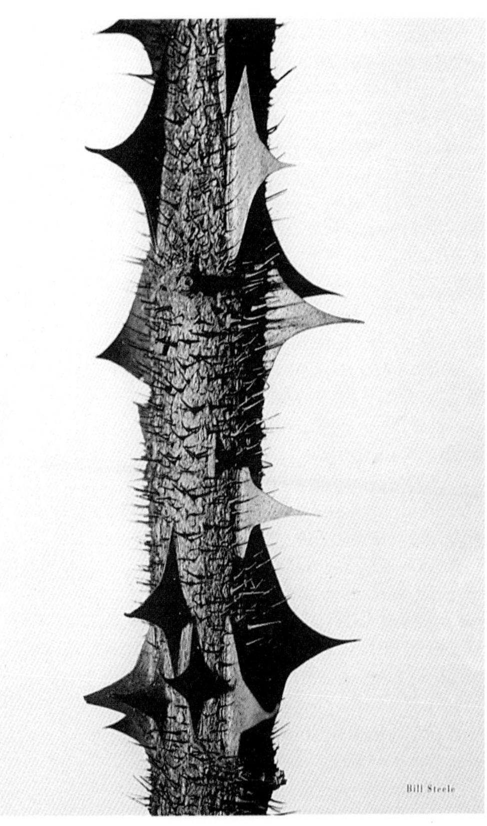

Spy

Spy's art direction is both imaginative and appropriate to its content. Within a disciplined typographic format based on Garamond, Alternate Gothic and Metro Black, and on a small budget, the art director creates a great variety of visual imagery which builds upon the mocking humour of the editorial. Spy, dedicated to demolishing the pretensions and perversions of New York society, has a retentive obsession for the minutiae of corruption which is presented in features stuffed full of tables, diagrams, sidebars set in 7pt and lengthy body texts, which run in parallel and often over many pages. Spy is not a browsers' magazine. This earnest documentation is painstakingly structured in print used as multi-layered and highly graphic information design. It has visual clarity but also the air of arcane complexity essential to Spy's eccentric persona, an identity given expression by tiny portraits inserted in tables (opposite, far right) and pictograms which punctuate the text to emphasise running gags and issue themes, as in the hand gun which doubles as a turning symbol (centre spread). The style, with its elaborate detailing and typographic embellishment, is "post-modern" yet decorative elements become functional signposts to editorial sections. The magazine spurns simplistic combinations of large pictures and unbroken bodies of text, but the maze of editorial components is relieved by strong openers with powerful headlines: "Big dumb white guys with guns" is the perfect lead to a feature on right-wing fraternal societies, and Alex Isley has given it the prominence it deserves.

Spy (USA)
June 1988
art director Alexander Isley

FRIENDLY NEIGHBORS
PERSONAL LIBERTY
FRESH AIR
Our First Annual Sea-to-Shining-Sea Summer Jamboree
MODERN CONVENIENCES
CLEAN LIVING
PIZZERIA
GOOD FOOD
70 SPY JUNE 1988

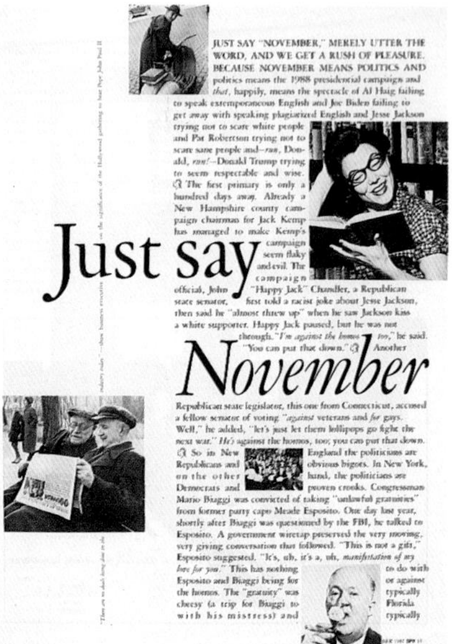
Just say November

JUST SAY "NOVEMBER," MERELY UTTER THE WORD, AND WE GET A RUSH OF PLEASURE. BECAUSE NOVEMBER MEANS POLITICS AND politics means the 1988 presidential campaign and *that*, happily, means the spectacle of Al Haig failing to speak extemporaneous English and Joe Biden failing to get *away* with speaking plagiarized English and Jesse Jackson trying not to scare white people and Pat Robertson trying not to scare sane people and—*run*, Donald, *run!*—Donald Trump trying to seem respectable and wise. The first primary is only a hundred days away. Already a New Hampshire county campaign chairman for Jack Kemp has managed to make Kemp's campaign seem flaky and evil. The campaign official, John "Happy Jack" Chandler, a Republican state senator, first told a racist joke about Jesse Jackson, then said he "almost threw up" when he saw Jackson kiss a white supporter. Happy Jack paused, but he was not through. "*I'm against the homos too*," he said. "You can put that down." Another Republican state legislator, this one from Connecticut, accused a fellow senator of voting "*against* veterans and *for* gays. Well," he added, "let's just let them lollipops go fight the next war." *He's* against the homos, too; you can put that down. So in New England the politicians are Republicans and obvious bigots. In New York, on the other hand, the politicians are Democrats and proven crooks. Congressman Mario Biaggi was convicted of taking "unlawful gratuities" from former party capo Meade Esposito. One day last year, shortly after Biaggi was questioned by the FBI, he talked to Esposito. A government wiretap preserved the very moving, very giving conversation that followed. "This is not a gift," Esposito suggested. "It's, uh, it's a, uh, *manifestation of my love for you*." This has nothing to do with Esposito and Biaggi being for or against the homos. The "gratuity" was typically cheesy (a trip for Biaggi to Florida with his mistress) and typically

BIG, DUMB WHITE GUYS WITH GUNS

When it comes to the rest of the country, we know we have a bad attitude. A decidedly *wrong* attitude. Fearful, ungenerous, incredulous, suspicious. Shame on us. But we also suspected that our long-standing perception—of a vast cultural Gobi populated by armed neo-Nazi lunatics scheming to establish an Aryan state, fez-topped Shriners on tiny scooters, a buffoonish president worthy of a Sinclair Lewis satire, small-town heroes squabbling over TV-movie rights to the story of their selfless bravery, the KKK practically in our backyard—was probably just a teeny bit unfair.

So, like many before us, we went in search of America. We were ready to renounce our skepticism, eager to learn. If the average citizen can enjoy a simple Memorial Day parade down Main Street, we reasoned, then so can we. We set out to find one. We did.

We also found a vast cultural Gobi populated by armed neo-Nazi lunatics scheming to establish an Aryan state, fez-topped Shriners on tiny scooters, a buffoonish president worthy of a Sinclair Lewis satire, small-town heroes squabbling over TV-movie rights to the story of their selfless bravery and, yes, the KKK practically in our backyard.

JUNE 1988 SPY 71

Spy (USA)
August 1988
art director Alexander Isley
illustrator Drew Friedman

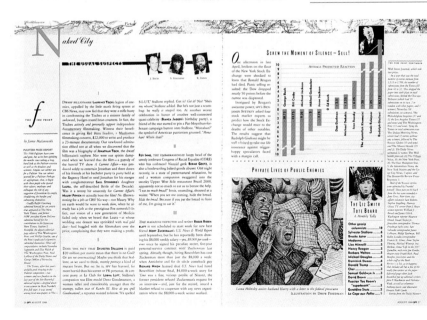

Naked City

THE USUAL SUSPECTS

SCREW THE MOMENT OF SILENCE—SELL!

PRIVATE LIVES OF PUBLIC ENEMIES

THE LIZ SMITH TOTE BOARD

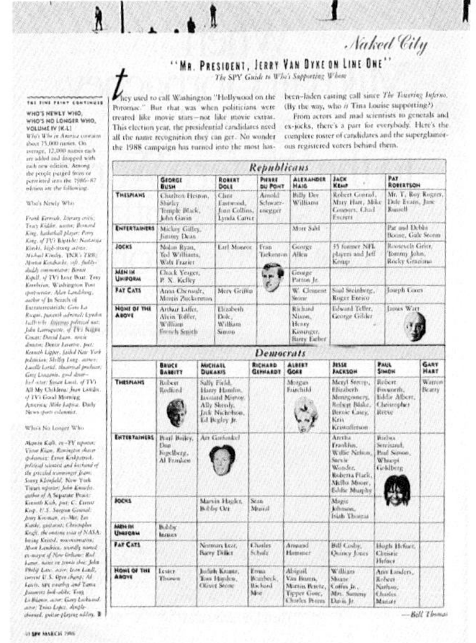

Naked City

"MR. PRESIDENT, JERRY VAN DYKE ON LINE ONE"

Spy (USA)
March 1988
art director Alexander Isley

Spy (USA)

April 1988

art director Alexander Isley

A self-mocking parody of Spy editorial design opens a feature on Post-Modern style with a jarring mix of evil pastel shades, typographic noise and pocket pictures as signs.

POSTMODERN DANCE

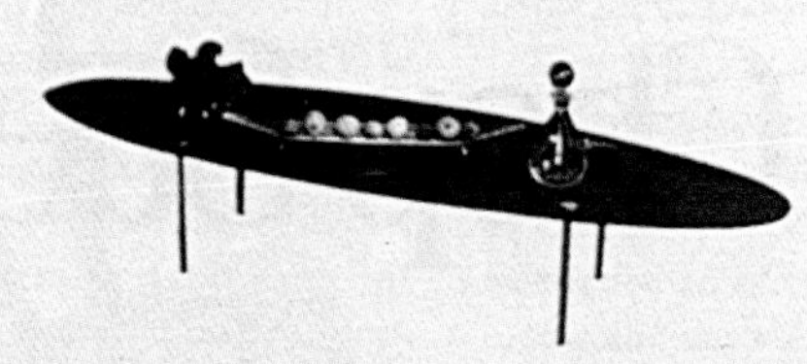

POSTMODERN PAINTING

Postmodern Graphics

Postmodern *ARCHITECTURE*

A SPY Guide

The Rise and Fall of a Great American Buzzword

Postmodern *DECORATION*

POSTMODERN *Furniture*

by Bruce Handy

Post— modern CLOTHING

The word *postmodern* used to mean something, in much the same way that *prehistory*, say, means things that happened in the epoch before history was invented, or that *canine* means "of dogs." *Postmodern* started life as a critical term. First in architecture, then in painting and dance, it referred to works that consciously rebelled against modernist style, often by paying homage to the once-shunned styles and genres of the past. ▶ To college professors and *Artforum* editors it still means that. To rock critics and slick-magazine-caption writers and wraithlike people standing around the lobby at the Brooklyn Academy of Music — well, it's hard to pin down what *postmodern* means to them. It can mean anything that's sort of old

Post~modern THEATER

POST~MODERN *Food*

to

POSTMODERN **Television**

POSTMODERN **MU-SIC**

Postmodern

Everything

POSTMODERN *ART*

Post~modern FICTION

King

In its heyday in the late 1980s King was a men's general interest magazine with some guts and a sharp, jaundiced eye for the darker side of modern life. Its design, by the Canadian Nigel Smith at Studio Sergio Sartori, reflected this editorial slant. King's informed reporting of bizarre social and political phenomena was presented in the German photojournal tradition of bold picture treatments and montage, but overlaid by a clean, highly stylized typography and an individual use of spot colour which gave the magazine its distinct visual indentity; this was bound together by decorative elements in the Memphis style, in marbled borders which defined separate editorial sections. The picture (right) headlined Cattavissimi – "the bad guys" – opens a feature on political tyranny in Central America with a forceful montage of portraits of El Salvadorean neo-fascist Roberto D'Abuysson, Contra leader Adolfo Calero, and Manuel Noriega: brutal faces over which an angry red tint has been laid. Two other spreads (opposite, below right and bottom) demonstrate King's uninhibited presentation of insanitary subjects. The magazine also provided very original coverage of men's fashion. Typical of the magazine's informative treatment is the use of subtle spot colour to pick out six different cuts of suit collar (opposite, above right).

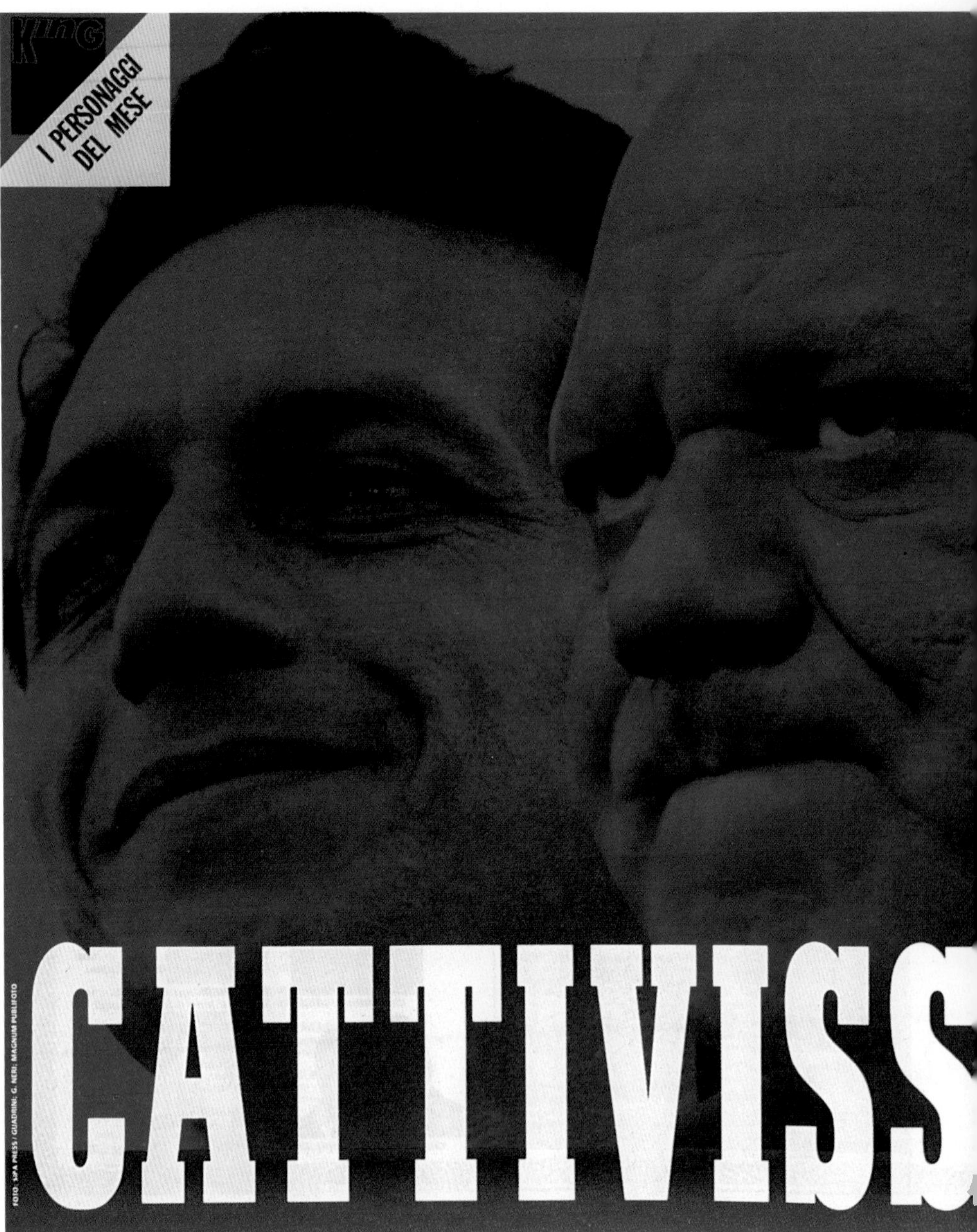

King (Italy)
April 1989
designer Nigel Smith/ Studio Sergio Sartori
photographers Sipa/G.Neri/Magnum

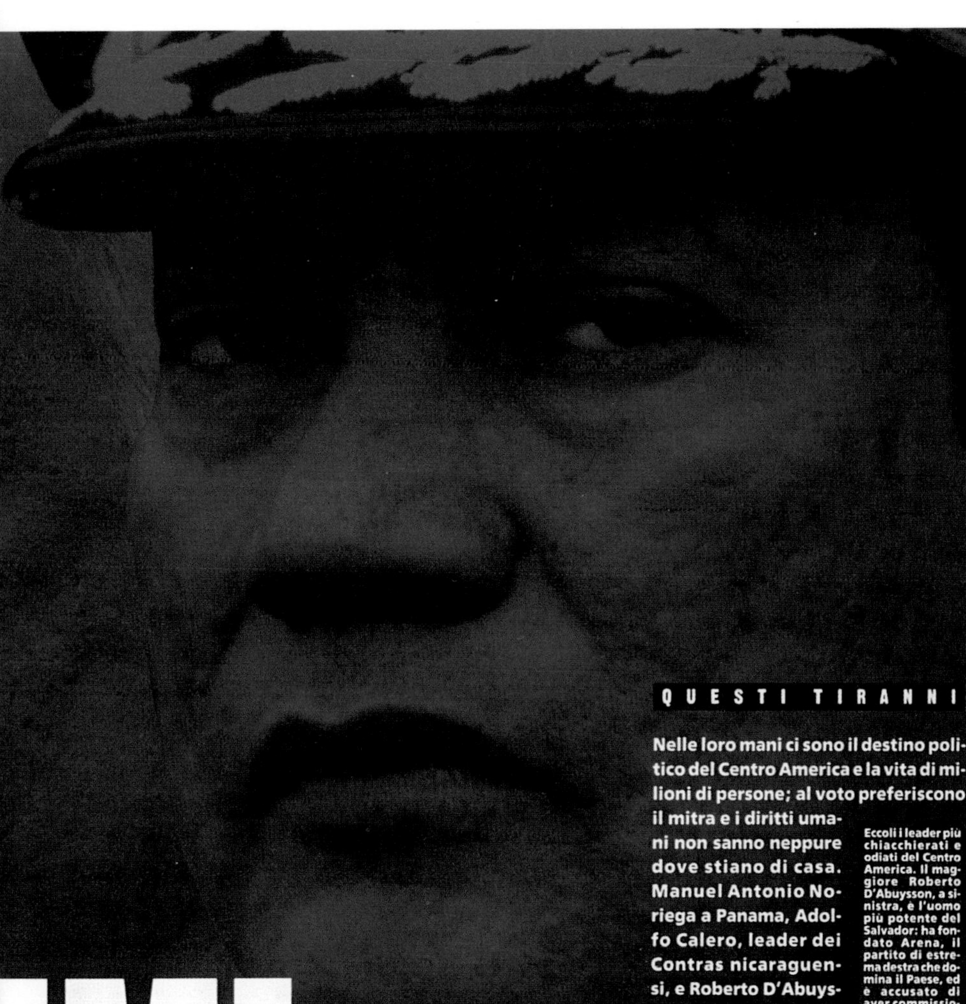

IMI

QUESTI TIRANNI

Nelle loro mani ci sono il destino politico del Centro America e la vita di milioni di persone; al voto preferiscono il mitra e i diritti umani non sanno neppure dove stiano di casa. Manuel Antonio Noriega a Panama, Adolfo Calero, leader dei Contras nicaraguensi, e Roberto D'Abuysson in Salvador usano ogni mezzo, anche il più spietato e brutale, per raggiungere il loro scopo. King è andato a intervistarli ponendo ai tre domande scomode sui loro traffici, sui loro sistemi di dominio, legali e no

Eccoli i leader più chiacchierati e odiati del Centro America. Il maggiore Roberto D'Abuysson, a sinistra, è l'uomo più potente del Salvador: ha fondato Arena, il partito di estrema destra che domina il Paese, ed è accusato di aver commissionato l'omicidio dell'arcivescovo Romero. Adolfo Calero (al centro) con l'appoggio della Cia guida da Miami la rivolta dei Contras contro il governo sandinista del Nicaragua. Manuel Antonio Noriega, il caudillo di Panama, è accusato dal governo americano di aiutare i narcotrafficanti e di riciclare dollari sporchi.

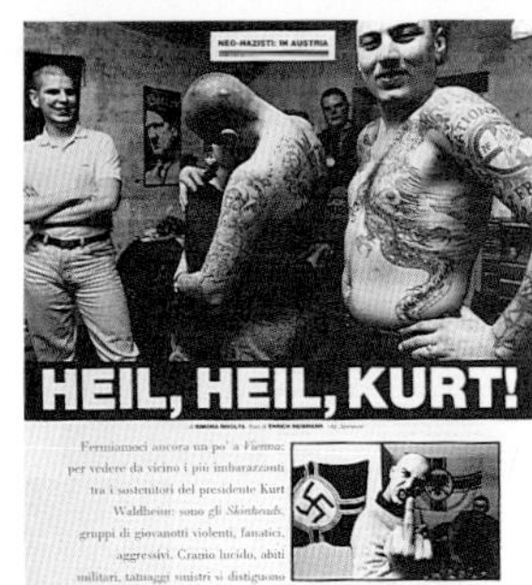

King (Italy)
May 1988
designer Nigel Smith/
Studio Sergio Sartori
photographer
Enrich Reismann

King (Italy)
May 1989
designer Nigel Smith/
Studio Sergio Sartori

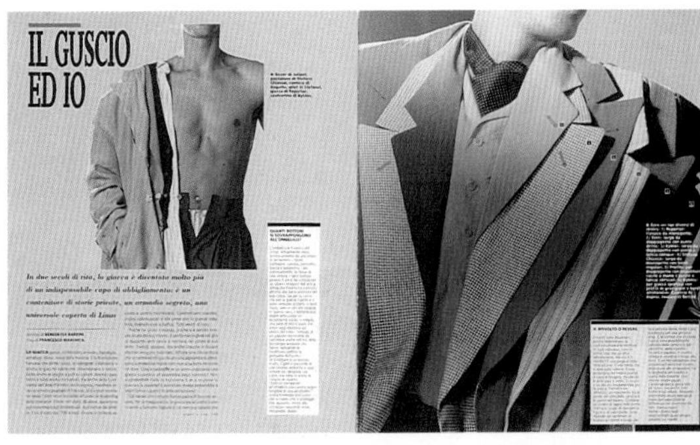

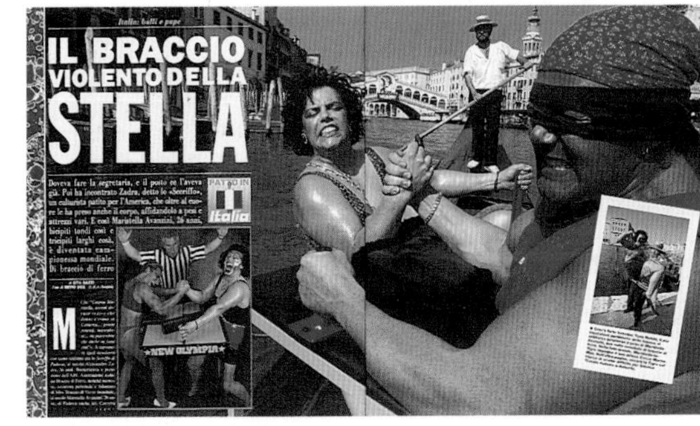

King (Italy)
October 1988
designer Nigel Smith/
Studio Sergio Sartori
photographer Nevio Doz

The Face

These three spreads from The Face, designed by Neville Brody, are from a special feature on Parisian art, style and fashion. The article is composed of a number of separate stories, each consisting mainly of pictures, captions and, in some cases, extended introductions. It is of the kind that requires decisive intervention by the art director if any sense is to be made of it. Brody's treatment is unusual in its picture placement, typography and page structure. The feature opens with a daring full-page heading in custom type (repeated in scaled-down form on subsequent pages to splice the feature together) facing a standfirst set in a size too small for such a wide measure but given generous leading. The inset cameos and miscellaneous page elements, such as byline, turn symbol and folio number, add graphic interest rather than clutter to a spread designed with great restraint. In the two following spreads the designer has dispensed entirely with conventional layout disciplines. One spread, for example (opposite), uses neither modular composition nor the common descending vertical order of head, standfirst and text. But despite their abstruse geometric logic the pages work brilliantly. They are well balanced along horizontal and vertical axes, the use of dogleg setting meshes the typographic elements together, and the bastard measures above and below photographic portraits work as plinths and columns. The overall effect, as befits the nature of the material, is of a set of exhibition panels which are read in a circular order dictated by the delicate composition.

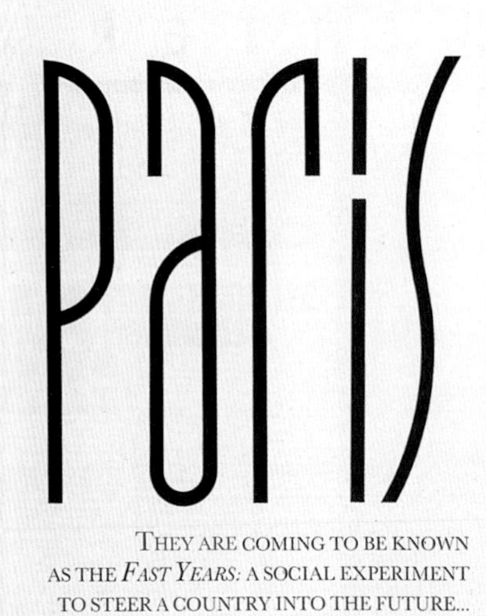

THEY ARE COMING TO BE KNOWN AS THE *FAST YEARS:* A SOCIAL EXPERIMENT TO STEER A COUNTRY INTO THE FUTURE...

Photography ANDREW MACPHERSON Text PATRICK ZERBIB

WHO SHAPES PARIS LIFE? EUROSTYLE TEENS, POST-MARXIST THINKERS, STARLETS AND STREET GANGS? ALL OF THESE. AND THE 24 PICTURED OVER...

S I D I K I B A K A B A

FREDERIC ANDREI WAS THE OPERA-LOVING POSTBOY IN JEAN-JACQUES BENEIX'S MOVIE *DIVA*, THE FRENCH FILM THAT HELPED DEFINE THE STYLE OF POP VIDEOS AND MOVIES IN THE EIGHTIES. HE'S JUST COMPLETED *PARIS MINUIT*, WHICH HE DIRECTED AND STARS IN.

ELIZABETH DJIAN IS THE STYLIST WHO GAVE *JILL* MAGAZINE ITS DISTINCTIVE CHARACTER, LENDING CLASS TO OUTRAGEOUS CLOTHES AND WIT TO CLASSICS. SHE STYLED OUR OPENING FASHION STORY.

PHILIPPE GAUTIER is one of a new generation of video artists, after Goude and Mondino, inspired by the comic book art that the French excelled at in the Seventies. Much sought after by advertisers, he has made clips for Telephone, Ray Lema and an award-winning short for Rita Mitsouko. His films are the product of collaborative effort between film-maker, designers and musicians, resulting in a unique kind of collective imagery. **"Over the last five years, Paris has exploded. There are creative people in every field, except perhaps music, which is weak. But it's still hard to find the means to do things. I borrowed money from the bank to make my first short film four years ago and I've just about finished paying it back. As for showing my work in London and New York, I'd like to but I still haven't done enough yet. I really want to work in the US where they have the best computer technicians specialising in synthetic images. That's my big project, a feature that integrates computer-generated imagery with live action; but you have to take your time about these things."**

JOANNA PAVLIS is an actress and model based in Paris. After studying acting in Washington, she went to New York and lived from "odd jobs, like everybody". Her career took off in Europe, when she modelled for *Vogue* and *Harper's* and appeared in short films in Paris. In her first feature, *Red Kiss*, she plays an American model who falls in love with Parisian photographer Lambert Wilson.

"I left New York four or five years ago. I thought I could avoid being a waitress here. Besides, I have a very European face. My family is Greek and Russian, so I felt maybe I wasn't quite right for the States. In Paris, people see cinema as an art, they argue about films, whereas in the States, they just want to know if an actor is 'bankable'. There is such a love for cinema here. People are always working, they are very professional. Of course, working in another language is hard; the only thing I can rely on is emotion. But that too is kind of easier here."

JACK LANG

AS MINISTER OF CULTURE DURING MITTERAND'S PRESIDENCY, JACK LANG ENVIGORATED THE ARTISTIC LIFE OF THE CAPITAL. HE BACKED CONTROVERSIAL SCHEMES AND FUNDED FRESH VENTURES. HE WORE A **LEWIS LEATHERS** JACKET IN PHOTOS AND PICKED THE LABEL OFF HIS GREY **LACOSTE** IN MEETINGS.

ANTOINE DE CAUNES

Antoine de Caunes is the producer and host of radio and TV shows. He is about to publish his first novel, a thriller set in the rock scene that jets between New York and Paris.

"I work and think in English. My book tells the story of a real New York detective. I wrote it in English and the hardest part of the job was to adapt it into French. At the moment I'm preparing a twice-monthly 90-minute rock show for US cable networks, but my big project is a film script, a comedy that could only be produced in America because of the high budget. I've sent a copy to Dan Aykroyd. I live and dream as an American, but I love coming back to Paris. That's where my roots are."

DIANE KURYS

Diane Kurys has had two international successes as a director with *Diabolo Menthe* and *Coupe de Foudre*. Her next production, filmed in English at Rome's Cinecitta, stars Peter Coyote, Greta Scaachi, Jamie Lee Curtis.

"I've had to accept that film is an international medium since the success of *Diabolo Menthe*. Since then, Paris has been my home, and America my second home. In Paris I have my family and friends, people you know from shoot after shoot. Since *Coup de Foudre*, I've had more and more American offers. Each time I ask myself if I should go, and it is tempting. In America my friends are more eclectic: artists and people who work in areas other than film. I couldn't imagine an effective relationship with anyone there. When the French go to sleep in Paris, the Americans wake up in Los Angeles."

ALAIN BASHUNG

Alain Bashung, a singer and – for France – an authentic rocker, has had an erratic career since his debut disc in 1968. Since his comeback eight years ago, he has become one of the most popular of a new generation of singer-songwriters. His latest album is "Crossing The Rio Grande".

"Paris is my first home but she doesn't satisfy me. I can't do everything here. I can't write. It's impossible. I make a few notes then I leave and hide in a hotel in Normandy. It's dangerous; you drink too much and you eat too much. Here, you can't work efficiently. In London you can record for 12 hours with a ten minute break and people don't make any problems. And I use Ian Dury's musicians; you don't have to explain the humour or the feeling to them a hundred times."

THE FACE 63

The Face (UK)

July 1986

art director Neville Brody

photographer Andrew Macpherson

Transworld Skateboarding

In all sports magazines the essential design problem is to get across the sense of movement, physical dynamism and excitement inherent in the subject. David Carson's radical solution at Transworld Skateboarding was to use highly abstracted imagery and a freeform typography that vividly expresses the culture and the action of the sport. In skateboarding, like dance, motion is everything, but its individualist nature limits the photographic possibilities to boy/girl on skateboard. As well as using the obvious fisheye and wide-angle lens shots, Carson crops viciously into detail, exploits motion blur and odd angles, photocopy degeneration, textured halftone screens and the application of lurid spot colour to create a wide variety of impressionistic visual effects. Pictures have primacy over words. Type is cut up, set small in an acre of white space, placed at oblique angles or dropped into the vertical: there is no regular form to the page, and legibility is often sacrificed to the creation of invigorating layout. Disobeying the rules, doing what you want, is part of skateboard culture and if this were not reflected in the magazine it would be failing its readership.

Andy Howell, a rookie pro without a board sponsor, sliding off the lower wall.

the stubbies
challenge
nsa pro-am championship
olympic velodrome
carson, california
september 26 & 27, 1987
by steven harnish

Transworld Skateboarding (USA)
1987
art director David Carson
photographs Brittain/OFoto

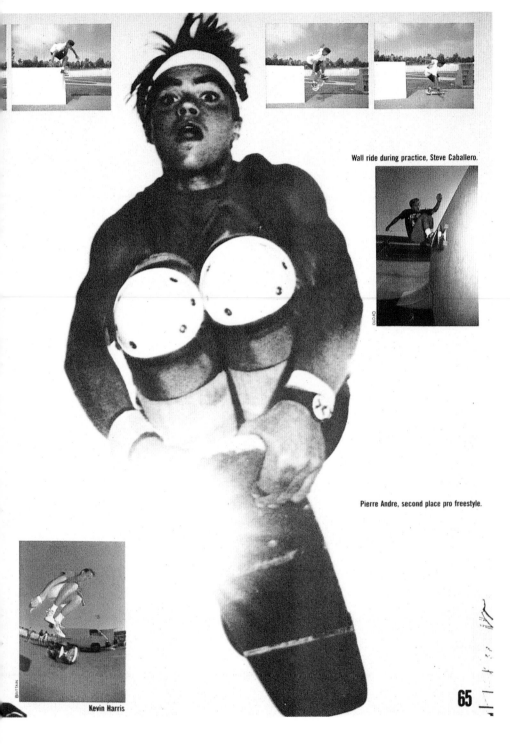

Wall ride during practice, Steve Caballero.

Pierre Andre, second place pro freestyle.

Kevin Harris

65

Transworld Skateboarding (USA)
1987
art director David Carson
photographers Grant, Vuckovich

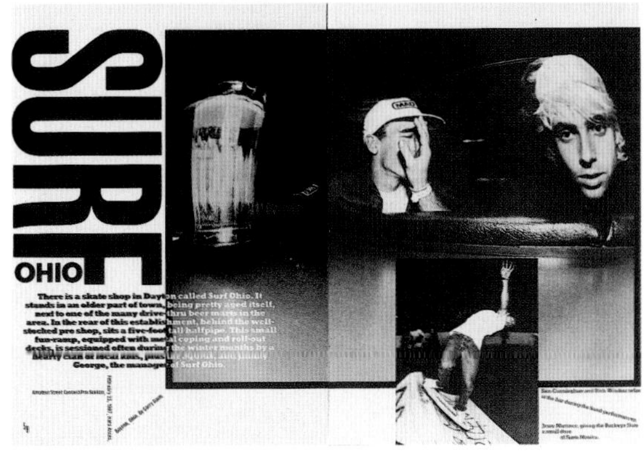

Transworld Skateboarding (USA)
August 1987
art director David Carson
photographer Swank

Emigre

Although the arts and graphic design magazine Emigre cannot be judged by conventional design criteria, the typographic experiments conducted within its pages have begun to exert an influence on the layout of commercial magazines. Emigre exploits its over-size format and the graphic capabilities of desktop publishing systems (see pages 224 – 31) to create novel page structures, textural layers and typographic stresses. Designer Rudy VanderLans also makes inventive use of offset litho print processes. Aesthetic priorities are dominant in this experimental and very beautiful magazine but Emigre has also evolved into an informative document of graphic techniques which provides an underlying discipline as well as inspiration. One spread (right) demonstrates an aspect of Emigre's unusual page structure: it contains four separate articles/ interviews, all of which are carried from the previous page and over into the next – they run in parallel, and are distinguished by different font, type size, measure, leading and shape. The principle is quickly picked up by the reader and creates fascinating interlocking forms on the page. An interview is reprinted verbatim (opposite, top) using rapid changes in type size and weight to represent verbal stress. To emphasise the distressed quality of Stefano Massei's photography to which a whole issue was devoted, one spread was printed on newsprint. Type is laid over the image, and type on type, integrating the composition and creating multi-dimensional layering.

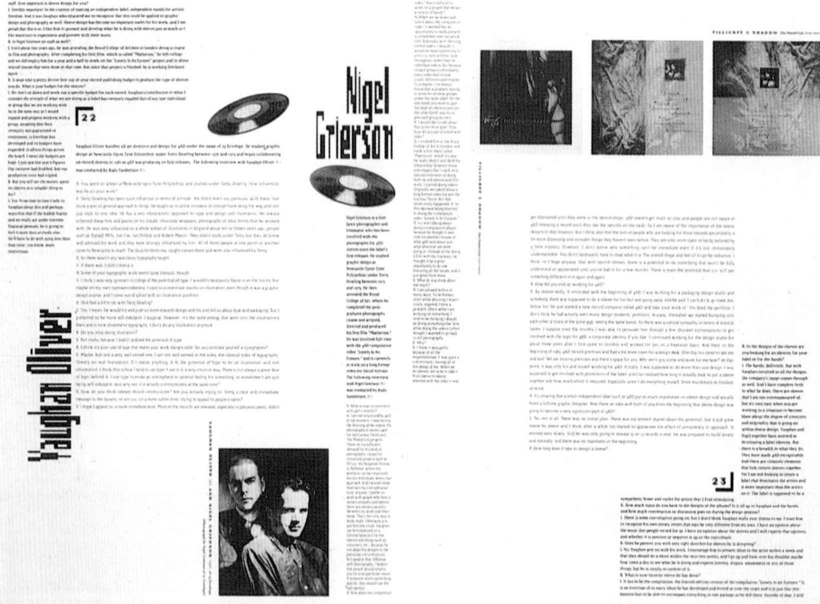

22

Nigel Grierson

Vaughan Oliver

23

Emigre (USA)
No. 9 1988
designer Rudy VanderLans
type designer Zuzana Licko

Johnny D.: **Hey, what's going on?** Emigre: I just want to hear your reaction to this page we received from Thirst. Rick Valicenti just... *Johnny:* **Who?** Emigre: Eh...Rick Valicenti, he designed this page and he used Mike Ditka as a symbol for Chicago. *Johnny: Oh, yeah I saw that.* Emigre: Now, Ditka is not exactly the most popular guy around at this point. Three losses in a row! How do you feel about Ditka as a symbol for Chicago? *Johnny: It's a bit weird especially when I see Ditka talk on Monday Night Football, sorta going* **Blah, Blah, Blah...** *But personally I think it's a great tribute to the guy. Because eh...* **sports is my life,** *you know; graphic design, I like it, I know a bit about it, but sports is my life, and I love the coach. You know, he's a real strong personality. Unfortunately things aren't going so well at present.* **So he loses three games. So what?** *He'll be back. He's pissed right now, because you know, he's never lost three games in a row. But the guy never gives up, never says no, he never quits. Chicago likes that and coach Ditka stands for what this city is all about. We're a real blue collar town. It's a tough place. Not like San Francisco, those wimps. They have an earthquake and they cancel the World Series, the fucking WORLD SERIES!* **Come on! Sports is my life, I couldn't deal with that.** Emigre: So you think Ditka's sorry he traded McMahon right now? *Johnny: Well, I know Mike Ditka, (I mean not personally, of course, we wouldn't get along). But eh...maybe in the back of his mind he might regret it a little bit. I don't know. Ditka's unpredictable. That's what we like about the guy. And anyhow, in San Diego they're gonna bench McMahon this Sunday.* **So what's there to be sorry about?!** Emigre: What do you think Valicenti means with that type on the bottom? *Johnny: Yeah, I'm a little bit pissed off about that, cause he's not clear about it. Is he making fun of the coach there with those letters at the bottom, "DA, blah?" I don't know...* Emigre: Well, what do you think he means by that? *Johnny:* **How the hell would I know?!** *Well maybe it's about how the coach is* CHICAGO / Rick Valicenti [Thirst] *always on television going like blah, blah, blah. He's always mouth'n off a lot. But eh...he's a motivator, he brings out the best in people. Sometimes he's aggressive, sometimes he's happy, sometimes he's selling cars, sometimes Dristan or house mortgages. Anything! But I think Valicenti's interpretation is eh...you know, what is the coach really saying? And it looks like you got a four letter word there or something.* Emigre: So you like the idea of replacing the Sears Tower with Ditka's face? *Johnny: Yeah, to hell with the Sears Tower. Ditka has a very strong presence in town. You see him everywhere, in the papers, on the news, all the time, the guy's everywhere.* Emigre: What do you think of that shot Valicenti used? Taken off a television screen, that's not the most flattering picture is it? At least he could have used some sort of promotional 8 by 10 glossy? *Johnny:* **Nah.** *Well, you know, on the one hand I say* **great,** *Ditka's face as a symbol.* **Chicago's big brother,** *in the city of big shoulders; that's great. But he's not making fun of the guy, or is he? But I guess coach Ditka does the same thing. That's the best part of it.* **He's talking to the press everyday,** *the cameras are on him all the time, he'll stick a piece of gum on the camera, he'll do this or that, he's always poking fun, and he's* **always** *on TV.* Emigre: So you consider this to be an appropriate design? *Johnny:* **What? You're asking for my approval? Is that it?** Emigre: Well, is it thumbs up for this one? *Johnny: Yeah, sure,* **come on,** *the coach gets a full page in some graphic design magazine,* **I think that's great!** *Although I don't know what the hell's going on in there. What the hell's that all about? You got strange photos and textures here and there. I don't know what route you guys travel on your way to work, and shit, that rag costs quite a fortune, I mean jeezus!* Emigre: Well the moment we can produce it for fifty cents a copy we'll sell them for two bucks a piece. *Johnny: Nah, don't worry, I like that entrepreneurial attitude, take whatever you can get. Anyway, I gotta check out. Talk to you later, and eh...* **don't forget about the friggin' World Series on Friday night, OK? LaDeDa.**

Emigre (USA)
no. 8 1988
designer Rudy VanderLans
photographer Stefano Massei

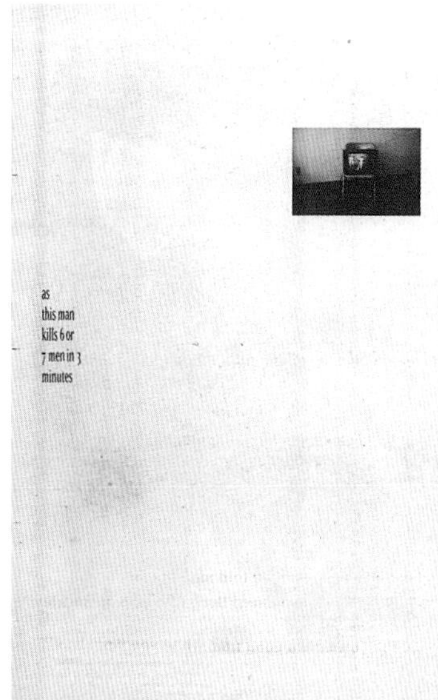

Emigre (USA)
no. 13 1989
designers Rudy VanderLans, Rick Valicenti
type designer Zuzana Licko

Apart

The German cultural magazine, or 'Menschen Enzyclopedia', Apart, follows a reductive design formula, a boiled-down essence of magazine structures which combines simplicity with an underlying subtlety of touch. The page is shorn of all unnecessary embellishment, it follows a rigid rectilinear geometry, and type and picture placement are determined by unbreakable rules of composition fixed by the grid. The system works because of the literary nature of the subject matter. The entire magazine is set in just two weights and two sizes of Futura. The cast-iron two-part grid bisects each page along the horizontal axis, giving four clear divisions to the spread. Each opening spread follows the same format: the top left quadrant is left as white space in which headlines at relatively small size are immediately visible; the bottom left is reserved for photography, the right-hand page for body copy. These strong divisions and the formal separation of text and image give the magazine a surprisingly fluid graphic continuity. The austerity of design provides a neutral platform for text and images, and a scaffolding for subtle graphic variations and beautiful photographic compositions. In the examples here, additional vertical divisions are imposed on the grid according to a 2-4-3 ratio. Folio numbers are set in a tint of black at full page height as a constructive element. In the picture quadrant (see opposite, bottom) picture size diminishes in a spiral according to the golden mean, with additional focus provided by a second colour over monochrome halftones.

Apart (Germany)
no. 10 1988
art director Mike Meiré

acht

neun

zehn

Apart (Germany)
no. 11 1988
art director Mike Meiré

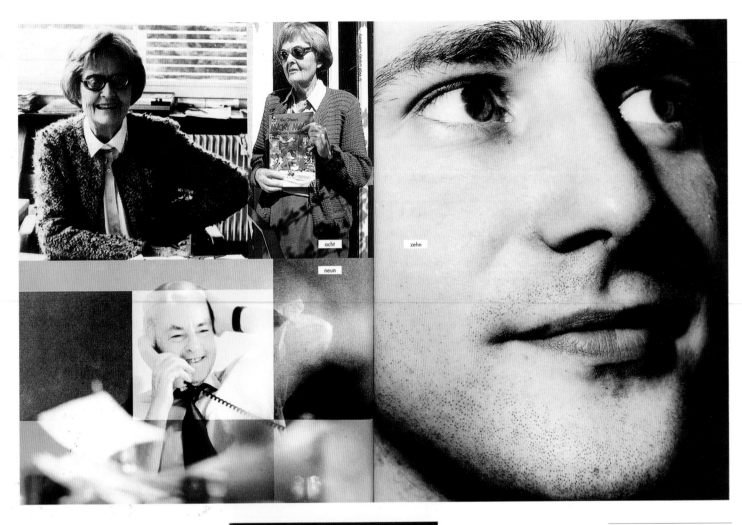

chet Baker

29

Apart (Germany)
no. 10 1988
art director Mike Meiré
photographer
Panni Charrington

Management Today

Management Today is a fascinating example of intimate dialogue between art director and readership, given spice by a tinge of antagonism. The designer, Roland Schenk, joined the magazine in the mid-1960s and, although Management Today has been through many peaks and troughs in that period, Schenk's best work was produced in the late 1980s, when editorial improved substantially, and through the nurturing of photographers of the calibre of Brian Griffin (see pages 198 – 223). Schenk and Griffin treat their subject, the businessman, "like a nude", persuading corporate chiefs into surreal or theatrical situations to make portraits which record fact but also tell a story. Schenk, taught in the German photojournal tradition, uses dramatic contrasts of scale and crops harshly into faces. The page design has a dramatic tension created by a precariously balanced asymmetric dynamic. The massive, tightly spaced grotesque headlines are precisely engineered as constructive building blocks which sheer into photographs. Colour is provided by aggressive reds. The style, reflecting the business ethos of the readership, projects masculinity and strength. Two spreads (opposite) demonstrate the effectiveness of Schenk's technique in a powerful unity of type, image and storyline. The headline is focused by the silent stare of the silhouette and its meaning repeated in the cut-up blocks of the photograph, a device carried through into the following spreads of the feature. The graphic weight of the red panel in which the heading is set is emphasised and delicately balanced by a slim leg of caption copy.

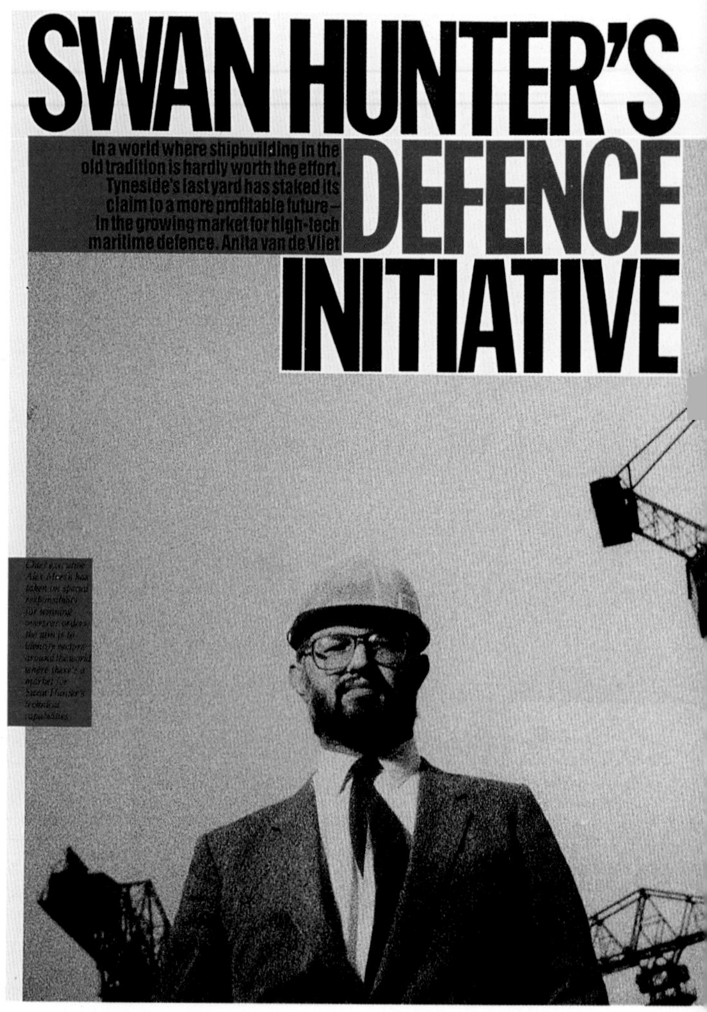

Management Today (UK)
February 1988
art director Roland Schenk
photographer John Claridge

'The last thing I would have done is buy a shipyard,' says Peter Vaughan disparagingly. Since Vaughan is a member of the four-strong management team which bought out Swan Hunter from British Shipbuilders two years ago, the innocent observer might be forgiven a twinge of perplexity. Swan Hunter is the last remaining shipbuilder on Tyneside, with 2,700 ships – including the *Illustrious* and the *Ark Royal* – and 125 years of shipbuilding experience to its name. On a lucky day, as on Wednesday 20th of last month when *HMS Chatham* was launched, you may see one of Swan Hunter's decidedly shipshape products sailing sleekly down the Tyne, cheered on by the men who made her. Towering above them stretch tall cranes, mighty sections of hull, steel-cutting works – indeed, all you might associate with a shipyard. So is Vaughan suffering, one wonders, from the sort of disordered perception which afflicted The Man Who Mistook His Wife For a Hat?

The case, happily, turns out to be less severe, a mixture of oversensitivity and proleptic vision. First, Vaughan and his brother Roger, Swan Hunter's deputy chief executive, respond irritably to descriptions of the company as part of the 'declining British shipbuilding industry'. On the contrary, says Roger stoutly, 'We see ourselves as part of a growing high-tech industry', responsible for some of the 'largest and most sophisticated products in the UK'. And second, although the company will continue to fight for any shipbuilding order it can get, its future profits, according to Peter, who is commercial director in charge of diversification, will not necessarily depend on building ships as such, but on the wider area of 'maritime defence', where Swan Hunter intends to sell its design and technical skills as much as physical products, acting as both consultant and manufacturer.

The consultancy sector is one where Roger Vaughan in particular can claim some expertise: he was one of the founders, and then managing director, of the small but successful A & P Appledore shipyard consultancy in the 1970s (see *Management Today*, October 1986), before rejoining British Shipbuilders as director of productivity in 1981. Now, at Swan Hunter, he explains, 'We're interested in working with naval customers, whether foreign or UK, on defence systems ideas at a very early stage. We can provide product design *and* building, or design a product for someone else to build, or offer long-term support and training. This shifts us from just picking up one middle sector of the business' (the actual building of the ships).

With virtually every maker of merchant ships subsidized, there's just no profit to be made from this side of the business

The reasons behind Swan Hunter's redefinition of business are clear enough. The shipbuilding market is notoriously one of the toughest in the world. Virtually every maker of merchant ships is now subsidized: 'There's no profit to be made out of it anywhere,' says Peter, adding scathingly, 'If the Koreans and Russians want to make floating boxes that carry oil, let them.' Warships, with their sophisticated electronics and weaponry installation are a different (and more profitable) matter, but here, too, the market is suffering from overcapacity – as the imminent closure of the Scott Lithgow yard bears witness.

Last September, Kleinwort Grieveson Securities published an extended research report on 'Warship Building and the Fleet'. 'The future for many of the warship building yards does not look too healthy,' writes analyst Robert Jarman. 'Two warship building companies in the US (Lockheed in Seattle and Todd on the West Coast and in Texas) have recently had to close yards for lack of USN surface-ship orders, and we would expect that trend to

57

Management Today (UK)
March 1988
art director Roland Schenk
photographer Stuart Redler

One of the biggest players in the UK construction market, John Laing faces many of the traditional family company problems. But a new strategy to decentralize operations gives managers entrepreneurial incentives. The aim is both to develop existing divisions and to start new ventures using outside expertise. Will this path enable Laing to break out of the building industry cycle? Annabella Gabb

LAING'S BUILDING BLOCKS

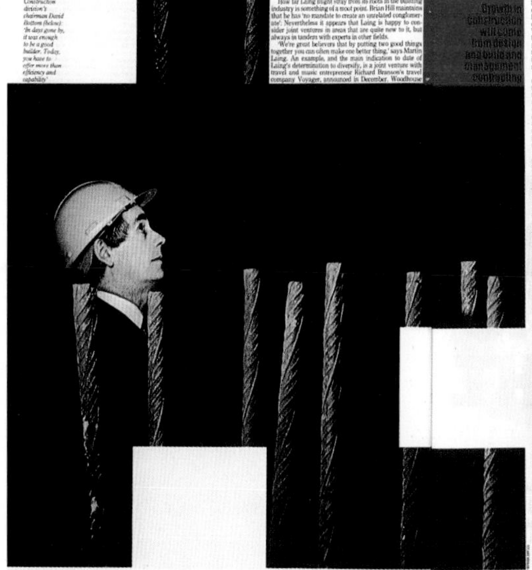

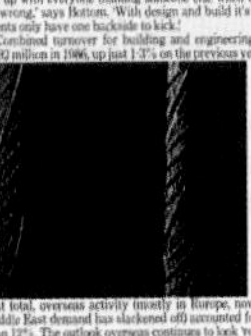

Blueprint

Blueprint and Metropolis (overleaf) are both large format, small circulation architecture/design magazines. They differ wildly in design, and while this can be ascribed to dissimilar editorial approaches – the former focuses on individual designers, the latter explores cultural themes – it is as much the product of diverging national characteristics. The American Metropolis, designed by Helene Silverman, is in the effusive spirit of Burtin and Beall. Blueprint is a development of the international style as adapted to European (and, in the 1960s, American) architecture magazines by such figures as Bill Slack and Massimo Vignelli. Blueprint's format, devised by Simon Esterson, is characterized by disciplined typography and a 4/5/8 grid which, although rigorously adhered to, allows considerable flexibility. These three examples, designed by art director Stephen Coates, show the very varied formal possibilities. The design elements are appropriately scaled to the A3 format: headlines are shot up to 100mm capital heights; pictures are allowed to fill the page. The grid offers powerful contrasts between narrow and wide columns, allows multiple picture sizes, and imposes a rectilinear construction appropriate to the presentation of high-quality architectural photography in conjunction with substantial texts. Blueprint's commissioned artwork is one of its great strengths, and its editorial philosophy is personified in Phil Sayer's graphic double-exposure portrait of Jasper Morrison (opposite) – the designer and his work.

Blueprint (UK)
April 1989
art editor Stephen Coates
photographer Peter Cook

Rowan Moore explores the silent industries of Stockley Park. Photographs Peter Cook

WORLD OF WORK

If you asked a computer to choose the world's best business location, it would probably come up with Stockley Park. Set in the magic overlap of Far Eastern and East Coast time zones, on which the prosperity of London seems to depend, it is also only four minutes from the world's busiest international airport. Three motorways on its doorstep put six universities, six business schools and thirteen technical colleges within an hour's drive. And according to the 1981 Census, quoted in "A Working Guide to Stockley Park", 14,289 highly trained people of "relevant occupation types" live within the catchment area.

Then again, you would need a computer's immunity to doubt actually to build there. The price of wonderful communications is an area composed of muddy offcuts of land, sliced up by successive generations of canal diggers, railway and road builders, and airport engineers. The place is governed by the mathematics of transport, but it looks like the Somme.

Armies of worms

The site itself was originally composed of rubbish: quarried for gravel to help build London, its pits were filled in return by the capital's domestic waste, which still emits noxious gases. The sheer physical effort of transforming this barren waste is one of Stockley Park's most impressive, if least glamorous, achievements. Some 25 million cubic metres of earth and debris were shuffled around the 350 acre site, and its top surface scraped off and rearranged. Armies of worms were imported to aerate the soil and, as the project would have exhausted the domestic topsoil market, the stuff had to be manufactured. Mature trees were imported from Belgium.

Norman Foster's lack of enthusiasm for the pitched roof is well known. At Stockley Park, he complied with the planners' insistence on one, but inverted it to make it invisible

Blueprint April 1989 35

Blueprint (UK)
March 1987
art editors Simon Esterson, Stephen Coates
illustrator Paul Cox

18 Blueprint March 1987

NEW YORK NOW

A SPECIAL REPORT BY JANET ABRAMS

New York is the twentieth century city. It is as old and graceful as the deco skyscrapers, as young and vulgar as the Trump Tower. Blueprint's award-winning American correspondent Janet Abrams traces the city through three generations: she talks to Philip Johnson, doyen of the old guard, traces the new establishment and meets the latest young lions. This special report begins with fragments of life in the city now. Drawings by Paul Cox.

Blueprint March 1987 19

Blueprint (UK)
November 1989
art director Stephen Coates
photographer Phil Sayer

Much of the furniture that captured the headlines in the 1980s was a tale of extravagance – of flamboyant invention and prices to match. Now, with colour supplements running reports on "refuseniks" who turn their backs on designer luxury for a spartan, clutter-free existence, and even Starck preaching the gospel of ecological restraint, ostentation looks increasingly out of keeping with the mood of the times. Rick Poynor talks to two designers whose work has always run counter to the prevailing currents and suddenly looks more relevant than ever. Jasper Morrison, pictured right, reduces form and technology to a point of almost child-like simplicity and expressiveness where nothing goes to waste, while Thomas Eisl, overleaf, refuses to settle for costly excess and is rediscovering the poetry in everyday objects. Portraits by Phil Sayer and Richard Faulks

EXCESS IS A BORE

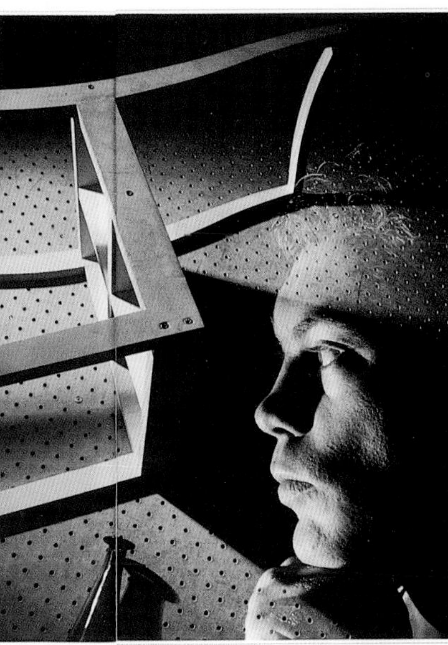

JASPER MORRISON

Keep it light

28 November 1989 Blueprint

Blueprint November 1989 29

Metropolis

Metropolis is a less sharply focused magazine than Blueprint (previous pages) and its design more ambitious. The magazine's eclectic editorial mix (swimsuits, garbage, industrial films) is reflected in the typographic format which changes issue by issue. That format is governed by the issue's dominant editorial theme (for garbage, for example, an industrial OCR face). The design is also more intrusive because it is subjective. The text is interpreted graphically through semantic forms, such as the two-deck pull-out quote (below, right) as typographic bikini. Whereas in Blueprint the headline, image and body text are coolly differentiated in two-dimensional construction, at Metropolis, Helene Silverman introduces jarring contradictions, text overlaid on pictures, multi-layer montages of found images: the page is less ordered, more challenging to the reader, and more visually exciting. What is lost in legibility is more than compensated for by the conceptual clarity and integrated visual dynamic of the design. Silverman's work is technically accomplished and informed by an intelligent sense of both American design tradition and the needs of the job in hand. The total design method used in Metropolis suits the magazine's intellectual stance and is in any case invention born of necessity: the associative montages of found images are a response to an art budget which disallows commissioned photography, and the lively luxury imparted by imaginative use of spot colour belies a general absence of four-colour editorial sections.

Metropolis (USA)
December 1988
art director
Helene Silverman
photographer Edward Stern

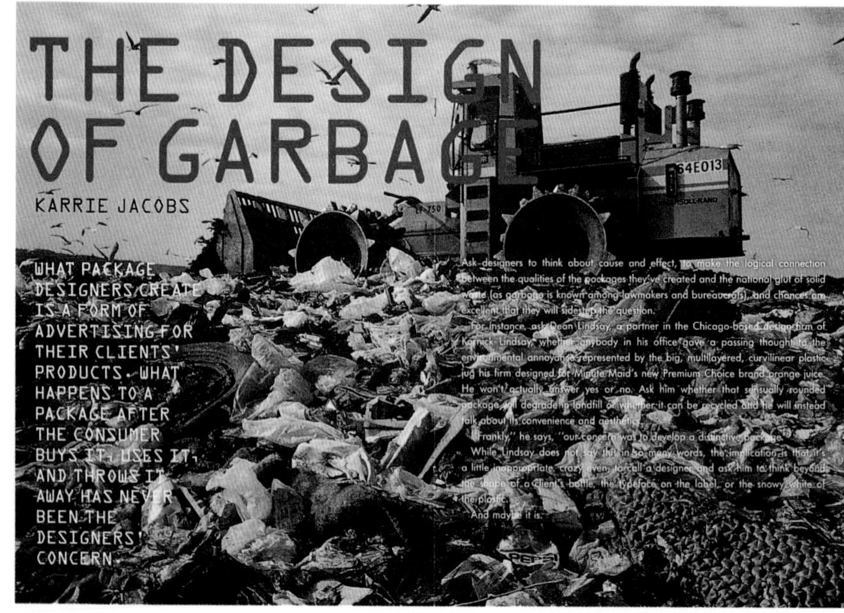

THE DESIGN OF GARBAGE

KARRIE JACOBS

WHAT PACKAGE DESIGNERS CREATE IS A FORM OF ADVERTISING FOR THEIR CLIENTS' PRODUCTS. WHAT HAPPENS TO A PACKAGE AFTER THE CONSUMER BUYS IT, USES IT, AND THROWS IT AWAY HAS NEVER BEEN THE DESIGNERS' CONCERN.

Ask designers to think about cause and effect, to make the logical connection between the qualities of the packages they've created and the national glut of solid waste (as garbage is known among lawmakers and bureaucrats), and chances are excellent that they will sidestep the question.

For instance, ask Dean Lindsay, a partner in the Chicago-based design firm of Kornick Lindsay, whether anybody in his office gave a passing thought to the environmental annoyance represented by the big, multilayered, curvilinear plastic jug his firm designed for Minute Maid's new Premium Choice brand orange juice. He won't actually answer yes or no. Ask him whether that sensually rounded package will degrade in landfill or whether it can be recycled and he will instead talk about its convenience and aesthetics.

"Frankly," he says, "our concern was to develop a distinctive package."

While Lindsay does not say this in so many words, the implication is that it's a little inappropriate, crazy even, to call a designer and ask him to think beyond the shape of a client's bottle, the typeface on the label, or the snowy white of the plastic.

And maybe it is.

Metropolis (USA)
November 1988
art director
Helene Silverman

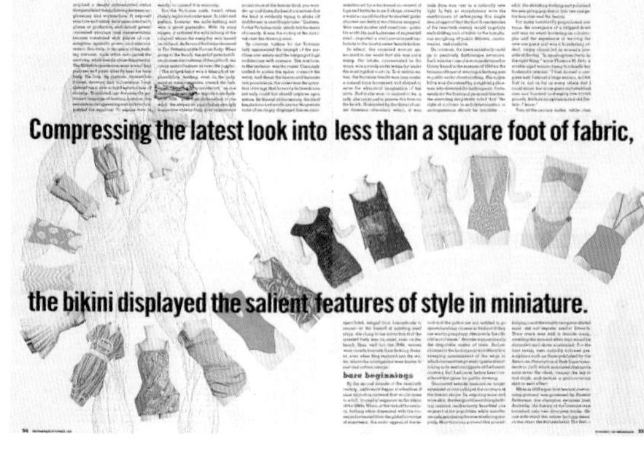

Compressing the latest look into less than a square foot of fabric,

the bikini displayed the salient features of style in miniature.

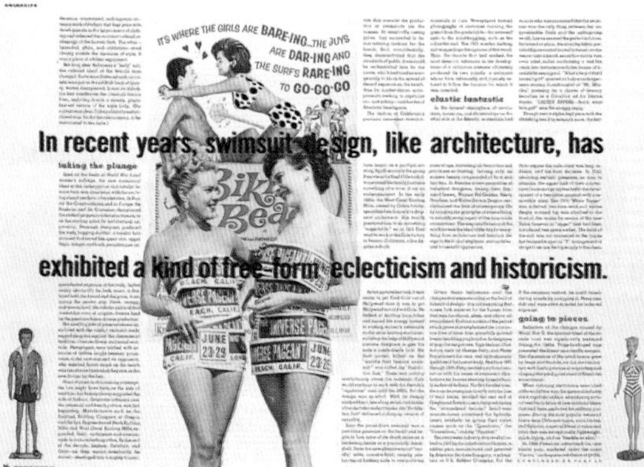

In recent years, swimsuit design, like architecture, has

exhibited a kind of free-form eclecticism and historicism.

Metropolis (USA)
May 1988
art director
Helene Silverman

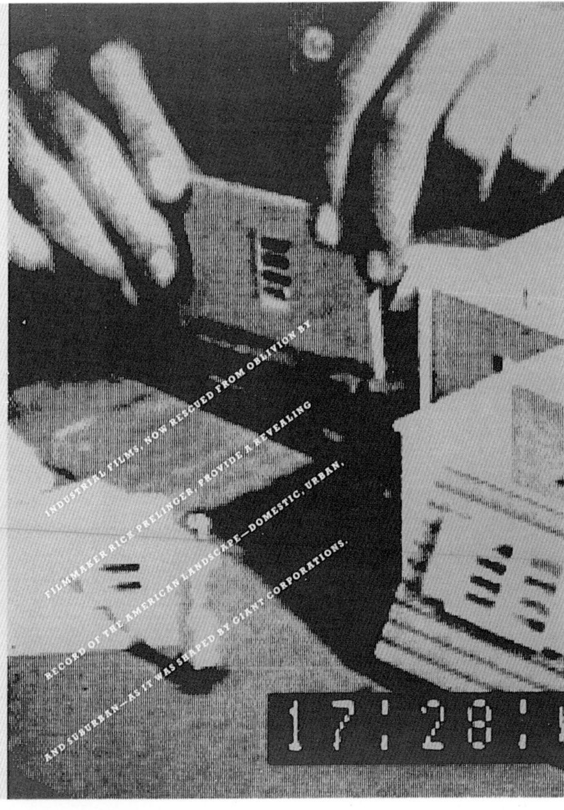

b r a v e [n e w] w o r l d

Rick Prelinger's office is abuzz with the drone of an airplane. This is no refined jet-engine whoosh, but the distinctive lawn-mower honk of early aviation. Prelinger, attired in his customary blue jeans and white button-down shirt, adjusts a knob on a TV set and the in-flight buzz is matched by black-and-white footage of countryside. The image is shaky—like a TV camera following a golf ball—and one imagines a nervous passenger pointing the camera overboard toward the fields and cottages while the pilot cuts a wide, generous turn.

These aren't just any buildings sprinkled against the fields below. They belong to Greenbelt, Maryland, Greenhills, Ohio, and Radburn, New Jersey—experimental communities built by a group of socially minded planners of the 1920s and 1930s. Loosely affiliated into a society of friends calling themselves the Regional Plan Association, designers and reformers such as Henry Wright, Clarence Stein, and Catherine Bauer advocated small cooperative towns nestled into natural settings as an alternative to the screeching trolleys, the slums, and the steam-powered mills of the city.

MIKE CANNELL

INDUSTRIAL FILMS, NOW RESCUED FROM OBLIVION BY FILMMAKER RICK PRELINGER, PROVIDE A REVEALING RECORD OF THE AMERICAN LANDSCAPE—DOMESTIC, URBAN, AND SUBURBAN—AS IT WAS SHAPED BY GIANT CORPORATIONS.

VIDEO PRINTS TAKEN FROM "CALL IT HOME"

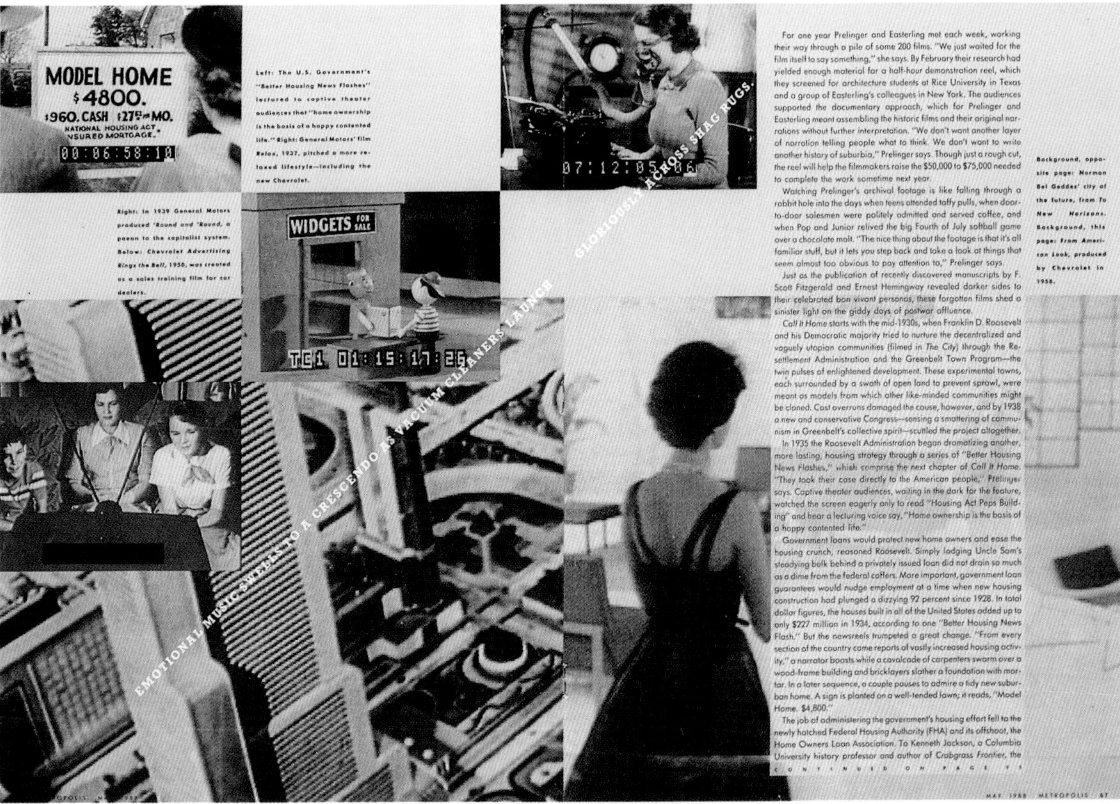

Left: The U.S. Government's "Better Housing News Flashes" lectured to captive theater audiences that "home ownership is the basis of a happy contented life." Right: General Motors' film Relax, 1937, pitched a more relaxed lifestyle—including the new Chevrolet.

Right: In 1939 General Motors produced 'Round and 'Round, a paean to the capitalist system. Below: Chevrolet Advertising Rings the Bell, 1950, was created as a sales training film for car dealers.

EMOTIONAL MUSIC SWELLS TO A CRESCENDO AS VACUUM CLEANERS LAUNCH GLORIOUSLY ACROSS SHAG RUGS.

For one year Prelinger and Easterling met each week, working their way through a pile of some 200 films. "We just waited for the film itself to say something," she says. By February their research had yielded enough material for a half-hour demonstration reel, which they screened for architecture students at Rice University in Texas and a group of Easterling's colleagues in New York. The audiences supported the documentary approach, which for Prelinger and Easterling meant assembling the historic films and their original narrations without further interpretation. "We don't want another layer of narration telling people what to think. We don't want to write another history of suburbia," Prelinger says. Though just a rough cut, the reel will help the filmmakers raise the $50,000 to $75,000 needed to complete the work sometime next year.

Watching Prelinger's archival footage is like falling through a rabbit hole into the days when teens attended taffy pulls, when door-to-door salesmen were politely admitted and served coffee, and when Pop and Junior relived the big Fourth of July softball game over a chocolate malt. "The nice thing about the footage is that it's all familiar stuff, but it lets you step back and take a look at things that seem almost too obvious to pay attention to," Prelinger says.

Just as the publication of recently discovered manuscripts by F. Scott Fitzgerald and Ernest Hemingway revealed darker sides to their celebrated bon vivant personas, these forgotten films shed a sinister light on the giddy days of postwar affluence.

Call It Home starts with the mid-1930s, when Franklin D. Roosevelt and his Democratic majority tried to nurture the decentralized and vaguely utopian communities (filmed in *The City*) through the Resettlement Administration and the Greenbelt Town Program—the twin pulses of enlightened development. These experimental towns, each surrounded by a swath of open land to prevent sprawl, were meant as models from which other like-minded communities might be cloned. Cost overruns damaged the cause, however, and by 1938 a new and conservative Congress—sensing a smattering of communism in Greenbelt's collective spirit—scuttled the project altogether.

In 1935 the Roosevelt Administration began dramatizing another, more lasting, housing strategy through a series of "Better Housing News Flashes," which comprise the next chapter of *Call It Home*. "They took their case directly to the American people," Prelinger says. Captive theater audiences, waiting in the dark for the feature, watched the screen eagerly only to read "Housing Act Peps Building" and hear a lecturing voice say, "Home ownership is the basis of a happy contented life."

Government loans would protect new home owners and ease the housing crunch, reasoned Roosevelt. Simply lodging Uncle Sam's steadying bulk behind a privately issued loan did not drain so much as a dime from the federal coffers. More important, government loan guarantees would nudge employment at a time when new housing construction had plunged a dizzying 92 percent since 1928. In total dollar figures, the houses built in all of the United States added up to only $227 million in 1934, according to one "Better Housing News Flash." But the newsreels trumpeted a great change. "From every section of the country come reports of vastly increased housing activity," a narrator boasts while a cavalcade of carpenters swarm over a wood-frame building and bricklayers slather a foundation with mortar. In a later sequence, a couple pauses to admire a tidy new suburban home. A sign is planted on a well-tended lawn; it reads, "Model Home. $4,800."

The job of administering the government's housing effort fell to the newly hatched Federal Housing Authority (FHA) and its offshoot, the Home Owners Loan Association. To Kenneth Jackson, a Columbia University history professor and author of *Crabgrass Frontier*, the

C O N T I N U E D O N P A G E 9 5

Background, opposite page: Norman Bel Geddes' city of the future, from *To New Horizons*. Background, this page: From *American Look*, produced by Chevrolet in 1958.

Structure, synthesis and meaning

It might be considered that page layout is a question of arranging the various components of the page – the headline, the text, the images – in a form which has logic and some kind of harmonious balance. It is, but it is more than this, just as architecture is something more than putting a roof over four walls to keep out the rain. Otherwise there would be precious little to be said on either subject. Nevertheless, to develop a critique of contemporary magazine design it is necessary to return to fundamentals.

The magazine format is the basis of visual identity but is by no means the sole expression of its individuality. The format, a regular typographic and spatial scheme, is a largely functional device which assists production and design and promotes recognition. The spatial scheme – the grid – divides space into modular sections over which type is placed according to more or less fixed specifications. It determines to a greater or lesser extent where type and images are positioned both according to editorial requirements (the nature of illustration, the length of articles, how they are combined within the page or the magazine, their relationship to each other, etc.), and according to the technical requirements of paper, print and budget. The typographic scheme, in the same way, provides a regular system of production, and of recognition – by creating an individual style for the magazine and distinguishing editorial from advertising. Conventional typographic structures determine style for the elements of a page: headline, to introduce the specific story and attract the reader to it; standfirst, as more detailed, but still brief introduction; and main text – which may be signalled by dropped capitals or small capitals and broken by running-heads and quotations, by column or vertical rules. In addition, there is the essential paraphernalia of captions, credits and direction-finding devices: straplines, folio numbers and turning symbols.

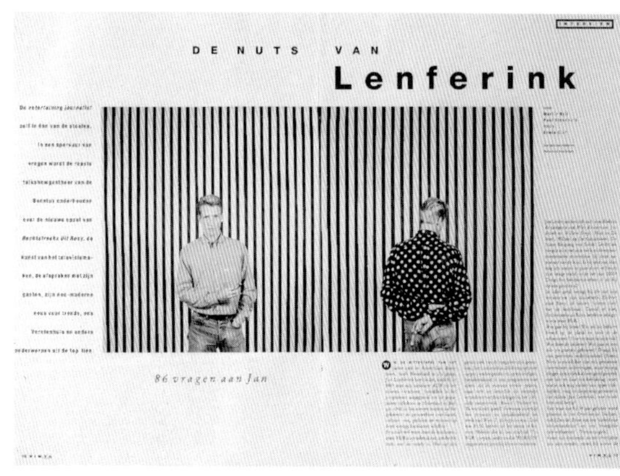

Vinyl (Netherlands)
1987
designers
Jacques Koewiden, Paul Postma
A perfectly balanced asymmetric design in which visual unity of type and image is created by echoing the vertical stripes of the picture in the wide line spacing of the standfirst type on the left-hand page.

This is to go back to absolute basics. Formats are nothing more than scaffolding on which to build and around which to create thematic and graphic variation, and many magazines succeed in achieving coherent design with no fixed format whatsoever or, like *Metropolis*, they change their typographic system with every issue. But a common error in magazine publishing is to equate format with design, to equate design with the construction of attractive patterns on a page, and to limit an appreciation of style to the associative qualities of type, whereby business magazines must have businesslike serifs, upmarket glossies parade classical type and fashion magazines put on an elegant Modern face. This is a most superficial form of styling, a misconception which has encouraged the "hired gun" approach to magazine design whereby consultants are employed to "re-design" and revive ailing magazine formats (and even ailing magazines!). But only the most rigid typographic and spatial schemes can determine the "look" of a magazine or its

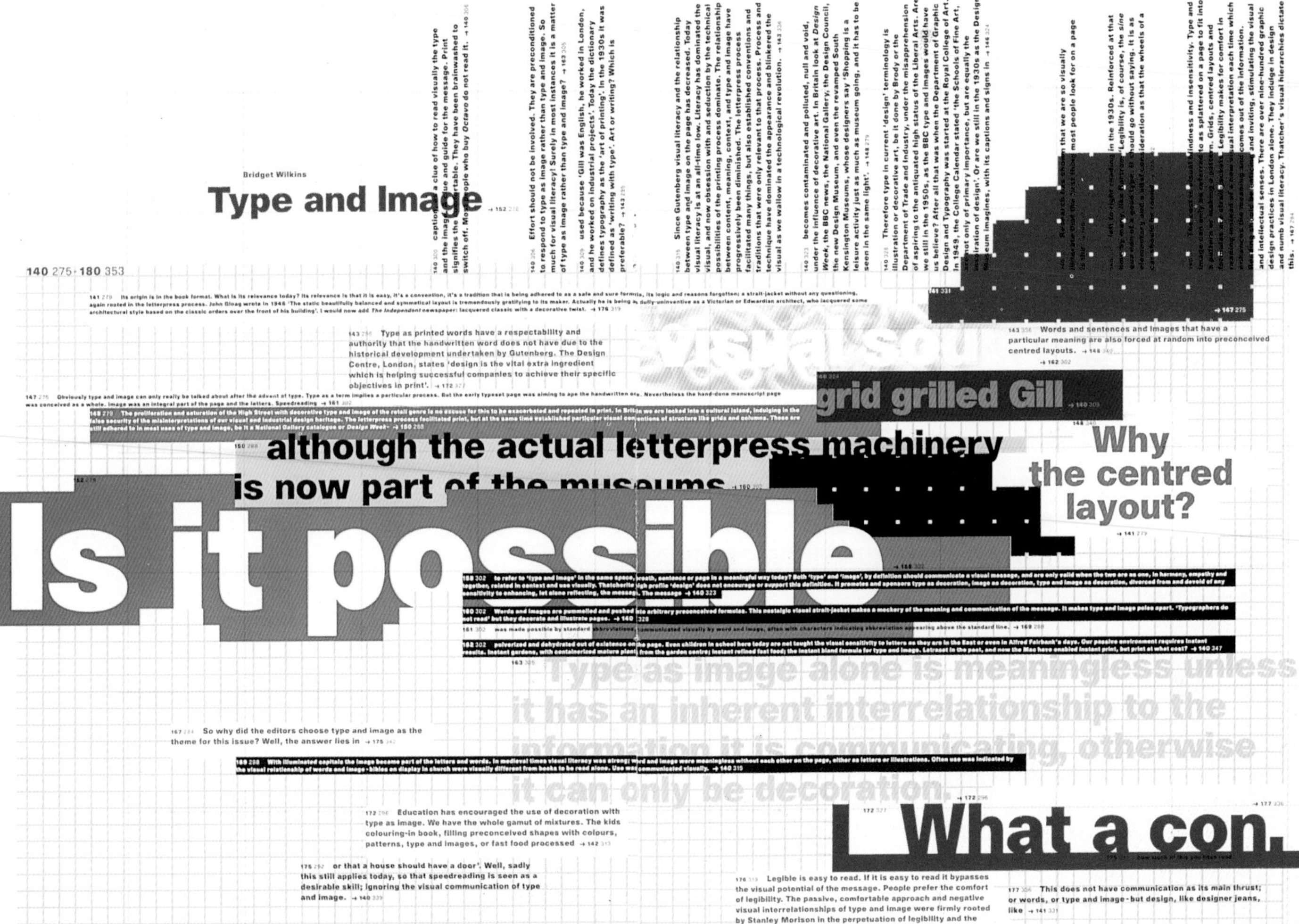

Octavo (UK)

no. 7 1990

designers Mark Holt, Hamish Muir, Michael Burke

An exploration in this typography magazine of a synthesis of type and image for the post-letterpress era. The discussion of the use of type to reinforce content, meaning and context is conducted through a barely penetrable maze of interlocking captions and footnotes designed to exploit the natural curiosity of the reader. This graphic manifesto for a new visual literacy states that "grids, centred layouts and formulas are strait-jackets" borne of obsolete print technologies, and it decries the goal of legibility as a passive, cultural backwater. "Reading", it states, "should be enticing and inviting, stimulating the visual and intellectual senses."

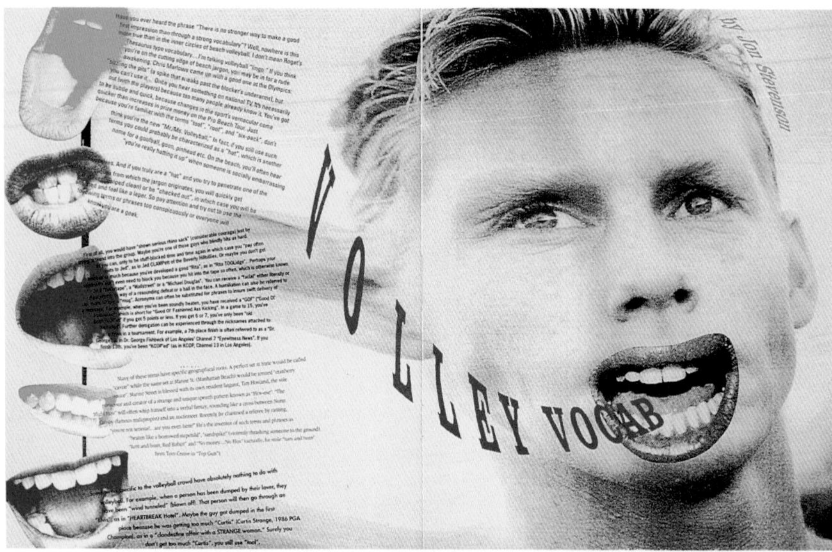

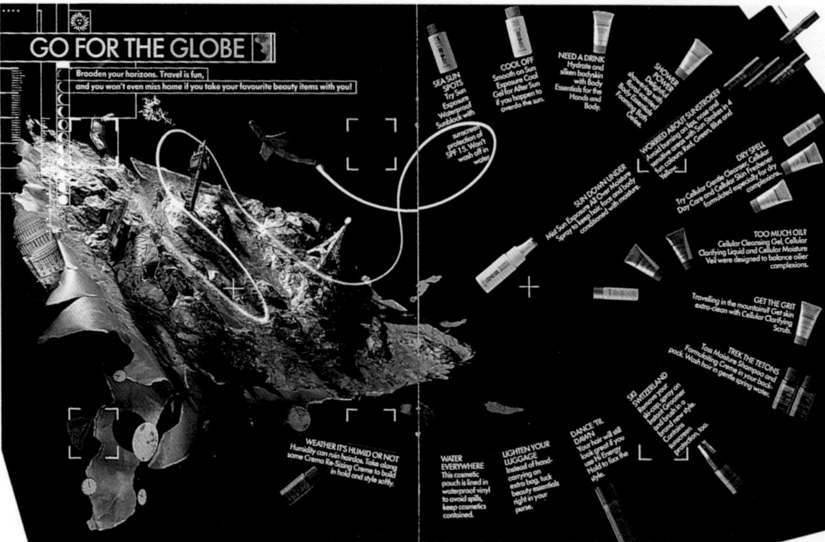

Pro Beach (USA)
Spring 1989
art directors
Carroll/Woo Design

Top: glossary of volley ball jargon graphically illustrated in a montage of mouths and expressive, freeform typography.

Headlines (UK/USA)
no. 4 1989
designers
David Ellis,
Andy Altman
photographer
Rocco Redondo

Above: for hairdressing trade magazine Headlines, Why Not Associates use three-dimensional staged photography and a vigorous sweep of angled captions to created a visually and contextually coherent resumé of cosmetics for travellers.

composition, such as those systems commonly devised for news weeklies and institutional journals. Magazines cannot be designed remotely. Layout is a function not only of format, but of planning, commissioning, art direction and graphic design. If it is to incorporate visual narrative and do anything other than parrot conventional structures, then skilful magazine layout requires close and sympathetic understanding of editorial of the kind which can only be reached on a day-to-day basis; layout, founded on a basic understanding of the technicalities of type and print, is the synthesis of typography and art, the expression of meaning through a coherent visual dynamic.

The traditional purpose of the format and the grid is to provide ease of production, consistency and clarity of form; a particular hierarchy of type was developed based on the objective function of each element of the page. Essentially, the headline is larger than the standfirst, the standfirst larger than the body text, etc., and body type is sized according to the column width. This is not, however, the sum of evolution in magazine typography. It so happened that the development of formatting coincided with the rise of Modernism, which presented ideas such as collage, modularity and dynamic equilibrium, which were most appropriate to the exercise of magazine layout. Late Modernists in the USA and Switzerland continued a scientific exploration of the dynamics of layout and visual perception, experimenting with contrasts of size, colour values, biomorphic forms, typographic symbol, depth and perspective. The American expressionist designers introduced representational forms and narrative typography. In the 1960s visual – as opposed to literary – journalism flourished in magazines and as a result many of the copywriting techniques of advertising were employed. And in the late 1970s and early 1980s we saw a potentially retrograde step, the revival of traditional symmetrical forms and a return to typography as the foundation of layout. Today, as in all the arts, there is no single identifiable strand which can be picked out as characterizing a "new" magazine design – other than its extraordinary variety, with contrasts of mannered minimalism, conventional Modernism, extravagant typographic ornament, self-reference, and intriguing digressions into unstructured collage of interlocking texts, symbol and image.

The magazines which illustrate this section are chosen because they personify trends in contemporary magazine design and for this reason do not necessarily conform to conventional structures or typographic hierarchies. Some do. They include examples of layered and "synthesized" structures which combine the elements of the page in one body, and of "de-structured" design, such as Fabien Baron's *Interview*, in which those elements are disintegrated either within the spread or across sequences of pages; examples of very graphic or artful approaches, and of restrained art direction in which the picture or text is allowed to do its work without interruption; examples of the way in which content dictates different page structures, and the different solutions required for news, pictorial features, literary features and fashion.

"Synthesis", a word at the heart of magazine design and layout, has two very closely connected meanings. In abstract terms, it is an expression of the overall design problem: the sum of technical conditions, editorial intention, words, images, sequence and continuity, which make up the design concept. Concretely, synthesis is the integration of the many elements of the page, including colour, form, type and illustration, into a single body with one meaning, as a form of collage; it is also the synthesis of all the articles within a magazine into a coherent sequence. Optical unity produces an integrated flow of information and creates a single object and a single character, out of the disparate visual and literary components of the page. It creates excitement and dynamism, and should allow the eye to see beyond surface meanings and successfully amalgamate a variety of complex signs and symbols. This is the opposite of merely placing an illustration on one page of the spread and the text on the other with no graphic or associative interconnection: an ostensibly workmanlike approach which fails to recognize that these heterogeneous elements are in fact working together to do one job. That approach is static and may have insufficient force to induce a response in the reader, who must do all the work of interpretation.

Bulldog (Japan)
October 1989
designers Yoko Tajima, Yasufi Yoshizawa

These pages are working hard, but not too hard; as well as the three pictures there are ten different typographic elements vying for attention. But despite its complexity, and because the components are so cleverly resolved, this lively spread works magnificently.

Collage and photomontage are twentieth-century art forms which were motivated by the breakdown of traditional social and belief systems, the destruction of religious understanding of human action by the new science of psychology, and the creation of a complex and often incomprehensible industrialized world. Representational art was an insufficient description or reflection of life. There was a need to reintegrate the broken facets of existence into a new whole. This was achieved through the creation of a new iconography of abstract plastic forms, of associative and contradictory elements which attacked the subconscious mind, which exploited the urge to bridge differences by finding similarities. It recognized that we see things not as separate entities, but in a dynamic relationship. Thus out of two contradictory elements we create associations and thence a meaning – why are the two things placed together? What is the object? Out of the fragments we create a new whole.

"Reintegration" of representational, symbolic and abstract forms is precisely what a magazine designer does in creating a layout, "welding objects and background into a dynamic plastic unity by interpenetration of color planes and lines".[1] Unlike classical symmetry, with its stolid proportions based upon the functional and formal requirements of architecture, plastic dynamism is founded on the need to express activity, tension and difference, and therefore operates with a more versatile arrangement of opposing forces. It is asymmetrical, but nonetheless in equilibrium, and it operates according to the laws of mathematical proportion no less than classical symmetry. There are, however, new weights in the balance: colour (red is heavier than yellow, lighter than black), diagonals, symbol, depth of perspective, texture, irregular form and line. A balance between these components can be achieved by instinct, experience and understanding, or according to the precepts of visual science, with the order of space derived from the golden mean or modular construction, and from the psychology of perception and the organization of signs.

The organization of the elements of the page as a single coherent object, within which flows an ordered sequence of information, is a creative act in which the designer must make his or her own value judgements, creating a set of priorities and links for the eye to follow and associative elements for the mind to capture. The act, however, begins with nothing more than a blank grid sheet, a galley of type and a set of images and, hopefully, an idea.

Grids and formats

The spreads shown here are all from weekly magazines, and all conform more or less to an archetypal magazine format which was developed for ease of production and consumption, although from the readers' point of view the utility of the structure derives as much from sheer familiarity as from any inescapable editorial logic. This is particularly so of the three news feature magazines – Time, Newsweek and Business Week – which follow three-column formats which in their essential details are strikingly uniform: in each case all typographic elements are locked in by column and frame rules; a running head at the top of the page is followed by a descending order of (sans serif) headline, standfirst and body copy. Note the fondness for dropped capitals. The women's weekly Best is an interesting downmarket variation, a five-column format crammed with text set solid, overlapping images and bright colour. This is the epitome of the "busy" page, well designed in news tabloid style. The spread from the women's magazine Me offers an informal and clever visual treatment of a well loved editorial perennial.

Best (UK)
8 June 1990
art director Anthony Cohen
photographer
Tony Stone/Worldwide

DOSSIER ACTIVITY BREAKS

KIDS ONLY

ADVENTURE HOLIDAYS

From canoeing to computing – give your children the experience of a lifetime and send them off on their own. It'll be a real challenge and they'll have great fun too

5 PAGES

RELATIONSHIPS

Are you still in love?

Tune into some on-the-sofa bodywatching and find out

Are you still starry-eyed and in love or on the brink of a break-up? Most experts agree that our bodies constantly betray our true feelings and, if you know what to look for, the way the pair of you sit in front of the TV set can provide some surprising insights

Love on the rocks

If this is how you sit in front of the box, then your days together could be numbered. The unfriendly crossed legs show all lines of communication between you are firmly closed (and probably have been for some time). Complete strangers sit next to one another like this — and, sadly, that's what you've become. Unless you take fast, drastic action, you could be heading for a permanent split.

Bosom buddies

Doormat danger

Anything goes!

Viewing Figures

Home sweet home?

Passion rules

He's the boss

Queen of the castle

Me (UK)
29 May 1989
art editor Sue Walsham
photographer
John Ingledew

Show Business

• COVER STORY

Movie Muscle

Ever searching for funds and profits, Hollywood increases its dominance over the global film industry, inspiring fear and imitators

By HOWARD G. CHUA-EOAN

Opening scene: Fade in to Cannes' promenade La Croisette, providing a scan of yachts, the ongoing film festival, and a boardwalk filled with men in business suits. The scene dissolves to a bar at the Carlton Inter-Continental and to three men in suits talking over drinks.

First man: If you wanna cut your risks, you'll need a star known all over. You've gotta go the way Hollywood's going: global. With the kinda money you're plunking down, you'll wanna global star.

Second man: Yeah. Big in the States. Bigger outside the States.

Third man: Who's that?

First: Arnie, of course.

Second: Yeah. Schwarzenegger.

Third: Bigger than Stallone?

First: Stallone's peaked.

Second: Arnold's your guy. In the '80s his movies grossed $1 billion worldwide.

First: He's popular in India, Russia, Europe—West and East.

Second: He's very big in Japan.

First: Yup. The men must think he's a sumo wrestler with muscle definition.

Second: And if audiences don't speak English, they won't notice the accent. You'll reap bonanzas selling video rights in the U.S., Italy, Taiwan, Afghanistan . . .

This fragment of a screenplay is clearly more fanciful than documentary, but it is the thought behind the script that counts. Global strategic planning does thrive, ringing wildest-dream cash registers in Cannes, where the annual festival ends this week, and even more so in the boardrooms of major and independent Hollywood studios and the transnational corporations that run much of the U.S. film industry today. Hollywood is no longer making movies solely for the American market, and studio bosses do not expect to recover the costs of their mammoth productions from domestic receipts alone. Overseas revenues that once amounted to a bonus have become a necessity. Says Duncan Clark, senior vice president of Columbia Tri-Star's international marketing division: "The costs of doing business are so high these days that we need to be involved in every possible profit center." Hollywood has always led the world movie market, but its dominance is now so great that it is crushing filmmakers in other countries.

The world's demand for American entertainment seems insatiable, and Hollywood is ever ready to please, titillate and excite for the price of a movie ticket. Last year box-office revenue from North American theaters amounted to over $5 billion, from overseas markets some $3 billion. In the sale of video versions, foreign buyers already account for more than 40% of the studios' revenues. "We may not be able to export our automobiles, but we are exporting our culture in the form of movies," says Thomas Pollock, chairman of MCA (Universal) Motion Picture Group. "By next year, close to 50% of our earnings will be coming from foreign marketplaces." Strauss Zelnick, president of 20th Century Fox, estimates that "within ten years, our overseas sales could well be larger."

Global receipts are particularly crucial to expensive movies. The producers of Schwarzenegger's latest epic, *Total Recall*, recouped their $60 million budget in part by selling overseas distribution and video rights even before the movie went into production. Sometimes, foreign grosses are higher than U.S. receipts. *Rambo III*, for example, did a tepid $55 million at home, but drew $105 million abroad. Paramount's *Indiana Jones and the Last Crusade* was a runner-up to Warner Bros.' *Batman* in North America last year—$197 million vs. $250 million—yet won the worldwide box-office stakes by raking in $260 million overseas. *Batman* did less well abroad, though with $150 million in foreign receipts it was hardly a flop.

Rather than waiting months for the latest U.S. blockbuster to hit their shores, Europe and Asia are sometimes getting seats at the premiere. In 1988 Universal opened *Back to the Future II* in the U.S., Europe and Japan simultaneously. The film made more than $300 million for the studio, and the receipts were available months earlier than usual, saving millions of dollars in interest. Tom Cruise's car-racing melodrama, *Days of Thunder*, will be in movie theaters in Japan in mid-June, just two days after its U.S. debut.

Stars like Schwarzenegger, Stallone and Cruise come at a steep price ($10 million or more in straight salary plus percentages of gross), but they give a movie name recognition worldwide in theaters and at video-rental counters. "If you're an established name who can generate broad identity," says Christopher Dixon, an analyst with the investment firm of Kidder, Peabody, "then the studios are willing to pay for it." The prestige of such megastars can sell up to 200,000 units of videotape per film. A case in point: when Mel Gibson was in a remote part of Thailand filming the soon-to-be-released *Air America*, villagers greeted the actor with shouts of "Mad Max." They had recognized him from tapes available at local video stores.

The most energetic practitioner of international movie dealmaking among independent producers is Carolco, the Hollywood studio that put together Stallone's *Rambo* series and has now turned its attentions to Schwarzenegger. Says Carolco vice president Thomas Levine: "We make movies that compete with the major studios in the international market. They have to contain a big element—like Arnold or Sly or Mel Gibson. That is what lets us compete. So there's not that much quibbling over salaries." The major studios think along the same lines. Don Simpson, coproducer of Paramount's *Days of Thunder*, admits that the movie "would not have been made without Tom Cruise. You don't go out and spend a lot of money to make a film starring somebody who cannot open the movie in every market."

The independents and the majors have a symbiotic relationship. Carolco, for example, sells distribution rights to major studios, which also pick up the enormous cost of promoting and marketing. The ma-

50 TIME, MAY 28, 1990 TIME, MAY 28, 1990 51

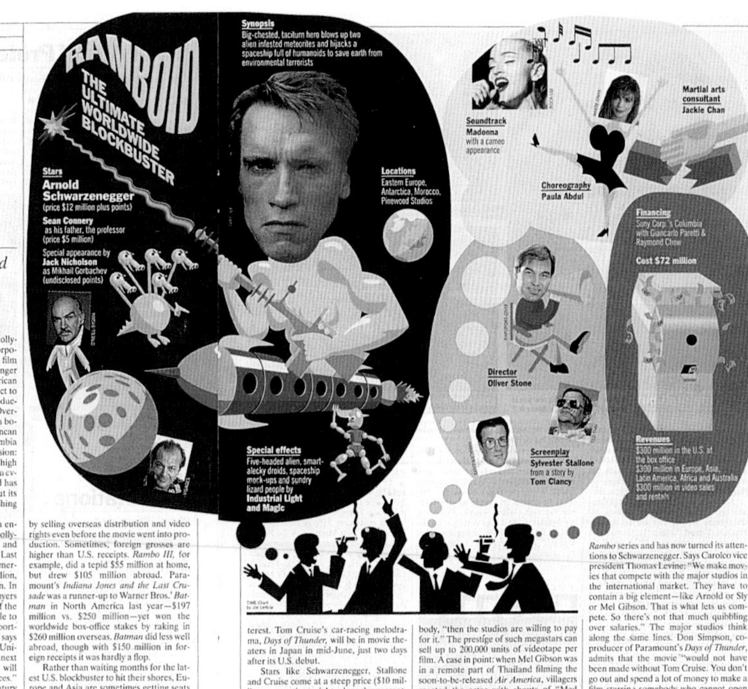

Time (USA)
International edition
28 May 1990
art director Rudolf Hoglund
illustrator Joe Lertola

ASIA

Stacking the Deck

Burma's military rulers are prepared for an election—but not for an opposition victory

Newsweek (USA)
International edition
28 May 1990
art director
Patricia Bradbury
photographers
Reuter/Piers Cavendish/
Kataruna Alanko

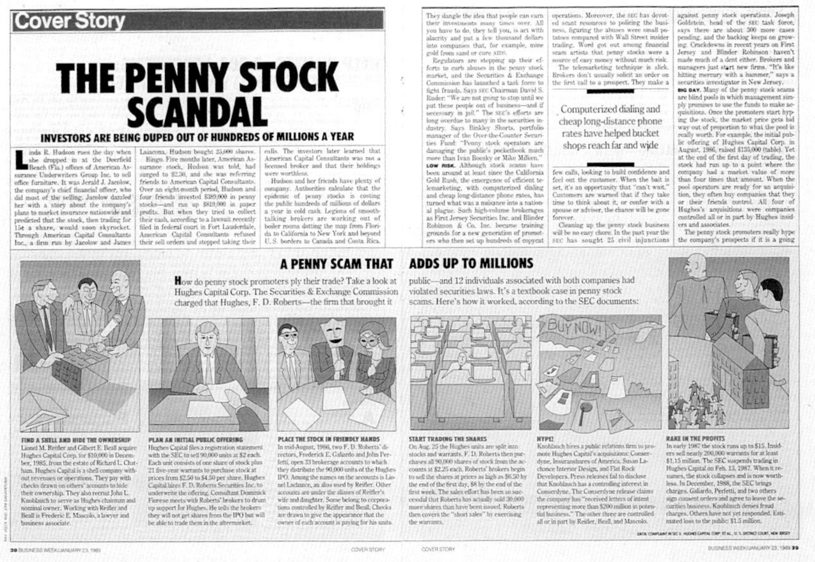

Cover Story

THE PENNY STOCK SCANDAL

INVESTORS ARE BEING DUPED OUT OF HUNDREDS OF MILLIONS A YEAR

Computerized dialing and cheap long-distance phone rates have helped bucket shops reach far and wide

A PENNY SCAM THAT ADDS UP TO MILLIONS

How do penny stock promoters ply their trade? Take a look at Hughes Capital Corp. The Securities & Exchange Commission charged that Hughes, F. D. Roberts—the firm that brought it public—and 12 individuals associated with both companies had violated securities laws. It's a textbook case in penny stock scams. Here's how it worked, according to the SEC documents:

FIND A SHELL AND HIDE THE OWNERSHIP

PLAN AN INITIAL PUBLIC OFFERING

PLACE THE STOCK IN FRIENDLY HANDS

START TRADING THE SHARES

HYPE!

RAKE IN THE PROFITS

Business Week (USA)
International edition
23 January 1989
art director
Malcolm Frouman
illustrators
Ray Vella, Joni Danaher

Grids and formats

The use of classical symmetry and sans serif typography advertises a literary conceit. The New Yorker, its design unchanged for half a century, is at least the genuine article. For this magazine, as for the Atlantic Monthly and the beautifully crafted World of Interiors, the centred layout and pyramidal hierarchy of type are intended to speak volumes about the traditional qualities of editorial and, above all, the quality of the readership. The French literary magazine Lire (which shares its design consultant with the Atlantic) is the exception. The offset headline and white space lighten the structure and, with the exception of the rather clumsy centred rule separating headline from standfirst, it achieves a balance of restrained decoration, openness and elegance which strikes the desired chord of middle-class progressive intellectualism.

The New Yorker (USA)
14 May 1990
art director Lee Lorenz

THE TALK OF THE TOWN

Notes and Comment

ON March 29th, President Bush made a speech about AIDS—his first on the subject since taking office—to a group of business and labor leaders. In it he said, among other things, that he supported a bill currently pending in Congress which forbids discrimination (chiefly in employment) against people with AIDS; that compassion and appropriate care should be extended to those with the disease; and that, in general, the government's health agencies were "on a wartime footing" in respect to the epidemic.

The President's remarks elicited a predictable pattern of response. As usual, few people criticized his use of military language—with its inherent, if perhaps unintended, promise of quick action, and its implied notion of an "enemy." And many were prompt to praise the symbolic importance of the speech. Donald S. Goldman, who is a member of the National Commission on AIDS, an advisory group appointed by Congress and the President, told the *Times* that although the talk was six years late the President had nonetheless "set a standard for himself" by adopting such a compassionate manner, and added, "It is important to note that the President made the speech."

Other commentators were not so kind. The President said that he had asked Congress for three and a half billion dollars for AIDS programs in 1991. Critics remarked that after Medicaid and Medicare entitlements and various miscellaneous expenses are deducted the Bush request comes to about one and three-quarters billion dollars. Others pointed out that the President had made no mention of a measure, sponsored by Senators Edward M. Kennedy and Orrin G. Hatch and supported by a range of AIDS experts, that would provide six hundred million dollars in federal disaster relief to cities hit hard by AIDS. And still others noted that the two legislative measures that had the President's support—the anti-discrimination bill and the money for AIDS programs—did not speak to the most pressing needs. Jeffrey Braff, who is the executive director of the Gay Men's Health Crisis, a social-service agency in New York, said, "What good does it do to stop AIDS discrimination in the workplace if people cannot get the proper medical care that allows them to live and work with AIDS? And what help is protection in housing if people with AIDS cannot afford long-term home care but, rather, are forced into overcrowded hospitals?"

Several weeks after the President's speech, the National Commission on AIDS issued a report that reiterated the complaints about the government's AIDS policies and added a few others, chiefly in the area of education. For instance, it said that, because of the regulations governing the makeup of local advisory panels on AIDS, federally funded educational materials often do not address target groups—intravenous-drug users, especially—in an appropriately frank manner. The commission's major allegation, however, was that the government is without an "effective national strategy" for dealing with the epidemic; that is, there is no leadership.

Lack of leadership is not unique to the AIDS situation, of course; it is something pointed out by advisory boards looking into almost any serious social question. The AIDS-leadership question, however, is much more complex. It's not just a matter of practical concerns—bureaucracies, scientific assumptions, legislative support—but also a matter of creating a climate in which leadership can emerge. It's difficult enough for politicians to step forward on issues less psychologically loaded; when it comes to AIDS, they must face individual and collective anxieties about almost everything—sex, race, drugs, death.

The question of AIDS leadership is also related to America's role in a changing international order—to a sense that the spotlight has been turned away from us, perhaps for good. Feelings of self-doubt can have devastating effects. For example, the recent coverage of the results, however preliminary, of a promising new treatment for AIDS—orally administered alpha interferon—might not have been so slow if the tests had been conducted at the National Institutes of Health, say, rather than at a clinic in Kenya. And would a govern-

Atlantic Monthly (USA)
December 1987
art director Judy Garlan
illustrator Edward Sorel

THE ATLANTIC MONTHLY

Memories of a fifties education

JOE COLLEGE

BY PHILIP ROTH

WHILE I WAS GROWING UP, MY FATHER WORKED AS an assistant manager in the Essex County, New Jersey, office of Metropolitan Life, earning about $125 a week in salary and commissions during his peak years. In the middle 1940s, as I made the transition from grade school to high school, a business risk he took wiped out the family savings. After long consultations with my mother, he had invested with some friends in a frozen-food distribution company, and for several years he continued by day as a Metropolitan insurance man while at night and on weekends, without drawing a salary, he went out on the refrigerated truck, trying to hustle frozen-food business in Jersey and eastern Pennsylvania. In addition to using up the family savings he'd had to borrow some $8,000 from relatives in order to pay for his share in the partnership. He was forty-five, and took the risk because it seemed unlikely that he could get any further with the Metropolitan, a corporation that in those days advanced very few Jews from the sales force into managerial positions. His education, through eighth grade, also seemed to him an impediment to promotion.

He had hoped that by the time his two sons graduated from high school, the new enterprise would have taken off and he'd be able to afford to send us both to college. But the business went bust quickly, and when I was ready for college he was still saddled with paying off his debt. Fortunately, in 1949 he was unexpectedly promoted by the Metropolitan to manage an office just outside Newark, in Union City. The district was doing virtually no business when he came in but offered a real financial opportunity if

DECEMBER 1987 ILLUSTRATIONS BY EDWARD SOREL 41

« A style de vie similaire, classe sociale homogène... » Illustration Yan Nascimbene pour « Lire ».

100

ALAIN MINC

La machine égalitaire

Peut-être vivons-nous les dernières grandes heures de la classe moyenne. L'ancien inspecteur des finances analyse les rouages de la « machine à limer les différences » qui homogénéise l'actuelle société française.

LE LIVRE

*« **LE PIRE EST DEVANT NOUS** mais la crise est sans doute passée », écrivait Alain Minc en 1982. La disparition de la croissance a stoppé le mécanisme qui faisait de la France un pays moderne. Elle a abouti à faire renaître des corporatismes et à en insuffler de nouveaux. Dans son essai,* L'après-crise est commencé, *Alain Minc évoquait déjà l'alliance tacite de ces corporatismes pour repousser la crise sur les exclus. Aujourd'hui, l'ancien inspecteur des finances précise ce nouveau paysage social de la France. Fondée sur une égalité de principe, la machine égalitaire républicaine porte en elle ses effets pervers : chômage et réapparition d'un « lumpen ». L'Etat providence pénalise de fait les marginaux, les « fins de droit », les retraités et les isolés. La Sécurité sociale ignore les nouveaux pauvres ; les prestations familiales, les systèmes de retraite privilègient les privilégiés. Il y a « quelque chose de pourri au cœur de l'Etat providence ». Autre incarnation du mythe égalitaire : l'école. Ses mécanismes cachés de sélection viennent renforcer la hiérarchie sociale existante. Le modèle égalitaire est à bout de souffle, diagnostique Alain Minc. Mais l'énarque libéral de gauche ne remet pas pour autant en cause l'idée d'égalité : c'est un nouveau modèle égalitaire qu'il soumet à la réflexion des politiques. La France doit se dégager de son immobilisme actuel et de ses deux corollaires, corporatisme et individualisme. La réduction des inégalités au sein du système fiscal et assurantiel, la prise en charge des exclus et surtout l'instauration de la concurrence pour mettre fin aux monopoles corporatistes : telles sont les propositions que Minc énonce avec une énergie à soulever des montagnes d'indifférence et de bureaucratie.*

La machine égalitaire, par **Alain Minc,** 284 p., Grasset.

L'EXTRAIT

Les libéraux du XIXe siècle voyaient dans la Révolution l'avènement de la classe moyenne, même si elle s'intitulait, pour eux, la « masse ». Depuis près de deux siècles, la société française n'a cessé de courir à la recherche de cette force dominante et insaisissable. Dès que se produit un raz de marée politique, chacun croit entrevoir l'incarnation de la classe moyenne. Jamais la société française n'a été plus proche de cette réalité vers laquelle elle continuera de tendre sans jamais l'atteindre, car, paradoxe des paradoxes, la classe moyenne risque de s'émietter dans les décennies à venir, bien davantage qu'elle ne l'est aujourd'hui : c'est d'ailleurs tout l'enjeu du débat encore souterrain sur l'idée même d'égalité. Le triomphe de la classe moyenne : il se mesure dans des réalités aux assonances inélégantes, salariat, féminisation, urbanisation, tertiarisation, socialisations,... et autres phénomènes en « ions ».

Le salariat, au premier chef : la France est longtemps demeurée un « mouton noir » sociologique parmi les pays les plus développés avec une population agricole, artisanale et commerçante prohibitive. Son ombre portée ne cesse de surplomber les réalités politiques et sociales, bien davantage que ne l'exigerait une démographie désormais en contraction. Ainsi près d'un actif sur trois était-il en 1960 un non-salarié ; ils ne sont plus désormais que 10 %. Peut-être avons-nous d'ailleurs atteint un plancher qui nous empêchera de connaître les taux de salarisation de 95 à 98 % habituels dans les pays anglo-saxons. Si, comme tout le laisse penser, les valeurs sont en train de s'inverser, plus individualistes, plus hédonistes, plus égotistes, le salariat ne devrait plus s'étendre sans limite.

Mais le salariat ne constitue évidemment pas la seule matrice de la classe moyenne. Plus important : le nivellement des salaires s'est accentué entre catégories socioprofessionnelles et au sein de chacune d'elles. De 1950 à 1967 la dispersion avait augmenté ; depuis 1968 — cela ne laisse guère de chance au hasard —, elle n'a cessé de se réduire. Ainsi le salaire des cadres supérieurs, qui représentait en 1950 2,89 du salaire moyen de l'ensemble des salariés et 3,63 en 1967, est-il tombé à 2,60 en 1980 et 2,53 en 1983. Pour les cadres moyens le ratio est

101

Lire (France)
October 1987
art director
Jean-Pierre Cliquet
illustrator Yan Nascimbene

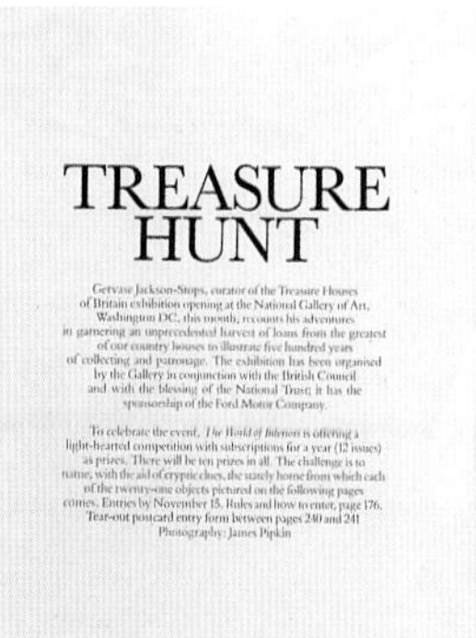

TREASURE HUNT

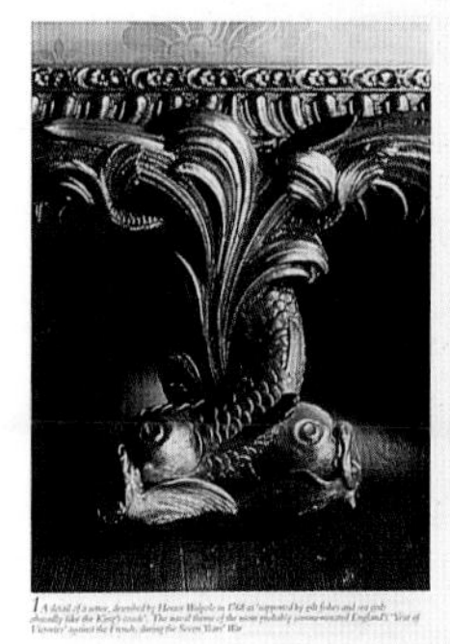

The World of Interiors (UK)
November 1985
creative director
Wendy Harrop
art director
Margaret Donegan
photographer James Pipkin

Grids and formats

The standard magazine feature grid has three columns. Why? Because 8-9pt is the smallest type legible to the average reader, and that size has an optimum column width of 12-14 picas; three such columns fit on an A4 page. But the three-column grid can be inflexible: it allows only three legitimate picture widths, and tends to create uniform and crammed pages. Here are three variations which overcome the problem. FAZ Magazin is actually greater than A4 size and can accommodate four columns, but the principle is the same. On each side of the spread the central column is omitted to create air and space for bastard picture measures. Extraordinary attention to typographic detail contributes to this beautifully integrated design. The columns act as pillars supporting both the carefully shaped left- and right-ranging captions, and the engravings and silhouettes which are grasped within the text by contoured setting as if embedded in cement. Each eyeline is precisely focused to direct the reader and hold the composition. The interior design magazine Intern simply lets unneeded page space lie fallow, retaining the structure of the page by superimposing the grid lines in a magenta tint. The structure of Diver, a literary review, is more complex. A subsidiary text, set bold in a wider central column, runs in parallel to the main feature. Together with the type running over line and half tone, this gives the layout variety and tonal contrast, as well as texture and a perception of depth.

AUFKLÄRER UND GOTTES SOLDAT: JOHANN FRIEDRICH OBERLIN

Von Thomas Mense

Eine knappe Autostunde ist es von seinem Geburtsort Straßburg bis in das Steintal in den Nordvogesen. Hier bilden die höchsten Erhebungen eine Wetterscheide und bescheren einen langen Winter, der dem Steintal den Ruf eines „elsässischen Sibirien" eintrug. Heute schlägt man daraus Kapital: Überall sehen wir Skilifte; das Steintal ist ein gefragtes Wintersportgebiet. Über Schirmeck und Rothau kommend, ist das kleine Fouday oberhalb des Tals der erste Ort seines Pfarrbezirks, der damals fünf Dörfer und drei Weiler hatte. Auf dem Kirchhof liegt Johann Friedrich Oberlin begraben. Witterungsfeste Blumen aus Keramik und Plastik schmücken die mächtige Grabplatte ebenso wie das schmiedeeiserne Kreuz mit der liebevollen Aufschrift: Papa Oberlin.

Vor hundertsechzig Jahren, am 5. Juni 1826, fand hier unter überwältigender Anteilnahme die Beerdigung dieses bemerkenswerten Mannes statt, dessen Ruf als charismatischer Pädagoge, Reformer und Geisterseher schon zu Lebzeiten in ganz Europa verbreitet war. Wir nehmen die Straße hinauf und biegen in halber Höhe des Tals ab in die Ortschaft, die an einen steilen Südhang gebaut ist. Ein kleines Schild „Musée Oberlin" weist den Weg.

Das Zentrum von Waldersbach ist eine schmale Straße, an der Bürgermeisteramt, Post, Schule, die schlichte Kirche und das Pfarrhaus liegen. Gepflegte Bauerngärten, Häuser mit akkurat gestapelten Holzvorräten, Katzen, die sich in der warmen Mittagssonne räkeln: Eine gemächliche Ruhe strahlt der Ort aus, es ist eine beschauliche, ländliche Idylle für erholungsbedürftige Städter. Viele junge Leute seien in die Städte gezogen, die Landwirtschaft ernähre hier nicht mehr viele, die Alten lebten noch hier und zeitweise einige Wochenendler, erzählt uns der junge Pfarrer. Ja, richtig, wir haben ein paar Häuser mit verschlossenen Läden gesehen. Das Museum befindet sich im Parterre des 1787 erbauten, großzügigen Pfarrhauses. Erst zwanzig Jahre nach seinem Amtsantritt, als die größte Not beseitigt war, hatte Oberlin in den Bau eines neuen Pfarrhauses eingewilligt. Wir laufen über die knarrenden Dielen des Museums, das ein liebevolles, skurriles Andenken an Oberlin bewahrt. Wir sehen den großen Kanonenofen, die Vitrinen mit dem selbstgebastelten pädagogischen Spielzeug, das Naturalienkabinett, Schulbücher, Landkarten, das Herbarium, den Rahmen mit den bunten Steinen, die Oberlin zur Charakteranalyse benutzte wie die zahlreichen Schattenrisse nach der Methode seines Freundes Lavater. Mit der kleinen Handdruckpresse druckte Oberlin Landkarten des Steintals und des Himmels und Bibelzitate: „Hört auf, euch zu sorgen um euer Leben, um das, was ihr essen werdet, oder um euren Leib, was ihr anziehen werdet" steht dort auf französisch. Wir werfen einen Blick in die mit Papieren, Tabellen, Briefen, Manuskripten vollgestopften Schubladen. Da findet sich, fest verschnürt in einem Bündel, das mehrseitige, in Schönschrift auf deutsch niedergelegte Programm Oberlins, das er sich bei seinem Amtsantritt 1767 gesetzt hatte: „Entwurf einer Verbesserung des Zustandes des Steinthals." Punkt eins lautet: „Die Beförderung der Gottes-Furcht u. Tugend", Punkt zwei: „Die Verbesserung der Gemüthskräfte, d. Geschmaks durch die schöne Einrichtung unserer Schuh-

Nutzen der Gelehrsamkeit: Oberlin verstand die Theologie als praktische Wissenschaft. Er predigte Gottesfurcht, und er bekämpfte die wirtschaftliche Not auf dem Lande

Segen des Fortschritts: Oberlin kam 1767 ins Steintal. Aus der Armenstube des Elsaß machte er eine blühende Gemeinde. Er verbesserte die Viehhaltung, legte Sümpfe trocken, baute Wege und gründete eine Kreditkasse

Frankfurter Allgemeine Magazin (Germany)

31 August 1990

art director
Hans-Georg Pospischil

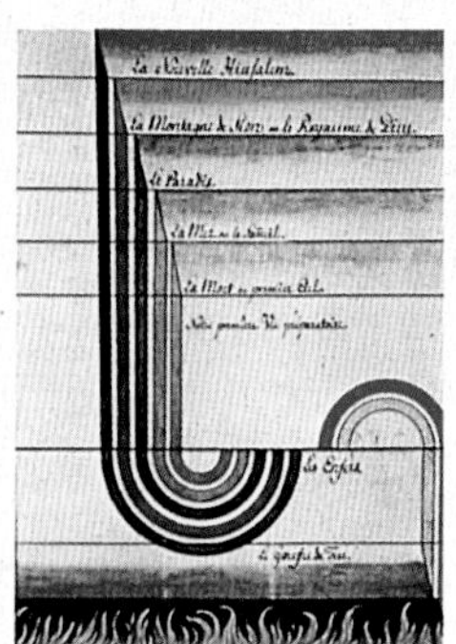

Stufen des Heils: Oberlin verband die Ideen der Aufklärung mit mystischen Spekulationen. Das Bibelstudium inspirierte ihn zur „Darstellung der verschiedenen Welten"

len." Auf eine faszinierende Weise haben die großen Ideen des Jahrhunderts an diesem Ort ihren Widerhall gefunden. Hier wurde Aufklärung zur Praxis, zu einem Stück konkreter Utopie, das das damals unwirtliche, abgelegene Steintal zu einem Mekka für eine illustre Schar von Besuchern aus ganz Europa werden ließ.

Der Elsässer Oberlin war nicht nur ein Grenzgänger zwischen Deutschland und Frankreich („Ich bin ein Deutscher und zugleich ein Franzose" heißt es in seiner Selbstcharakteristik), zwischen Katholizismus und Protestantismus (er nannte sich oft einen „evangelisch-katholischen Geistlichen"). Mühelos verband der protestantische Landpfarrer auch die Ideen der neuen Philosophen mit pietistisch-mystischem Gedankengut, das im achtzehnten Jahrhundert durch Offenbarungen von zahlreichen Geistersehern wie Swedenborg und Oetinger die Köpfe der Zeitgenossen ebenso in Aufruhr versetzte wie das Denken Voltaires, Diderots, Rousseaus und anderer. 1818 wurde Oberlin für seine Verdienste um die Landwirtschaft mit der Ehrenmedaille ausgezeichnet, 1819 zum Ritter der Ehrenlegion ernannt. Selbst Zar Alexander I. hatte von Oberlin gehört und

Lob des Herkommens: Oberlin stammte aus einer angesehenen Straßburger Familie. Am Vater, einem Gymnasiallehrer, rühmte er den „liebevollen Ernst"

Offenbarung des Glaubens: Oberlin, dessen Mutter „ganz weltlich gesinnt" war, ließ sich die Visionen seiner Gemeindemitglieder erzählen. Aus den Träumen der Geisterseher schuf er „Landkarten des Jenseits"

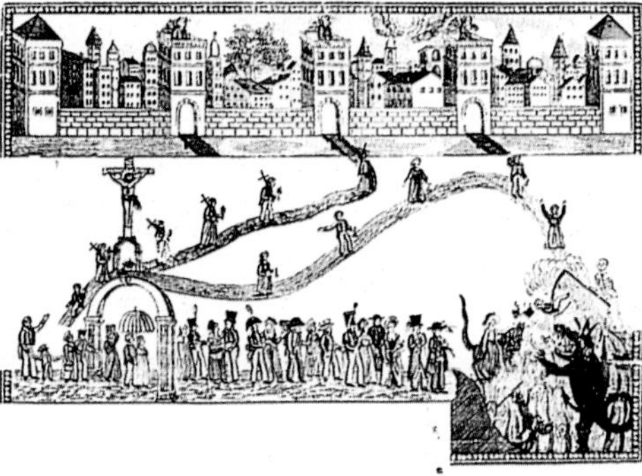

stellte aus Bewunderung 1813 einen Schutzbrief für das Steintal aus, als russische Truppen nach Frankreich einmarschierten.

Auf Oberlin stößt man heute vornehmlich durch einen seiner bekannten Gäste, den Sturm-und-Drang-Dichter Jakob Michael Reinhold Lenz. Dessen Besuch im Januar/Februar 1778 zeichnete Büchner in seiner Novelle „Lenz" fast sechs Jahrzehnte später minutiös anhand von Oberlins Aufzeichnungen nach. (Übrigens hielt Büchners Brautvater, Pfarrer Jaegle, an Oberlins Grab die Predigt.) „Den 20. Jänner ging Lenz durch's Gebirg." – So beginnt Büchners kongeniale Einfühlung in den verzweifelten Lenz. Dieser eiferte Goethe nicht nur in der Dichtung, sondern auch im Leben nach. Vergeblich suchte er die Liebe der von Goethe verlassenen Friederike Brion. Als Goethe Lenz 1776 wegen einer „Eselei" aus Weimar ausweisen ließ, irrte dieser durch das Land, von Freund zu Freund, ohne Fuß fassen zu können. Ein Brief des Pädagogen und Dichters Pfeffel, dessen Assistent Lerse ebenfalls dem Straßburger Sturm-und-Drang-Kreis 1770/71 angehört hatte, zeichnet ein frühes Bild von Oberlin und zeigt, welch große Hoffnungen in ihn gesetzt waren: „Ein simpler, weiser, menschenliebender, kurz ein wahrhaft apostolischer Mann. Ohne Ansprüche auf Genie (sic) und Berühmtheit wirkt er in seiner Sphäre langsam wie ihn die Vorsehung unterstützt. Er hat das Steintal, das elsässische Sibirien, schon zur Hälfte umgeschaffen, den höchst armen und verwilderten Einwohnern Liebe zur Arbeit, zum Lesen und zu aufheiternden Künsten, und, was unendlich mehr ist, zu Sitten und Tugenden eingeflößt. Was Lenz tun wird, wollen wir sehen. Oberlin ist der Mann, und vielleicht der einzige Mann, der ihm, wenn sein Kopf erlaubt, Geschmack an einer anhaltenden und nützlichen Arbeit beibringen kann."

Den Geschmack an einer anhaltenden und nützlichen Arbeit beibringen – das war das handfeste Programm zeitgenössischer Theologie, nach der der Landpfarrer zum Sozialpädagogen wurde. Er war Ökonom, Landwirt, Kaufmann, Arzt, Erzieher, ja nicht selten schriftstellernder Aufklärer. Er war ein Theologe, wenn nicht der Befreiung, so doch der (praktischen) Aufklärung gemäß dem physiokratischen Wirtschaftsden-

Reform der Erziehung: Oberlin wollte die Schule zur Pflicht machen. 1770 entstanden in Waldersbach in den Vogesen die ersten Kleinkinderschulen

37

Intern (The Netherlands)

no. 2 1987

designer Reynoud Homan

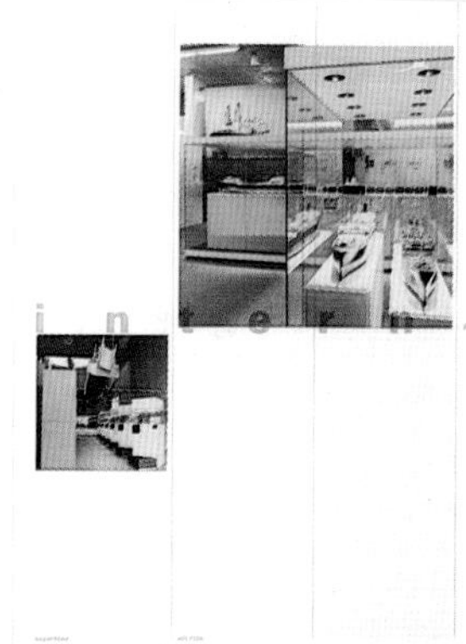

Diver (The Netherlands)

1989 (special issue)

designers Toula Antonakos, Rik Comello, Hans Bockting

Grids and formats

Certain aspects of magazine structure, such as the headline ruling all beneath it, are too often taken for granted. Even the headline can be dispensed with. The two Wire spreads incorporate a headline/standfirst hybrid, which collapses the typographic structure into a simpler form and gives editors a chance to say more about the subject. There is also a less abrupt transition from heading to text. The lead in the Jenkins ear story, illustrated by a portrait which fairly leaps out of the page, runs easily into the text. Paul Elliman's spare compositions, simple typography and inspired picture placement follow no fixed system and fall into structures improvised out of the material available and built on collaboration between art director and editor. Neville Brody uses a similarly reductive technique at Arena (see page 202). By contrast, Phil Bicker's Face spread contains all of the expected components of headline, standfirst, byline, body copy, but not in the conventional monolithic form. The page has an interlocking architectural order in which the head and delta-shaped standfirst are cantilevered out of body text. The intended order of reading, however, remains intact. In Straight No Chaser, the portrait and standfirst are placed at right angles to the main text, in order to exploit the panoramic width of landscape binding. The complex arrangement is resolved by reversing the first letter of the head out of the photograph.

The Face (UK)
October 1989
art director Phil Bicker
photographer Juergen Teller

CANNES – PRONOUNCED CON – IS A SUN-KISSED HEAP OF LEGO BUILDINGS

From a lonely Catholic girl to the gang of three, she drank and danced her way through Bananarama until one day she realised she didn't like the music any more. Finding salvation through The Smiths and new playmates

banana shaken

through The Eurythmics, she became Siobhan Fahey – wife of Dave, mother of Sam, sister of Shakespear, and the Eighties' last great re-invention

76 / THE FACE

safe sax

Straight No Chaser (UK)
no. 4 1989
designer Ian Swift
photographer
Antonio Mattesini

The War of Jenkins' ear:

on his latest record. But Mark Sinker

Billy Jenkins, wharf-rat

finds the man with the Voice

of the new British jazz,

of God less ferocious than he sounds.

takes a scratch at Miles

"SKETCHES OF SPAIN'? I've never heard it! What *does* it represent? I picked on it for the visual thing. For a distinctive sleeve. I don't know whether . . . well, I don't mean to insult these people, because I haven't met them, as my Grandad used to say. But I'm dubious about labelling pieces in a pretentious or an unthought way. Or a traditional way. I think, I can't talk like that. And people tend to romanticise about locations. William Walton did a London Symphony – but he must have done it in a country cottage! It doesn't sound like London to me, albeit the London of the 1920s.

"I thought, let's be realistic, let's document the truth. We *record* in a realistic way, without compressing or digitalising. I put my musicians in parts where they can use their talents naturally. So it's real to me."

So this is the Reverend Billy. He isn't as furious as his tone in print. He mumbles his

28 WIRE MAGAZINE

Photography by Simon Durrant

Wire (UK)
March 1988
designer Paul Elliman
photographer
Simon Durrant

Herman Leonard is one of the masters of jazz photography. Working through the 40s and 50s with many of the greatest musicians of the day,

ABOVE: Lester's pork pie
ABOVE RIGHT: Stan Getz
FAR RIGHT: James Moody

40 WIRE MAGAZINE

WIRE MAGAZINE 41

Wire (UK)
February 1988
designer Paul Elliman
photographer
Herman Leonard

Grids and formats

Grid design continues to be a source of innovation. The large-format (340 x 240mm) Gap Casa has a 4/6 column grid which provides nine legitimate picture measures and allows a lot of text to be incorporated into very open layouts. This is achieved by leaving empty column sections, and by floating 4-column setting on to the 6-column grid. The typographic scheme is equally complex (the page, right, combines no fewer than ten variations in face, weight and style) but this mass of elements is controlled with sufficient skill to impose order and style. The use of justified setting at such a narrow measure is a more dubious practice. Grids are normally notional devices, but in Report, a large-format arts magazine published in Seoul, the grid is made concrete, a dominant graphic feature of eight black and white bars to the page, in which the economical Korean alphabet is punctuated by photographic detail.
The grid is repeated throughout the magazine, peeling away, as in the opening spread, to reveal the image "beneath" it. Cento Cose is, by contrast, an extemporaneous construction with no perceivable underlying scheme. The control provided by digital design systems promotes the use of "gridless" layout, a common feature of contemporary magazine design. The two spreads shown here are before (top) and after (bottom) a restyling dictated entirely by typographic fashion: the setting has changed from rectangular to biomorphic, and type from modern condensed grots to decorative serifs, yet the overall page structure remains identical.

Gap Casa (Italy)
April 1988
art director Paola Bianchi

Piccole e grandi cronache dal mondo risuonano fra Gap Casa, i corrispondenti esteri e le redazioni delle più interessanti riviste di design nel panorama internazionale.

TAMTAMTAMTAMTAMTAMTAMTAMTAMTAMTAMTAMTAM

Francia: nuovi strumenti per l'analisi di mercato al servizio dell'industria del mobile

PARIGI

Quale arredo produrre e dove venderlo? La risposta viene dalla distribuzione e dall'indagine dei nuovi stili di vita francesi.

LO STILE E IL CONSUMO

In assenza di una seria indagine di mercato, l'UNIFA, il sindacato francese dei mobilieri, ha promosso e realizzato il 'panel' dei distributori, idoneo a valutare il cambiamento della domanda dell'acquirente. I sociostyles rivelano cinque fasce di mercato corrispondenti ad altrettante 'mentalità'.

Il modesto ricorso a ricerche di mercato da parte dei fabbricanti di mobili è un problema rilevato costantemente in Francia, sin dalla fine del periodo di grande espansione economica conclusosi nei primi anni 70. In questo periodo, la questione dell'adeguamento del prodotto ai desideri del consumatore, quello di un scelta ragionata dei canali di distribuzione e quello di una politica dell'immagine non venivano avvertiti. La situazione si è radicalmente modificata in seguito all'inversione congiunturale dell'80-81, che ha provocato non solamente una riduzione complessiva del volume delle vendite, ma anche modificazioni profonde del mercato: disinteresse per i mobili di genere tradizionale, soprattutto da parte dei giovani; dirottamento delle disponibilità economiche verso altri settori (tempo libero, viaggi,...); obsolescenza delle reti di distribuzione rispetto ai cambiamenti di comportamento dei consumatori.
Per ovviare alla mancanza di strumenti di mercato in grado di apprezzare queste evoluzioni, l'UNIFA (il sindacato francese che raggruppa i mobilieri) ha organizzato un panel, così da poter valutare quantitativamente i cambiamenti della domanda di mercato, e fatto realizzare studi qualitativi in grado di individuare la natura delle nuove aspettative dell'acquirente.

IL PANEL DEI DISTRIBUTORI

Il panel dei distributori è uno strumento creato nel 1982. Si tratta di un sistema di controllo del mercato che permette di seguire l'evoluzione totale delle vendite, in fatturato e in

Nell'80 la tendenza si capovolge: motivazioni e reazioni

Il panel dei distributori risulta uno strumento d'analisi importante, ma i produttori non sempre lo utilizzano come servirebbe.

67

GIORNALE ATTUALITÀ • PRODOTTI

CALENDARIO DELLE FIERE

APRILE

FIERE: MACEF PRIMAVERA

L'estetica entra in cucina

NUOVA METALMOBILE

Sgabello monotubo

CONSORZIO ITALIANO PRODUTTORI COPPI IN COTTO

Componenti architettoniche dell'identità ambientale

AREA

"Incontro" componibile

39

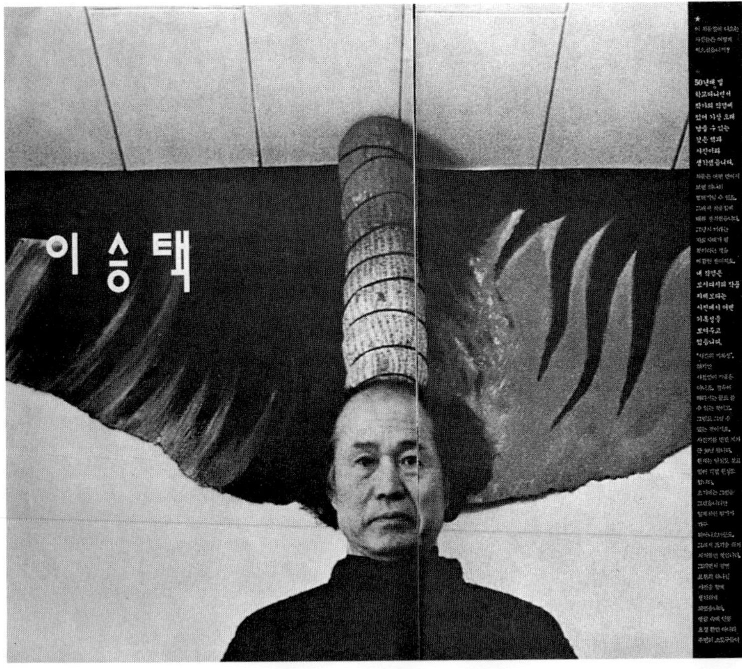

Report (Korea)
8 February 1989
designer Ahn Graphics

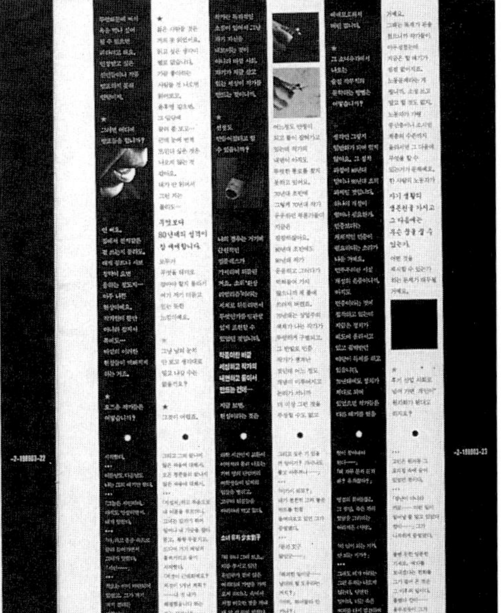

Cento Cose (Italy)
May 1989
art director
Renzo Castiglioni

Cento Cose (Italy)
August 1990
art editor Laura Marras

Type and meaning

Eliminating the use in print of decorative embellishment as a signature of wealth and class was a primary aim of the modernist avant-garde. Likewise, the revival of baroque types and borders, small vignettes and pastel colours in the 1980s was an aesthetic response in sympathy with the new culture of consumption, calculated to flatter and attract an affluent target readership, but not always to serve the specific content of editorial. In this sense, the aristocratic rhetoric of post-modern "home" and "style" magazines is editorially passive design (the exception here is the rococo styling of type in Italian Vogue, which refers directly to the subject matter). Commercial sense dictates that style as fashion fetish has an important place in magazine design as a means of eliciting recognition from the right kind of readers. This style is undeniably bourgeois, a showy decorativism sometimes very well done, but tending to be overbearing, and often drowning structural cohesion in a rich but dissolute banquet of ornament. The new baroque assumes an understanding of technical possibility in print, but not necessarily of form, or of communication of substance.

Esquire (USA)
June 1990
art director Rip Georges
illustrator James McMullan

Metropolitan Home (USA)
January 1990
art director Don Morris
photographer
Dominique Vorillon

REPLANTING DOWN-HOME ROOTS

DOMITEAUX theory: The simplest forms are the most powerful, as in his foursquare porch and chimney. See Resources

To build history into a house, a forward-thinker chooses shapes that don't change, textures that do

Mark Domiteaux
DALLAS, TEXAS

THE NINETIES ARE ABOUT PARING down, about making choices," says architect Mark Domiteaux. In designing his own home, he says, "I want to make the best of those choices." For Domiteaux, a partner in the Dallas firm Metro Architects, that means fashioning a "great hall" where the living room/kitchen/dining area is a long, window-lit sweep of space. That means using unfancy, industrial materials that, imaginatively handled, can seem right at home, such as concrete blocks or corrugated metal. And that means unabashedly looking to the past for inspiration, to Dallas' earliest stucco and brick houses, built to stand up to the weather, with durable materials and strong, direct shapes. To pack the most space into family life, Domiteaux deliberately kept the house's three bedrooms small, tucked off the great hall—but each in its own wing with a lot of windows and a shaded porch. The place is uncluttered, easygoing—"as comfortable," the architect maintains, "as an old pair of jeans."

DEEP IN the heart of Texas, Mark Domiteaux (below) sculpts with concrete blocks that unabashedly state what they're made of.

Produced by Newell Turner and Susan Weinberger
Written by Aaron Betsky; Photos: Dominique Vorillon

86 • METROPOLITAN HOME • JANUARY 1990

Emois (France)
October 1987
art director
Rosamaria Del Vecchio

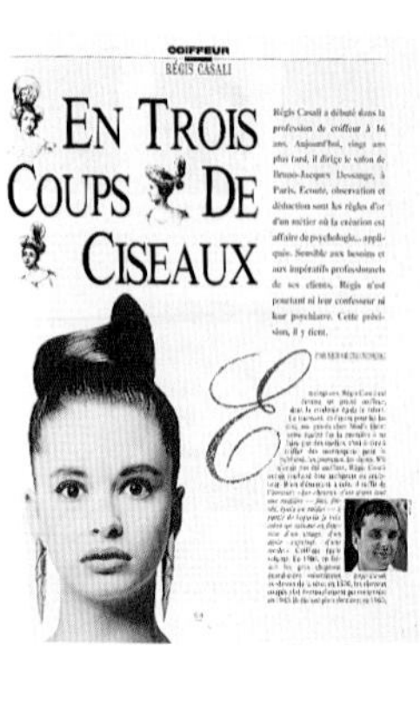

COIFFEUR
RÉGIS CASALI

EN TROIS COUPS DE CISEAUX

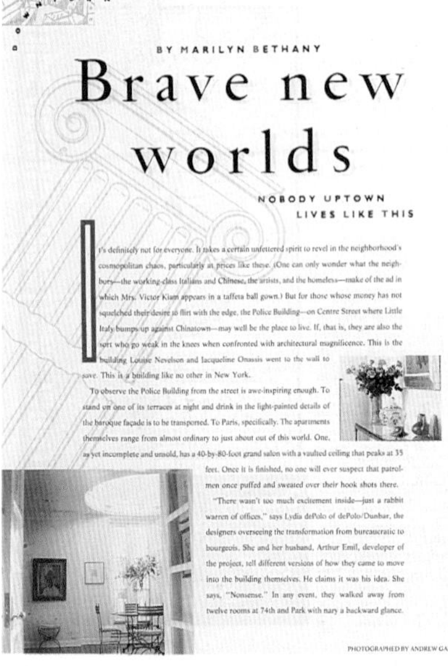

DOWNTOWN

BY MARILYN BETHANY

Brave new worlds

NOBODY UPTOWN LIVES LIKE THIS

It's definitely not for everyone. It takes a certain unfettered spirit to revel in the neighborhood's cosmopolitan chaos, particularly at prices like these. (One can only wonder what the neighbors—the working-class Italians and Chinese, the artists, and the homeless—make of the ad in which Mrs. Victor Kiam appears in a taffeta ball gown.) But for those whose money has not squelched their desire to flirt with the edge, the Police Building—on Centre Street where Little Italy bumps up against Chinatown—may well be the place to live. If, that is, they are also the sort who go weak in the knees when confronted with architectural magnificence. This is the building Louise Nevelson and Jacqueline Onassis went to the wall to save. This is a building like no other in New York.

To observe the Police Building from the street is awe-inspiring enough. To stand on one of its terraces at night and drink in the light-painted details of the baroque façade is to be transported. To Paris, specifically. The apartments themselves range from almost ordinary to just about out of this world. One, as yet incomplete and unsold, has a 40-by-80-foot grand salon with a vaulted ceiling that peaks at 35 feet. Once it is finished, no one will ever suspect that patrolmen once puffed and sweated over their hook shots there.

"There wasn't too much excitement inside—just a rabbit warren of offices," says Lydia dePolo of dePolo/Dunbar, the designers overseeing the transformation from bureaucratic to bourgeois. She and her husband, Arthur Emil, developer of the project, tell different versions of how they came to move into the building themselves. He claims it was his idea. She says, "Nonsense." In any event, they walked away from twelve rooms at 74th and Park with nary a backward glance.

PHOTOGRAPHED BY ANDREW GARN

IN THE DINING ROOM OF PUBLIC-RELATIONS EXECUTIVE BERNARD CHAPPARD, DESIGNER LYDIA DEPOLO POSITIONED THE TABLE BENEATH THE SKYLIT CUPOLA SO DINERS CAN TAKE IN THE VIEW

New York (USA)
25 December 1989
design director Bob Best
photographer Andrew Garn

Vogue (Italy)
December 1989
art director Juan Gatti

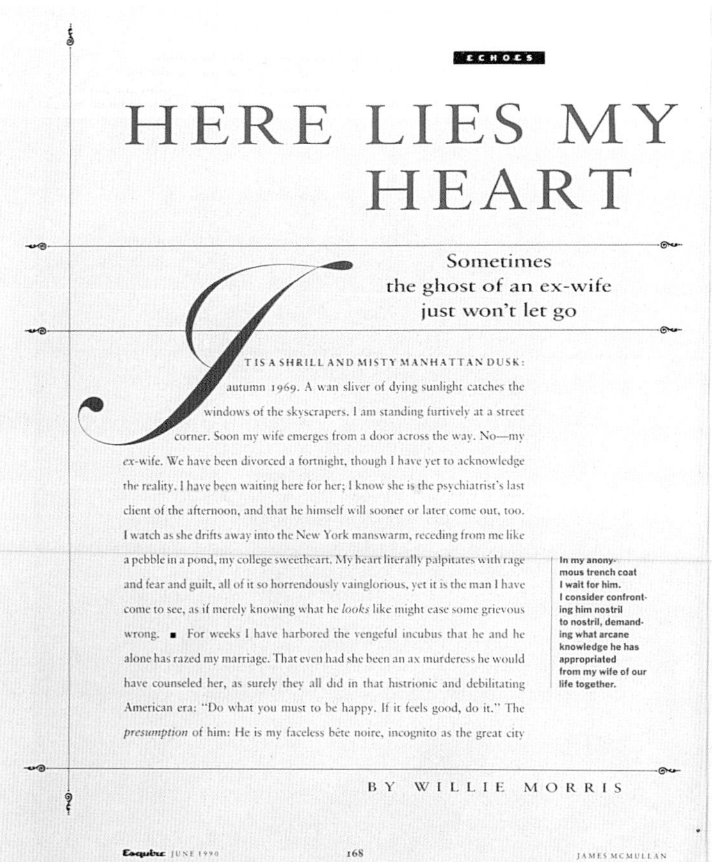

ECHOES

HERE LIES MY HEART

Sometimes the ghost of an ex-wife just won't let go

IT IS A SHRILL AND MISTY MANHATTAN DUSK: autumn 1969. A wan sliver of dying sunlight catches the windows of the skyscrapers. I am standing furtively at a street corner. Soon my wife emerges from a door across the way. No—my *ex*-wife. We have been divorced a fortnight, though I have yet to acknowledge the reality. I have been waiting here for her; I know she is the psychiatrist's last client of the afternoon, and that he himself will sooner or later come out, too. I watch as she drifts away into the New York manswarm, receding from me like a pebble in a pond, my college sweetheart. My heart literally palpitates with rage and fear and guilt, all of it so horrendously vainglorious, yet it is the man I have come to see, as if merely knowing what he *looks* like might ease some grievous wrong. ■ For weeks I have harbored the vengeful incubus that he and he alone has razed my marriage. That even had she been an ax murderess he would have counseled her, as surely they all did in that histrionic and debilitating American era: "Do what you must to be happy. If it feels good, do it." The *presumption* of him: He is my faceless bête noire, incognito as the great city

In my anonymous trench coat I wait for him. I consider confronting him nostril to nostril, demanding what arcane knowledge he has appropriated from my wife of our life together.

BY WILLIE MORRIS

Esquire JUNE 1990 168 JAMES MCMULLAN

Type and meaning

Here we have a very different aesthetic: it is big and bouncy, masculine, youthful and dynamic, and to a degree "classless" although the modernist letterforms used are not popular, but have a strong intellectual bias. There is a degree of irony involved in that Helvetica, which was designed as an objective medium for the written language which signified nothing in itself, has in these examples lost its corporate neutrality and gained a very specific human character through the use of constructive typographic composition. The integrity and vitality of these tightly woven layouts is achieved entirely through inventive use of type and without recourse to fussy detail or any superficial styling. Thus the aesthetic can be determined not only by type style, but also by the manner in which type is used. Nonetheless, the techniques illustrated here have little to do with function or structure: they are stylized expressions of general editorial outlook. There is, for example, a clear distinction between the poise of Tempo, the relatively adult gloss of Arena (see also overleaf) and the anarchic composition of Underground, which has a younger readership. Each of these magazines has a young, educated and, with the exception of green consumer magazine Oko-Test, male-oriented audience. This fact is clearly communicated in the design.

Arena (UK)
November 1989
art director Neville Brody
photographer
Eamonn McCabe

From its heroic origins in

Ein Kilo Heroin. Ein V-Mann. Ein Justizskandal. Wie deutsche Drogenfahnder eine unschuldige Frau in den Knast brachten. Und warum sie keiner rausholt.

der fall schwarzer

Tempo (Germany)
September 1989
art director Lo Breier

Olympic cyclists by *Guardian* picture editor Eamonn McCabe, the doyen of sports photographers

the arenas of Ancient Greece, sport has become one of the grails of the twentieth century, worshipped by a global TV audience, endorsed by corporate money, and pursued with sometimes reckless determination by athletes. In this special sports supplement,

port

Arena engages the realms of sweat, skill and immortality. We meet two American worldbeaters – Carl Lewis and Bo Jackson – remember the greatest football match ever played, freeze-frame eight young boxers, scale the heights of speed climbing and take a wry look at sporting chic in *Vanity*. A muscle-flexing 30-page sporting extravaganza

Contributing Editor **Richard Williams**

Underground (UK)

September 1987

designer Rod Clark

THE VULTURES

DAN

THE CROWS

THE JEREMIAHS

MORRISONS

THE ONLOOKERS

THE MONKEY RUN

LICK THE TINS

total

Oko-Test (Germany)

July 1985

designers

Christof Gassner,

Sabine Muller, Monika Weiss

Vor 13 Jahren fielen auf Nordenhams Weiden die Kühe tot um. Gestorben an Bleivergiftung. Heute bemüht sich die Stadt um ein ökologisches Image. Eine Reportage über den Alltag nach der Katastrophe.

12

Wundermittelchen gegen dicke Schenkel und Angst sind »nur« wirkungslos und teuer. Problematisch wird es bei exotischen Arzneien gegen Krebs oder gegen Asthma.

Die meisten Tomatensäfte enthalten zuviel Salz. Es soll angeblich den Geschmack verfeinern. Wir vermuten: Die Hersteller wollen den faden Geschmack billiger Tomaten überdecken.

ÖKO TEST

Magazin für Alltagsökologie

Berichte

ÖKO-TESTS

Magazin

Rubriken

Inhalt

Weiß eigentlich noch jemand, wie Kartoffeln schmecken? Nein, nicht Salzkartoffeln. Auch nicht die Pommes aus der Frittenbude. Die schmecken nach Salz. Kennen Sie den Kartoffel-Geschmack? Oder nehmen wir Tomatensäfte. In dem ÖKO-TEST, den Sie in diesem Heft finden, stellten wir als Hauptzutat der meisten Säfte Salz fest. Mit Salz wird der fade Geschmack der Lebensmittel-Massenprodukte überdeckt. Durch zuviel Salz haben wir das Würzen verlernt und uns des natürlichen Geschmacks der Speisen entwöhnt. – Der zweite ÖKO-TEST dieses Heftes sollte sich eigentlich mit Müslis beschäftigen. Das Testergebnis verschob das Thema: Es geht um den Zucker. Über den Zucker könnte man beinahe dasselbe schreiben wie über Salz: Mit Zucker wird der fade Geschmack der Lebensmittel-Massenprodukte überdeckt. Durch Zucker haben wir uns des natürlichen Geschmacks der Speisen entwöhnt. Aber zum Zucker gibt es noch mehr zu sagen. Zucker ist eine Droge, die bereits Kleinkindern verabreicht wird, Sinnesempfindungen prägt und das erste Suchtverhalten im Leben hervorruft. Die Affäre mit den gezuckerten Kindertees – Säuglinge bekamen Karies, Kleinkinder Kiefervereiterungen – ist meist als Betriebsunfall empfunden worden. Tatsächlich war sie ein Alarmsignal gegen ein sehr ungesundes Ernährungssystem. – Die Industrie soll endlich deklarieren, wieviel Zucker und Salz sie den Fertigprodukten zufügt. Und sie muß aufhören, im Zusammenhang mit Zucker und Salz von Gesundheit zu sprechen. Wir müssen lernen, bewußter mit Zucker und Salz umzugehen. Das ist nicht nur eine Frage der Gesundheit, sondern auch des Genusses.

Arena (UK)
March-April 1989
art director Neville Brody
photographer
Norman Watson

photography **norman watson** assisted by **david simms**
fashion by **david bradshaw** hair **tony allen** for toni & guy
models **jairo** (bananas, paris), **alain** (select), **marine** (we, paris)

ALCAZAR
Right: Double breasted jacket in blue cotton silk mix £609; shallow 'V' neck sweater in blue cotton crepe, £214; both by Claude Montana and available at L'Uomo Regine, London

L'ALSACE AUX HALLES
Left: Single breasted gilet in white cotton £155; polka dot shirt with mother of pearl buttons in navy, £220; black trousers in rayon silk mix, £225; all by Commes des Garcon and available at Commes des Garcon and L'Homme, Manchester

Á LA COUPOLE
Middle: Single breasted evening jacket by Yves Saint Laurent, £300, from Rive Gauche and Moss Bros, London; white cotton shirt by Commes Des Garcon, £145, from Commes des Garcon and L'Homme; wristwatch by Hermes

é Noir

Type and meaning

Typographic styling overlays the standard structure of every magazine with certain associative emphases and accents. This is one aspect of formatting; art direction implies something more, the articulation of the story. One way is through expressive combinations of word and image (see, for example, page 203); another is to exploit the semantic qualities of type, with or without a fixed format, to interpret editorial content subjectively, to communicate meaning, or merely to provide thematic variation. These layouts illustrate three different kinds of concrete typography which might be described as aural, associative and figurative. The first, from Interview, is a brilliant exposition of visual poetry, an ideogrammatic, typographic rap. It uses varied type sizes, overlaid to force the perspective, to recreate the rhythm, cadence and volume of rap. In this case the layout is executed within the magazine's normal typographic format. El Europeo uses a simple, roughly constructed combination of levelled gun and typewriter face which together create an immediate symbolic association with hard-boiled crime writing. The i-D spread, using type distortion and a masked-out, liquid background, makes a more direct figurative link between typography, word and meaning.

Public Enemy's first record, *Yo! Bumrush the Show*, went gold. Their second record, *It Takes a Nation of Millions to Hold Us Back*, went platinum. The single "Fight the Power" (from their third and most recent album, *Fear of a Black Planet*) was the musical theme of Spike Lee's *Do the Right Thing*. *Fear of a Black Planet* went platinum in one week. These figures might not be so impressive if the act were a middle-of-the-road act, but Public Enemy pulls no punches, and there is no shortage of controversy over their lyrics. They have become cultural heroes, representing the truth of urban youth in no uncertain terms: "Elvis was a hero to most/but he never meant shit to me you see/Straight up racist that sucker was/Simple and plain/Motherfuck him and John Wayne"—from the single "Fight the Power."

In early 1983 a mobile D.J. collective known as Spectrum City was roaming around Roosevelt, Long Island, playing hip-hop in the parks and broadcasting their highly influential Super Spectrum Mixx Show on the Long Island radio station WBAU every Saturday night. At the forefront of all the action was a powerhouse jester/M.C. named Flavor Flav, whose antics and energy brought him into local prominence. It was also in Spectrum City that **Flavor Flav** began his collaboration with producer Hank Shocklee and another resident of the 'Velt, named Chuck D. Chuck had studied the speech patterns of minister Louis Farrakhan, and by blending this dynamic oratory with a keen political consciousness and a Madison Avenue knack for phrasemongering, Chuck established himself as one of the most powerful voices in rap. In 1986 Flavor Flav, Chuck D, and a D.J. named Terminator X formed Public Enemy. As his name suggests, Flavor Flav was the perfect counterpart to Chuck D's heavily militant, hard-core approach to rap. Sometimes Flavor Flav adds spice, accent, or salt, but most often his voice is inserted as a kind of hydraulic adrenaline boost, loopy and cartoonlike against Chuck's straight-ahead drilling. A master at playing "the dozens" (a ritual requiring speedy wit to out-insult your opponent), Flavor Flav can be as biting as he is hilarious. But as he proves on the recent hit single "911 Is a Joke," when Flavor Flav takes over the role of lead rapper, he commands serious respect.

I'm black
and i'm
proud
i'm ready
and hyped plus I'm
amped
most of my
heroes don't appear
on no stamps
sample
a look back
you look
and find
nothing but rednecks
for 400 years
if you check
don't worry
be happy
was a
number
one jam...

Interview (USA)
September 1990
creative director Tibor Kalman
designer Kristin Johnson
photographer David Lee

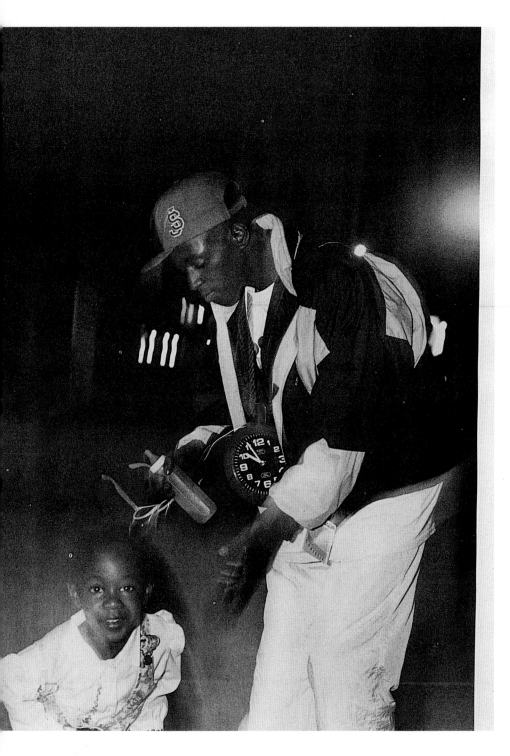

El Europeo (Spain)
April 1990
art director Javier Urena

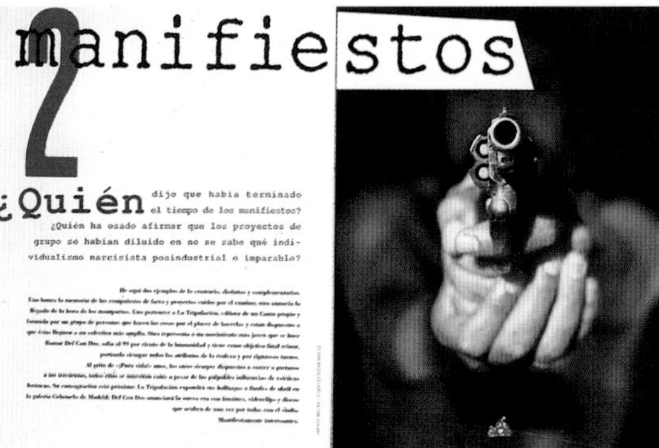

2 manifiestos

¿Quién dijo que habia terminado el tiempo de los manifiestos? ¿Quién ha osado afirmar que los proyectos de grupo se habian diluido en no se sabe qué individualismo narcisista posindustrial e imparable?

Deep Water

is water dangerous?

The i-D Good Water Guide

We've learned to live with food scares, but water scares? After Perrier's bubble burst, both bottled water and tap water have been shown to be bad for your health. Does the answer lie in water filters, and why have people started buying water from polar glaciers? Exactly how safe is it to drink?

the Perrier scare wasn't a health crisis so much as an image problem

i-D (UK)
May 1990
art director Stephen Male
art editor Neil Edwards
photographer Nils Vik

Type and meaning

The Japanese men's fashion and general interest magazine Piacere Rakan has as its title an obscure combination of Italian and Japanese which translates literally as "pleasure devil". It is produced to very high print standards which allow the subtlest gradations of colour and tone, and fine picture reproduction at the small sizes typically used in Japanese magazines. This provision is exploited in a very exact and carefully detailed design, with beautiful typographic constructions of Japanese and roman characters (here endearingly mistranslated into English). Type is layered upon background textured either by elegant freehand brush-strokes or by machined geometric forms, creating pages of exquisite refinement. Nonetheless, the most interesting feature of the main spread is not the typography but the conceptual idea which informs the design: the real art is in the powerful evocation of the headline in such a reductionist visual image as a half-face and car-door pillar.

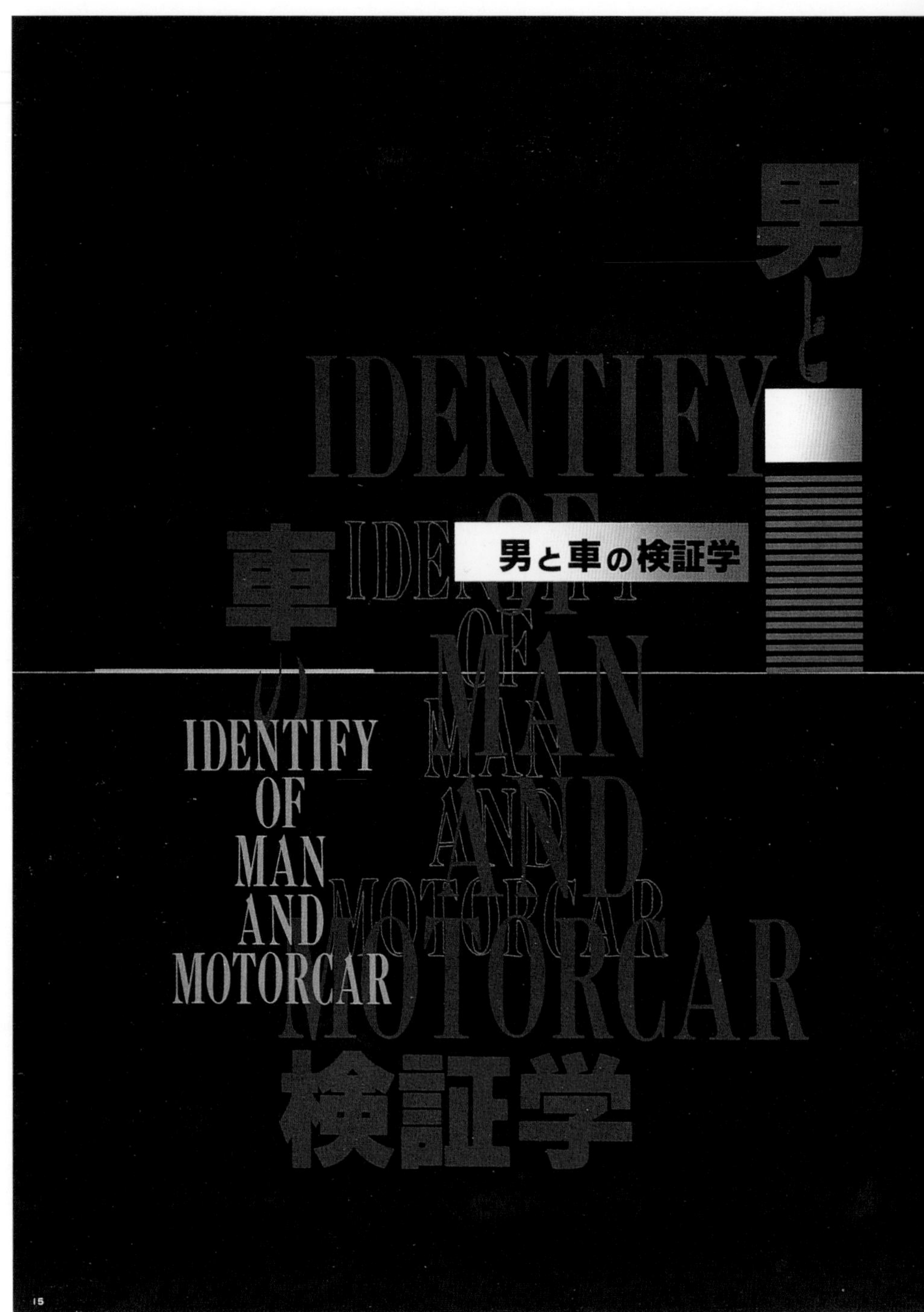

Piacere Rakan (Japan)
February 1989
art director Mitsuru Ueda

Piacere Rakan (Japan)
June 1988
art director Mitsuru Ueda

Type and meaning

Four more examples of putting type to work as a graphic component. The editorial page from Pubblicità Domani, an advertising trade magazine (left) offers a clever solution to the problem of enlivening editorial matter with limited visual potential. As a means of creating an air of easy familiarity, the inclusion of a picture of the editor on the leader page is nothing new. It also flatters his or her ego, but more often than not manifest vanity causes the device to fall flat. These intimate pocket portraits, however, are witty, and fit neatly into the graphic plot which signposts the section title as a series of dropped capitals within the body copy. Elle uses a similar technique to make the most of limited space. Like many fashion magazines it carries in its front section a long series of single-page features facing right-hand advertising matter. These pages must be clearly distinguished as editorial, relatively unobtrusive, yet attract readers' interest. Again, the solution is to mesh type and image tightly together, both physically and conceptually. In this carefully planned design, the headline becomes a participant in the image, knocked off the page by a mallet with its shaft inserted neatly into the column gutter. Rolling Stone art director Fred Woodward uses type as illustration in much the same way as Fabien Baron (see page 134). The decorative Georgian capitals (opposite) are clearly a stylistic statement, yet they also work as a constructive graphic device, as does the type in the other Rolling Stone spread, with its smooth, page-high, split "O" which, whether intended or not, is a mirror for Sinead O'Connor's shaven head.

Rolling Stone (USA)
18 May 1989
art director Fred Woodward
type designer
Dennis Ortiz-Lopez

CROQUET, THE ONCE GENTEEL PASTIME, HAS BECOME A VERY SERIOUS MATTER

WICKED WICKETS

BY GLENN O'BRIEN

I have seen the future and it looks a lot like the past, except longer," a great baseball player, Dan Quisenberry of the Kansas City Royals, once said. That's the way the future looked last summer at the All-Maine Croquet Championships in Cape Elizabeth, Maine. The carefully manicured croquet courts were laid out next to the postmodern-Victorian architecture of the luxurious Inn by the Sea. The players emerged from horse-drawn carriages: the men in their white flannels, straw hats, and kid gloves; the women in long dresses puffed out by crinoline petticoats.

Wait a second—this *was* the past, a staged fashion demonstration of how people dressed for croquet in the 19th century. The real players, the tough, serious tournament players, also wore mostly white but there were clear signs that this was the present, if not the future, of the sport. Some wore heavy-duty sneakers and shorts, and looked ready for a few sets of tennis. The top-seeded croquet player looked like Ben Hogan in a golfing cap, another had rock-and-roll-length hair. But there was still something timeless about the mallets propelling balls across the perfect bent grass through the wickets. Here was a sport untouched by new technology, steroids, weight lifting, scholarships, under-the-table payments, or free agency.

Not so long ago croquet was an endangered sport. Around the turn of the century, however, it was all the rage, a family pastime played throughout the U.S. and Britain. It was so popular that critics frothed about the game's dangers to society. One 19th-century commentator wrote: "The ingenuity of man has never conceived anything better calculated to bring out all the evil passions of humanity than the so-called game of croquet."

What could be evil about this genteel game? Perhaps moralists were appalled by the fact that croquet could be played by men and women on equal terms, leading to God knows what sort of intimacies. It's an equal-opportunity sport in which men enjoy no advantage, neither speed nor strength being a requisite; today, one of the country's better players is a 72-year-old woman, Nelga Young. It is a game of killer instinct, however, and that may have something to do with the "evil passions" associated with the game. Everyone who has played in a backyard is familiar with "sending" an opponent's ball. In tournament play, the abuse of an opponent's ball is elevated to a sadistic art; as a major strategic move that ruins opponents' plans, it's practiced often and with devilish delight.

Then, after two world wars and a depression and the rise of golf and tennis, croquet became a leisure-class sport essentially confined to Palm Beach, Newport, and the enclaves of those too rich to be famous or to have "lifestyles." Croquet eventually acquired a tame, unsporting image. People with a toy-like croquet set in the attic or in the garage misunderstood the game, thinking that it was restful recreation for senior citizens or even a simple game for tots. Then the sport started to grow again. Clubs of serious croquet players were formed in New York in 1967, in Palm Beach in 1969, and in Bermuda in 1970. Slowly the word spread that croquet was really a world-class game of great refinement, subtlety, and well-mannered cruelty. It was a secret that was bound to get out.

In 1986, some 300,000 croquet sets were sold, according to the U.S. Croquet Association. There are now more than 300 croquet clubs in the U.S., most with their own courts. While meticulously groomed courts—not mere lawns—are required for serious play, a serviceable one will fit into a modest backyard and can be set up much more cheaply than a tennis court.

What's responsible for the resurgence? Players are discovering that the game is neither tame nor simple, that it is a tremendously complex, skilled art, requiring the coordination and "touch" of billiards along with the strategic skills of chess.

One brake on the popularity of croquet has been confusion about its basic regulations: Players rarely agree on the rules. Actually, it has several sets of rules, depending on where and with whom you play. Players in the U.S. declared their independence from the British Croquet Association rules at the turn of the century, marking the devolution of croquet into a whole bunch of games. Ten years ago, there were at least five variations in use; now, two are considered to be the main versions.

The issue of rules has been so notoriously mixed up from the beginning that Alice found the same anarchic quality in the kind of croquet played in Wonderland. "I don't think they play at all fairly," she says, "and they all quarrel so dreadfully one can't hear oneself speak—and they don't seem

Croquet is now a world-class sport. Mallet, balls, Hammacher Schlemmer, NYC; stylist, Anita Calero.

LEN DELESSIO

Elle (USA)
June 1988
publication director
Regis Pagniez
art director Phyllis Schefer
photographer Len Delessio

Pubblicità Domani (Italy)
May-June 1990
design director Italo Lupi
art director Andrea Fanti

Rolling Stone (USA)
14 June 1990
art director Fred Woodward
photographer
Andrew Macpherson

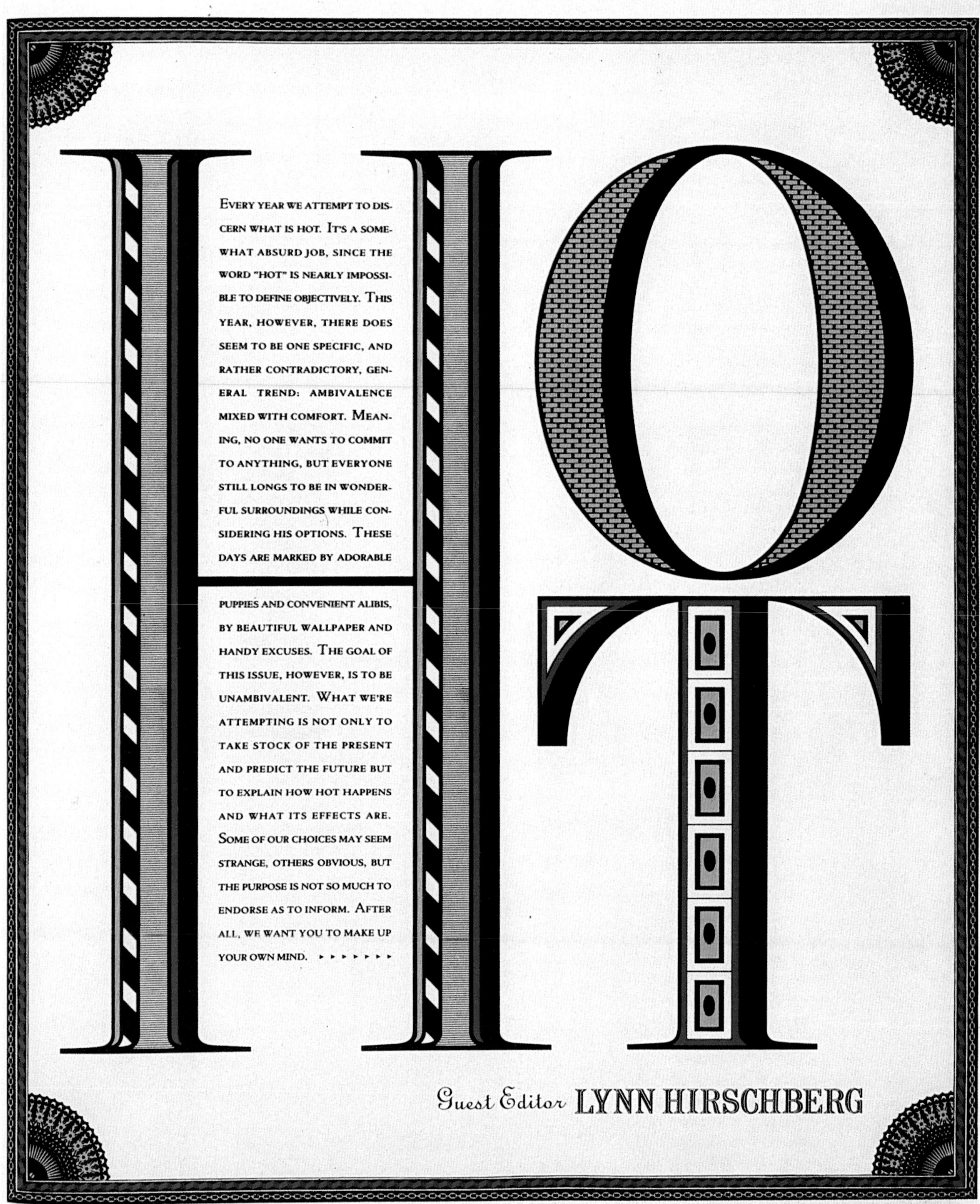
HOT
Every year we attempt to discern what is hot. It's a somewhat absurd job, since the word "hot" is nearly impossible to define objectively. This year, however, there does seem to be one specific, and rather contradictory, general trend: ambivalence mixed with comfort. Meaning, no one wants to commit to anything, but everyone still longs to be in wonderful surroundings while considering his options. These days are marked by adorable puppies and convenient alibis, by beautiful wallpaper and handy excuses. The goal of this issue, however, is to be unambivalent. What we're attempting is not only to take stock of the present and predict the future but to explain how hot happens and what its effects are. Some of our choices may seem strange, others obvious, but the purpose is not so much to endorse as to inform. After all, we want you to make up your own mind.
Guest Editor LYNN HIRSCHBERG
Alphabet by Dennis Ortiz-Lopez
Rolling Stone, May 18th, 1989 · 51

Contents pages

The cover is a poster and the contents page a guide, superfluous in some respects given that most readers flip through the magazine from back to front. That said, of all pages in a magazine this one has the most clearly defined function, requiring a typographic clarity which makes manifest the structure of the magazine, highlights departments and special features, and the pages on which to find them. The architecture magazine Domus has a solution to the problem of relating content to location and much else besides. A tabular format identifies, from left to right, author, page number, title, building location, architect and photographer. The cover story is highlighted between two heavy rules. This page also incorporates the editorial masthead, yet it has plenty of open space, graphic purity and visual interest. Each of the pages illustrated here makes an attempt to provide a visual as well as a literal association with editorial content. In the case of FAZ Magazin, this is done by the simple expedient of scattering coloured eggs over the page to provide an allusion both to Easter and an article on colour theory, as well as bring life to a page of text. Spy's design is cluttered with vignettes but the essential information is immediately apparent. This delicate balance between order and intrigue is brought into focus by Junie's contents page; its delightful maze of information and images is inimical to clarity but a magnet for the attention of its teenage girl readership. The innovative Traveler has dispensed entirely with the tabular contents list, locating holiday destination and page number on a cartographic display.

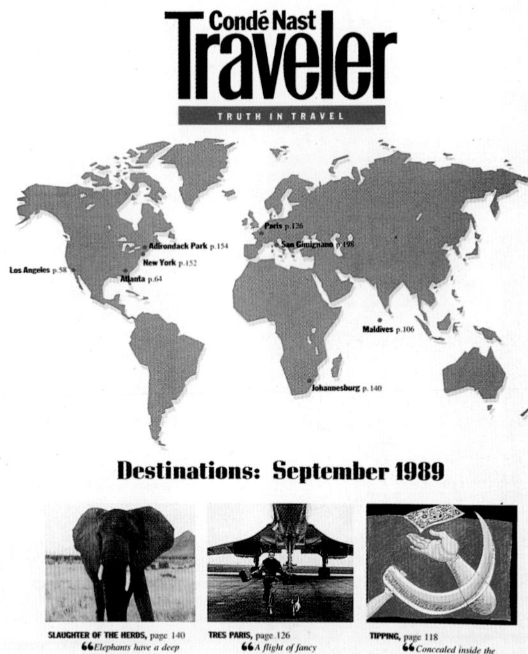

Condé Nast
Traveler
TRUTH IN TRAVEL

Los Angeles p.58
Adirondack Park p.154
New York p.152
Atlanta p.64
Paris p.126
San Gimignano p.198
Maldives p.106
Johannesburg p.140

Destinations: September 1989

SLAUGHTER OF THE HERDS, page 140
"Elephants have a deep comprehension of death and often return to where a member of the herd has fallen"

TRES PARIS, page 126
"A flight of fancy comes finally to rest, having exhausted purse, imagination, and Ouzo"

TIPPING, page 118
"Concealed inside the palm is a twice-folded bill. The customer maintains direct eye contact"

NEWS...BRIEFING...DEPARTMENTS...FEATURES...SERVICE

6

Condé Nast TRAVELER

Traveler (USA)

September 1989

design director
Diana La Guardia

Domus (Italy)
July-August 1986
art director Italo Lupi

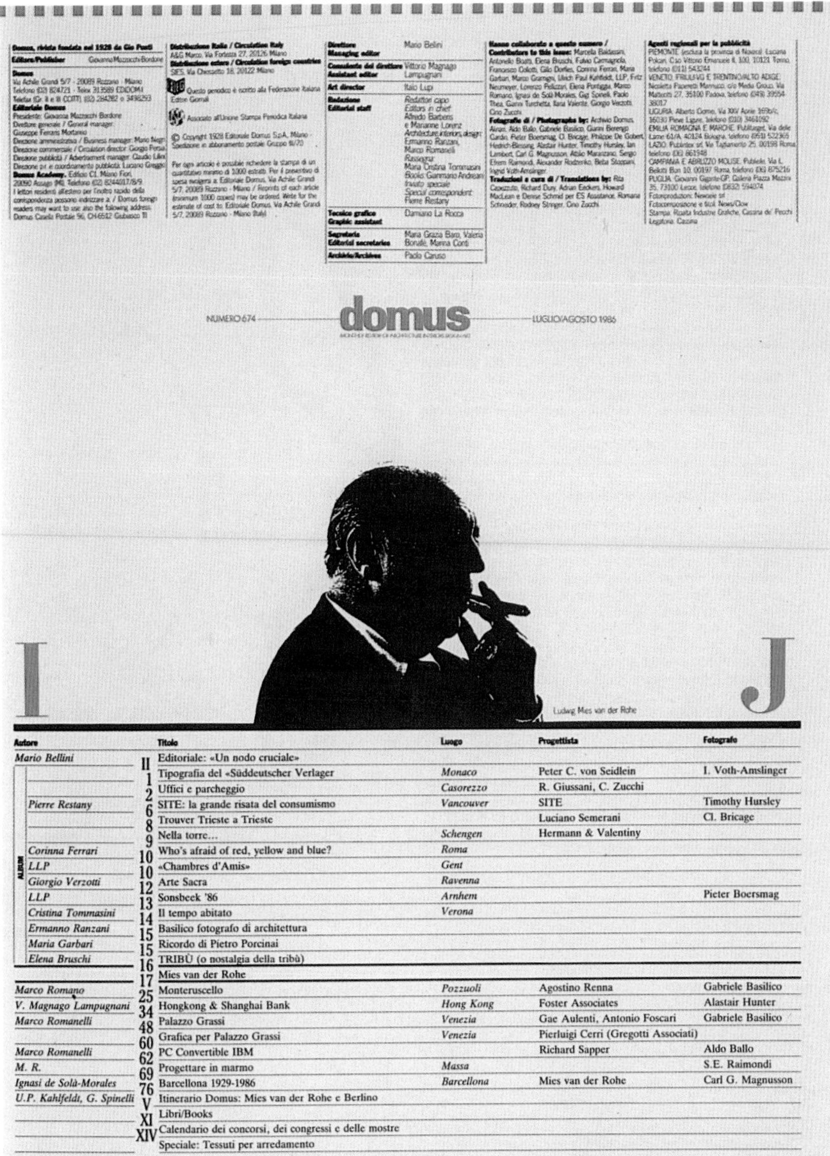
NUMERO 674 — domus — LUGLIO/AGOSTO 1986

Ludwig Mies van der Rohe

Autore		Titolo	Luogo	Progettista	Fotografo
Mario Bellini	II	Editoriale: «Un nodo cruciale»			
	1	Tipografia del «Süddeutscher Verlager	Monaco	Peter C. von Seidlein	I. Voth-Amslinger
	2	Uffici e parcheggio	Casorezzo	R. Giussani, C. Zucchi	
Pierre Restany	6	SITE: la grande risata del consumismo	Vancouver	SITE	Timothy Hursley
	8	Trouver Trieste a Trieste		Luciano Semerani	Cl. Bricage
	9	Nella torre...	Schengen	Hermann & Valentiny	
Corinna Ferrari	10	Who's afraid of red, yellow and blue?	Roma		
LLP	10	«Chambres d'Amis»	Gent		
Giorgio Verzotti	12	Arte Sacra	Ravenna		
LLP	13	Sonsbeek '86	Arnhem		Pieter Boersmag
Cristina Tommasini	14	Il tempo abitato	Verona		
Ermanno Ranzani	15	Basilico fotografo di architettura			
Maria Garbari	15	Ricordo di Pietro Porcinai			
Elena Bruschi	16	TRIBÙ (o nostalgia della tribù)			
	17	Mies van der Rohe			
Marco Romano	25	Monteruscello	Pozzuoli	Agostino Renna	Gabriele Basilico
V. Magnago Lampugnani	34	Hongkong & Shanghai Bank	Hong Kong	Foster Associates	Alastair Hunter
Marco Romanelli	48	Palazzo Grassi	Venezia	Gae Aulenti, Antonio Foscari	Gabriele Basilico
	60	Grafica per Palazzo Grassi	Venezia	Pierluigi Cerri (Gregotti Associati)	
Marco Romanelli	62	PC Convertible IBM		Richard Sapper	Aldo Ballo
M. R.	69	Progettare in marmo	Massa		S.E. Raimondi
Ignasi de Solà-Morales	76	Barcellona 1929-1986	Barcellona	Mies van der Rohe	Carl G. Magnusson
U.P. Kahlfeldt, G. Spinelli	V	Itinerario Domus: Mies van der Rohe e Berlino			
	XI	Libri/Books			
	XIV	Calendario dei concorsi, dei congressi e delle mostre			
		Speciale: Tessuti per arredamento			

Spy (USA)
June 1989
art director B. W. Honeycutt

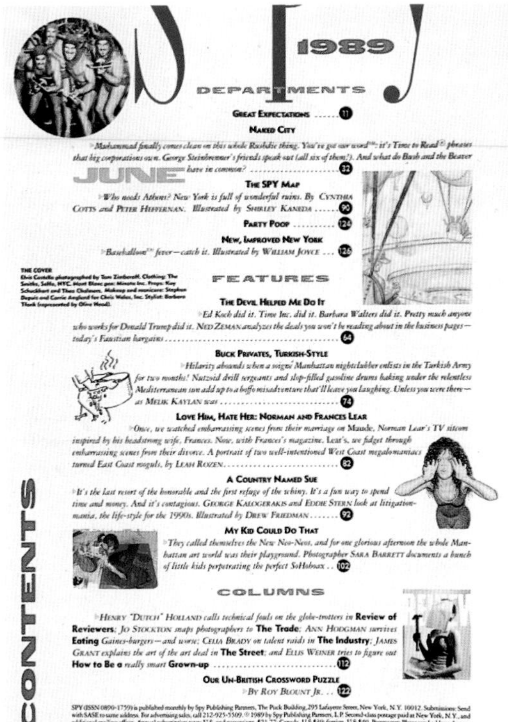
JUNE 1989

CONTENTS

DEPARTMENTS

Great Expectations 11

Naked City
Muhammad finally comes clean on this whole Rushdie thing. You've got our word™: it's Time to Read© phrases that big corporations own. George Steinbrenner's friends speak out (all six of them!). And what do Bush and the Beaver have in common? 32

The SPY Map
Who needs Athens? New York is full of wonderful ruins. By Cynthia Cotts and Peter Heffernan. Illustrated by Shirley Kaneda 90

Party Poop 124

New, Improved New York
Baseballoon™ fever—catch it. Illustrated by William Joyce ... 126

THE COVER
Elvis Costello photographed by Tom Zimberoff. Clothing: The Smiths, Saffo, NYC. Mont Blanc pen: Minato Inc. Props: Kay Schuckhart and Theo Chalmers. Makeup and manicure: Stephen Dupuis and Carrie Angland for Chris Wales, Inc. Stylist: Barbara Thank (represented by Olive Hood).

FEATURES

The Devil Helped Me Do It
Ed Koch did it. Time Inc. did it. Barbara Walters did it. Pretty much anyone who works for Donald Trump did it. Ned Zeman analyzes the deals you won't be reading about in the business pages—today's Faustian bargains 64

Buck Privates, Turkish-Style
Hilarity abounds when a soigné Manhattan nightclubber enlists in the Turkish Army for two months! Nutzoid drill sergeants and slop-filled gasoline drums baking under the relentless Mediterranean sun add up to a boffo misadventure that'll leave you laughing. Unless you were there—as Melik Kaylan was 74

Love Him, Hate Her: Norman and Frances Lear
Once, we watched embarrassing scenes from their marriage on Maude, Norman Lear's TV sitcom inspired by his headstrong wife, Frances. Now, with Frances's magazine, Lear's, we fidget through embarrassing scenes from their divorce. A portrait of two well-intentioned West Coast megalomaniacs turned East Coast moguls, by Leah Rozen...... 82

A Country Named Sue
It's the last resort of the honorable and the first refuge of the whiny. It's a fun way to spend time and money. And it's contagious. George Kalogerakis and Eddie Stern look at litigation-mania, the life-style for the 1990s. Illustrated by Drew Friedman...... 92

My Kid Could Do That
They called themselves the New Neo-Neos, and for one glorious afternoon the whole Manhattan art world was their playground. Photographer Sara Barrett documents a bunch of little kids perpetrating the perfect SoHohoax .. 102

COLUMNS

Henry "Dutch" Holland calls technical fouls on the globe-trotters in Review of Reviewers; Jo Stockton maps photographers to The Trade; Ann Hodgman survives Eating Gaines-burgers—and worse; Celia Brady on talent raids in The Industry; James Grant explains the art of the art deal in The Street; and Ellis Weiner tries to figure out How to Be a really smart Grown-up 112

Our Un-British Crossword Puzzle
By Roy Blount Jr. ... 122

SPY (ISSN 0890-1759) is published monthly by Spy Publishing Partners, The Puck Building, 295 Lafayette Street, New York, N.Y. 10012. Submissions: Send with SASE to same address. For advertising sales, call 212-925-5509. © 1989 by Spy Publishing Partners, L.P. Second-class postage paid at New York, N.Y., and additional mailing offices. Annual subscription rates: U.S. and possessions, $21.77; Canada, U.S.$30; foreign, U.S.$40. Postmaster: Please send address changes to SPY, P.O. Box 359139, Palm Coast, FL 32035-9139. For subscription information, call: 1-800-423-1780. Member, Audit Bureau of Circulations.

Junie (Japan)
October 1989
designer Mitsuru Ueda

JUNIE No.107 October 1989
完ペキシステムノート
14 新鮮！ベーシック・ファッション
51 ファッション小物にこだわり商品学
63 What's POP
ベッドって寝るためだけじゃつまらない！
71 "眠らせないで、私のハート"恋したの！
103
131 TREND20
108 作ろう Sandwiches

Frankfurter Allgemeine
Magazin (Germany)
27 March 1986
art director
Hans-Georg Pospischil
photographer Volker Hage

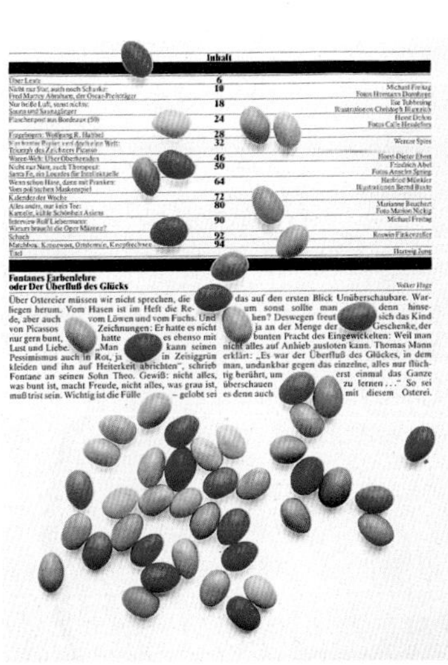
Inhalt

Fontanes Farbenlehre oder Der Überfluß des Glücks

The cover

Panorama (Spain)
August 1988
art director Angel Vico
photographer Paco Llata

This picture weekly cover featuring Tour de France winner Pedro Delgado has all of the classic ingredients: celebrity, heroism, topicality, colour and a multitude of prominent but carefully arranged copy tasters including that essential word "exclusive".

The best magazine cover is the memorable cover, the kind (as a designer once said) "that sticks in your mind so well it can be drawn from memory".[1] But ask any publisher and you will be told that, on the contrary, the best cover is the one that sells, and a straw poll of any newsstand will show that a publisher's idea of what sells is the human face looking out at the reader and lots and lots of cover lines.

The cover is the area of magazine design that is most closely controlled, causes maximum agony, and is the most potent source of conflict between the aesthetic ambitions of the designer and the base motive of profit, for on this one page, which must signal both editorial character and content, hangs the fate of up to 40 per cent of a magazine's circulation. Will it be picked up off a bookstall by the casual browser? Will it deter or attract committed readers? The answer to these questions is known only to that pair of slipshod sciences we call popular prejudice and received wisdom, according to which the cover must have a full face, preferably lifesize, the eyes staring full at the camera (pupils exactly 6cm/2½in apart) above a charming and attractive smile. The face must have personality, be unthreatening and a mirror image of the reader (or more accurately, the reader's physical and social aspirations) and it should be surrounded by as many tasters as can be squeezed into the left, right or bottom of the page. It would be helpful if the face were that of the Princess of Wales (reputedly a guaranteed 20 per cent boost to circulation), but if the lady was used last month or is otherwise engaged then Madonna, Linda Evangelista or Tatjana Patitz will do.

The stifling conservatism of contemporary cover design is grounded in fear of failure and the sure knowledge that if one does what one's competitors do then at least one can't do any worse. And in defence against innovation the management has a pocketful of old wives' tales (and statistics) which will prove that the last time fluorescent green was used sales dipped disastrously. Equally, immediately the competition exhibits "daring" then *everybody* follows suit next month. *Tatler*, in 1987, started a vogue for what had been the publisher's anathema, black and white photography. Fabien Baron rekindled the craze at *Vogue Italia* in 1989, in his case using monochome with constancy and panache.

Cover design reveals interesting national characteristics. The Italians are untrammelled by convention and show inventive use of both images and logotypes; the French have a distinct preference for full-figure model shots; the Americans and English for the full face; and the Japanese for torso and head – often of more than one individual.

David Bailey said that at *Vogue* in the 1960s, "On the same day, six photographers shot a cover," usually including himself, Bert Stern, Avedon and Penn. "Six photographs would be put up on the wall and one was chosen. The light was always on the model's right, and her eyes were looking towards it, to draw the viewer to the type. A psychoanalyst called Doc looked at the covers, and if he didn't like one it just didn't go on."

These conventions showed signs of breaking down in the late 1980s, thanks largely to the influence of the Italians. "Psychological" testing of covers on market research samples prior to release is to some extent discredited and editors have recognized that 20 separate cover lines cannot be read easily by the browser and detract from the visual image. Terry Jones turned the model's back to the camera for the first issue of *Donna*. When *Vanity Fair* was relaunched in 1983 by the most

Vogue (Italy)
July-August 1989
art director Fabien Baron
photographer Albert Watson

Few fashion magazines have the nerve to depart from the full-face cover shot. Vogue Italia is an exception, using a wide variety of compositions and a range of colourways from dayglo to monochrome. The magazine happily breaks cardinal commercial rules as in this exuberant, graceful and notably faceless silhouette by Albert Watson.

conservative of US publishing houses it attempted a brave but botched experiment in sophisticated soft-sell cover presentation. Unfortunately it chose to use weak and rather obtuse images, and within four or five issues the magazine had slunk back to the Hollywood personality shot with multiple cover lines. *Vogue* (US), under the art direction of Derek Ungless, varies cover photography between full figure and full face. Regis Pagniez at *Elle* (US) has experimented with harsh crops and multiple images, and always employs brief cover lines executed cleanly and with restraint.

This is, however, grasping at straws. "Personality" and headshot cover photograpy dominates popular women's weeklies and monthly glossies, men's monthlies, music magazines, popular arts and movie reviews, and is becoming increasingly prevalent in trade and business magazines, no doubt for sound commercial reasons. The opportunities available in these cases are therefore fairly limited. What is required from the designer – apart from considerable political aptitude – is an attractive and dynamic image, cropped to create maximum force and balance, an acute colour sense, and the ability to combine a large number of competing lines of type in a small space. Obviously, the pictorial and typographic treatment differs significantly between the glossy fashion books and popular weeklies. *Best* and *Panorama,* for example, project a very different image from *Vogue*: a hard sell cacophony of blocked type and all-capital headlines – "busy" covers – which should not, however, be equated with disorder. Even very similar magazines exhibit subtle variations of image. The typography of *Elle* UK and *Elle* US is identical, but the picture choice and use of colour show clear individual characteristics related directly to the outlook of their readers: one favours plain "English rose" types and muted colours; the other prefers rich colour and darker, tomboyish models.

The conceptual cover presents a very different design problem, for which the exhortation to a memorable image has absolute relevance. It requires planning, the ability to think laterally, clever copywriting and, above all, first rate execution, for a good idea sloppily carried out is worse than useless. George Lois and Carl Fischer were the masters of this technique, in which abstract ideas are made concrete by epigrammatic rebus pictures. Both worked in advertising and naturally they borrowed advertising methods for use on *Esquire*, for the magazine cover is a form of advertising, a poster which displays the wares inside. Photomontage and staged or trick photography were applied as illustration of the issue's major feature. Surrealist incongruity was used to shock. Visual pun, repetition, cultural reference and metaphor and representational devices were employed with simplicity and intensity. These images, such as "The passion of Muhammad Ali", an elegiac representation of the boxer as Saint Sebastian, belong to the symbolic iconography of twentieth-century art, a process of making that Juan Gris described as "passing from the general to the particular", a reinterpretation and "reintegration" of signs in new contexts to create new meanings. It is an essential skill in the design of covers of magazines whose content does not lend itself to literal visual expression, particularly business, trade, technical and political journals. The process is not necessarily expensive, complicated or time-consuming. It merely requires an agile mind. *Time Out*, the London review and listings magazine, covered a massive range of subject matter from politics to eating out, for which its designer, Pearce Marchbank, turned out a stunning set of narrative cover designs on a weekly basis, usually at 24 hours notice from camera shoot to page film. They were nevertheless carefully planned and executed, and to speed up the process the designer fixed a (proportionally reduced) copy of the magazine logo to the camera shutter, to provide a precise representation of the graphic combination of type and image in the viewfinder. Many of these covers were produced against stiff editorial opposition. One, a cover entirely in a solid four-colour green, with the word "jealousy" in very small type in the centre, provoked despair in the editorial department. Yet it stood out so well on the newsstands the issue sold out.

The rise of the figurative cover at the expense of the narrative is not easy to explain. Management timidity is undoubtedly the most profound cause, and the strength of public relations machines has been a strong influence. In addition, the daily exposure to a barrage of visual images creates the danger of falling into cliché,

Spy (USA)
April 1988
art director Alexander Isley
photographers Deborah Feingold/ Joe McNally

Irony and humour in cover design are by no means dead. This two-part cover for Spy's "nice issue" (an elaborate April fool) relies for its success entirely on the readers' appreciation that Donald Trump is the magazine's bête noir. The property developer's downfall on page 3 is beautifully executed, complete with the collapse of the barcode.

Tatler (UK)
May 1989
art director
Dorothy Ann Harrson
photographer/designer
Michael Roberts

Two powerful symbols – target and woman – combine to make a compelling visual image. This is not Tatler's usual cover style but the novel adaptation of comic-book art is guaranteed to give prominence on the newsstand.

and a corresponding preference for graphic abstraction and oblique symbolic reference, as opposed to the crude simplicity of the graphic pun. But although we rarely see today anything to compare with the art of Rand, Wolf, Lois, Marchbank or *The Sunday Times Magazine* in its heyday, a number of magazines still succeed in making alternatives to the "face" cover work. *Stern* regularly produces strong narrative graphic forms, and has done so for many years, as has *Avenue* and *The Atlantic*. *King* has developed an interesting combination of collage and figurative photography; *Metropolis*, the New York architecture magazine, uses descriptive photomontage; and *Tempo* makes excellent use of documentary and staged photography. Few magazines today execute the punning cover with sufficient subtlety and impact: perhaps the exceptions are *Spy*, with its famous faces montaged into absurd situations, and *Management Today*. The style does, nevertheless, remain popular in computer and technical magazines which have to convey very abstract ideas to their readership and, as a result, rely heavily on illustration and trick photography. The news supplements are strong adherents to documentary and illustrative photography, most notably *Sette Giorni*, the *Boston Globe* and *Washington Post* magazines. Abstract illustration is a valuable mainstay in the art, design and architectural press, as exemplified by *Sur Express*, *Domus*, *Art Forum* and, less frequently, *Progressive Architecture*.

To the figurative, narrative and abstract, we can add a fourth alternative, the text-based cover. Typographic constructions can make a powerful contrast to the array of visual images on the newsstands, and are used with considerable effect by *Business Week* (USA) and *Business* (UK).

Where magazines do not depend on newsstand sales, i.e., when they are subscription based or controlled circulation, the possibilities for experiment with cover design are unlimited, as long as the essential recognition factors remain in place. The logotype, for example, does not need to sit at the top of the page. Photographic and illustrative abstractions are perfectly acceptable, and cover lines may be pared to the minimum – preferably to a single effective taster of the copy inside. They should nevertheless aspire to memorability. This remains the most effective benchmark of good cover design. What makes a cover memorable, however, and how directly it affects the emotions, intellect or aesthetic sensibility, is a matter which can only be determined by the final arbiter, the circulation figures.

Full face covers

Faces sell magazines, through recognition of either self or celebrity. Standard full-face shots can be seen by the dozen on any newsstand, but these examples offer something different, relying on emotion rather than charm or familiarity, and thereby evoking a powerful response. Even Interview's single celebrity shot of Johnny Depp has been made barely recognisable by a harsh crop, and it works because of its overt anger. So does the i-D cover which shocks through aggression, its impact exaggerated by the word "Warning!" impressed over a contorted face, straggling hair, liquid lips and eyes. It is hard to envisage such a picture on the cover of Vogue, but i-D's nonconformist readership can easily sympathise with a negative image. The Face cover, by contrast, is a beautiful expression of serenity, enhanced by overexposure, gold colouring and a quiet mantle of cover lines. Edge exploits the natural fascination invoked by an incongruous image: the surreal montage of face and oven dial illustrate a major feature on Tokyo with a wry comment on life in the City.

Edge (Japan)
Spring 1990
designers
Tomo Osaka, Yoshie Nara, Yasushi Nakayama

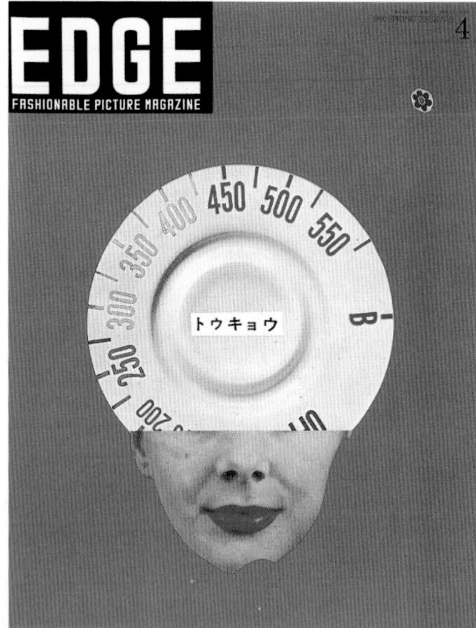

i-D (UK)
May 1990
art director Stephen Male
photographer
Jean Baptiste Mondino

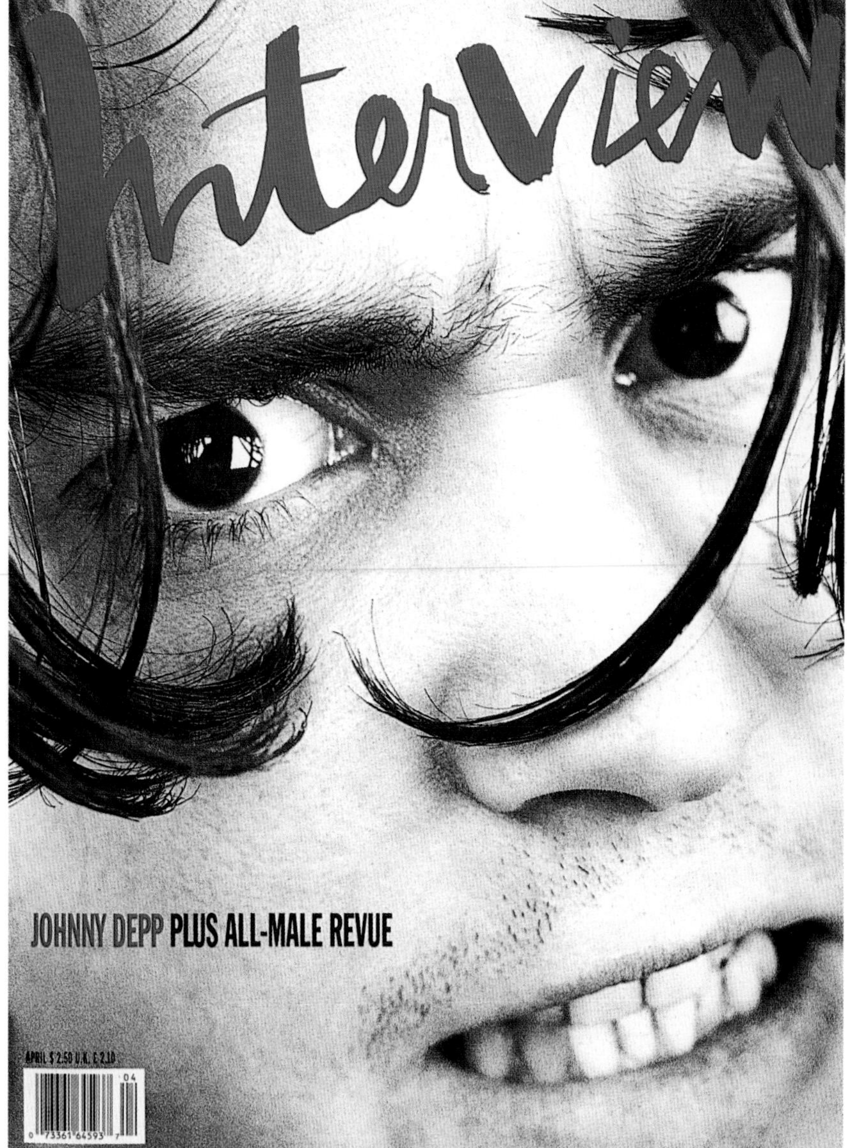

Interview (USA)
April 1990
creative director Fabien Baron
photographer Wayne Maser

The Face (UK)
January 1989
art director Phil Bicker
photographer Phillip Dixon

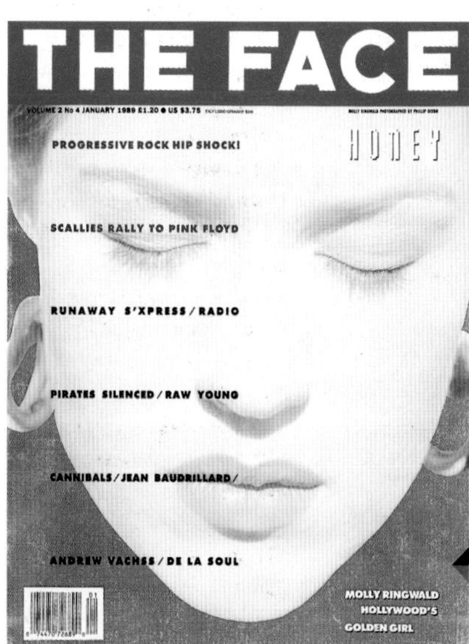

Montage and illustration

Six further variations on the face as cover art, all illustrative in form, ranging from venture capital journal QED's anthropomorphic machine to MET's disembodied eyes. They include two superb examples of narrative photomontage, Management Today's depiction of BBC director-general Michael Checkland as Mrs Thatcher's mouthpiece, and Nitin Vadukul's graphic evocation of the influence of political lobbyists for InterCity. Most of these magazines do not rely heavily on newsstand sales although each have striking covers. Frankfurter Allgemeine Magazin is a newspaper supplement and this enables its art director to use predominantly black covers which would not work on the shelves, yet do have classical distinction.

Frankfurter Allgemeine Magazin (Germany)
14 July 1989
art director Hans-Georg Pospischil
illustrator Heinz Edelmann

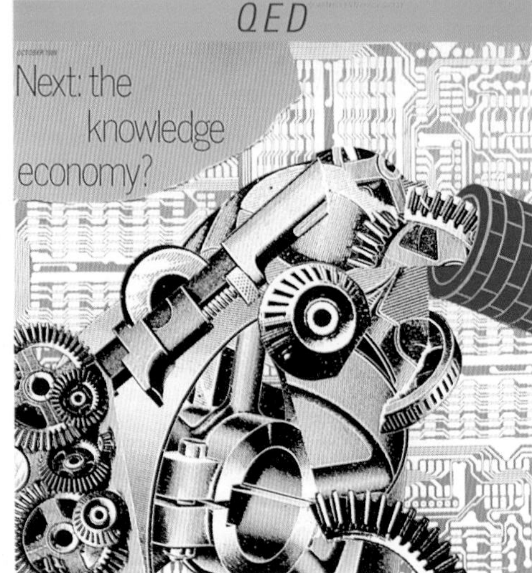

Quarterly Enterprise Digest (UK)
October 1989
art director Mike Lackersteen
illustrator Dan Fern

Lire (France)
June 1988
art director and illustrator
Jean-Pierre Cliquet

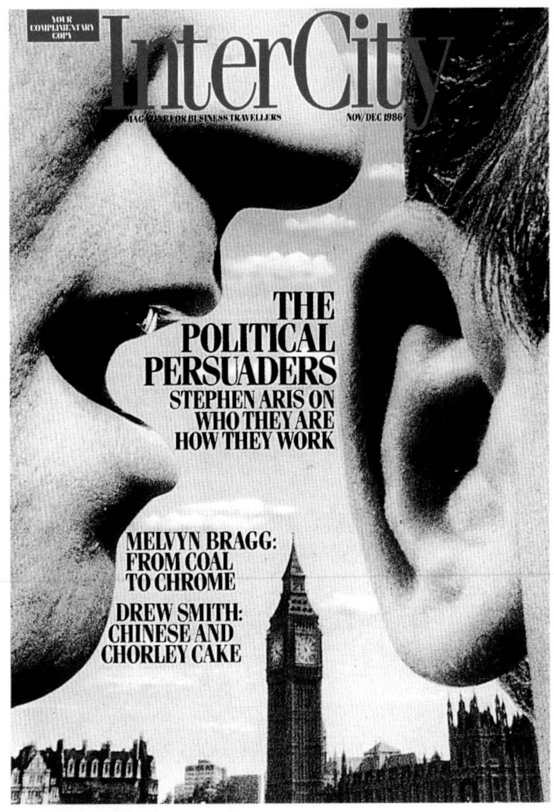

Management Today (UK)
February 1988
designers WRPS
art director Roland Schenk

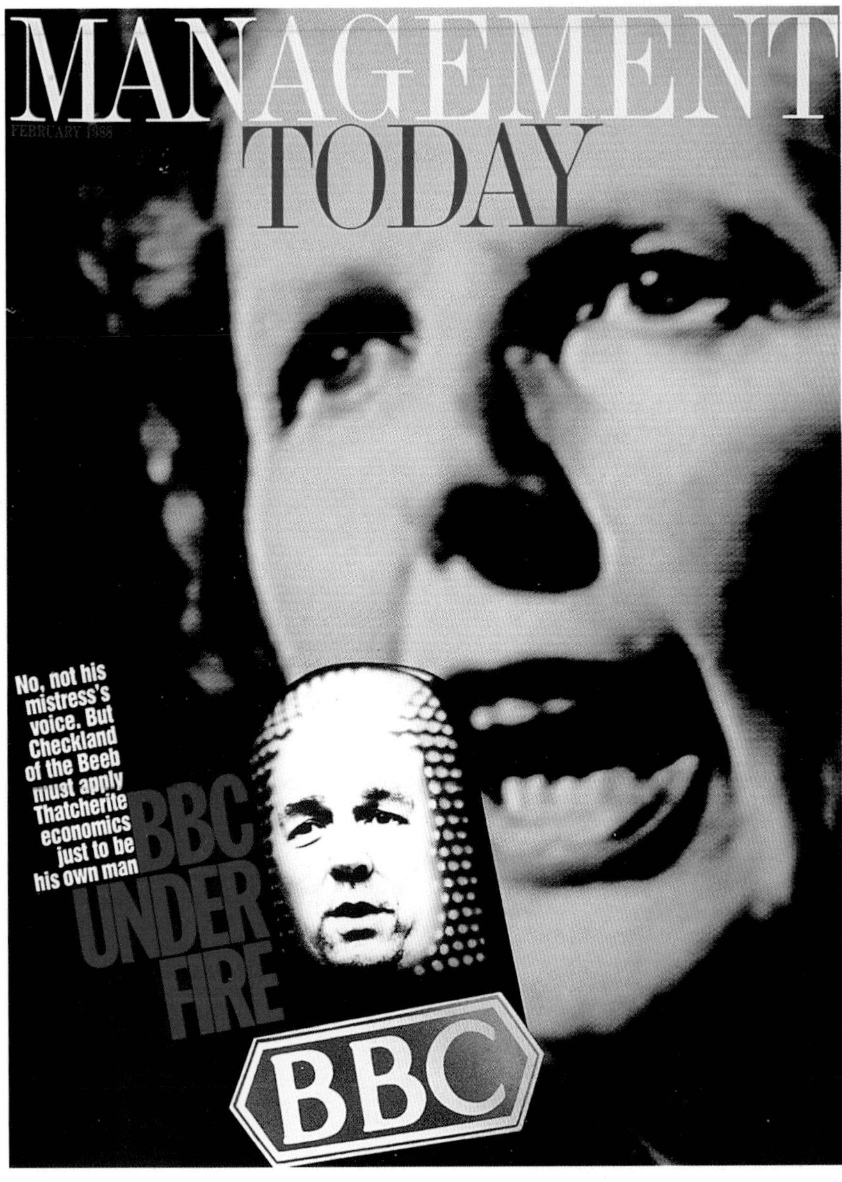

InterCity (UK)
November-December 1986
art director
Mike Lackersteen
illustrator Nitin Vadukul

Money, Economy & Time (Japan)
no. 12 1990
art director
Osama Yamashita

Against convention

Conceptual illustration (as in QED's man-machine on the previous page) and abstract or montaged cover design is generally seen only on the covers of subscription or controlled circulation magazines. With the exception of the literary review Diver, with its abstract interpretation of suspense by Ko Sliggers, these examples are all from design or architectural magazines which can afford to take a more relaxed and inventive approach to cover design. The position of mastheads, for example, need no longer be fixed at the top of the page. Quaderns slaps both logo and coverlines on the side of Carlo Mollino's car. This cover's strength is in its simple execution and beautiful printing in red and metallic inks. Both Items and Metropolis use montage to illustrate a variety of editorial topics. In the latter, a range of issue themes are combined in a coherent image built from pictures culled from old copies of Fortune magazine. Copy tasters, which can be distracting, are in this case paraded boldly as an integral graphic feature of five black bars.

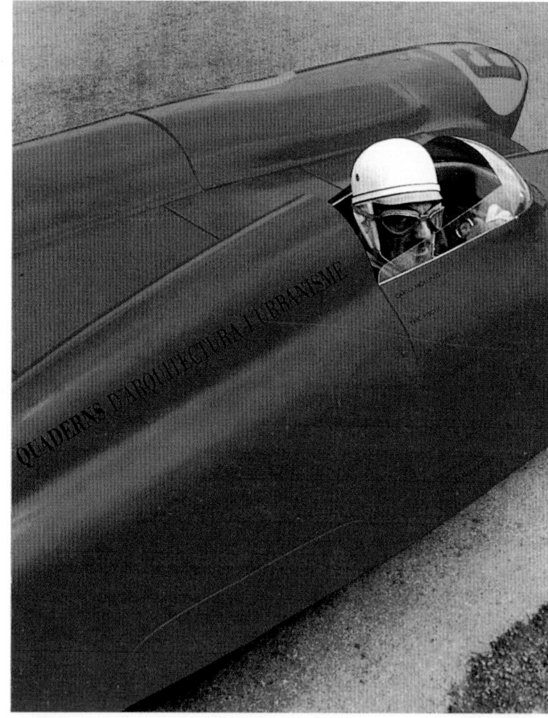

Quaderns (Spain)
no. 174 1987
designers
Joaquim Nolla, Josep M. Mir
photograph of Carlo Mollino by Invernizzi

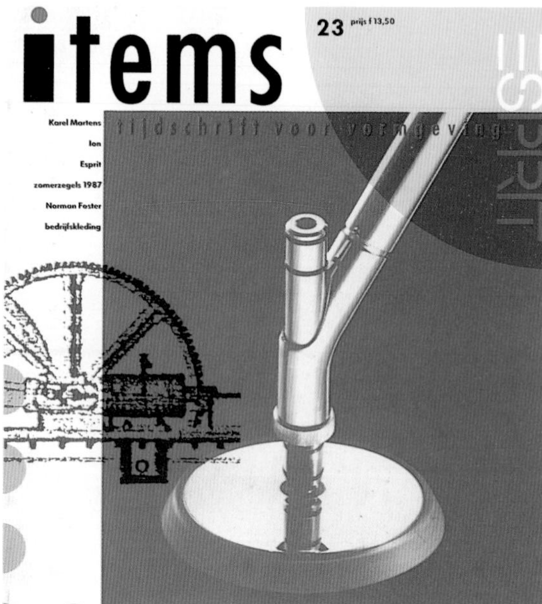

Items (The Netherlands)
no. 23 1987
designer
Vormgeversassociatie

THE ARCHITECTURE & DESIGN MAGAZINE OF NEW YORK

METROPOLIS

NOVEMBER 1987 $3.95

WAITING TO BE TRANSPORTED

MECHANIZED BODY BUILDING

ARCHITECTURE AND THE MACHINE

HOUSING THE MILITIA

DEVICES FOR LISTENING

transformations

Metropolis (USA)
November 1987
art director
Helene Silverman

Diver (The Netherlands)
vol. 2 no. 2 1985
designer and illustrator
Ko Sliggers
art director Hans Bockting

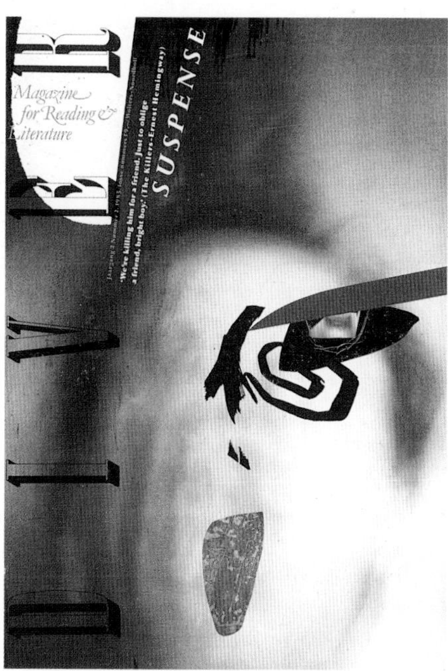

Text-based covers

Typographic covers have the benefit of directness. The cover, after all, is a poster advertisement for the editorial – a concise contents page – and in the case of Bulldog, which uses the cover to describe the entire contents in considerable detail, this injunction is taken to its logical conclusion. The result actually works, and has been executed with great sensitivity to colour and typographic detail. Transworld Skateboarding has an equally honest and straightforward approach, simply shouting its name out four times followed by cover blurbs under the platitudinous heading "cover blurbs". Underground succeeds in telling the potential buyer a great deal about both its content and editorial style in a multi-dimensional and interlocking construction of logotype, cover lines and images. This is a powerful graphic poster which makes up for the absence of a single strong image by making a dominant feature of a pictographic stick of dynamite, strikingly drawn in forced perspective. Business, by contrast, uses a succinct typographic pun to promote a single feature. Avenue's approach is as direct but more subtle: this cover makes a play on the functional similarity of magazine wrapper and theatre curtain. Both shield and are drawn aside to reveal their contents. The illusion is cleverly enhanced by a specially drawn trompe l'oeil logotype.

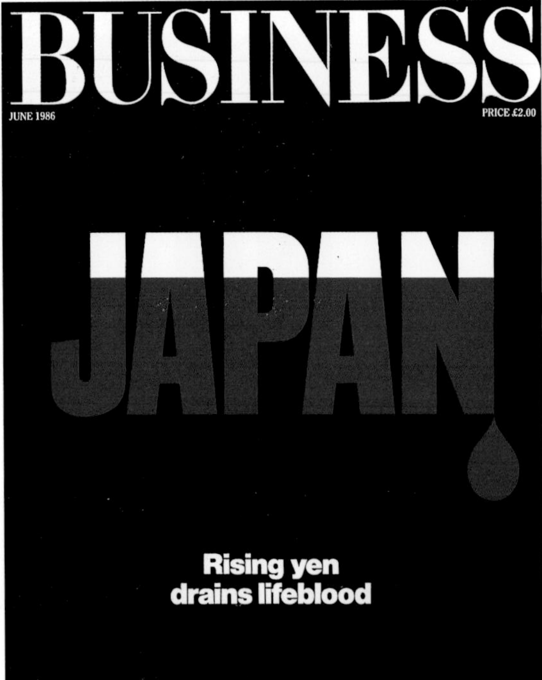

Business (UK)
June 1986
art director
Debra Zuckerman

Avenue (The Netherlands)
May 1988
art director
Hans van Blommestein
photographer Leo Hol

Transworld Skateboarding (USA)
August 1987
art director David Carson

Bulldog (Japan)
October 1989
designers Yoko Tajima,
Yasufi Yoshizawa

Underground (UK)
May 1987
designer Rod Clark

Photography and illustration

There is always a strong temptation to appreciate magazine photography for its intrinsic qualities rather than for the way it is put to work. But while the intensity of many of the layouts shown in this book is imparted by a single forceful picture which has been given the simplest graphic treatment, others, and often the most effective, incorporate distinctly inferior images which have nevertheless been used to a purpose and with inspiration. Photography is the backbone of pictorial magazines, and its primary role is journalistic: it must work with the text and within the composition. And it can also serve as background texture or as a dynamic component of form, or typographically as a unit of visual punctuation. Its usage is subject to the same journalistic considerations as all other aspects of magazine design: does it tell a story? And if so, how? Does it give enough information? How does one photograph work with others to create contrast, drama and narrative? Will it quickly grab the readers' attention? How does it work with the type, and within the layout? Will it reproduce well?

Photography and illustration in magazines are part of the unified concept, and reverence for the sanctity of photography is usually misplaced because the photograph is there to do a job and not to sit around on the page looking pretty. The "gallery" approach to photography, which was characteristic of early magazines immediately after the introduction of halftone reproduction, was superceded through integration with other visual components by the modern movement. Sometimes we see the old idea recurring, as when the border and sprocket holes of 120 format film are used as a frame, "proving" the integrity of an unadulterated, uncropped image. Sometimes this is done in dumb homage to current fashion, sometimes as a form of decoration, but always the implication is that the image can stand alone, outside and above the design.

But the designer is under no obligation to preserve the image intact. The relationship between designer and photographer can be ambiguous and sometimes contradictory, and is similar to that between editor and author. With photography, as with writing, the designer is to a considerable degree interpreting and altering the original. There are two eyes involved, and they might not always be looking for the same things, although it is eminently preferable that they should be. Use of photography, therefore, requires both sensitivity and courage, the knowledge of when to leave a picture alone and when to turn it to a different purpose. It requires the largely instinctive ability to recognize a good photograph together with the logical understanding of how it will fit within the context of the editorial content and design.

Photography is one of the most important contributors to the character of a magazine, and those art directors and designers who succeed in building up a firm relationship with photographers rarely have to struggle to design their pages after the event. The page is designed in concept in the commissioning process, and in reality in the photographer's lens. It is this part of the designer's job that most involves nurturing and releasing the skill of others, and the most successful prize their ability to balance detailed briefing with a ready acceptance of the photographer's own creative contribution. Each must understand the others' role and talents and feed off the other, as did the greatest exponents of synthesized magazine photography and design, Avedon and Brodovitch. The powerful visual identity of certain magazines is a direct result of such close relationships: *Elle*, an apparently "under-

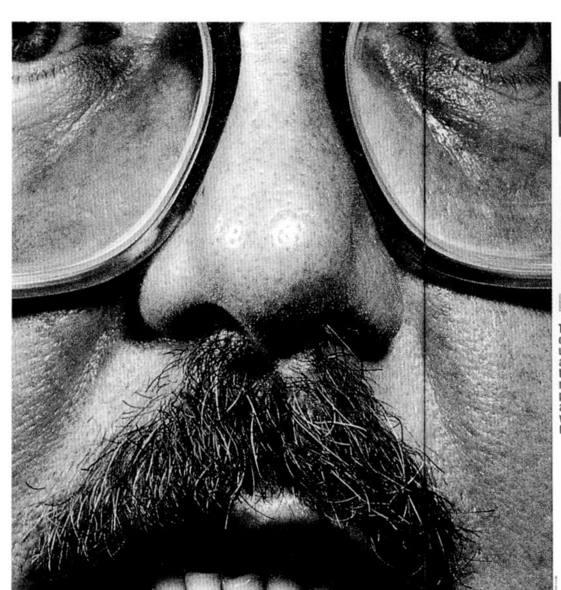

THE NEW FACE OF TRADE UNIONISM

The GMB, like competing trade unions, is making an all-out effort to reconstruct its membership: the policy promises to alter the union's whole character. Geoffrey Foster

A spacious detached house in the suburbs, it might easily be the home of a successful GP. But appearances are deceptive. Go through the door and the interior is too austere even for medical consulting rooms. In fact, the building houses one of the 10 regional offices of the General, Municipal, Boilermakers and Allied Trades Union (GMB), the third biggest union in Britain with over 800,000 members, a grand old bulwark of the movement and pillar of the Labour Party.

On the wall of the makeshift waiting room hangs the region's tasselled banner, redolent of marching men and defiant slogans. 'Unity is Strength' it proclaims, around a representation of two hands clasped in friendship. But the banner is out of date. It was embroidered before the Boilermakers (and allied trades) joined up with the General and Municipal Workers in 1982. And since then, the union has dropped its heroic handshake in favour of the simple initials GMB, with two little matchstick figures, hand-in-hand to symbolize unity, incorporated into the M; and the motto has been softened to the less aggressive 'Working Together'.

These changes are far more than cosmetic, although they're that, too. They are symptomatic of adjustments that are taking place throughout the labour movement as the unions (not all, certainly, but many of them) come to terms with the realities of the 1980s. Gone, at least for the time being, are the days when major unions could bring ministers to heel; when the British Government was only too ready to treat with them as partners in a 'social contract' – which some unions actually observed. Since 1979, the Thatcher Government has done more than any of its predecessors to regulate British trade unions, and they have been powerless to resist. Otherwise, the Government has to a large extent ignored them.

Employers have, in many cases, followed suit. Talk to captains of industry today, and you could well get the impression that the trade unions, which loomed so large in their thinking in the 30 years to 1979, had ceased to exist. Down the line, middle managers have often created chan-

GMB general secretary John Edmonds (far left) launched the drive to bring in part time workers and females

Will Thorne (small picture), first general secretary of the GMWU, led a union that was both male and manual

Management Today (UK)
December 1987
art director Roland Schenk
photographer Brian Griffin

A remarkable spread given power by the close association of word and image. The simple expedient of a cruelly tight crop transforms a bland face into a brute. This is art direction as propaganda, bordering on character assassination, but the same effect can be used to achieve entirely different results, as is shown by a spread from Interview **(see page 201).**

designed" magazine, gets its strong look from an idiosyncratic use of colour, very tight cropping, and most of all from the well thought out compositions of experienced editorial specialists of the stature of Toscani, Marc Hispard and Gilles Bensimon; the melange of *i-D* is as much the product of the clashing fashion photography of Marc Lebon and Nick Knight as its heavy graphic overlay; the large format *Blueprint* has prospered through the inspired patronage of original portrait and architectural photography; while the bold tectonic style of *Management Today* is offset by the humorous little dramas played out in Brian Griffin's portraiture.

Naturally there are occasions, sometimes all too frequent, when necessity must become the mother of invention, when the images are inadequate for the task, when the budget only runs to stock shots, and in certain types of photography, such as news action, when everything is unpredictable. By latching onto a detail, by blowing up a photograph to "unnatural" size, or through a severe and incongruent crop, it is often possible to turn an unpromising picture into a memorable image. Alternatively, there is recourse to montage or to the recently popularized small picture – the picture as punctuation and signalling device.

As a means of directing eye response, photography is an essential weapon in the graphic armoury: the classical – and most obvious – method is to use the eyeline of a headshot to point the reader to the text (which corresponds to one of those unwieldy "rules" of page composition – that the sightline must never be moving out from the page). Photography also provides depth and texture. By dramatically varying the scale of images a third dimension can be imparted to the page. Photography as background texture underlying the

Stern (Germany)

no. 38 1989

art director
Wolfgang Behnken

photographer
B. Fichel/C. Ploesser

This is magazine photography at its best. The picture documents and takes the reader into a hidden world, it has dramatic content and composition, stunning colour, and is allowed to speak for itself by art director Wolfgang Behnken.

type can provide an additional layer of graphic interest and evocation.

It is true for all types of magazine photography – action, portrait, fashion, still life, architectural, technical, art – that the content, shape, lighting values and texture of the image must work to resolve its inherent journalistic qualities with the architecture of the page. Cropping, for example, concentrates the eye on that part of the photograph which contains the essential visual information, or throws an image into a particular perspective (metaphorically speaking), yet it also provides a means of exerting constructive force within the composition, just as contrasts of light and shade contribute to the balance of the layout. However, the primary factor in the juxtaposition of photography has to be the necessity to create narrative interaction between images, so that they are organized to create meaning either in their relationship with the text or, as a sequence of events and through contrary or sympathetic association, with each other.

Photography's supremacy in magazine illustration lies primarily in its properties of mechanical reproduction, which facilitate both speed of production and a taut and homogeneous composition of the page elements. But in its objective and documentary character it has a material reality with which drawn illustration cannot hope to compete. Photography provides visual information, but this does not mean, however, that it cannot also evoke emotion or take on representational forms. While editorial photography has on the one hand striven for greater realism, action and immediacy, there has also been a contrary movement towards impressionism and abstraction to serve conceptual rather than straightforward narrative purposes. "The photographer can subordinate the characteristics of the lens and the film or plate to his photographic intentions",[1] to achieve realism, lyricism, humour and darkness, to use grain and focus, blur and colour distortion, angle and perspective, and lately, digital manipulation, to the end of directly describing mood and context. Photography and illustration are increasingly converging in this respect. Illustration is a more individualistic and subjective form based on personal experience and interpretation; its message is usually indirect and rhetorical.

The use of illustration in magazines was originally documentary and, when it was superceded in this role by photography, the narrative form became dominant, initially in the very literal style of fiction illustration which had been prevalent from the Victorian age. Illustrators were required to describe specific scenes using a sentimental or romantic naturalism, and Norman Rockwell's work for the *Satuday Evening Post* is a classic of the type. In 1946, at *Seventeen*, Cipe Pineles initiated a more liberal system of commissioning by giving artists *carte blanche* to create a personal interpretation of magazine fiction, resulting in an increase in subjective, conceptual, abstract and expressionist forms. She was followed in this by Henry Wolf at *Esquire* and, as the popularity of the work of such artists as Ben Shahn, Saul Steinberg, Robert Weaver and Sidney King grew, romanticism became confined to the not-too-torrid fiction of women's weeklies. However, in the business press there had already been a significant move towards abstraction and highly graphic illustration. At *Fortune*, throughout the 1930s, the cover and run of book had been used to display the work of established modern artists, such as Rivera, Léger, Garretto and Lewandowski. At the *Radio Times*, in England, the inherent interpretive gap between aural and visual media prompted a most imaginative use of editorial illustration, in covers and feature illustration by E. McKnight Kauffer, Paul Nash, Stanley Herbert, Edward Ardizzone, Eric Fraser and, after the Second World War, by Ronald Searle and Robin Jacques. But it was again at *Fortune*, after 1945, that modernist abstract illustration came into its own, exemplified by the work of Herbert Matter, Herbert Bayer, Lester Beall and George Giusti, the significance of which was in its holistic graphic approach. Illustration was seamlessly integrated with text and photography as diagrammatic and conceptual art. In this way illustration was used as collage, incorporating all the graphic elements – sometimes including photography – and involving close cooperation between art director and artist, together with a strong understanding of the subject matter.

With the exception of Giusti, the "illustrators" mentioned above were graphic designers who understood that illustration must work with the text and be seen to be doing so within the compositional arrangement. Unlike a painting, editorial illustration has a very specific connection with an associated narrative. There is no reason why illustration should be rectangular in form, no reason why it should it be "framed"; instead, it is infinitely preferable that the literal connection be mirrored in the graphic construction of the page. This maxim is by no means restricted to the scientific and conceptual illustration created in *Fortune*. It can be applied to all editorial illustration, although the temptation to treat illustration as fine art – a work in itself – often proves all too strong. In contemporary magazine design text and illustration are too commonly seen as complementary but nonetheless very separate entities. *Frankfurter Allgemeine Magazin* is one rare example of a showcase of fine illustration which is incorporated adroitly within the graphic scheme. Art director Hans-Georg Pospischil uses the work of artists such as Heinz Edelmann and Hans Hillmann with sensitivity, but without undue respect for its sanctity.

It is often the case that the editors of one magazine can singlehandedly impel the development of illustration through intelligent commissioning, as well as using that illustration to create a strong visual identity. *Esquire* and *FAZ* are good examples. In the recent period the responsibility for this has often fallen to magazines devoted to the popularization of science, precisely because they communicated many concepts that could not be photographed. In the late 1970s and early

Interview (USA)
March 1990
creative director Fabien Baron
photographer Michel Comte

A second variant on the close-cropped portrait: this opening to a question-and-answer interview focuses attention on the eyes and the smile and becomes, with the headline set under the eye, a clear statement about the character of the subject.

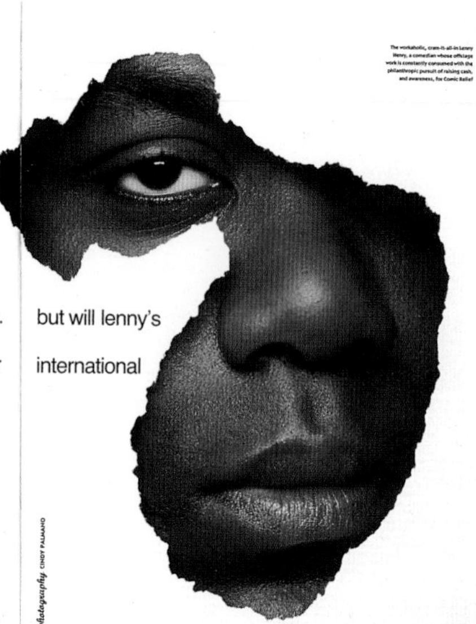

has **lenny henry** been immersed in the mainstream too long? this **paper tiger** obviously thought so, as he spent a week in february recording *lenny live and unleashed*, a stand-up movie to be released this summer. but will lenny's international eagerness to please sabotage his bid for fame? *sean o'hagan* asks the questions

I've just asked Lenny Henry if he bruises easily. There's a long pause as he stares at the floor. All the answer I need. What annoys him the most then, critics or the smart arses on the street? "Smart arses are no problem because they're usually dead funny. Scousers are the worst – 'Saw yer on telly last night, Lenny. It were shite!' No mercy. I've had guys come straight in the dressing room right after a show – 'Whaddya think yer doing? Eh? That were crap! Get a day job.' And it's like, 'Ta, pal. Thanks a lot.' Bam! Your ego's destroyed, crumpled up on the floor. That's bad."

Worse than a professional hatchet job?

"What *really* irks is people saying I'm a softie. I don't cuss and swear and I'm not overtly political so I'm Mr Softie. That *irks*. It doesn't hurt, it *niggles*. It's like: what do you want me to do? I'm not Mr Pontification. That's not *me*. If you don't like it, then . . ."

Like no other British funny guy, apart, maybe, from the reconstructed Jasper Carrot, Lenny Henry straddles pre- and post-'alternative' comedy like a benign colossus. His recent live show at London's Hackney Empire gathered up all the loose ends of a journeyman career that has spanned the parallel universes of scampi and chips and *Saturday Night Live*.

The reconstructed Lenny Henry steers a course through old-school professionalism, right-on politics, family entertainment and sophisticated subversion. Henry is a phenomenally successful comedic everyman whose only problem is an over-eagerness to please. Everybody. All the time.

"I just want to get better, broaden out. I go and see someone like John Sessions doing Napoleon and it's '*What?!*' Dawn (French, his wife) is always saying to me, 'Steady on, Len, don't take it so personal,' but I can't help it. I see someone do a great show and I'm thinking, I gotta get more organised, I gotta work harder. I'm desperate to broaden out."

Lenny Henry's marathon one-man show reflects both his eagerness to please and his obsessive desire to cover the waterfront. Despite the wealth of character and observation in creations like Deacus, Delbert and Theopholis, it's the stand-up that stimulates most. Here the labyrinthine imagination of the true comic genius merges with the absurdity of the everyday. The voice wraps itself round a thousand accents and the face registers ▶

ARENA 132 SPRING

photography cindy palmano

Arena (UK)
May-June 1989
art director Neville Brody
photographer
Cindy Palmano

This metaphorical image harks back to American graphic expressionism of the 1960s. The use of torn paper to denote black man breaking into white man's world is by no means original – Henry Wolf used it for a Show cover featuring Lena Horne – but Cindy Palmano's portrait of Lenny Henry, cleverly alluding to the map of Africa, demonstrates the potential for communicating subtle ideas through visual images.

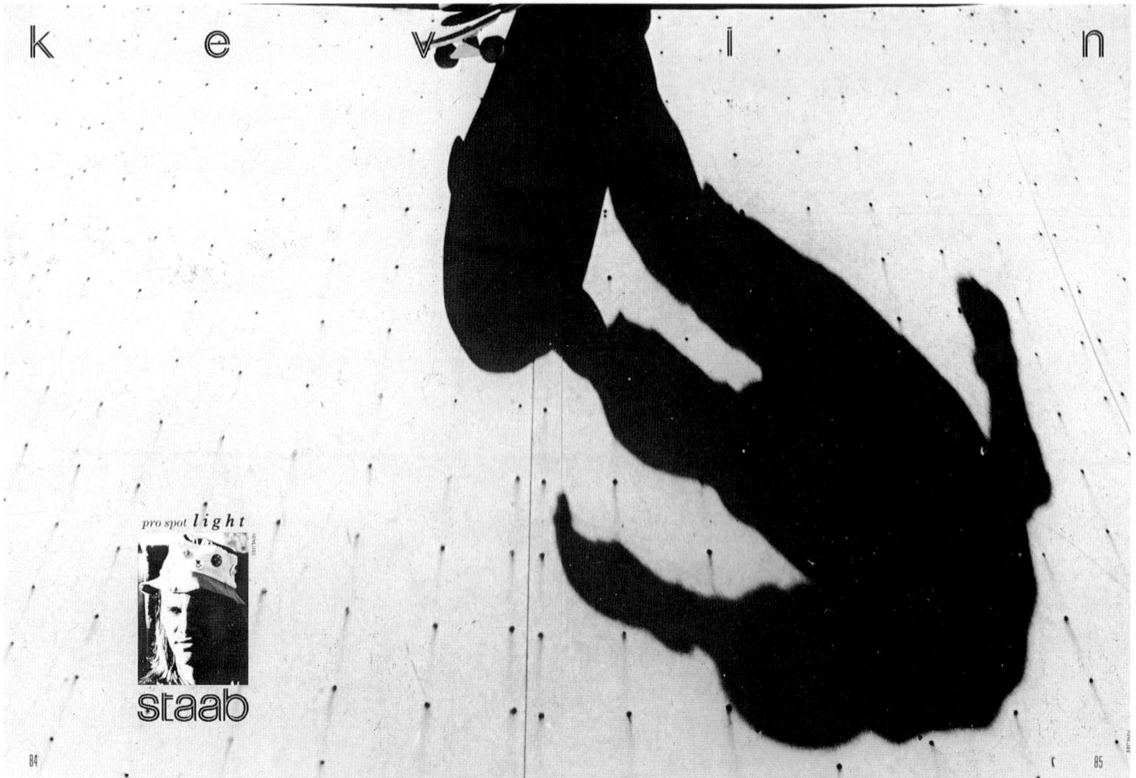

Transworld Skateboarding (USA)
art director David Carson
photographer Brittain

Here, photography is used for its illustrative rather than journalistic properties: the image excites curiosity, but would benefit from some explanation (compare the spread opposite). Either this is a reference to the existential nature of skateboarding, or its subject is an enigma in the sport. Unfortunately, the effect is weakened by eccentric typography which gives the appearance of advertisement rather than editorial.

Perfect (France)
October 1988
art director Bruno Richet
photographer Serge Rivoallon

This is a classic example of the obscure triumphing over the obvious: there could be no better way of expressing the fragile grip on life of a freestyle rock-climber than this graphic close-up. Without the headline the image is rendered meaningless: together, the force of text and image is magnified immeasurably.

1980s, *New Scientist* in Britain, and *Psychology Today* and *PC* in the USA developed strong reputations for their use of metaphorical imagery to explain enigmatic scientific and technical ideas. Conceptual illustration has become a most important niche into which photography (photomontage excepted) cannot fit, and it was in this area that a new generation of illustrators, who appeared in the late 1970s, were able to work with licence. They included, in Britain, a remarkable crop of graduates from the Royal College of Art: Sue Coe, Russell Mills, Ian Pollock, Robert Mason; and in the United States Brad Holland and Matt Mahurin. The air-brushed hyper-realism and one-dimensional fabulism of the 1960s was replaced by very individual styles and what Chris Jones, art director of *New Scientist*, described as "astonishingly individual integrity and strength of purpose, combined with an aggressive personal commitment that often depicted a form of social realism".[2]

It is probably true to say that, in the absence of such a personal, subjective view, illustration has no edge over photography. There has to be some strong individual contribution to the text. Illustration can act as a "humanistic" or textural counterpoint to photography, it can proffer some stylistic identity, or editorial continuity, as in the application of pocket illustrations as page headers. But to justify its presence it has to provide commentary, caricature, atmosphere, or emotion, or reveal thought through metaphor: it has to do something that photography cannot do.

Photos : Serge Rivoallon
La folie des hauteurs
La grimpe c'est le sport qui monte. Mais attention plus besoin des Alpes pour s'éclater. Un simple mur suffit, au besoin celui de votre salon. Un vrai sport. Un Hymalaya de sensations. Même si vous n'atteignez jamais les sommets...essayez !

Photographic narrative

Photojournalism brings into focus the two essential forms of pictorial narrative: combination and sequence. In the former the pictures are combined on a spread (see overleaf); in the latter the story unfolds page by page. Both methods derive from cinematic montage. The sequential technique, in which double-page pictures are set against a narrow column of caption type, has been exploited magnificently by Wolfgang Behnken at Stern who refines the story to its essence of full-bleed photograph and short, crisp caption. This sequence on the Spanish Foreign Legion ("Death is their living") has all of the essential qualities of photographic documentary: contrasts of perspective in long shots, tightly cropped close-ups, narrow and wide angles, and variations in subject and mood. It makes a set of contrasting pictures which build up to communicate vividly a life of harsh discipline, danger and fear.

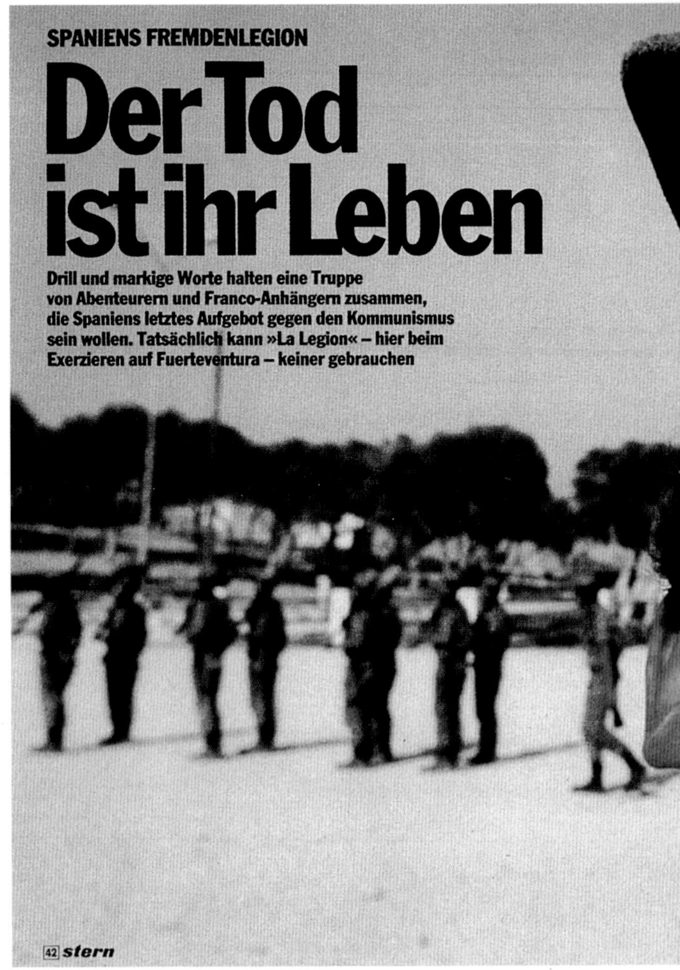
SPANIENS FREMDENLEGION

Der Tod ist ihr Leben

Drill und markige Worte halten eine Truppe von Abenteurern und Franco-Anhängern zusammen, die Spaniens letztes Aufgebot gegen den Kommunismus sein wollen. Tatsächlich kann »La Legion« – hier beim Exerzieren auf Fuerteventura – keiner gebrauchen

42 stern

Stern (Germany)
no. 10 1989
art director
Wolfgang Behnken
photographer
Spanish Connexion

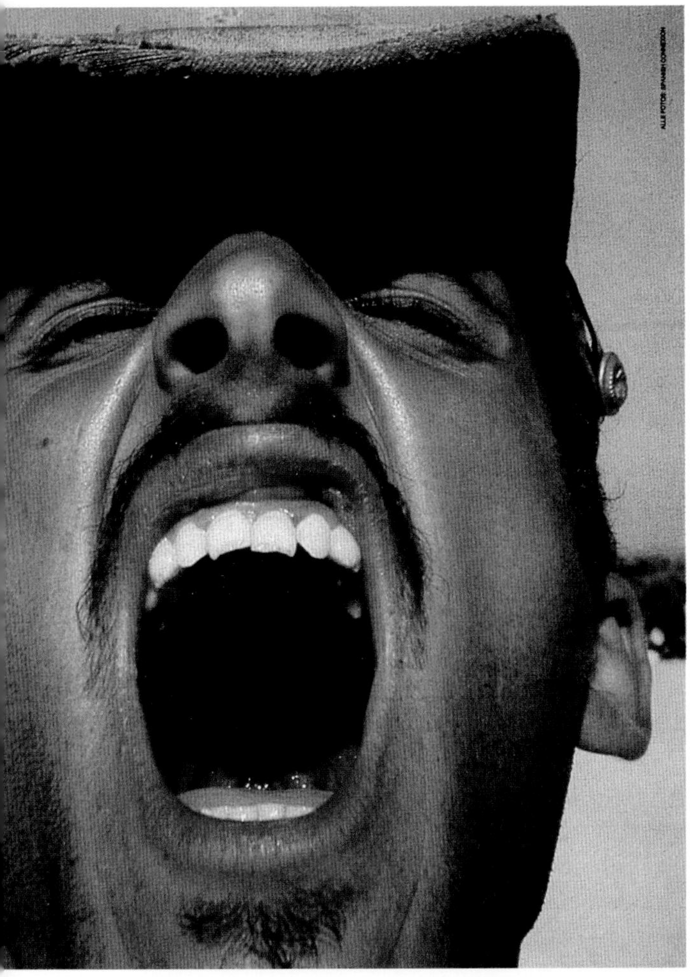

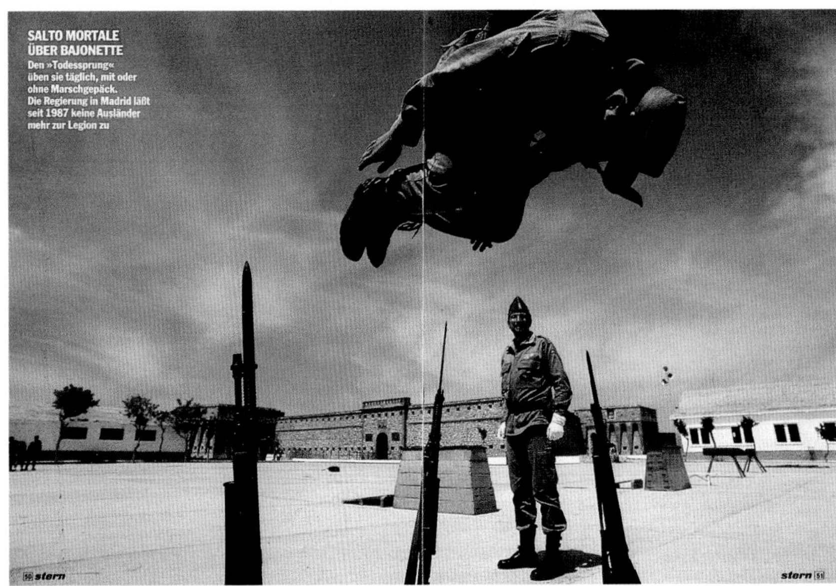
SALTO MORTALE
ÜBER BAJONETTE
Den »Todessprung«
üben sie täglich, mit oder
ohne Marschgepäck.
Die Regierung in Madrid läßt
seit 1987 keine Ausländer
mehr zur Legion zu
stern
stern

AUF
VERLORENEM
POSTEN
Stundenlang liegt
dieser Soldat getarnt
im Wüstensand und
wartet auf einen Feind,
der nie kommen wird.
Auf Fuerteventura lernen
die Söldner, wie sie
Guerilleros außer Gefecht
setzen können
stern

Photojournal technique

Here are four variations of photographic layout in popular picture/feature magazines. The active aircrash spread from Panorama (right) is laid out in the classic Paris Match style which attempts to summarize the entire story in the opening spread. The main picture, which puts the drama in context, is superimposed by text, captions, inset diagrams and detail shots which take the reader close up to the action. Actuel (far right) uses diagonal angles and tightly butted pictures to create movement and vigour. The relationship of this apparently incongruous set of images becomes clear only on reading the text. The make-up of VSD, a feature magazine, incorporates a substantial body of text. Again, there is a lot going on, but the layout has coherence. The dominant image, a cut-out within countoured body type, adds depth and perspective, pulls the elements of the page together, and acts as a pivot for the eye between heading and text. Ajo Blanco is a rather different case, in which photojournalistic emphasis is given to a single-bleed image intended to encapsulate a feature which, with the exception of headline and short standfirst, does not get underway until the subsequent spread.

Panorama (Spain)

27 March 1989

art director Angel A. Vico

photographer Sipa Press

Cinco conversaciones antes del accidente aéreo

EL MINUTO DE LA MUERTE

La angustia de los pilotos, grabada en las 'cajas negras'

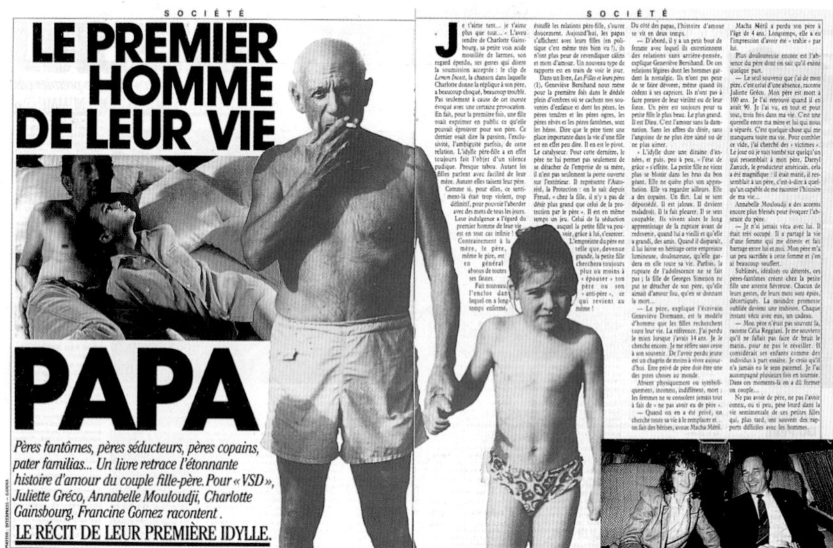

SOCIÉTÉ

LE PREMIER HOMME DE LEUR VIE

PAPA

Pères fantômes, pères séducteurs, pères copains, pater familias... Un livre retrace l'étonnante histoire d'amour du couple fille-père. Pour « VSD », Juliette Gréco, Annabelle Mouloudji, Charlotte Gainsbourg, Francine Gomez racontent.

LE RÉCIT DE LEUR PREMIÈRE IDYLLE.

Le Nouveau VSD (France)

1 October 1987

designer unknown

photographer Interpress/Gamma

Actuel (France)
September 1981
designers
Betite, Donon, Laugier
photographer
AP/Liu Heung Sh'ing

Ajo Blanco (Spain)
March 1990
designer Manel Lopez
photographer Pascal le Pipe

Fashion photography

Fashion photography mirrors fashion, in its horror of cliché as well as in its content. The genre moves in perpetual cycles, from location to studio work, from colour to monochrome, from harsh contrasts to soft focus, from abstraction to journalistic narrative. Sudden shifts and 180-degree rotations in approach have occurred regularly since editorial fashion photography superseded illustration in the 1930s, of which the most dramatic came after the Second World War with the removal of fashion from studio sets to the street (it was no coincidence that this occurred simultaneously with Coco Chanel's New Look). Surreal and photojournalistic devices, such as extreme contrasts of scale, of detail and long shot, became the dominant influences. Avedon, Bassman and Derujinsky began experiments with blur, radical angles and incongruous juxtaposition, and Penn developed his dramatic macro-lens beauty "stoppers" which remain one of the strongest features of US Vogue (opposite). The overriding priority, however, was characterized by 1960s Vogue editor Diana Vreeland's exhortation to "take pictures that sell frocks", a journalistic imperative that informs the middle and upper range of fashion magazines exemplified by Vogue and Elle. This thinking is apparent in Peter Lindbergh's and Patrick Demarchelier's street location work and reportage for Vogue and, in the classic manner, in Toscani's sculptural compositions and close-up detailing which give Elle such a strong visual cohesion and dynamic graphic character.

Elle (USA)

October 1985

publication director Regis Pagniez

photographer Toscani

Vogue (USA)
September 1989
art director Derek Ungless
photographer Irving Penn

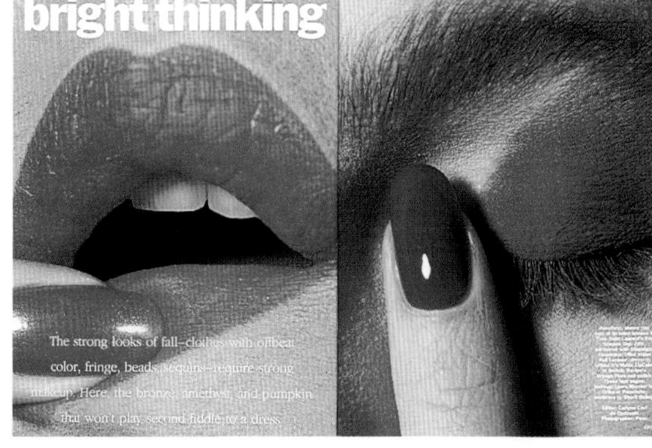

bright thinking

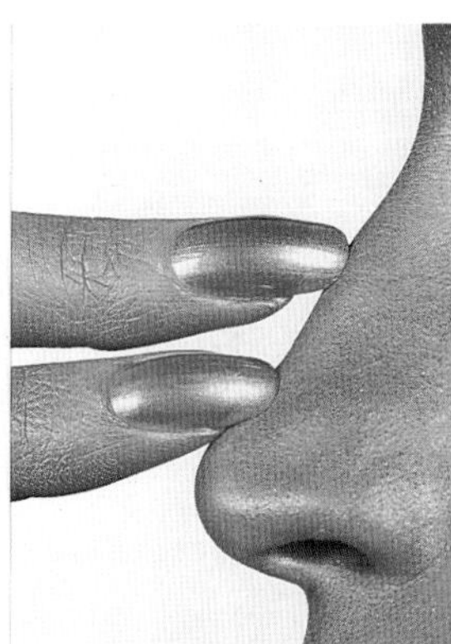

COLORFALL

THE MANY MOODS OF COLOR BY MADELEINE CHAPSAL

When my mother was working with Madeleine Vionnet as a haute-couture pattern designer in the 1930s, the house was filled with yards of crepe and muslin. There must have been at least 30 different shades of each color.

I still have hundreds of swatches of Mother's exquisite fabrics, but the colors do not affect me anymore. It's not that they aren't pretty—I simply wouldn't like to wear them. But when I go to Christian Lacroix, Yves Saint Laurent, Chanel, Sonia Rykiel, Valentino, or Agnès B., I'm totally mesmerized by the colors I see.

If color has the power to communicate, charm, and motivate, it also spells out desire. I remember how excited we were when designers like Pierre Cardin, Jacques Fath, and Christian Dior audaciously began combining greens and blues after World War II. We had always thought that was verboten.

The most daring of all was Givenchy, with his red, fuchsia, yellow, and mauve combinations. Later, Yves Saint Laurent started combining the uncombinable: Prince of Wales suits with flowered

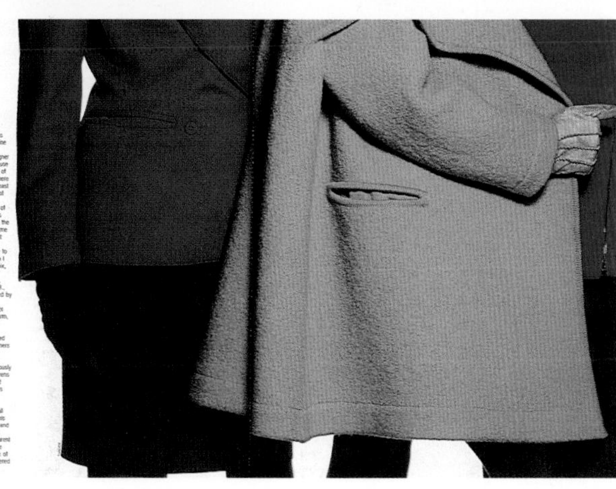

Elle (USA)
September 1988
publication director
Regis Pagniez
photographer Toscani

Fashion photography

Contemporary fashion photography is informed by the ideas of anti-fashion and street fashion which, when introduced by Punk in the mid-1970s, produced a profound change in editorial philosophy. Fashion editors and stylists, with Ray Petri and Simon Foxton in the vanguard, intervened more aggressively as interpreters of style, and no longer considered themselves bound to show images dictated by Parisian couture. Article, accessory and location were united to create a coherent imagery – or what could be described as a specific cultural iconography. This was a reversal of the post-war movement's ideal of a photography "independent of properties or of any other attractions extrinsic to the subject and composition". It took a less literal view of the journalistic purposes of fashion photography which, accordingly, became more impressionistic and stylized. The new imagery was invented and perfected at i-D with the graphic portrayal of avant-garde street and club-inspired fashion. Type and image were combined to evoke a vibrant, ad-hoc, ragamuffin style of the kind perfected by Marc Lebon. Even when studio-bound the photography, like the typography, is mobile and apparently spontaneous. There is clearly a strong trend towards the use of photojournalist mannerism, in which fashion is related as fictionalized narrative as developed by Stephen Meisel and Michel Haddi (see pages 213, 214). This pseudo-realism, an urge towards technical experiment and an ever-present strand of abstract idealism characterize the new fashion photography.

i-D (UK)
May 1990
art director Stephen Male
art editor Neil Edwards
photographer
Jean Baptiste Mondino

i-D (UK)
June 1986
art director Terry Jones
art editor Moira Bogue
photographer Nick Knight

i-D (UK)
September 1985
art director Terry Jones
designers Moira Bogue, Stephen Male
photographer Marc Lebon

i-D (UK)
June 1989
art director Stephen Male
art editor Neil Edwards
photographer
Kate Garner/Satellite

Fashion photography

In spite of the universal availability of colour, monochrome photography is increasingly valued as imparter of verité – and as a means of differentiating editorial from advertising. Its use has been encouraged by the superb quality of four-colour monochrome printing flash-dried on double-coated papers. This is also the most striking feature of fashion art direction at Arena, where Neville Brody has successfully exploited the harsh masculinity and broody atmosphere of Juergen Teller's coarse-grained, high-contrast images (opposite); see also Jean Baptiste Mondino's lurid eroticism (page 210). By contrast colour, once regarded as a source of excessive realism in fashion photograpy, has been exploited afresh through the application of darkroom and digital effects. The surrealistic compositions of Stephane Sednaoui, Nick Knight and Satoshi Saikusa constitute a new level of creative interpretation in which the "fashion" encompasses more than mere clothes, and becomes a function of the photographer's technical virtuosity and imagination.

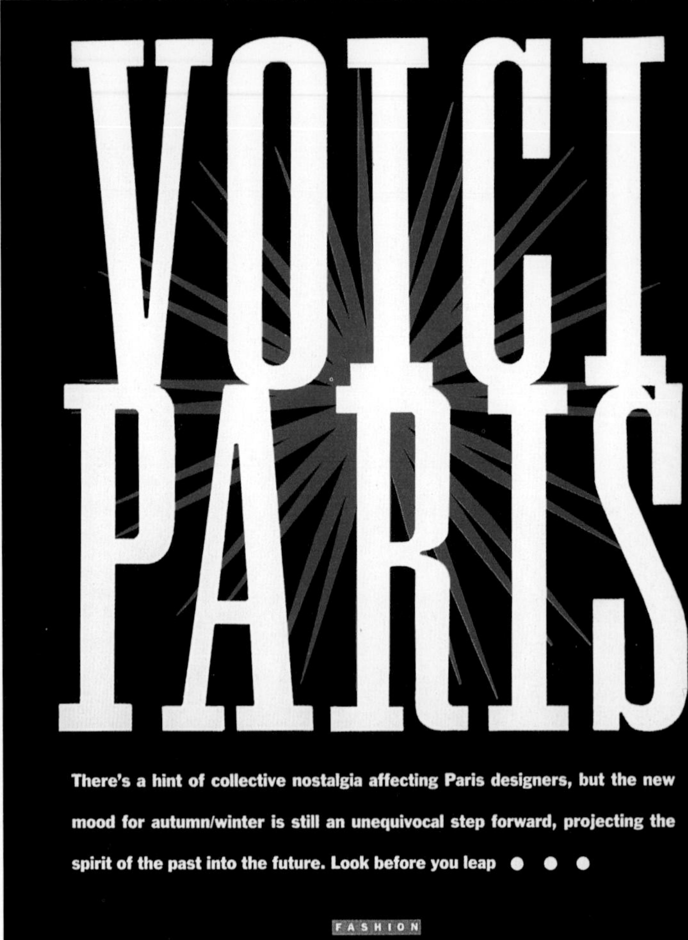

VOICI
PARIS
There's a hint of collective nostalgia affecting Paris designers, but the new mood for autumn/winter is still an unequivocal step forward, projecting the spirit of the past into the future. Look before you leap
FASHION

The Face (UK)
June 1988
art director
Phil Bicker/Elisabeth Djian
photographer
Stephane Sednaoui

Arena (UK)
May-June 1989
art director Neville Brody
photographer Michel Haddi

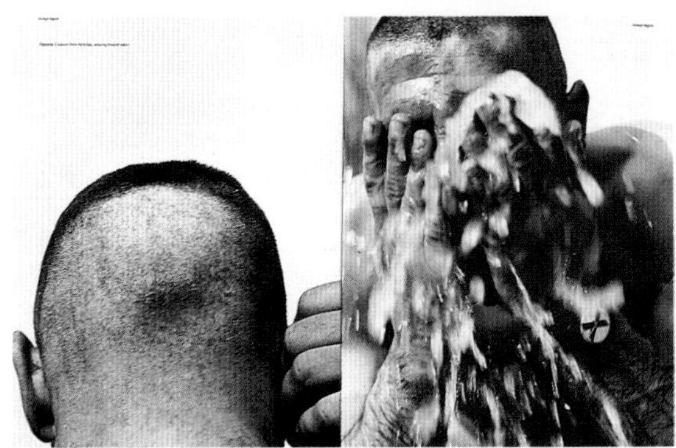

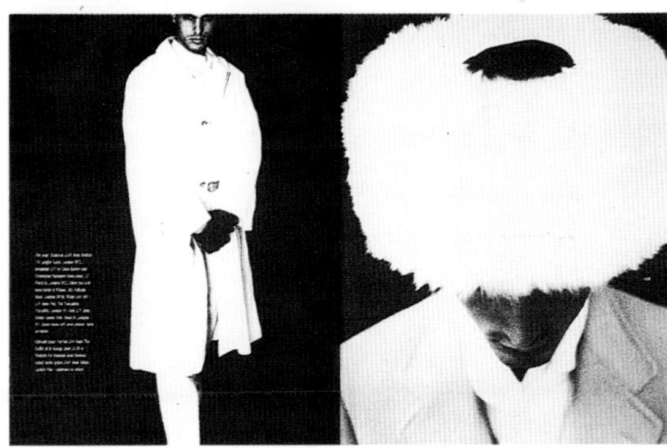

Arena (UK)
January-February 1988
art director Neville Brody
photography Juergen Teller

Fashion photography

Italian Vogue has for many years been an adventurous patron of new and experimental fashion photography. Under the liberal art direction of Fabien Baron and Juan Gatti a new generation of photographers as stars has emerged to follow in the steps of Steichen, Horst, Avedon, Penn, Hiro, Bailey and Bourdin. Italian Vogue's abstracted, monochromatic style has brought out the best of established talents such as Peter Lindbergh and Herb Ritts, and of the newer breed – Albert Watson, Nick Knight, Javier Vallhonrat and Steven Meisel. Vallhonrat (right) is a most proficient master of light. He builds a romanticized chiaroscuro which harks back to Steichen and Hoyningen-Huene, yet is softened by blur and metallic solarized colour effects. The most prolific of Vogue's contributors, Albert Watson (opposite), is also indisputably the most versatile photographer working today, a brilliant studio and location photographer who combines a strong journalistic grasp with a keen sense of movement and sculptural form. He is an equally adept portrait artist, and in his understanding of magazine page composition is an inheritor of the editorial tradition established by Avedon and Toscani.

Vogue (Italy)
March 1989
art director Fabien Baron
photographer
Javier Vallhonrat

Vogue (Italy)
February 1989
art director Fabien Baron
photographer
Albert Watson

Vogue (Italy)
May 1990
art director Juan Gatti
photographer Steven Meisel

Illustration

Frankfurter Allgemeine Magazin is still one of the finest platforms for European illustration. Art director Hans-Georg Pospischil regularly commissions three or four works for one article and gives artists of the quality of Paolo Piglia, Christoph Blumrich and the American Brad Holland considerable scope for interpretation. Heinz Edelmann and Hans Hillmann, whose work is shown here, are the most frequent contributors to the magazine and are closely attuned to the art director's method of working. Pospischil commissions illustration very early in the planning stage, often before the article is written and, when he can, he discusses his intended layout with the artist. This close liaison between illustrator and designer produces tightly integrated graphic schemes, as in the examples by Edelmann on this page which, although not entirely typical of the artist's expressionist style, show very clearly the nature of the process in which illustration becomes a graphic as well as narrative device.

Frankfurter Allgemeine Magazin (Germany)
19 January 1990
art director
Hans-Georg Pospischil
illustrator Hans Hillmann

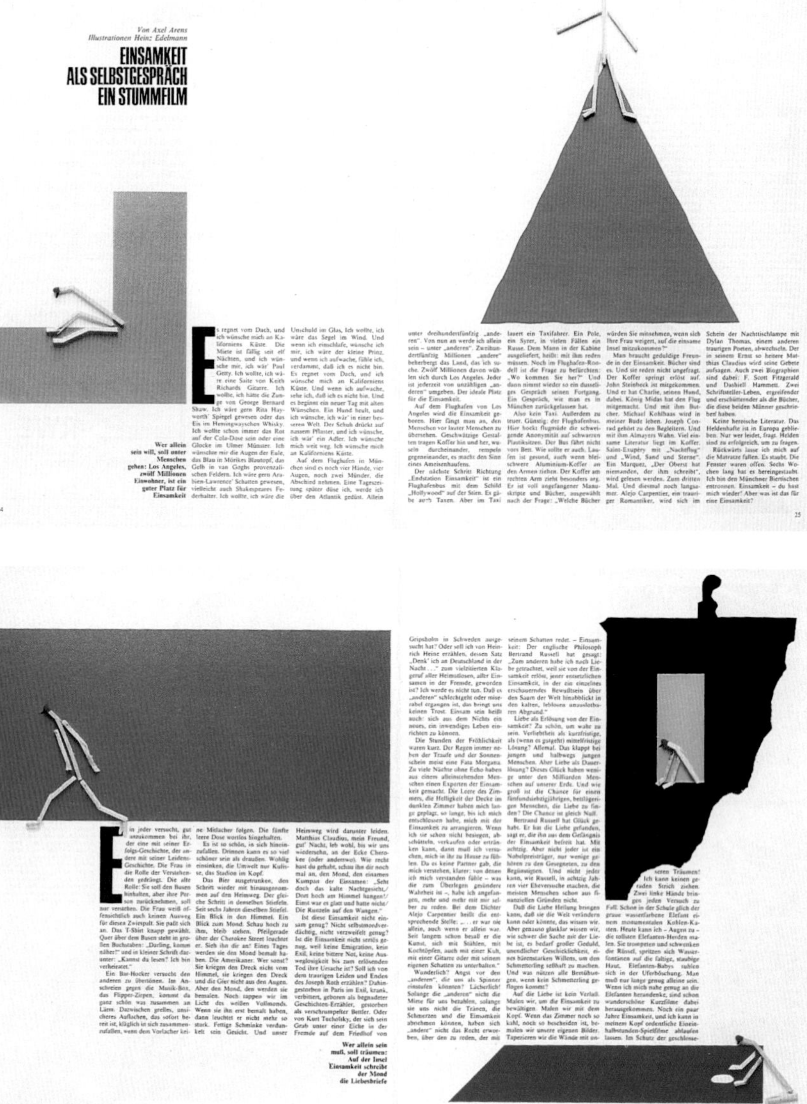

Von Axel Arens
Illustrationen Heinz Edelmann

EINSAMKEIT
ALS SELBSTGESPRÄCH
EIN STUMMFILM

Frankfurter Allgemeine Magazin (Germany)
4 October 1985
art director
Hans-Georg Pospischil
illustrator Heinz Edelmann

ICH BIN DAS JÜNGSTE GERICHT, UND ICH WILL RACHE

Der Detektivroman als religiöse Gattung

Detektivromane gehören, ohne allen Zweifel, zur Erbauungsliteratur.

Wie der Detektiv durch die Unterwelt schreitet, richtend und strafend, so stellen wir uns Gottes Engel vor. „Gäbe es mehr seinesgleichen, die Welt wäre ein Ort, so sicher, daß man darin leben könnte“, erklärte Raymond Chandler. „Durch diese staubigen Straßen muß ein Mann gehen, der selbst nicht schäbig ist, der eine reine Weste hat und keine Angst.“

Nach altem Brauch gibt es am Schluß eines Detektivromans ein Jüngstes Gericht en miniature. „Charlotte, ich bin jetzt das Gericht und der Richter“, erklärt Mike Hammer, „so schön du auch bist, so sehr ich dich auch fast geliebt hätte, ich verurteile dich zum Tode.“ Das ist ein Zitat aus einer neunseitigen Anklagerede. Danach wird Charlotte Manning von Mike Hammer erschossen. Kein Mord also, sondern eine Hinrichtung, Strafe. Zwischendurch würzt allerlei Fieses den Text, schließlich wird aber ein durch und durch moralisches Exempel statuiert. Seinen rabiaten Detektiv rechtfertigend, rechtfertigt Mickey Spillane sich selber. Die Welt muß doch wieder in Ordnung kommen. Was dagegen? Na also. Im Prinzip fällt die Bestrafung des Bösen zwar in die Kompetenz der himmlischen Gerechtigkeit. „Die Rache ist mein“, spricht der Herr durch Moses Mund, „ich will vergelten.“ Damals muß er noch direkt eingegriffen haben, später wenigstens indirekt, zum Beispiel durch Erleuchtung eines Detektivs, der daraufhin prompt das Kreuzverhör erfunden hat. Der Detektivroman ist die literarische Konsequenz aus der Erschütterung der Zuversicht ins Funktionieren oder gar ins Vorhandensein einer Instanz, welche sittliche Ordnung eingesetzt hat und auch durchsetzt. Woody Allen hat das Lamento über diesen Verlust travestiert, indem er den Mechanismus des Detektivromans benutzte:

Damit die Welt wieder ins Lot kommt, wandeln Gottes Engel durch die literarische Unterwelt, richten und strafen mit eigener Hand

Von Hans Daiber
Illustrationen
Hans Hillmann

20

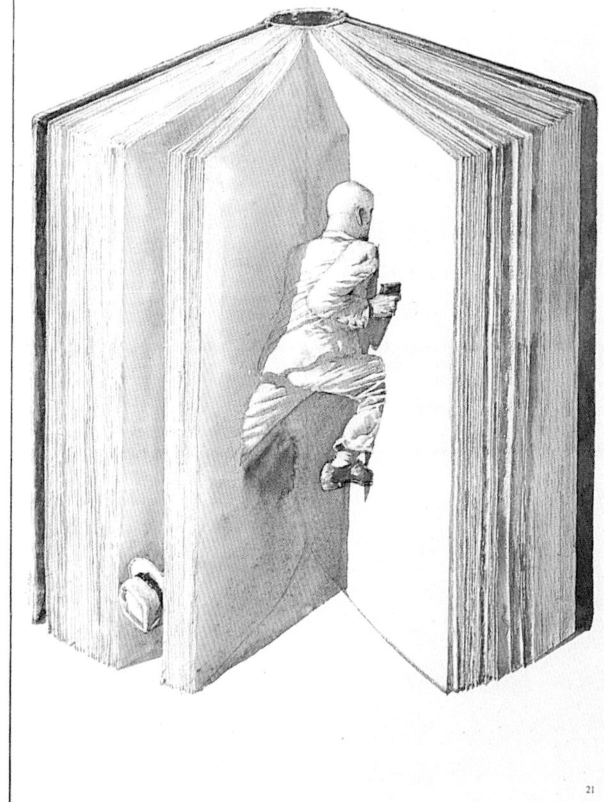

21

Beim Auftrag angefangen, einen Mörder zu finden, bis zur Tötung des Übeltäters. Nietzsche hat (im Herbst 1886) verkündet, Gott sei tot. Woody Allen fand rund achtzig Jahre später heraus, wer Gott getötet hat: Claire Rosenzweig, Philosophiestudentin, eine langhaarige und langbeinige Blondine, bei deren Anblick „Speicheldrüsen in den dritten Gang schalten“. Natürlich bettelt Claire am Schluß um ihr Leben, aber der Detektiv, jeder Zoll ein Gottesverweser, läßt sich nicht erweichen. „Wenn das Höchste Wesen erledigt wird, muß jemand bestraft werden.“ Logo. In klassischen Fällen werden zwischen Todesschuß und Tod dem Sünder seine Todsünden vorgehalten, damit er, wenn nicht in Reue, so doch im Bewußtsein seiner Verworfenheit dem überirdischen Kollegen anheimfällt.

Gewiß, man liest Kriminalromane, weil sie „spannend“ sind. Ist es aber wirklich spannend, wer wen warum ermordet hat? Durchaus nicht, meinte Wysten Hugh Auden: irgendeine „magische Funktion“ habe die Gattung. Freilich gibt es Tricks, die Anteilnahme zu verstärken: Erotik, Exotik, Luxus oder Elend, merkwürdige Charaktere. Im Prinzip geht es aber um moralische Qualitäten, um Schuld und Unschuld. Das Reizvolle, sagte Auden, sei der sittliche Konflikt zwischen Gut und Böse, zwischen uns und „jenen“. Da gibt es die pharisäische Reaktion, das echte oder trügerische Bewußtsein, ein besserer Mensch zu sein, oder auch das heimliche Eingeständnis: da wäre auch ich in Versuchung gefallen, da hätte auch ich geschossen. Diese Mitschuldtheorie entspricht der Ansicht, daß Dramen „reinigend“ auf das Gemüt des Betrachters wirken: Man frevelt und büßt mit dem Helden; als Gedankentäter nimmt man voll Mitleid und Furcht an Verfehlung und Strafe teil.

Gilbert Keith Chesterton hat diese Haltung auf einen Detektiv projiziert, den Father Brown. Der liest keine Spuren, der brilliert nicht mit Deduktionen, hat keine kriminalistische Routine, er kennt dafür das menschliche Herz. Intuitiv scheint er das Richtige zu treffen. Doch es ist keine Intuition, es ist moralische Erfahrung, die ihn obsiegen läßt. Er kennt die Schlechtigkeit der Welt, weil er sich selbst als potentiellen Verbrecher empfindet; nur sein strebendes Bemühen, verbunden mit der Gnade Gottes, hält ihn auf dem Tugendpfad. Modell stand ein irischer Priester, der Chesterton zum Katholizismus führte. Damals waren Detektivromane moralische Jagdgeschichten, meinte Agatha

ICH TÖTE, DENN ICH BIN GERECHT

22

Damit dem Verbrecher seine Schandtaten klarwerden, ist der Todesschuß aus der Waffe seines Verfolgers nicht das letzte, das er zu hören bekommt

23

Illustration

The magnificent portrait of Van Morrison (opposite) is not an illustration but a photograph, heavily distressed in the darkroom by illustrator Matt Mahurin, and upon which art director Fred Woodward has placed a sympathetic typographic construction of dog-eared "V" and "M" to create an imposing opening spread. Arguing over whether this is photography or illustration is unnecessary: it is photography used subjectively, as illustration. The adulterated portraits by Jeffrey Fisher for Business (below right) work in a similar manner: overpainted vignettes unify a mixture of painted and photographic portraits in a feature on the history of industrial innovation. Professional Investor (right) and QED (opposite, below right) both include combinations of illustration and photography, as collage, to create the kind of conceptual illustration which is an essential visual ingredient of the business and trade press. The Japanese MET uses negative prints in sharp relief to create a three-dimensional background to the page which provides graphic texture.

Professional Investor (UK)
November 1989
art directors
Esterson Lackersteen
art editor Bridget Riley
illustrator Volker Strater

Sector survey *Commercial property*

The coming soft landing for property

As the end of the latest commercial property boom approaches, Michael Brett reveals why, unlike 1973, the downturn won't be so vicious

When the property pulse is out of synch with that of securities it can disconcert the investment manager

Business (UK)
September 1988
art director
Debra Zuckerman
illustrator Jeffrey Fisher

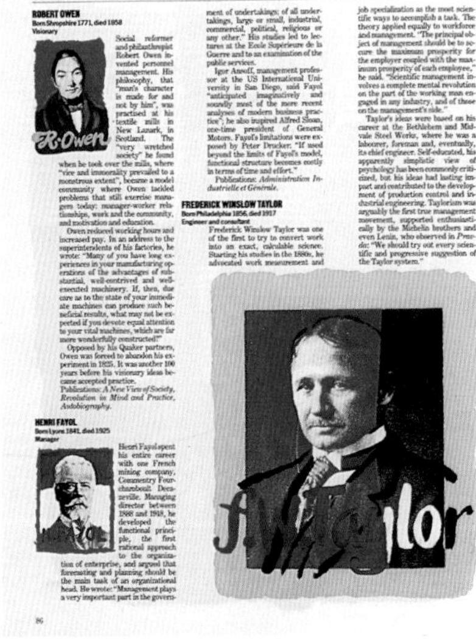

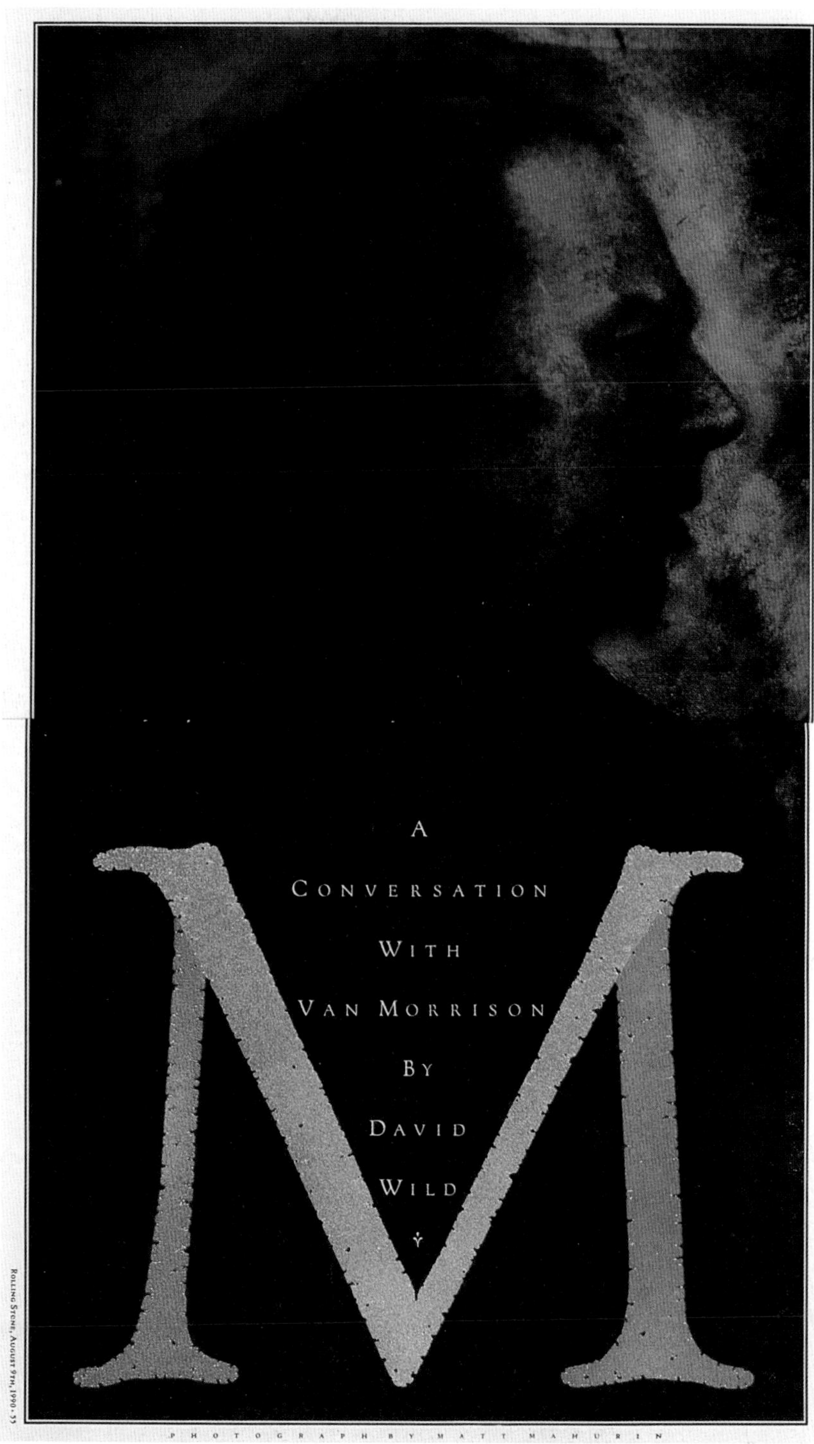

Rolling Stone (USA)
9 August 1990
art director Fred Woodward
illustrator Matt Mahurin

Money, Economy & Time (Japan)
no. 12 1990
art director Osama Yamashita

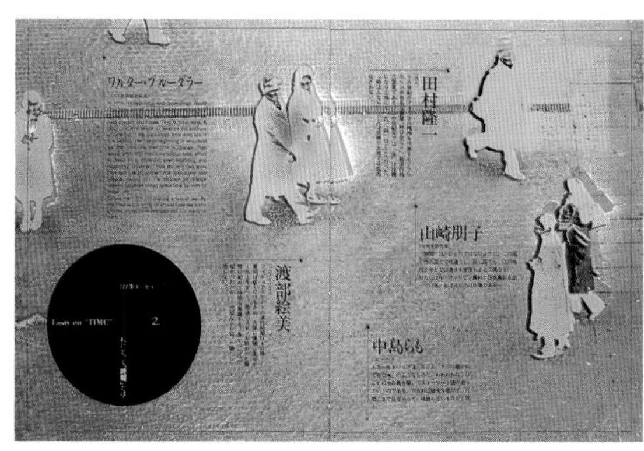

Quarterly Enterprise Digest (UK)
February 1989
designer Mike Lackersteen
illustrator Andrew Douglas

Charts and diagrams

The diagram is the most direct form of graphic communication, the purest form of visual journalism and an intense challenge to the designer. As a means of making complex information intelligible, the chart or map can provide both qualitative and quantitative understanding. The diagram can also impart visual excitement and, while the designer should aim for objective interpretation, there is also the possibility of creating drama, emphasis and, of course, exaggeration or distortion. Diagrams in magazines can do much more than provide information. Traveler presents hard fact in tables and maps with an air of authority in its graphic detail and luxury in its use of colour. But the Spy map (opposite) exploits the form to put over an elaborate visual joke on the Mafia, and does so with unerring accuracy and attention to detail. This is one of a series of imaginative and always impertinent charts published in each issue. Wigwag uses a traditional form of diagram, the family tree, in a similar manner, here presenting the genealogy of the American automobile as the gorgeously coloured fruit of a gnarled oak. The style is attractive, the execution informative, and the result is a memorable image.

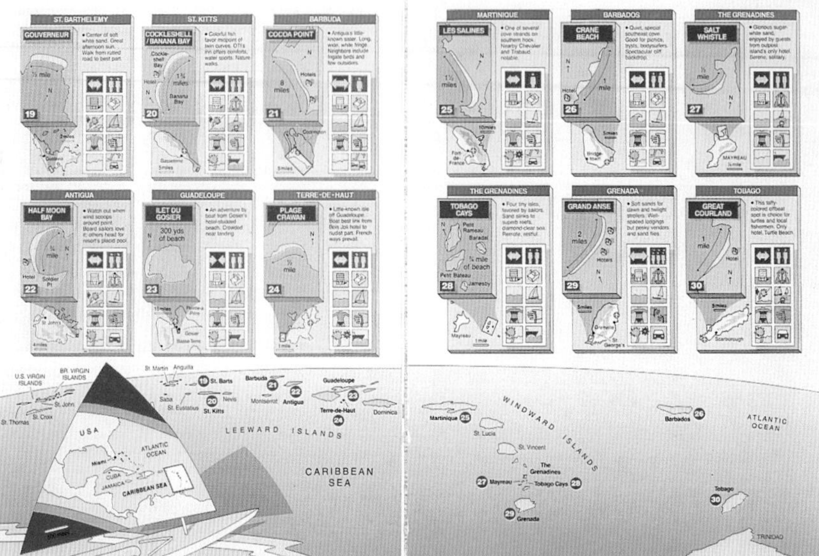

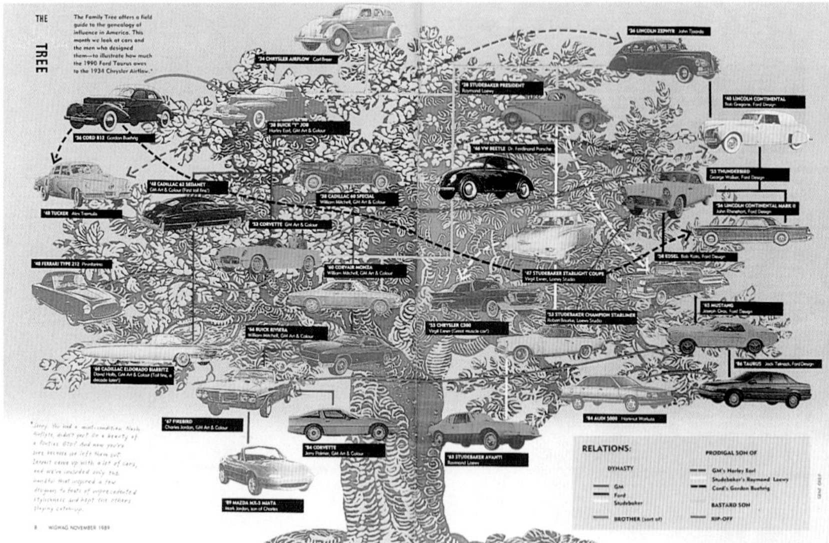

Top: Traveler (USA)
November 1987
design director Lloyd Ziff
illustrator John Grimwade

Above: Wigwag (USA)
November 1989
art director Paul Davis
illustrator Gene Greif

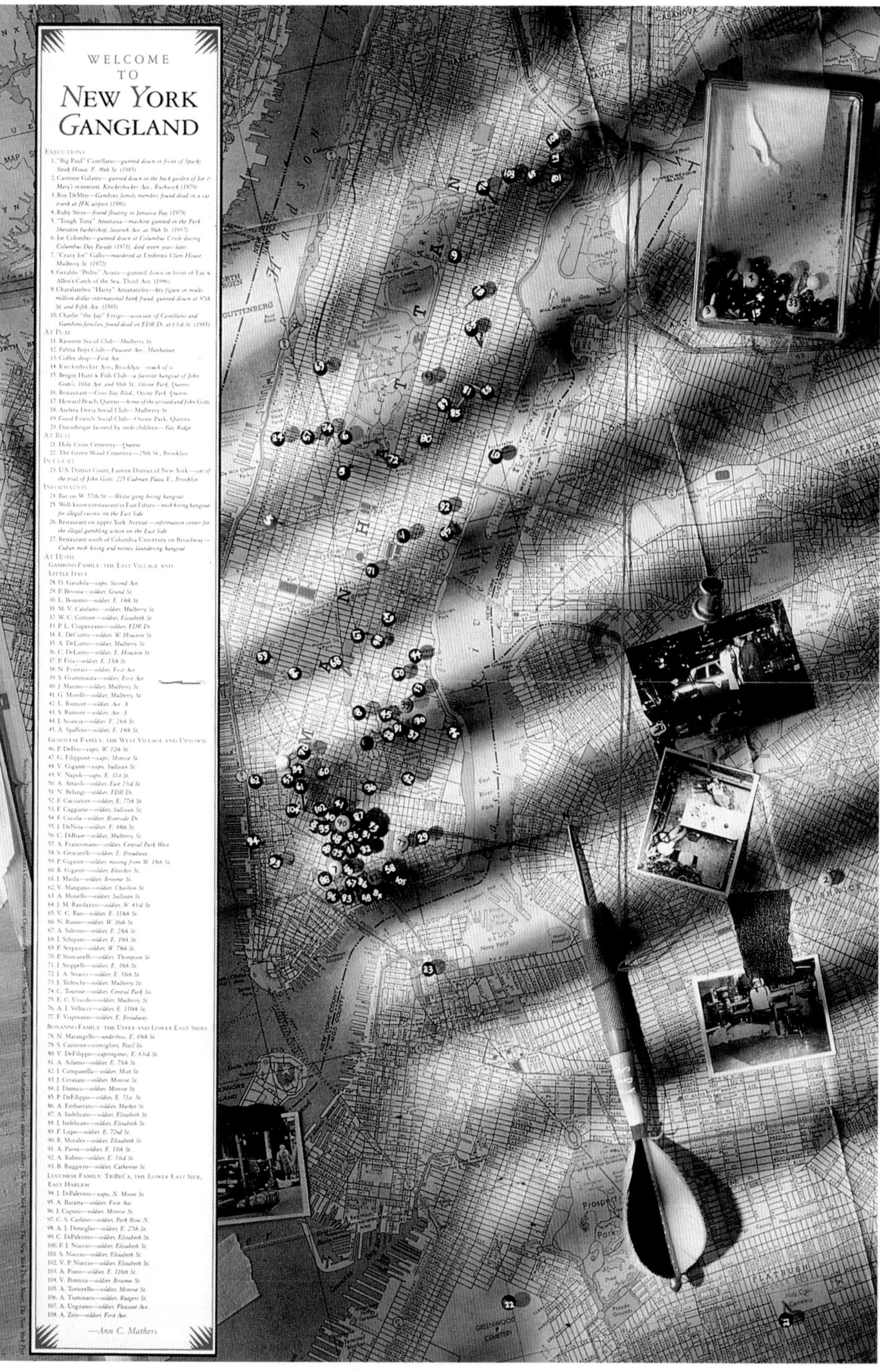

Spy (USA)

October 1986

design directors
Drenttel Doyle Partners

Charts and diagrams

The diagram from the computer magazine Mac User uses flow chart, pictograms and text to produce an informative representation of the software and hardware components of desktop publishing. It is, appropriately, an excellent application of the equipment it describes. Management Today (opposite) makes frequent use of diagrams which, although presented in this objective and informative style which emphasises the magazine's authorative editorial values, act equally well at the level of illustration. The organization chart graphically illustrates the corporate complexity of BP prior to the wholesale disposal of unwanted subsidiaries, shown in yellow. The presentation is dynamic and exploited as a strong graphic element within the design of the page; so is the three-dimensional cartographic chart, which is not squared up in a retentive ruled box, but allowed to float as an integral feature of the headline. National Geographic (right) has probably the largest chart-making department of any magazine in the world. This elaborate three-dimensional example is typical of its popular realist style; the diagram is illustrative and to a degree informative, but in this case there might be some doubt as to whether anything is achieved that the written word could not do.

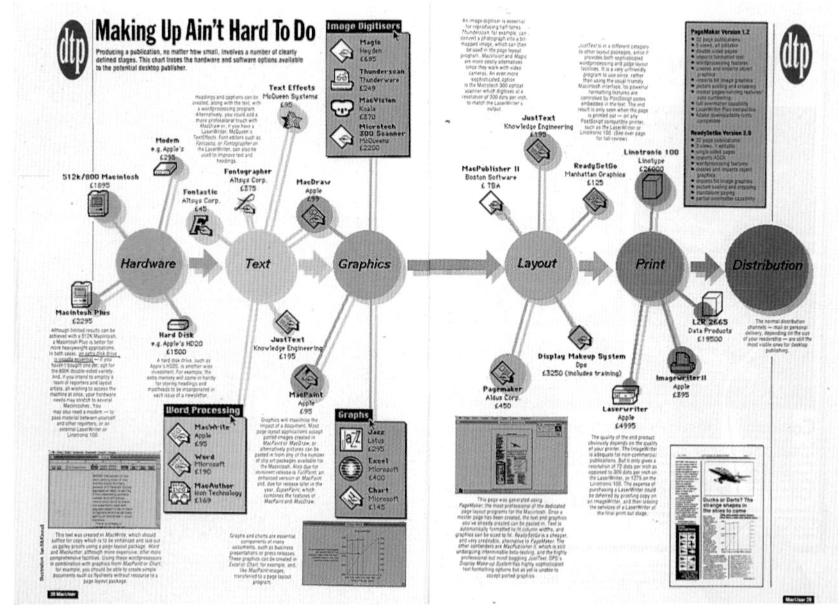

Mac User (UK)
July-August 1986
art editor Hazel Bennington
illustrator Ian McKinnell

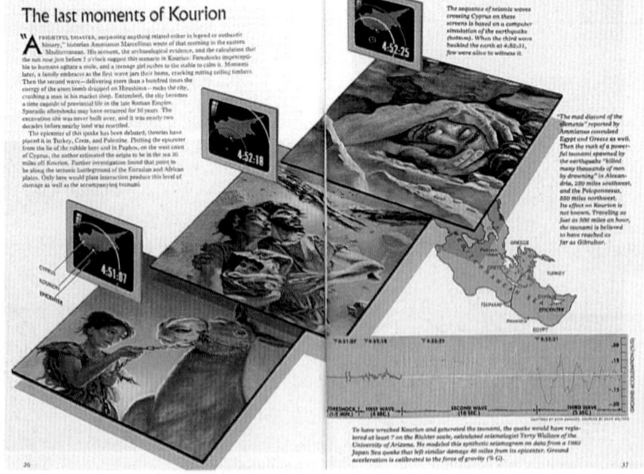

National Geographic (USA)
July 1988
design/illustration editors
Gerard Valerio,
W. Allan Royce
illustrators
Bryn Barnard, Davis Meltzer

HORTON'S TOUGH TRIUMPH

Robert Horton chopped a lot of dead wood off Standard Oil, turning doubters into fans of BP's man in the US. Timothy Harris

'The best view in Cleveland,' chortles Robert Horton, as he looks from his windows on the 15th floor of the BP America headquarters buildings. The view, in fact, is dull, stark and industrial. Stretching to the horizon like a watery desert is a drab Lake Erie, bisected by the white wake of a single ship. On its waterfront are huge brown vacant lots and Cleveland's rundown football stadium.

At such moments, Horton, the master salesman and current chairman of BP America, is giving one more lift to Cleveland, a city he adopted as fervently as it adopted him. When sharing the view with Horton, a beholder feels that Cleveland is filled with both achievement and renewal, not the derided capital of America's Rust Belt. Explains one visitor: 'Horton gets you excited seeing things his way.'

The evident rapport Horton has with Cleveland is startling, given the tremors that greeted his arrival as chairman and CEO a little over two years ago. Brought in by BP to resuscitate the ailing Standard Oil, in which it held a majority stake, Horton risked alienating executives, staff and the Cleveland community by embarking on a mighty round of sell-offs, closures and rationalisation. But Horton, who returned to London last month to resume his role as one of seven BP managing directors, left Cleveland with accolades from the locals. Cleveland's mayor George Voinovich, for example, described Horton as a role model for responsible corporate executives everywhere. Meanwhile, Horton's peers in the Cleveland Chamber of Commerce voted him the city's outstanding business executive.

Although these are, admittedly, regional kudos for a man who remains chairman of Cleveland's largest company, the solid achievements that won Horton these praises indicate he is ready for even more responsibility at BP, the world's third-largest oil company. In London, Horton will again be a managing director, but with a difference. This time, he will head operations in the US and UK. Plus, he will be in charge of BP Group Government and Public Affairs, which gives him responsibility for BP's image worldwide. On a limited basis, this is just the sort of international role that the chairman of

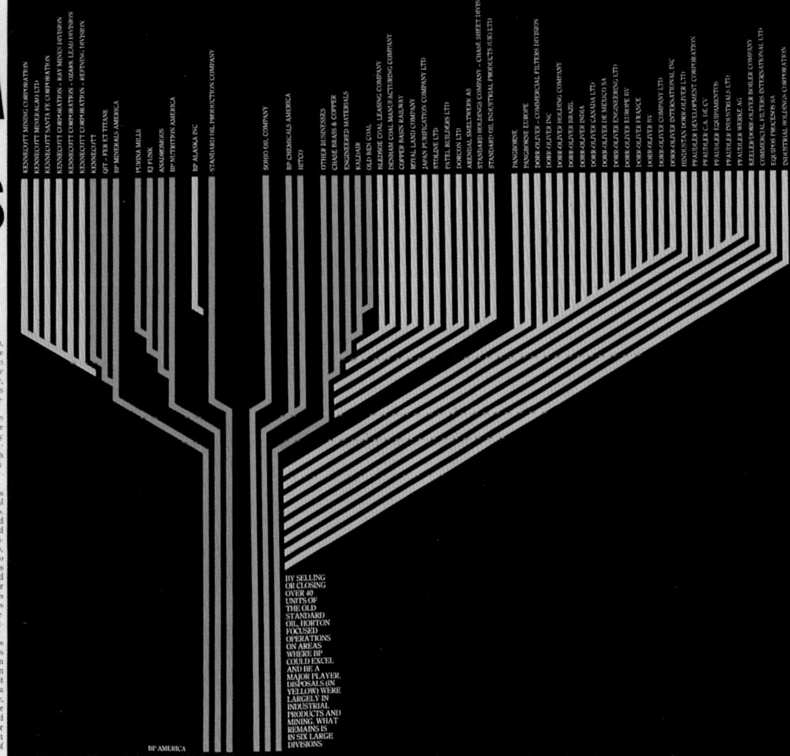

Management Today (UK)
May 1988
art director Roland Schenk
illustrator Mike Robinson

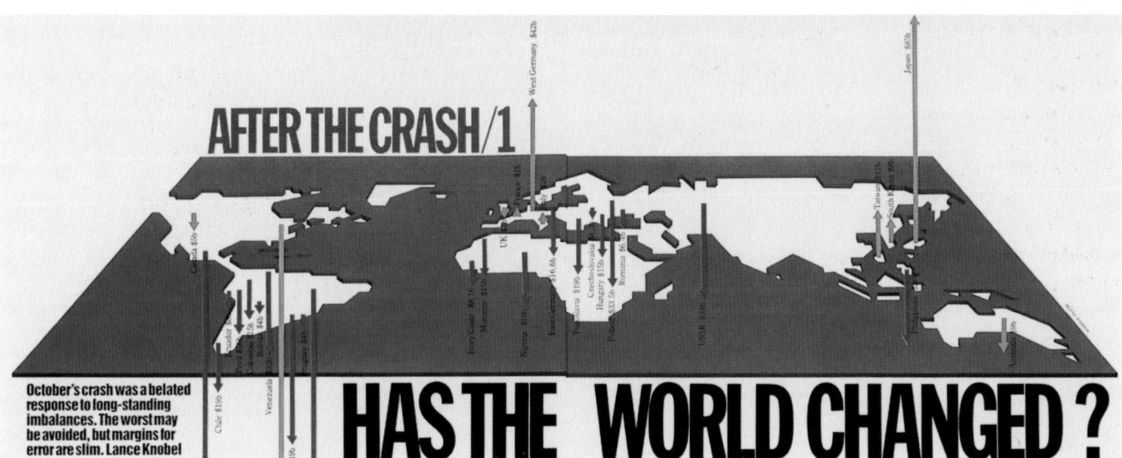

October's crash was a belated response to long-standing imbalances. The worst may be avoided, but margins for error are slim. Lance Knobel

HAS THE WORLD CHANGED ?

Although it may be painful for some investors, the October crash has had a salutary effect on thinking about the world's economic situation. Nothing during the surging bull market has made so clear the precarious tightrope that the economy has been traversing, for these were also years of profound instability. While the world's markets spiralled steadily upwards, many indicators failed to show the same confidence: currency rates fluctuated wildly, interest rates were on a rollercoaster, commodity prices plunged relentlessly. And deep structural problems, notably the now infamous twin deficit in the US and third world debt, loomed.

What has puzzled many observers of the crash is that these economic fundamentals did not change dramatically to provoke the market slide. In fact, many of the problems seemed to be righting themselves, however glacially. The crash can be seen as a belated recognition of fairly grim global reality, and it may now provoke more serious examination of how to correct the problems and return the world to a more secure, stable economic state.

There does seem to be widespread agreement that the crash was largely inevitable. Economist John Kenneth Galbraith, drawing parallels with 1929, wrote just after the crash, 'The overwhelming factor was greed, which turned suddenly into fear' once it became clear the speculative bubble had burst. Felix Rohatyn, director of Lazard Frères and the man generally credited with rescuing New York City from bankruptcy, in a post-crash speech highlighted 'Continued irresponsible fiscal behaviour on the part of government combined with continued irresponsible behaviour on the part of the financial community, throughout the world.'

The crash itself, as most economists agree (see p. 30), will probably have a negligible economic effect, at least in Britain. In the US, however, that might not be the case. Citicorp chairman John Reed, in an interview with *Business Week*, was less sanguine than most: 'The thing that bothers me is that we've seen a loss of the order of $1 trillion of value in the US and more overseas. And we can't find any blood. . . . Hey, $1 trillion disappears, there's got to be more pain than we've seen.' But the problems the crash foreshadows will certainly have a dramatic effect.

Fortunately, even the most pessimistic observers think the 1987 crash will not produce the same results as the 1929 debacle. The lessons of the Great Crash seem, at least minimally, to have been learned: instead of tightening the monetary grip, in the aftermath of the recent crash US authorities relaxed their stance; trade protectionism is still largely discredited. The modern equivalent of a Smoot-Hawley protective tariff remains unlikely (even in 1930, a petition by 1,028 economists urged President Hoover to veto Smoot-Hawley, but such sensible advice did not prevail). But though a second Great Depression is not imminent, problems may ensue.

Understandably, the impact may be greatest in the US, where things have gone so profoundly wrong. Many Americans received a shock in the crash, not just because of the $1 trillion wiped out, but because of the rude awakening from the dream of the Reagan years. In a prescient article in the October (pre-crash) *Atlantic* magazine, former US commerce secretary Peter Peterson details how, while real consumption per worker has risen by $3,100 since 1980, $2,150 of that pleasurable rise has been funded by cuts in domestic investment and foreign debt. As Peterson pithily puts it, the US had replaced the 1970s motto of 'tax and spend' with a new one of 'borrow and spend'.

The difficulty the US faces is that the size of the problem has grown to almost unmanageable proportions. The budget deficit of $165 billion and a current account deficit of $160 billion have combined to suck in huge amounts of foreign funds to keep the US economy going. By the end of 1987, the US was a net debtor of $400 billion, a radical reversal from their record creditor status in 1981 of $141 billion. No matter what economic action is taken, most observers expect US indebtedness to reach $1 trillion in the 1990s, which will be over 20% of GNP.

Such a situation is unsustainable, even for an economy as large and vital as America's, because at some point

Surpluses in Japan and West Germany have led to deficits elsewhere. With foreign debt spiralling up, the continuing instability of the global economy is clear

Management Today (UK)
January 1988
art director Roland Schenk
illustrator Mike Robinson

Into the unknown: magazines for an electronic age

Digital technology is a great big unknown, and after all, a mystery is the most stimulating force in unleashing the imagination.
Rudy VanderLans, *Emigre* magazine

Digital composition is not quite as new as we might think. Back in the 1970s there was a concept called "area composition" which was hailed as a break-through in magazine production technology, but the plaudits were premature. Area composition was a crude form of computer-aided design in which grids and typographic formats were specified by clumsy control codes in a manner too inflexible to be of practical use, except, at best, in periodicals with extremely regular editorial structures such as listings and directories. The idea was put on the shelf for a while. The full ramifications of digital composition were not then fully understood: it was felt that the computer might "absorb some of the tasks [the designer] never liked in the first place, freeing him for more creative work".[1] As such, the computer would only ever be understood as a workhorse, and never as a creative tool.

Today, we still cannot hope to grasp the ultimate potential for digital systems in magazine production. Computers set the type, scan images, paint colour and texture, aid interactive page layout and then generate the colour film. That's where it stops. There is a big hole between pre-press and print. Plates are still produced photographically, and printing is a messy mechanical process. And it will remain so, even when plates etched by laser and dry offset lithography (which will slash set-up times) become a practical proposition.[2] We must conclude, therefore, that it is the need to print on paper that today sets the limits to electronic design. To make a genuinely revolutionary transformation in graphic design, the delivery system has to change. We have to move from paper to the screen.

That scenario is a little premature, although we shall return to it. There is, in the meantime, a considerable amount to say about the way in which computers, the Macintosh pre-eminent amongst them, have changed the face of magazines.

Do new methods of production actually change form? Of course they do. We have the experience of photocomposition as proof. Movable metal type was banished from all but the few remaining craft print shops five hundred years after its invention. Photocomposition has shown less endurance, and is bowing out to digital setting a mere thirty or forty years after its introduction on a widespread commercial basis, but in its time photocomposition ignited a true revolution in graphic design. Although the technology was not made practicable until 1936, the concept was first described in 1893 and with commercial lithography it was to become the driving force behind the new typography.[3] The two technologies gave designers a hitherto unimagined ability to manipulate type and combine it with image.

Photocomposition was more flexible and dynamic than metal and encouraged structural and semantic versatility. The most important effect of lithographic and photomechanical print processes was to remove the compositor's monopoly on design: the hand was separated from the eye. Like all technical advances, these upset traditional methods of working, destroyed old disciplines, de-skilled craft and altered the division of labour. Naturally, they provoked the extreme and opposing reactions which typically greet change: reckless ambition and acute anxiety. Computers in design offices induce an identical response today.

Although digital composition has been a commonplace in newspaper offices since the late 1970s, and some Apple II-based systems were used in magazine design early in the following decade, it was not until the arrival of a fully configured Apple Macintosh with suitable software, in around 1987, that computerized design came into its own. The related flatbed digital scanning technology, of both low resolution monochrome and high resolution colour types, was introduced only a little earlier. So there is at most three years practical experience to draw on.

Although it will effect change, digital composition need not affect form or style in any way whatsoever. It is possible to produce quite conventional layouts. The typographic controls available in the third and fourth releases of desktop publishing software (*c.* 1990) are equal and greater in precision (at 0.06 points) to those available in phototypesetting systems. There are, however, two stages at which normal disciplines may break down: firstly, the designer has to pay more careful attention to the kind of typographic detail that would normally have been attended to by a trained compositor, such as hyphenation, kerning and character compensation, and which is now controlled by automatic (and fallible) computer defaults – but if a machine encourages a designer to think about type this cannot be such a bad thing; and secondly, and this is more of an editorial point, the galley correction stage is omitted and so a rigorous system of twice (or thrice) reading of the page proof has to be implemented. In all other respects, such as the availability and fidelity of type, and typographic and spatial formats, there is no necessity to change normal practice. There is, however, the possibility to do so and both to improve and adapt design as well as production.

The most obvious facilities of the computer, such as its ability to shadow, outline and cast shade and texture over type, are probably its least interesting, and perhaps its most regrettable. The changes that computerized production will effect on design are much more profound, because it transforms the act of making.

The design process is one of elimination of choices and maximization of possibility, of understanding what is possible and choosing between possibilities. Because the resulting idea has to be implemented in print those choices have, in the conventional production process, to be conveyed to a technician – to a typesetter or filmmaker. This produces a dependancy, a communication problem, and a separation of skills. Digital composition re-unites the idea and its making in one process. It also unites all of the components of the product in a single system: the writing, the editing, the type, the images and the colour. By integrating these processes and components the designer is given much greater control over production and consequently, many more design choices. Clearly this brings with it difficulties as well as benefits: careful discrimination is required if we are not to be overwhelmed by possibility. However, in the act of synthesizing the elements of the page the benefits are immeasurable.

The computer is primarily an interactive visualization and design tool and it assists both editorial and design. It is possible to edit text and compose the layout on screen simultaneously. Thus, the effect of any typographic construction such as contoured type aligned around a picture, or concrete typography, which would once have had to be carefully and painstakingly cast off and marked up, can be analysed and edited instantly. The effect of overlaying or masking out type and its interaction with images is apparent on screen.

Emigre (USA)

no. 10 1988

designer Susan Lally

This spread, entitled "A fraction of American culture from fifteen minutes of radio", is from a special issue of Emigre by students of Cranbrook Academy of Art. The design goes beyond the bounds of conventional print typography, with a dense layering of barely legible type and fractured images which represent brief snatches of banal radio show talk.

(10:31 PM / STATION 730, HAL)

(10:32 PM / STATION 730, LIZ)

(10:33 PM / STATION 730, HAL)

of *ah* stuff

(10:35 PM / STATION 730, LIZ)

92 94 96 98 100 102

(10:43 PM / STATION 730, LIZ) ... seen them they get off the air

that sounds like

(HAL) It certainly isn't and the unfortunate fact I think al

(LIZ) Yes, indeed.

(STATION 989) I want to drive a Honda everyday.

(10:43 PM / STATION 730) ... they get off the airplane and the first thing they do is comb their ... to the camera and do 20 seconds

(HAL) Well, I, I'm often distracted by a deep seated feeling *um* most of the television anchors at the network level *ah* could not complete the map, the blank map of Europe, certainly ... a blank map...

5 55 311 4742 11 1

ne and the first thing they

stuff that sounds like they're an expert on the country and they haven't even gone through customs yet.

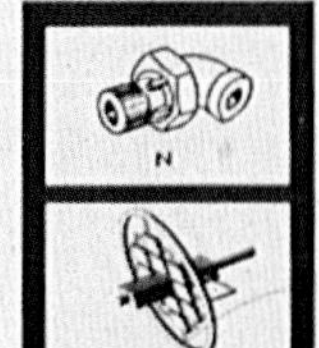

Photography can be manipulated and adapted to a variety of purposes – illustrative, decorative, and constructive – and processed, over-painted or montaged. Using paint systems, texture, symbol, plastic form and line can be added directly to the layout and colour choices experimented with on screen. The knowledge of the effect of design choices, which was once achieved only through the hard-won experience of seeing it in print, is now available within the machine. This does not mean that design becomes "easier", or that talent and creativity become redundant; on the contrary, they are released from technical constraints; the individual should learn much more quickly and should be able to evolve new and better solutions to old problems. We will as a result see new combinations and new forms.

In the metal-set/letterpress process, type and image were conceptually and physically separated; in photocomposition/offset these elements were physically combined, but processed by different people using different, if related, technologies. In digital composition the process of producing type and image is fully re-united. The creation of layout, once subject to the constraints of time and communication, has itself become dynamic and interactive. The thought and the act become almost simultaneous.

How this will affect form is still unclear. A distinct aesthetic has already arisen out of experimental work with computers but certain of its characteristics may turn out to be nothing but the product of immaturity. Common features are the layering of text, complex and irregular grid systems, rotation and warping of type in three-dimensional perspective, the use of textured backgrounds, hieroglyphs, graduated tones, often used within a self-conscious typographical style which reflects the limitations of early computer sytems – the primitive aliasing and stepped shapes of low-resolution bit maps.[4]

This "new primitive" typographical style was a very honest and workmanlike approach to such restrictions which, however, no longer apply. It was true that even when smooth-curved Postscript[5] printer fonts became available it was often not possible to get an accurate representation of the type on screen. In this case, it was sensible to continue using the crude bit-mapped fonts which were represented truly as they were printed. Now, however, with the new outline fonts, screen representation is usually good enough to ensure that what you see on it will be the same as the printed result, but the primitive style has persisted. One good reason for this is that the bit-mapped fonts were a genuinely positive contribution to the development of typography, and one which would never have arisen but for the computer; they have a unique and powerful simplicity which makes a welcome change from the smooth sophistication which is the common goal of conventional typography.

The return to primitive values has been justified in *Emigre* magazine, which has made itself a centre of experimentation in digital design, in that "computer technology has advanced the state of graphic art by such a quantum leap into the future that it has brought the designer back to the most primitive of graphic ideas and methods.... This return to our primeval ideas allows us to reconsider the basic assumptions made in the creative design process, bringing excitement and creativity to aspects of design that have been forgotten since the days of letterpress. We are once again faced with evaluating the basic rules of design that we formerly took for granted."[6]

This approach is in diametrical opposition to the "technician" school of computer graphics, prevalent in the television industry, but also in print, which treats the computer as a hyper-realist special effects machine which does what we do now, but "better", whereas the new primitives seek to effect both quantitative and qualitative change. If this school has a weakness it is in a tendency in certain of its followers to use bit-mapped type as an expression of modernity. Primitive type is, however, one of the less significant aspects of the design of *Emigre*. Of much more interest is its unusual parallel structure, in which articles and interviews run together, in a hybrid braced and modular grid, through the length of the magazine. Thus it questions a "basic assumption" about how a magazine should be assembled, and questions a methodology which is rooted in functional requirements which are no longer relevant, for it is practically impossible to construct a magazine in this way without the assistance of digital technology. Only when parallel structures have been tried will we know if they aid comprehension.

If a new and enduring aesthetic emerges, it will be derived from those intrinsic qualities of the computer, such as its ability to perform repetitive tasks, its ability to provide accurate visualization, and its sheer productive power; and these capabilities will act together to make magazines quicker and cheaper to produce and change their function and structure. The more obtrusive idiosyncrasies that we see in much computer-based design today are those which stem from its limitations, and from the over-exuberance typical of anyone who has been given a new toy. Those stylized aspects of the "new aesthetic" which exist for their own sake, because they can be achieved *only* with digital composition yet have no useful function, will tend to atrophy away. Those that have purpose will endure.

There is a further aspect to the "new aesthetic", in its simultaneity and dense layering of type and texture, that cannot be explained away simply as an objective response to modern methods of production; rather, it is an anticipatory exploration of the potential of future technologies. For only in electronic media like television or the new computer-based "multimedia" is it possible to realize the true potential of computer-aided design. Designers who use computers to compose for print see, every day in their work, kinetic qualities which cannot be translated to the page. On the screen type moves, appears and disappears, flashes white on black, while images which have been scanned into the system can be dragged around or filled with colour, pulled to pieces and reassembled. Today we are attempting to reproduce some of those effects on paper but ultimately this can only be a source of frustration. With the truly electronic magazine, this embryonic new typography will finally come into its own.

What is an electronic magazine? It is designed in the computer and delivered by computer; that is, the magazine is read from a visual display. The few prototypes that have already been constructed use "hypermedia" systems as a framework. Hypermedia is really nothing more than a set of software applications which all work together in one big program; for example, database retrieval, wordprocessing and mathematical spreadsheets, and paint, animation and sound systems, so that many different kinds of information can be drawn together. The programs can be customized very easily, using simple English-language commands, to create individual information systems – individual magazines. Hypermedia is essentially the controlling arm of the multimedia concept, which is the synthesis of many kinds of media – text, video, photography, illustration, sound – as one medium, within the computer.

Multimedia is destined to become an essential means of overcoming the problem of organizing the vast amount of information to which we have access in a single vehicle for distribution, cross-referencing and presentation. The idea arose out of the convergence of several digital technologies. Sound, video and graphics can be produced and controlled digitally; personal computers are becoming powerful enough to manipulate and display high resolution animated graphics and video; and optical storage disks provide us with a compact memory medium with vast capacity. The first electronic magazines will probably be distributed as compact discs.

The implications for information design, graphic design and art are immense. As far as graphic design is concerned, many of the existing rules of typography become redundant. Instead of emboldening, italicizing, or enlarging type for emphasis, it will be possible to use far more effective and precise means of catching the eye, by flashing a headline or caption up on the screen, for example, or by making type move or wink. Purists may detest such ideas, but consider that it should be possible to create very complex information hierarchies using just one size and weight of type. And because digital information systems are three-dimensional, typography may become cinematic: time will be a new factor in design. Type can scroll up or down the screen, and it can have depth where successive layers of information are placed one on top of the other. There are many ways of achieving this, but "hot text" is one example, whereby if further information is required, the reader clicks on the relevant word and an explanatory subtext is superimposed on the screen or the reader is taken off down a new path.

The magazine format should be ideally suited to hypermedia, which can handle many different kinds of information structure but is least suited to the kind of linear narrative that appears in books. The magazine combines linear narrative with parallel levels of information – pictures, captions, main text and sub-texts – which are usually designed to be browsed or studied according to the whim of the reader and, although its articles are usually self-contained, they generally have some common denominator. In hypermedia, the structure may be strictly linear, i.e., moving serially from page to page, or three-dimensional, with layers which offer the reader the chance to move into deeper levels or move off on some tangent of interest, or to another subject. The reader may be taken along a very strict course, or allowed to wander or browse. There are many complex design issues here, mainly involving how the reader is guided through the maze, and when and how the reader is interrupted, which will only be solved with practice. Some solutions, such as the "metaview", which is a kind of 3D contents page, have already been devised.

Prototype electronic versions of *The Economist*, and Condé Nast *Traveler* and *20-20* magazines were

The Economist
February 1990
designers Multimedia Inc.

This contents and feature page are from an experimental digital edition of The Economist. The electronic magazine is prepared and viewed in hypermedia, an interactive database incorporating sound, video and text, and is distributed on compact disc.

devised in 1990 by the London-based Multimedia Corporation. These original design experiments followed the existing formats quite closely but nevertheless threw up some interesting ideas. They were prepared on Macintosh and "printed" on compact disc. The first thing one notices about these magazines is that the contents pages have no numbers. The reader simply points with the mouse at the story of interest, or in the case of *Traveler*, points at a holiday location on a map of the world. Like many conventional contents pages, *The Economist* version highlights three stories with pictures. Again, the reader points to whichever picture is of interest, but in this case the "picture" is a video film and it changes regularly to illustrate another article. Thus the whole contents can be visually highlighted. Once inside the magazine, the reader scrolls through the story. This incorporates hot text, which when pointed at brings up subsidiary texts and images, so that a name, when clicked, may introduce a portrait and short biography to the screen. As the reader scrolls through the text, the relevant charts and illustrations appear, driven in animated sequences to give greater understanding. Short video sequences can be inserted, as can sound – thus music critics will one day be able to play to readers the music they are describing. Such elements may be introduced by the designer according to timed sequence, or according to readers' actions and habits, or left to readers to discover for themselves. There is evident potential here for creating surprise and emphasis, as well as to give maximum assistance in the discovery of information.

The electronic magazine raises some fundamental questions about how people will use magazines, the most important point being that magazines could become mutable, and interactive: the reader could add comment or amend fact, add to or change the images, cross reference, cut and paste information from one magazine to another; or the publisher could send out regular updates which alter the material, and provide indexes to existing material. It is, in fact, impossible to predict at this early stage what might occur. Initially the existing magazine concept will dominate how they work and look, just as the first cars looked like horse-drawn carriages. As far as the design is concerned, it is evident that new skills will be required and there will be considerable crossover between different design disciplines and new specializations. Art direction is likely to become a much more complex process and more akin to television production. The change in the production and delivery mechanisms will introduce radically new forms as video and computer animation merge with graphic design. And this takes no account of the cultural impact of this second machine age on art and design. New technologies effect subtler and deep-seated alterations in the way we think; they are inevitably linked to changes wrought in the larger world by related technical improvements, especially when we are confronted by such challenging ideas as interactive information systems and artificial intelligence. What shapes design is subject not only to production technology and how it is used, but also to the role that media plays in society, which tends to adapt just as profoundly.

The major obstacle to electronic magazines remains the immobility and expense of the delivery mechanism, the computer. To make the idea work properly we need a computer that rolls up and fits into the pocket like a magazine, and is as cheap as a magazine. Some such graphics-driven personal information machine should be available in a very few years, perhaps only one or two. The other problem remains the relatively poor legibility of screens, most of which cannot cope with 9pt text and smaller. Only certain types of magazines will translate well to the new medium. Literary magazines will certainly not. The paper magazine is not dead and will not die in the forseeable future. Its magnificent qualities of convenience, readability, colour, the very smell of the ink and the texture of paper will see to that.

The Economist

February 1990

Leaders

Germany benign ?
Soviet empire-unbuilding
A shield for Hongkong
De Klerk's chance
Tight money, sad markets

Moon race

Drug traffic

Sugar crisis

Business, finance and science

Business this week
Business
Finance
Science & Technology
Economic & Financial indicators
Books & Art
Letters

World politics and current affairs

Europe
Japan's gangsters
Britain
American survey
Asia
international

Steps to German unity

unhappy period between 1871 and 1945. Far popular is the idea outlined by the chancellor, Mr **Helmut Kohl**, for gradual moves to a German Federation.

There is the predictable effect on German politics of an extra 16m people who have had 40 years of dictatorship, not democracy.

With the imminent German economic and monetary union, the rush to the West has dropped showing that East Germans are

One, two, three ... crash

Notes

Preface
1 Symposium, *Magazine Design, the Rationalist's Dream?* ed. Steven Heller, AIGA Journal of Graphic Design, Vol. 3, No. 3, 1985.

Prologue: a new synthesis
1 Philip B. Meggs, *A History of Graphic Design*, New York, 1983.
2 Steven Heller and Seymour Chwast, *Graphic Style from Victorian to Post-Modern*, Harry N. Abrams, New York, 1988.
3 Paul A. Bennett, "Will Bradley", *Penrose Annual*, Vol. 49, 1955.
4 Paul Hogarth, "The artist as reporter", *Penrose Annual*, Vol. 55, 1961.
5 A. Smith, *The Newspaper: An International History*, London, 1979.
6 "The artist as reporter", op. cit.
7 In 1871, the Swede Carl Gustaf Vilhelm Carleman used a grid-patterned screen to reproduce a halftone image in the July issue of the *Nordisk Boktryckeri-Tidning*. This was, according to Rune Hasser, probably the first time that a text and a screen-printed halftone image were ever simultaneously used in a popular magazine. See *A History of Photography*, ed. Lemagny and Rouille, Cambridge University Press, 1987.
8 Patricia Frantz Kery, *Great Magazine Covers of the World*, New York, 1982.
9 *Printing Progress: a mid-century report*, International Association of Printing House Craftsmen, Ohio, 1959.
10 "The artist as reporter", op. cit.
11 Ibid.
12 Photogravure is an adaptation of the eighteenth-century intaglio technique, whereby photographic reproduction is used to produce cylindrical printing plates in which the image is cut in small cells in depth rather than in relief.
13 S. H. Steinberg, *500 Years of Printing*, third edition, Penguin Books, London, 1974.
14 *A History of Photography*, op. cit.

A dynamic iconography: magazines and the modern movement
1 The plastic image is a sum of the physiological and psychological responses to the dynamics of geometry, symbol and light. It is defined by Gyorgy Kepes as "... a forming; a dynamic process of integration, a 'plastic' experience. The word 'plastic' therefore is... used to designate the formative quality, the shaping of sensory impressions into unified, organic wholes.... The plastic image has all the characteristics of a living organism... it is a whole, the behaviour of which is not determined by that of its individual components, but where the parts are themselves determined by the intrinsic nature of the whole. It is, therefore, an enclosed system that reaches its dynamic unity by various levels of integration; by balance, rhythm and harmony." Gyorgy Kepes, *Language of Vision*, Paul Theobald and Co., Chicago, 1944.
2 These three artists represented the major strands of modern graphic design which coalesced into the new typography at the Bauhaus in the mid-1920s. Theo van Doesburg was born Christian E. M. Kupper in Utrecht, The Netherlands, in 1883. Lázló Moholy-Nagy, a Hungarian, taught at the Bauhaus from 1923. The Russian, Lazar Markovitch Lissitzky, 1890-1941, was with Alexander Rodchenko the leading member of the constructivist movement and founder of "the new objectivity". See Herbert Spencer, *Pioneers of Modern Typography*, London, 1969.
3 The manifesto is reprinted in full in Reyner Banham, *Theory and Design in the First Machine Age*, The Architectural Press, London, 1960.
4 Elementarism in the "modern" sense is based around the ideas explored in Malevitch's suprematist compositions of "fundamental suprematist elements – simple geometric forms that are the basic units of composition", ideas combined with El Lissitzky's understanding of the object as art. See *Theory and Design in the First Machine Age*, op. cit.
5 Allen Hurlbert, *Layout: the Design of the Printed Page*, Watson-Guptill, New York, 1977.
6 Van Doesburg's Dadaist writings in *De Stijl* were disguised behind the pseudonyms I. K. Bonset and Aldo Camini.
7 Hurlbert, op. cit.
8 In particular, in the communist photojournal *Arbeiter Illustrierte Zeitung*. See pages 30-43.
9 Quoted in John Willett, *The New Sobriety: Art and Politics in the Weimar Period*, Thames and Hudson, London, 1978.
10 From El Lissitzky's *Russland*, Vienna, 1930, quoted in *Theory and Design in the First Machine Age*, op. cit.
11 Mondrian considered that the oblique was a departure from the fundamental principles of De Stijl, insisting that the oblique expressed "eternal movement" and destroyed the "cosmic equilibrium and harmony" which was the goal of his compositional studies. See *Theory and Design in the First Machine Age*, op. cit.
12 See Varvara Rodchenko and Aleksandr Lavrentiev, *The Rodchenko Family Workshop*, ed. Carrell et al., New Beginnings, Glasgow, 1989.
13 Attilio Rossi, introduction to *Campo Grafico 1933-1939*, Electa, Milan, 1983.

The big picture: photojournalism between the wars
1 F. H. K. Henrion, "Whither graphic design?", *Penrose Annual*, Vol. 56, 1962.
2 During the Second World War *Match* was used as a fascist propaganda magazine. After liberation the magazine was re-named *Paris Match* in order to shake off its sullied reputation.
3 A. Rodchenko, "Predosterezheniye (Warning)", *Novy Lef*, no. 6, 1928, quoted in *A History of Photography*, op. cit.
4 Willi Muenzenberg, *Der Arbeiter-Fotograf*, 1931, quoted in *Photography/Politics: One*, Photography Workshop, London, 1979.
5 Attilio Rossi, introduction to *Campo Grafico 1933-1939*, op. cit.
6 *AIZ*'s history dates from 1921. The magazine was founded out of two earlier titles, *Sowiet-Russland im Bild* (1921-2) and *Sichel und Hammer* (1923-4). It ended its days in Prague as *Die Volks Illustrierte* (1936-8).
7 P. W. Korner and J. Stuber, *Germany: Arbeiter-fotographie*, reprinted in *Photography/Politics: One*, op. cit.
8 Heinz Willmann, *Geschichte der Arbeiter-Illustrierten Zeitung 1921-1938*, East Berlin, 1975.
9 Neither Rodchenko nor El Lissitzky was a full-time designer at *SSSR Na Stroike*; both worked as freelances and between them they designed some two dozen issues. The contents of each issue were decided by the editorial board (a collective on which the dominant figure was Maxim Gorky, until his death in 1936). The board then briefed as many as three or four designers and each had to make a separate pitch for the job. Rodchenko, for example, submitted 3 x 4 in. maquettes and only if they were approved was he given the job of designing the issue.
10 *SSSR Na Stroike* was closed down during the Second World War, and re-started in 1949. In 1950 the name was changed to *Soviet Union* but it never approached the quality of its heyday in the first half of the 1930s.
11 The phrases are extracted from the *Life* prospectus written by Henry Luce, reprinted in Loudon Wainwright, *The Great American Magazine: An Inside Story of Life*, New York, 1986.
12 Willi Muenzenberg, "Tasks and Aims", *Der Arbeiter-Fotograf*, 1931, quoted in *Photography/Politics: One*, op. cit.
13 *Picture Post 1938-50*, ed. Tom Hopkinson, Penguin Books, London, 1970.
14 Ibid.
15 Stuart Hall, "The Social Eye of Picture Post", *Working Papers in Cultural Studies 2*, Birmingham, 1972.
16 See Tom Hopkinson's introduction to *Picture Post 1938-50*, op. cit.
17 *The Great American Magazine*, op. cit.
18 Ibid.
19 Ibid.
20 According to Allen Hurlbert, in addition to Hollister, T. M. Cleland, M. F. Agha and Henry Dreyfus were employed as consultants on the design of the original *Life* format. See *Publication Design*, revised edition, New York, 1976.
21 Originally the idea was to allow the slug to "float" week by week in different parts of the cover page, according to the composition of the photograph, and to vary the colour. In practice, the slug stayed firmly in the highly visible top left corner, and the colour remained red until the issue of 29 November 1963, when a black masthead and border marked the death of President Kennedy.
22 Dime prospectus, reprinted in *Life: the First Fifty Years*, ed. Philip B. Kurnhardt Jr, Boston, 1986.
23 *The Great American Magazine*, op. cit.
24 Tom Hopkinson, introduction to *Picture Post 1938-50*, op. cit.

The first age of the art director: Cleland, Agha and Brodovitch
1 *The Great American Magazine*, op. cit.
2 Allen Hurlbert, *Publication Design*, op. cit.
3 M. F. Agha, introduction to *Magazines USA* catalogue, extract reprinted in *AIGA Journal*, Vol.3, No.3, 1985.
4 John Farleigh, *It Never Dies*, quoted by Allen Hutt in *Newspaper Design*, Oxford University Press, Oxford, 1961. Hutt is careful to wrap conditions around Farleigh's eclectic proposition. He adds, "Variety as here extolled is limited typographically in two ways, technical and aesthetic; the first derives from the requirements of the printing process (including the desired and/or possible paper), the second from the doctrine of fitness for purpose, particularly germane to the multiplicty of magazine 'personalities', if it may be put that way."
5 Lorraine Wild, "Modern American graphics II: the birth of a profession", *ID*, July/August, 1983.
6 Sarah Bodine and Michael Dunas, "Dr M. F. Agha, Art Director", in *AIGA Journal*, Vol.3, No.3, 1985.
7 See "Dr M. F. Agha, Art Director", op. cit.; other sources indicate a birth date of 1896.
8 M. F. Agha, "Leave European art in Europe", *Advertising Arts*, January 1932, quoted in Remington and Hodik, *Nine Pioneers of American Graphic Design*, MIT Press, 1989.
9 In his introduction to *Magazines USA* catalogue (op. cit.), Agha admitted his debt to advertising arts: "The influence of advertising on the design and architecture of magazines goes far beyond a mere floor plan... advertising, during the last thirty years or so, has developed eye-catching, tradition-breaking techniques, mostly borrowed from the post-World-War-One modern art: bleed pages, giant gatefolds, abstract symbolism, off-beat plots, syncopated piggy-back typography, giant faces, Victorian revivals, giant body-type, and various other creative dingbats. The glorious sport of eye-catching was fashionably called visual communication."
10 Andy Grundberg, *Brodovitch*, in *Documents of American Design*, Harry N. Abrams, New York, 1989. This is the definitive account of Brodovitch's life and work.
11 Frank Zachary, in conversation with the author, December, 1988.
12 Ibid.
13 This is Zachary's explanation for the demise of *Portfolio*: "Brodovitch ordered so many stats he broke us." *Portfolio* carried no advertising and was dependent on altruistic backers in Cincinatti.

The New York School: 1945-68

1 Ken Garland, "Structure and Substance", *Penrose Annual*, Vol. 54, 1960.

2 John Van Hamersveld, quoted in Roger Black, "Type and words: 20 years of publication design", *Print*, November/December, 1986.

3 Will Burtin, "Integration, the new discipline in design", *Graphis*, 27, 1949.

4 Ibid.

5 Ibid.

6 Bradbury Thompson, *The Art of Graphic Design*, Yale University Press, 1988.

7 Ibid.

8 Herb Lubalin, "Herb Lubalin's Typography Issue", *Print*, May/June, 1979.

9 *The Art of Graphic Design*, op. cit.

10 This text, in *Portfolio*, introducing examples of concrete typography, calligraphy and classical typography, is unsigned, but was almost certainly written by Brodovitch himself.

11 "Modern" is used here in the English sense: i.e. the fine-cut serifs developed by Diderot and Bodoni, which are also known by the contraction Didoni.

12 *Mademoiselle*, for example. Thompson was also fond of using shaded outline and knife-edge serifs.

13 Ruari MacLean, *Magazine Design*, Oxford University Press, Oxford, 1969.

14 Otto Storch, "Art directing the family magazine", *Art Directing for Visual Communication and Selling*, Art Directors Club of New York, 1957.

15 Ibid.

16 "Revolutionary" was Wolf's own description of the developments in magazine design in this period, in a conversation with the author in December, 1988. The same word is used by Phillip Meggs in his *History of Graphic Design*, op. cit., and it is justified in respect of the introduction of graphic expressionism to magazine design, and of the sheer quantity of good work being produced in this period: the ground-breaking, however, had already been done in the previous two decades.

17 In his first few years at *Esquire*, Wolf was described not as art director but "art assistant".

18 Henry Wolf, *Visual Thinking: Methods for Making Images Memorable*, American Showcase, New York, 1988.

19 Henry Wolf in conversation with the author, December, 1988.

20 There were certain aspects of type to which Wolf paid particular attention. Unhappy with the size of the *Esquire* logotype, which reduced space for photography, he had a lettering designer take off 1/16 in every month for eight months, until he was "found out" by the editor: having stripped off 1/2 in from the width, he was forced to stop. A further feature of Wolf's cover design was his clever incorporation of the "Esky" logo into the graphic scheme. The logo was designed in 1933 by Elmer Simms Campbell, and later re-worked by Paul Rand.

21 Will Hopkins, in conversation with the author, February, 1989.

22 Allen Hurlbert, *Layout*, Watson-Guptill, New York, 1977.

22 David Moore was art director of *America Illustrated* for over ten years, from the mid-1960s to 1977.

The new rationalists: a European revival

1 The magazine *Neue Grafik* (*New Graphic Design*), the trilingual "house journal" of the international style, was the most important point of distribution for Swiss typographic ideas. It was edited by Richard Lohse, Josef Müller-Brockmann, Hans Neuburg and Carlo Vivarelli.

2 Over three years the magazine's title was simplified from *Man About Town* to *About Town*, to *Town*.

3 Allen Hutt, *Newspaper Design*, op. cit.

4 Quoted in Charles Harrison, *English Art and Modernism 1900-1939*, Allen Lane, 1981.

5 The first phrase is Beatrice Warde's, from *The Crystal Goblet*, Sylvan Press, 1955. The neo-Georgian swipe is Nikolaus Pevsner's; see "Reactions in Anglo-German design 1900-1930", *Penrose Annual*, Vol. 43, 1949.

6 F. H. K. Henrion in conversation with the author, November, 1988.

7 The Royal College of Art's college magazine *Ark* also "had a huge effect [on commercial magazines] in both its look and subject matter", according to Ken Garland, especially in the period 1958-9. Art editors and contributors included Len Deighton, Alan Fletcher and Roger Coleman.

8 Kenneth Garland, "Illustrated periodicals", *Design*, 135, March, 1960.

9 A succession of talented art directors applied and developed Lustig's format for *Industrial Design*, including Martin Rosenzweig, James Ward and Peter Bradford.

10 Kenneth Garland, "Structure and substance", *Penrose Annual*, Vol. 54, 1960. It is interesting to note that Pevsner (op. cit.), writing eleven years earlier, was less certain of the direction in which English design should look for inspiration. "We need not go beyond the moment when the modern movement in typography and architecture came over to England. It represented the second stage in the process of Germany's paying back of what she had once received from England. Has she more to give now? I doubt it. Where then should this country turn? To America? We hope not. On the whole Georgian timidity is perhaps preferable to bogus streamlining. To Scandinavia and Switzerland? Perhaps, although it should not be forgotten that what is good for Basel and Gothenburg may not be adequate for London – unless London is ready to resign herself to being the eminently cultured capital of a small country."

11 Kenneth Garland, "Illustrated periodicals", op. cit.

12 Tom Wolsey emigrated to the United States in 1973, although he remains a British citizen. He returned to advertising and at the time of writing is Vice President Art of Ally & Gargano, Inc.

13 Tom Wolsey in conversation with the author, New York, 1987.

14 The words "Man", "About" and the date of issue were slipped into the characters of "Town" as a means of cleaning up the masthead and, as Wolsey put it, "making the unwanted words atrophy away". Wolsey used a similar technique for the masthead of the short-lived weekly *Topic*, which he designed in 1961.

15 A "Lucy" was a *camera lucida*, a projection system for enlarging and tracing photographs.

16 By comparison, in the early 1960s at the American monthly *McCall's*, Otto Storch had an art staff of ten, whereas at *Town* Tom Wolsey was working with a single assistant.

17 See Steven Heller, "Willy Fleckhaus", *Graphis*, No. 249, May/June, 1987.

18 An anecdote related by at least two former assistants: Derek Birdsall and Will Hopkins. An example of such exigency was when Fleckhaus, presented with a poor photograph of Yves Montand, blew up across two pages a detail of the actor's Gitane-wielding hand.

19 Thomas Schroder, editor of *FAZ Magazin*, in "*Frankfurter Allgemeine Magazine*", *Graphis*, No. 244.

20 Ibid.

21 Wolsey's tenure at *Queen* was brief, from July 1963 to July 1964: his relationship with Stevens was not that enjoyed by his predecessor, Mark Boxer. Wolsey's successor, Max Maxwell, was followed by Willie Landels in 1965.

22 See Robin Kinross, "The New Tradition", a review of Richard Hollis's career, *Blueprint*, No. 46, April, 1988.

23 Miller's arrival at *Vogue* coincided with a period of disruptive change in art staff as well as editorial, following the departure of its long-serving art director, John Parsons, in 1964. Max Maxwell (also from *Queen*) became art director in the interim between Parsons and Terence Whelan (who joined in 1965) and Peter Stillwell from 1966. Stillwell and Whelan were, in turn, followed by Barney Wan.

24 Ruari MacLean, *Magazine Design*, op. cit. In Britain, 150,000 is a substantial circulation figure for an up-market general interest monthly.

25 David King in conversation with the author, April, 1989.

26 Significantly, Rand started his career in newspapers, setting up the first dedicated graphics department at the *Daily Express* in 1959.

27 See Jeanette Collins, "Journalism and design: a marriage can be arranged", *Penrose Annual*, Vol. 68, 1975.

1968 and after: underground and up again

1 In *Fortune*'s case this was largely the result of moving from monthly to fortnightly publication in 1974.

2 In human terms there was very little continuity in design across the two decades. For example, of the designers active in the early and mid-1960s, Wolf and Wolsey, disenchanted with magazines, had gone into advertising art direction; Garland to the corporate design sector and books; Fleckhaus to book design and teaching; David King to book design (he left *The Sunday Times Magazine* in 1972, working briefly on *City Limits* and *Crafts* magazine); Peccinotti, Knapp and Kane to photography. Hurlbert became a publishing director – he died in 1983, as did Fleckhaus. The designers working on magazines in the 1960s and still doing so are few. Of the French, there are Jean Demachy and Regiz Pagniez (in 1990 they were, respectively, editorial directors of French and US *Elle*). Of the English, there are Roland Schenk, still at *Management Today* in 1990, and Michael Rand, at *The Sunday Times Magazine*; David Hillman is now an editorial design consultant at Pentagram, and Derek Birdsall returned to magazine design with the formatting of *The Independent Magazine* in 1989. In America, Milton Glaser provides a link to the 1960s, as did Will Hopkins who ceased magazine work only in 1988.

3 The underground press was not strictly an illegal press, despite the efforts of an alliance of "moral" campaigners, the police and courts. *OZ* editors were convicted under the Obscene Publications Act in 1971 following publication of its "Skoolkids" issue. In the same year *IT* was prosecuted for "conspiring to corrupt and debauch public morals" and "conspiring to outrage public decency" for carrying homosexual contact advertisements. And, of course, numerous charges of obstruction were brought by the police against street sellers of the left and alternative press.

4 Richard Neville had published a magazine of the same name in Australia since 1963.

5 The switch to psychedelia in the third issue of *OZ* apocryphally followed Martin Sharpe's first experience with LSD. See Jonathon Green, *Days in the Life: Voices from the English Underground*, Minerva, London, 1988.

6 *IT* parallels *OZ* in many respects: it was launched (in newspaper format) in the same year and folded in 1972, one year before *OZ*. Many of the staff of the two magazines were interchangable and in times of financial and legal trouble (all too regular) they shared production and print facilities.

7 Richard Adams, quoted in *Days in the Life*, op. cit.

8 Jerome Burne, quoted in *Days in the Life*, op. cit.

9 Felix Dennis, quoted in *Days in the Life*, op. cit.

10 Split-fountain divides the ink supply so that two colours may be printed simultaneously on one roller.

11 John Goodchild and Martin Sharp were primarily responsible for the design and artwork of *OZ*. Marchbank, who also designed the news format *Friends*, took over the design of *OZ* during the obscenity trial. *OZ* is the best documented of these magazines: the staff of *IT* and the short-lived *Ink* and *7 Days*, etc., did not publish their identity for fear of prosecution.

12 Barney Bubbles was a contributor to *OZ* No. 38, one of the finest of the later issues, and also became art director of *Friends* after Marchbank left for *Time Out*. Born Colin Fucher, Bubbles' pictorial graphic style spanned the otherwise unbridgeable divide between modernism and psychedelia. He died in 1983.

13 "Snare-pictures" or "Snare-art" was a new phrase for the old Dada practice of creating accidental or subversive combinations from found images and objects. See "Snareart", *OZ & Other Scenes*, special issue, 1967.

14 Allen Hurlburt, "Editorial Design in America", *Graphis*, No. 149, Vol. 26, 1971.

15 Roger Black, "Type and words: 20 years of publication design", *Print*, November/December, 1986.

16 "Fitting new formats", *Art Direction*, March, 1977.

17 From an interview with Milton Glaser by Alan Fletcher on the redesign of *Esquire*, in David White, "All the graphics that's fit to print", *Design*, May, 1978.

18 Milton Glaser, quoted in *Cut* magazine, Vol. 1, No. 1, Winter, 1988.

19 *OZ*, *IT*, *Ink* and *Friends* had all disappeared by 1973, the last to become a seminal source for advertising creative directors in London during the 1970s. Although most of the underground magazines folded (with the exception of music magazines such as *ZigZag*), left-wing newspapers survived, even if they did not prosper.

20 *instant DESIGN 1966-1986*, exhibition catalogue, Centro per le arti visive e Museo d'arte contemporanea di Villa Croce, Genoa, 1987.

21 See Christine Walker, "Between the lines: design has a new look", *Design*, January, 1983.

22 Driver was assistant art director and then art director of *Radio Times* from 1969 to 1981. Previously he worked at *Harper's Bazaar* (three issues only), *Drive* and the BOAC in-flight magazine *Welcome Aboard*. In 1990 he was design director at Times Newspapers, London.

23 Like many of those associated with *Radio Times* in this period, Holmes emigrated to the USA, where he joined *Time* magazine.

24 Terry Jones in conversation with the author, May, 1989.

25 *instant DESIGN 1966-1986*, op. cit.

26 A contraction of "culture-tabloid"; see Steven Heller, "New Culturetabs", *i-D*, March/April, 1987.

27 *Hard Werken*'s core members are Gerard Hadders, Willem Kars and Rick Vermeulen.

Journalism and art

1 Quoted in *Nine Pioneers of American Design*, op. cit.

2 Robert Harling, quoted in Harold Evans, *Newspaper Design*, Heinemann, London, 1973. Harling's remarks were directed specifically to newspaper designers, but in the context of this quotation, generally to "any typographical designer, graphic designer, layout artist, or whatever..." Harling was for many years designer of the magazine *Art & Industry*; see pages 102-123.
3 Alexey Brodovitch, *Portfolio*, op. cit.
4 Allen Hutt, *Newspaper Design*, op. cit. (my emphasis).
5 Roger Black, "Type and Words: 20 years of Publication Design", *Print*, November/December, 1986.
6 Walter Gropius, *The New Architecture and the Bauhaus*, Charles Bronford & Co.

Stucture, synthesis and meaning
1 Gyorgy Kepes, *Language of Vision*, op. cit.

The cover
1 David Hillman, in conversation with the author, 1989.

Photography and illustration
1 J. Müller-Brockmann, *The Graphic Designer and his Design Problems*, Niggli/Hastings House, New York, 1983.
2 Chris Jones, "Art in the world of science: a personal view", *Art Meets Science: the cover art of New Scientist*, exhibition catalogue, IPC Magazines Ltd, London, 1986.

Into the unknown: magazines for an electronic age
1 Allen Hurlbert, "Magazine design in the Seventies", *Penrose Annual*, Vol. 70, 1977-8.
2 Conventional offset lithography requires a combination of water and ink (ink is attracted to the surface of the plate to be printed, water repelled). The difficulty in obtaining the correct proportions of ink and water, and thereby the correct density of ink on the page, is a cause of delay in printing. In dry offset, only ink is required.
3 According to Meggs, op. cit., El Lissitzky "correctly predicted that Gutenberg's system belonged to the past, and photomechanical processes would replace metal type and open new horizons for design as surely as radio had replaced the telegraph." The first commercially available phototypesetting system was introduced as early as 1936 by the Photolettering Company in the USA.
4 A bitmap is an array of memory corresponding to the picture elements of the screen. Fonts with resolution restricted to that of the screen give a genuine, rather than symbolic, representation of the image.
5 Postscript is a common typographic "language" used in computers and laser printers to describe high resolution "smoothed" digital fonts. Type One or "outline" Postscript fonts give a fairly accurate screen description at any point size.
6 Editorial leader, "Graphic designers and the Macintosh computer" issue, *Emigre*, No. 11, 1989.

Bibliography

Books

Ades, Dawn, *Photomontage*, London: Thames & Hudson, 1976.

Banham, Rayner, *Theory and Design in the First Machine Age*, London: The Architectural Press, 1960.

Bojko, Szymon, *New Graphic Design in Revolutionary Russia*, New York: Praeger, 1972.

Brosseau, Ray, *Looking Forward: American Magazines 1895-1905*, New York: American Heritage, 1970.

Carrell et al., *The Rodchenko Family Workshop*, Glasgow: New Beginnings, 1989.

Click, J. W. & N. Baird, *Magazine Editing and Production*, Iowa: W.C. Brown, 1979.

Dennett, T. & J. Spence (eds.), *Photography/Politics: One*, London: Photography Workshop, 1979.

Di Grappa, Carol (ed.), *Fashion Theory*, New York: Lustrum Press, 1980.

Elson, Robert T., *Time Inc.: The Intimate History of a Publishing Empire*, New York: Athenean, 1968.

Evans, Harold, *Newspaper Design*, London: Heinemann, 1973.

Friedman, Mildred et al., *Graphic Design in America: A Visual Language History*, Minneapolis: Walker Arts Center/Abrams, 1989.

Fulton, Marianne, *Eyes of Time: Photojournalism in America*, New York: NY Graphic Society, 1988.

Garland, Kenneth, *Graphics, Design and Printing Terms*, London: Lund Humphries, 1989.

Gerstner, Karl, *The New Graphic Art*, London: Alec Tiranti, 1959.

Glaser, Milton, *Graphic Design*, New York: Overlook Press, 1973.

Gordon, George, *The Language of Communication*, New York: Hastings House, 1969.

Gray Smith, Cortland, *Magazine Layout: Principles, Patterns, Practices*, New York, 1977.

Green, Jonathon, *Days in the Life: Voices from the English Underground*, London: Minerva, 1989.

Grundberg, Andy, *Brodovitch*, New York: Harry N. Abrams, 1989.

Harrison, Charles, *English Art and Modernism 1900-1939*, London: Allen Lane, 1981.

Hefting, Paul (ed.), *Designers 11: Hard Werken, Wild Plakken*, Eindhoven: Lecturis, 1981.

Helbert, Clifford L. (ed.), *Printing Progress: A Mid-Century Report*, Cincinnati: IAPHC, 1959.

Heller, Steven (ed.), *Innovators of American Illustration*, New York: Van Nostrand Reinhold, 1986.

Heller, Steven & Seymour Chwast, *Graphic Style: from Victorian to Post-Modern*, New York: Harry N. Abrams, 1988.

Hofmann, Armin, *Graphic Design Manual*, New York: Van Nostrand Reinhold, 1965.

Hopkinson, Tom (ed.), *Picture Post 1938-50*, London: Penguin Books, 1970.

Hurlbert, Allen, *The Grid*, New York: Van Nostrand Reinhold, 1978.

Hurlbert, Allen, *Layout: The Design of the Printed Page*, New York: Watson-Guptill, 1977.

Hurlbert, Allen, *Publication Design*, New York: Van Nostrand Reinhold, 1976.

Hutt, Allen, *Newspaper Design*, London: Oxford University Press, 1960.

Jones, Chris, *Art Meets Science: The Cover Art of New Scientist*, London: New Scientist, 1986.

Jones, Terry, *Instant Design/A Manual of Graphic Techniques*, London: ADT, 1990.

Kepes, Gyorgy, *Language of Vision*, Chicago: Paul Theobold, 1944.

Kery, Patricia Frantz, *Great Magazine Covers of the World*, New York: Abbeville Press, 1982.

Kurnhardt, Philip B. (ed.), *Life: The First Fifty Years 1936-1986*, Boston: Little, Brown & Co., 1986.

Lemagny & Rouille, *A History of Photography*, London: Cambridge University Press, 1987.

Luther Mott, Frank, *A History of American Magazines (1741-1930, 5 Vols.)*, Cambridge: Harvard University Press, 1957.

MacLean, Ruari, *Magazine Design*, London: Oxford University Press, 1969.

MacLean, Ruari, *Typography*, London: Thames & Hudson, 1980.

Malossi, Giannino (ed.), *Instant Design 1966-1986*, Genova: Museo d'Arte Contemporanea, 1987.

Meggs, Philip B., *A History of Graphic Design*, New York: Van Nostrand Reinhold, 1983.

Müller-Brockman, J., *The Graphic Designer and His Design Problems*, New York: Arthur Niggli/Hastings House, 1983.

Naylor, Gillian, *The Bauhaus*, London: Studio Vista, 1968.

Perfect, C. & G. Rookledge, *Rookledge's International Typefinder*, London: Sarema Press, revised edn., 1990.

Peterson, Theodore, *Magazines in the 20th Century*, Urbana: University of Illinois, 1964.

Rand, Paul, *A Designer's Art*, New Haven: Yale University Press, 1985.

Remington, R. & B. Hodik, *Nine Pioneers in American Graphic Design*, Cambridge: MIT, 1989.

Schacht, John H., *A Bibliography of the Study of Magazines*, Urbana: University of Illinois, 1976.

Siepmann, Eckhard, *Montage: John Heartfield*, Berlin: Elefanten Press, 1977.

Smith, Anthony, *The Newspaper: An International History*, London: Thames & Hudson, 1979.

Spencer, Herbert, *Pioneers of Modern Typography*, London: Lund Humphries, revised edn., 1982.

Staal G. & H. Wolters (eds.), *Holland in Vorm: Dutch Design 1945-1987*, Den Haag: Stichting Holland in Vorm, 1987.

Steinberg, S. H., *500 Years of Printing*, London: Penguin Books, 1974.

Sterling, C. H. & T. R. Haight, *The Mass Media*, New York: Aspen Institute Guides, 1978.

Taft, William H., *American Magazines for the 1980s*, New York: Hastings House, 1982.

Tebbel, John, *The American Magazine: A Compact History*, New York: Hawthorne, 1969.

Thompson, Bradbury, *The Art of Graphic Design*, New Haven: Yale University Press, 1988.

Tschichold, Jan, *Asymmetric Typography*, New York: Reinhold, 1967.

Vitta Zelman, Tilde (ed.), *Campo Grafico: 1933-1939*, Milan: Electa Editrice, 1983.

Waibl, Heinz, *Alle Radici della Comunicazione Visiva Italiana*, Como: Centro di Cultura Grafica, 1988.

Wainwright, Loudon, *The Great American Magazine: An Inside History of Life*, New York: Knopf, 1986.

White, Cynthia, *Women's Magazines 1693-1968*, London: Joseph, 1968.

Willett, John, *The New Sobriety 1917-1933*, London: Thames & Hudson, 1978.

Willmann, Heinz, *Geschichte der Arbeiter Illustrierten Zeitung 1921-1938*, Berlin (Ost): Dietz Verlag, 1974.

Wingler, Hans M. (ed.), *Herbert Bayer: Das kunstlerische Werk 1918-1938*, Berlin: Bauhas-Archiv, 1982.

Wolf, Henry, *Visual Thinking*, New York: American Showcase, 1988.

Wolseley, Roland, *Understanding Magazines*, Ames: Iowa State University, 1969.

Wozencroft, Jon, *The Graphic Language of Neville Brody*, London: Thames & Hudson, 1988.

Magazines and Periodicals
Anon., "Art Editors: Eight Interviews," *Designer*, January 1985.

Anon., "Hall of Fame: Mehemed Fehmy Agha," *NY Art Directors Club*, 1972.

Anon., "Hall of Fame: Alexey Brodovitch," *NY Art Directors Club*, 1972.

Anon., "Hall of Fame: Will Burtin," *NY Art Directors Club*, 1974.

Anon., "Lester Beall," *Graphis*, No. 40, 1952.

Anon., "Lui: a Bestseller Magazine from Paris," *Novum*, July 1973.

Anon., "Neville Brody: New Spirit, New Wave," *Architectural Review*, August 1986.

Anon., "Sipa: 20 Years of Photojournalism," *Zoom*, No. 49, 1990.

Anon., "Stern & Wolfgang Behnken," *Idea*, No. 133, November 1975.

Arden, Paul, "Max Exposure – photo special," *Direction*, March 1989.

Baynes, Ken, "Are Consumer Magazines a Good Buy?" *Penrose Annual*, Vol. 59, 1966.

Bennett, Paul A., "Will Bradley," *Penrose Annual*, Vol. 49, 1955.

Bernard, Walter, "Influences," *AIGA Journal*, Vol. 4, No. 2, 1988.

Black, Roger, "Good Type: Making Your Own Fonts," *AIGA Journal*, Vol. 4, No. 2, 1988.
Black, Roger, "Type and Words: 20 Years of Publication Design," *Print*, November-December 1986.

Black, Roger, "The Yuppies' Favorite Typeface," *AIGA Journal*, Vol. 5, No. 1, 1987.

Bodine, S. & M. Dunas, "Dr M. F. Agha, Art Director," *AIGA Journal*, Vol. 3, No. 3, 1985.

Booth-Clibbon, Edward (ed.), *Design and Art Direction Annual*, 1955-89.

Brown, Richard, "Nigel Holmes: Time's Graphic Statistician," *Penrose Annual*, Vol. 73, 1981.

Burtin, Will, "Integration, The New Discipline in Design," *Graphis*, No. 27, 1949.

Clarke, C. F. O., "Alvin Lustig, Cover Designs," *Graphis*, No. 24, 1948.

Cleverdon, Douglas, "The Publications of the BBC," *Penrose Annual*, Vol. 46, 1952.

Collins, Jeanette, "Journalism and Design: A Marriage can be Arranged," *Penrose Annual*, Vol. 68, 1975.

Colyer, Martin, "Putting on a Bold Face: Neville Brody," *Blueprint*, May 1985.

Crawford, Ashley, "Milton Glaser," *Cut*, Vol. 1, No. 1, Winter 1988.

Davis, Brian, "Clive Crook: Observing Design," *Creative Review*, September 1984.

Ermoyan, Suren, "How Magazine Art Directors Build Readership," *Art Direction for Visual Communication*, 1957.

Garland, Kenneth, "Illustrated Periodicals: An International Survey", *Design*, No. 135, March 1960.

Garland, Kenneth, "Structure and Substance," *Penrose Annual*, Vol. 54, 1960.

Geissbühler, Stephan, "New Wave in Graphic Design," *Graphis*, No. 229, 1984.

Glaser, M. & I. Chermayeff, "Some Thoughts on Modernism: Past, Present & Future," *AIGA Journal*, Vol. 5, No. 2, 1987.

Guerrin, Michel, "Photo et Journalisme," *Photographies*, No. 11, March 1989.

Gwyther, M. & J. Myerson, "A Tale of Two Simons: Esterson and Costin," *Creative Review*, April 1986.

Heller, Robert, "The Sunday Times Magazine: The Drive Downmarket," *Design & Art Direction*, October 1984.

Heller, Steven, "A Designer's Epiphany," *AIGA Journal*, Vol. 5, No. 3, 1987.

Heller, Steven, "New Culturetabs," *Industrial Design*, March-April 1987.

Heller, Steven, "Willy Fleckhaus," *Graphis*, No. 249, May-June 1987.

Heller, Steven (ed.), "Symposium: Magazine Design, The Rationalists Dream?" *AIGA Journal*, Vol. 3, No.3, 1985.

Henrion, F. H. K., "Whither Graphic Design?" *Penrose Annual*, Vol. 56, 1962.

Hogarth, Paul, "The Artist as Reporter," *Penrose Annual*, Vol. 55, 1961.

Hook, Michael, "Press Quest: The Growth of Pan-European Publishing," *Campaign*, 27 January 1989.

Hurlbert, Allen, "Art Directing the Picture Magazine," *Art Direction for Visual Communication*, 1957.

Hurlbert, Allen, "Editorial Design in America," *Graphis*, No. 149, 1970-71.

Hurlbert, Allen, "Magazine Design in the Seventies," *Penrose Annual*, Vol. 70, 1977.

Hutt, Allen, "The First Word on Magazine Design," *Penrose Annual*, Vol. 63, 1970.

Johnstone, Mog, "Exploding Magazines/Alternative Magazines," *City Limits*, 14-20 May 1982.

Jones, Herbert, "Don't Overlook the Underground Press," *Penrose Annual*, Vol. 66, 1973.

Jones, Herbert, "The Magic Power of Magazines," *Penrose Annual*, Vol. 52, 1958.

Kaufmann, Michael, "Typographic Anarchy," *Creative Review*, March 1985.

Kinross, Robin, "The New Tradition," *Blueprint*, No. 46, April 1988.

Kinser B. & L. Sommese, "Herb Lubalin und das Typo Journal U&lc," *Novum Gebrauchsgraphik*, No. 6, 1981.

Kolpe, Max, "Hans Leistikow," *Gebrauchsgraphik*, October 1920.

Konigsberg, David, "Elle Conquers with Style," *Graphis*, No. 250, July-August 1984.

Lubalin, Herb, "Herb Lubalin's Typography Issue," *Print*, May-June 1979.

Lucio-Meyer, J. J., "The Layout of Queen Magazine," *Gebrauchsgraphik*, June 1967.

Mason, Tony, "Editorial Style Loses Out," *Design & Art Direction*, November 1984.

May, John, "The Newest Journalism: Actuel," *Blueprint*, March 1986.

McDonald, William B., "Elle: A New Trend in French Magazine Design," *Graphis*, No. 93, January-February 1961.

Meggs, Philip B., "Demilitarization of Graphic Design (Ramparts)," *AIGA Journal*, Vol. 4, No. 3, 1985.

Morris, Dean, "The Graphic Language of Neville Brody," *Communication Arts*, September-October 1988.

Myerson, Jeremy, "Perfect to the Letter: David King," *Creative Review*, September 1985.

NY Art Directors Club Annual, 1930-86

Ognjenovic, Danica, "Variety Artist: Catherine Denvir," *Creative Review*, September 1986.

Pevsner, Nikolaus, "Reactions in Anglo-German Design 1900-1930," *Penrose Annual*, Vol. 43, 1949.

Pitts, Bill, "A Guide To George Lois," *NY Art Directors Club*, 1978.

Poyner, Rick, "Open to Interpretation: Illustration at the RCA," *Blueprint*, October 1988.

Poyner, Rick, "The State of British Graphics," *Blueprint*, No. 46, April 1988.

Quarry, Paul, "The Instant Graphics of the i-D Ideas Man," *Design and Art Direction*, September 1986.

Rand, Paul, "Good Design is Good Will," *AIGA Journal*, Vol. 5, No. 3, 1987.

Ridler, Vivian, "Magazine Survey," *Penrose Annual*, Vol. 43, 1949.

Roberts, "*The Push Pin Studios*," *Graphis*, No. 80, 1958.

Scher, Paula, "The Mystery of Conde Nasty," *AIGA Journal*, Vol. 2, No. 4, 1984.

Schroder, Thomas, "Frankfurter Allgemeine Magazin," *Graphis*, No. 244, July-August 1986.

Schroder, Thomas, "Willy Fleckhaus, in Memoriam," *Graphis*, No. 227, September-October 1983.

Sikes, Gini, "The Design Doctors," *Metropolis*, June 1987.

Silverman, Helene, "Design o' The Times," *Industrial Design*, March-April 1988.

Snyder, Gertrude, "Herb Lubalin: Art Director, Graphic Designer & Typographer," *Graphis*, No. 235, 1984.

Stermer, Dugald, "What Happened to Magazine Design?" *AIGA Journal*, Vol. 3, No. 3, 1985.

Storch, Otto, "Art Directing the Family Magazine," *Art Direction for Visual Communication*, 1957.

Sutnar, Ladislav, "Work," *Gebrauchsgraphik*, October 1931.

Sweeney, Pat, "Not Just a Pretty Face: Brody, Harrop, Jones," *Media Week*, 9 August 1985.

Thompson, Bradbury, "Art Directing the Fashion Magazine," *Art Direction for Visual Communication*, 1957.

Thompson, Philip, "The Alternative Press Comes to Heel?" *Design*, No. 353, 1978.

Twisk, Russell, "Getting it Right: the Reader's Digest Editorial Formula," *The Listener*, 12 May 1988.

VanderLans, R. & Z. Licko, "The New Primitives," *Industrial Design*, March-April 1988.

VanderLans, R., "Graphic Designers and the Macintosh Computer," *Emigre*, No. 11, 1989.

Vignelli, Massimo, "The Pendulum Swings Both Ways," *AIGA Journal*, Vol. 3, No. 4, 1986

Walker, Christine, "Between the Lines: Design's New Look," *Design*, January 1983.

Waterhouse, Robert, "Free Cure for GPs: New Doctor Magazine," *Design*, February 1971.

Wells, S. et al., "Zine-Age Kicks: DIY Magazines," *New Musical Express*, 12 October 1985.

Whelan, Bride (ed.), *Society of Publication Designers' Annual*, 1986-89.

White, David, "All the Graphics that's Fit to Print," *Design*, No. 353, May 1978.

White, Lesley, "The Custodians of Style," *Campaign*, 27 June 1986.

Wild, Lorraine, "Modern American Graphics II: The Birth of a Profession," *Industrial Design*, July-August 1983.

Wolf, Henry, "Henry Wolf, Magazine Art Director & Designer," *Graphis*, Vol. 19, No. 109, 1963.

Yoxall, H. W., "Fashion Photography," *Penrose Annual*, Vol. 43, 1949.

Picture credits

Every effort has been made to trace the copyright holders of the images reproduced in this book. The author and publishers would like to thank the following for their kind permission to reproduce the illustrations listed here by page number:

Apart-Verlag, Königsdorf: 150-1
Architectural Press, London: 83 (left)
Arnoldo Mondadori Editore SpA, Milan: 171
The Atlantic Monthly Co., Boston: 164 (bottom)
Avenue, Amsterdam: 196 (bottom)

Bauhaus-Archiv, Berlin: 23 (middle: left and right)
BBC Publications, London: 110
Bellerophon Publications Inc., New York: 156-7, 195 (right)
Bibliotheek der Rijksuniversiteit te Leiden: 29
Bibliothèque Nationale, Paris: 18
Business People Publications Ltd, London: 196 (top), 218 (bottom)

City Limits, London: 112 (top)
The Condé Nast Publications Inc., New York: 49 (Courtesy Vanity Fair. Copyright © 1934, renewed 1962), 66 (Courtesty Vanity Fair. Copyright © 1945, renewed 1973), 67 (Courtesy Vogue, Copyright © 1957, renewed 1985), 68-7 (Courtesy Vogue, Copyright © 1957, renewed 1985), 184 (Courtesy Condé Nast Traveler. Copyright © 1989), 209 (Courtesy Vogue © 1989), 220 (Courtesy Condé Nast Traveler. Copyright © 1987)
Cowles Communications, New York: 79

David King Collection, London: 12, 21, 24, 30-8, 96-101
Dennis Publishing Ltd, London: 222 (top)
Design Council, UK: 83 (right), 111
Design Publications Inc., New York: 64
Diamond Sales Inc., Japan: 193, 219

Ediciones Panorama SA/Grupo Z, Madrid: 186, 206
Editoriale Domus SpA, Milan: 80, 185 (top left)
Edizioni Conde Nast SpA, Milan: 132-5, 173 (bottom), 187, 214-5
Eight Five Zero, London: 159
El Europeo/SA Editorial Gráficas Espejo, Madrid: 179
Elle Publishing/Hachette Publications Inc., New York: 182 (top), 208-9
Emigre Graphics, Berkeley: 148-9, 226-7

The Face, London: 117, 144-5, 168, 191 (right), 212-3
Frankfurter Allgemeine Magazin GmbH, Frankfurt am Main: 166-7, 185 (bottom right), 192 (top), 216-7

Gakushukenkyu-sha, Japan: 190
Gruner + Jahr AG & Co, Hamburg and London: 114, 162 (top), 200, 204-5

Haags Gemeentemuseum, The Hague: 25, 28
Hachette/Fillipachi Publications Ltd, Neuilly-sur-Seine: 89
Hard Werken, Rotterdam: 121
Harper's Magazine Foundation, New York: 128 (top)
The Hearst Corporation: 50 (© 1954), 51 (© 1940), 52-3 (© 1954), 54 (© 1955), 55 (© 1950), 67 (top) (© 1946), 74 (middle), (© 1959), 75 (bottom) (© 1959), all by courtesy Harpers Bazaar; 74 (© 1957), 75 (top right), (© 1958), 109 (© 1980, 1983), 173 (top), (© 1990), all by courtesy Esquire
Hulton Picture Company, London: 43 (text: © Syndication International; photographs: © Planet, Daily Herald, GPU)

i-D Magazine, London: 118, 119, 179, 190, 210-1
Interview Inc., New York: 136-7, 178-9, 191, 201
IPC Magazines, London: 95, 162 (bottom)

Jahreszeiten-Verlag GmbH, Hamburg: 174 (bottom)

Kamakurashobo, Japan: 185
Kindler & Schiermeyer Verlag GmbH, Munich: 90-4

Le Nouveau VSD, Paris: 206 (bottom)
Library of Congress, Washington DC: 15
Lire-Groupe Express et Cie, Paris: 165 (top), 193 (top left)

Madame Figaro, Paris: 129
Management Publications Ltd/Haymarket Publishing Group Ltd, London: 152-3, 193 (bottom left), 199, 223
Mary Evans Picture Library, London: 17, 19, 81
McCalls Corporation/McCalls Magazine: 70, 71 (Courtesy of Otto Storch)
McGraw-Hill Inc., New York: 163 (bottom right)
Meredith Corporation, London: 172 (middle, right)
Montetore Ediciones, SA, Barcelona: 207 (bottom)
Multimedia Corporation, London: 230

National Geographic Society, Washington DC: 222 (bottom)
National Magazine Company, London: 88
New International Media Srl, Milan: 182 (left)
News America Publishing, Inc., New York: 108, 172 (bottom)
Newsweek Inc., New York: 163 (bottom left)
The New Yorker Magazine Inc., New York: 164 (top)
Nuova ERI-Edizioni RAI, Milan: 142-3

Perfect, Neuilly: 203
Playboy, New York: 76

Rakan Press, Japan: 180-1
Ringier SA, Zurich: 172 (left)
Rochester Institute of Technology, New York, Department of Graphic Design: 63 (© Upjohn Company, Michigan)

Smith & Street Publications, Inc.: 65 (top left and right) (Courtesy of Bradbury Thompson)
Société du Journal Actuel SA, Paris: 207 (top)
Spy Publishing Partners, New York: 128 (bottom), 138-41, 185 (top right), 188, 221
Stedelijk Museum, Amsterdam: 20, 22
Stichting Openbaar Kunstbezit, Amsterdam: 194 (bottom)
Stichting Skrien Filmschrift, Amsterdam: 115
Straight Arrow Publishers, Inc., New York: 107, 182-3, 219
Straight No Chaser, London: 168

Thames & Hudson, London: 23 (© M. Anikst)
Time Inc. Magazines, New York (FORTUNE™): 42, 44-7, 58-62, 163 (top)
Time Out Magazines Ltd, London: 112 (bottom)
Times Newspapers Ltd, London: 96-101
TitanSports Inc., Stamford: 131 (bottom)
Typographische Monatsblatter: 82 (top)

United States Information Agency,

Washington DC: 78
Wagadon Ltd, London: 174-5 (top), 176-7, 202 (top), 213
Wire Magazine Ltd, London: 169
Wolters-Noordhoff bv, Groningen: 167, 195 (left)
Wordsearch Ltd, London: 123, 154-5
World Photo Press KK, Japan: 161, 197
Westvaco Corporation, New York: 65 (bottom)

Index

Numbers in *italics* refer to captions

WITHDRAWN